MOUNTAIN BIKE!

The Mid-Atlantic States
New York to West Virginia

MOUNTAIN BIKE!
The Mid-Atlantic States New York to West Virginia

A GUIDE TO THE CLASSIC TRAILS

JOE SURKIEWICZ

Menasha Ridge Press

Library of Congress Cataloging-in-Publication Data:

Surkiewicz, Joe.
Mountain bike! the Mid-Atlantic States : New York to West Virginia : a guide
to the classic trails / Joe Surkiewicz. — 1st ed.
p. cm.
Includes index.
ISBN 0-89732-305-X
1. All terrain cycling—Middle Atlantic States Guidebooks.
2. Bicycle trails—Middle Atlantic States Guidebooks.
3. Middle Atlantic States Guidebooks.
I. Title.
GV1045.5.M53S87   1999
796.6'3'0974—dc21   99-38556
CIP

Photos by the author unless otherwise credited
Maps by Bryan Steven Jones
Typography by Robert Clay White, Manuscript Ink™
Cover photo by Dennis Coello
Cover and text design by Suzanne Holt

Menasha Ridge Press
700 28th Street South
Suite 206
Birmingham, Alabama 35233

All trails described in this book are legal for mountain bikes. But rules can change—especially for off-road bicycles, the new kid on the outdoor recreation block. Land-access issues and conflicts between cyclists, hikers, equestrians, and other users can cause the rewriting of recreation regulations on public lands, sometimes resulting in a ban of mountain bike use on specific trails. That's why it's the responsibility of each rider to check and make sure that he or she rides only on trails where mountain biking is permitted.

CAUTION

Outdoor recreational activities are by their very nature potentially hazardous. All participants in such activities must assume the responsibility for their own actions and safety. The information contained in this guidebook cannot replace sound judgment and good decision-making skills, which help reduce risk exposure, nor does the scope of this book allow for disclosure of all the potential hazards and risks involved in such activities.

Learn as much as possible about the outdoor recreational activities in which you participate, prepare for the unexpected, and be cautious. The reward will be a safer and more enjoyable experience.

I thought all the wilderness of America was in the West till the ghost of the Susquehanna showed me different. No, there is a wilderness in the East; it's the same wilderness Ben Franklin plodded in the oxcart days when he was postmaster, the same as it was when George Washington was a wildbuck Indian-fighter, when Daniel Boone told stories by Pennsylvania lamps and promised to find the Gap, when Bradford built his road and men whooped her up in log cabins. There were not great Arizona spaces for the little man, just the bushy wilderness of eastern Pennsylvania, Maryland, and Virginia, the backroads, the black-tar roads that curve among the mournful rivers like Susquehanna, Monongahela, old Potomac and Monocacy.

From *On the Road*, Jack Kerouac

CONTENTS

List of Maps   xi
Ride Location Map   xiv
Map Legend   xvi
Acknowledgments   xvii
Foreword   xviii
Preface   xx
Ride Recommendations for Special Interests   xxiv

INTRODUCTION   1

Trail Description Outline   1
Abbreviations   3
Ride Configurations   4
Topographic Maps   5
Trail Etiquette   6
Hitting the Trail   7
And Now, a Word about Cellular Phones . . .   9

DELAWARE   11

1 Iron Hill County Park   12
2 Lums Pond State Park   15
3 Middle Run Valley Natural Area   18
4 White Clay Creek State Park   20
5 White Clay Creek Trail   22

SOUTHERN MARYLAND AND THE EASTERN SHORE   26

6 Assateague Island   27
7 Blackwater National Wildlife Refuge   30
8 Cedarville State Forest   34
9 Jug Bay Natural Area   37
10 St. Mary's River State Park   41

THE MARYLAND SUBURBS OF WASHINGTON, D.C. 44

11 Schaeffer Farm Trail 45
12 Seneca Creek State Park 48
13 Black Hill Regional Park 51
14 C&O Canal Towpath 54
15 Cabin John Trail 59
16 Capital Crescent Trail 62
17 Cosca Regional Park 66
18 Gambrill State Park 69
19 Greenbrier State Park 72

BALTIMORE, MARYLAND 76

20 Baltimore and Annapolis Trail Park 77
21 Patuxent Research Refuge North Tract 79
22 Patapsco Valley State Park—McKeldin Area 82
23 Patapsco Valley State Park—Avalon Area 85
24 Seminary Trail 88
25 Overshot Run Trail 91
26 Northern Central Railroad Trail 94
27 Liberty Watershed 97
28 Susquehanna State Park 101
29 Fair Hill Natural Resources Management Area 104
30 Hashawha Environmental Appreciation Center 108

GREEN RIDGE STATE FOREST, MARYLAND 111

31 Green Ridge MTB Trail 112
32 Stafford–East Valley Roads Loop 115
33 Mertens Avenue Area 118
34 North of Interstate 68 121

SAVAGE RIVER STATE FOREST, MARYLAND 124

35 Meadow Mountain O.R.V. Trail 125
36 Poplar Lick/Elk Lick Loop 128
37 Monroe Run Loop 131

THE LAUREL HIGHLANDS OF PENNSYLVANIA 134

38 Race Loop 135
39 North Woods Ramble 139
40 Kuhntown Loop 141

MICHAUX STATE FOREST, PENNSYLVANIA 144

41 Pole Steeple Loop 145
42 ATV and Log Sled Trails via Piney Ridge Road 147
43 Long Pine Reservoir Loop 149

44 Caledonia Loop   152
45 Mont Alto State Park Loop   154
46 Old Forge Loop   158

STATE COLLEGE, PENNSYLVANIA   161

47 Tussey Mountain to Whipple Dam   162
48 Penn Roosevelt to Alan Seeger and Back   164
49 State College to Alan Seeger and Back   167
50 State College to Whipple Dam and Bear Meadows   170
51 Dirt Road Tour   172
52 John Wert Path   175
53 The State College Epic Ride   176

BALD EAGLE STATE FOREST, PENNSYLVANIA   180

54 Cowbell Hollow/Top Mountain Trail   180
55 Bear Gap Ride   183

SOUTH-CENTRAL PENNSYLVANIA   186

56 Whitetail Mountain Biking Center   187
57 Gettysburg National Military Park   190
58 Rocky Ridge County Park   193
59 Spring Valley County Park   196
60 Kain Park   198
61 York County Heritage Rail Trail   202
62 Stony Creek Wilderness Railroad Bed Trail   205
63 Conewago Recreational Trail   208

JIM THORPE, PENNSYLVANIA   211

64 Lehigh Gorge State Park   212
65 Switchback Trail   215
66 Mauch Chunk Ridge   217
67 Weekend Warrior   220
68 Summer's Loop   223

PHILADELPHIA, PENNSYLVANIA   226

69 Fairmount Park—Kelly and West River Drives   227
70 Schuylkill Trail   230
71 Valley Forge National Historical Park   233
72 Ridley Creek State Park   236
73 Nottingham County Park   239
74 Hibernia County Park   241
75 French Creek State Park   244
76 Blue Marsh Lake   247
77 Tyler State Park   250

NEW JERSEY   253

78 Wharton State Forest   255
79 Lebanon State Forest   258
80 Delaware and Raritan Canal State Park   261
81 Round Valley Recreation Area   264
82 Allamuchy Mountain State Park   267
83 Delaware Water Gap National Recreation Area   270
84 Blue Mountain Lake Trail   274
85 Kittatinny Valley State Park   277
86 Sussex Branch Trail   279
87 Paulinskill Valley Trail   282
88 Stokes State Forest   283
89 High Point State Park   286
90 Wawayanda State Park   290
91 Ringwood State Park   293

THE CATSKILLS AND SHAWANGUNKS OF NEW YORK   296

92 Minnewaska State Park   297
93 Wallkill Valley Rail Trail   299
94 Vernooy Kill Falls Trail   301

POCAHONTAS COUNTY, WEST VIRGINIA   303

95 Greenbrier River Trail/Marlinton to Sharp's Tunnel   304
96 Red Run   306
97 Prop's Run   309
98 Snowshoe   312

SPRUCE KNOB, WEST VIRGINIA   315

99 Grants Branch to Gandy Creek Loop   316
100 Big Run Loop   318
101 Allegheny Mountain/Seneca Creek Loop   320

CANAAN VALLEY, WEST VIRGINIA   323

102 Plantation Trail   324
103 Canaan Loop Road (Forest Service Road 13)   327
104 Camp 70 Road   331
105 Olson Fire Tower   334
106 Canaan Valley State Park   337
107 Timberline   339

Glossary   343
Index   348
About the Author   356

LIST OF MAPS

1 Iron Hill County Park 13
2 Lums Pond State Park 16
3 Middle Run Valley Natural Area 19
4 White Clay Creek State Park 21
5 White Clay Creek Trail 24
6 Assateague Island 28
7 Blackwater National Wildlife Refuge 31
8 Cedarville State Forest 35
9 Jug Bay Natural Area 38
10 St. Mary's River State Park 42
11 Schaeffer Farm Trail 46
12 Seneca Creek State Park 49
13 Black Hill Regional Park 52
14 C&O Canal Towpath 56
15 Cabin John Trail 60
16 Capital Crescent Trail 63
17 Cosca Regional Park 67
18 Gambrill State Park 70
19 Greenbrier State Park 73
20 Baltimore and Annapolis Trail Park 78
21 Patuxent Research Refuge North Tract 81
22 Patapsco Valley State Park—McKeldin Area 83
23 Patapsco Valley State Park—Avalon Area 86
24 Seminary Trail 90
25 Overshot Run Trail 90
26 Northern Central Railroad Trail 95
27 Liberty Watershed 98
28 Susquehanna State Park 102
29 Fair Hill Natural Resources Management Area 105
30 Hashawha Environmental Appreciation Center 109

31 Green Ridge MTB Trail 113
32 Stafford–East Valley Roads Loop 116
33 Mertens Avenue Area 119
34 North of Interstate 68 122
35 Meadow Mountain O.R.V. Trail 126
36 Poplar Lick/Elk Lick Loop 129
37 Monroe Run Loop 132
38 Race Loop 136
39 North Woods Ramble 140
40 Kuhntown Loop 142
41 Pole Steeple Loop 146
42 ATV and Log Sled Trails via Piney Ridge Road 148
43 Long Pine Reservoir Loop 150
44 Caledonia Loop 153
45 Mont Alto State Park Loop 155
46 Old Forge Loop 159
47 Tussey Mountain to Whipple Dam 163
48 Penn Roosevelt to Alan Seeger and Back 165
49 State College to Alan Seeger and Back 168
50 State College to Whipple Dam and Bear Meadows 171
51 Dirt Road Tour 174
52 John Wert Path 174
53 The State College Epic Ride 177
54 Cowbell Hollow/Top Mountain Trail 181
55 Bear Gap Ride 184
56 Whitetail Mountain Biking Center 188
57 Gettysburg National Military Park 191
58 Rocky Ridge County Park 194
59 Spring Valley County Park 197
60 Kain Park 200
61 York County Heritage Rail Trail 203
62 Stony Creek Wilderness Railroad Bed Trail 206
63 Conewago Recreational Trail 208
64 Lehigh Gorge State Park 213
65 Switchback Trail 216
66 Mauch Chunk Ridge 218
67 Weekend Warrior 221
68 Summer's Loop 224
69 Fairmount Park—Kelly and West River Drives 228
70 Schuylkill Trail 231
71 Valley Forge National Historical Park 234
72 Ridley Creek State Park 237
73 Nottingham County Park 240
74 Hibernia County Park 242

75 French Creek State Park   245
76 Blue Marsh Lake   248
77 Tyler State Park   251
78 Wharton State Forest   256
79 Lebanon State Forest   259
80 Delaware and Raritan Canal State Park   262
81 Round Valley Recreation Area   265
82 Allamuchy Mountain State Park   268
83 Delaware Water Gap National Recreation Area   271
84 Blue Mountain Lake Trail   275
85 Kittatinny Valley State Park   278
86 Sussex Branch Trail   280
87 Paulinskill Valley Trail   280
88 Stokes State Forest   284
89 High Point State Park   288–89
90 Wawayanda State Park   291
91 Ringwood State Park   294
92 Minnewaska State Park   298
93 Wallkill Valley Rail Trail   300
94 Vernooy Kill Falls Trail   302
95 Greenbrier River Trail/Marlinton to Sharp's Tunnel   305
96 Red Run   307
97 Prop's Run   310
98 Snowshoe   313
99 Grants Branch to Gandy Creek Loop   317
100 Big Run Loop   319
101 Allegheny Mountain/Seneca Creek Loop   321
102 Plantation Trail   325
103 Canaan Loop Road (Forest Service Road 13)   328
104 Camp 70 Road   332
105 Olson Fire Tower   335
106 Canaan Valley State Park   338
107 Timberline   340

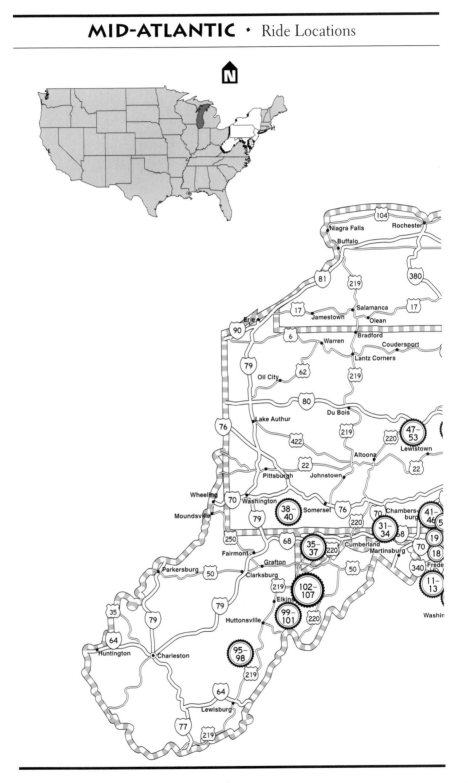

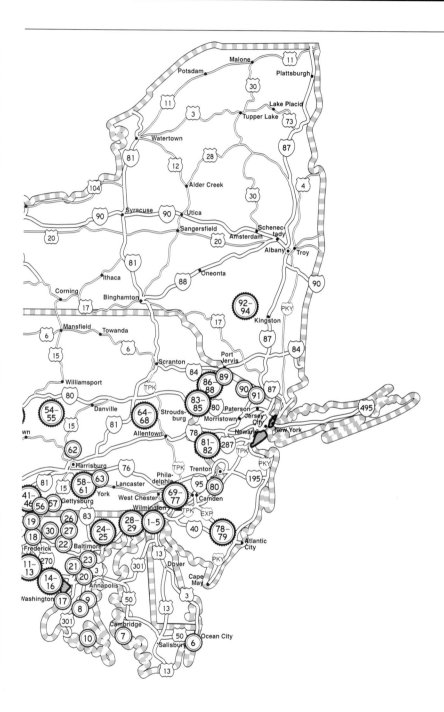

AMERICA BY MOUNTAIN BIKE · Map Legend

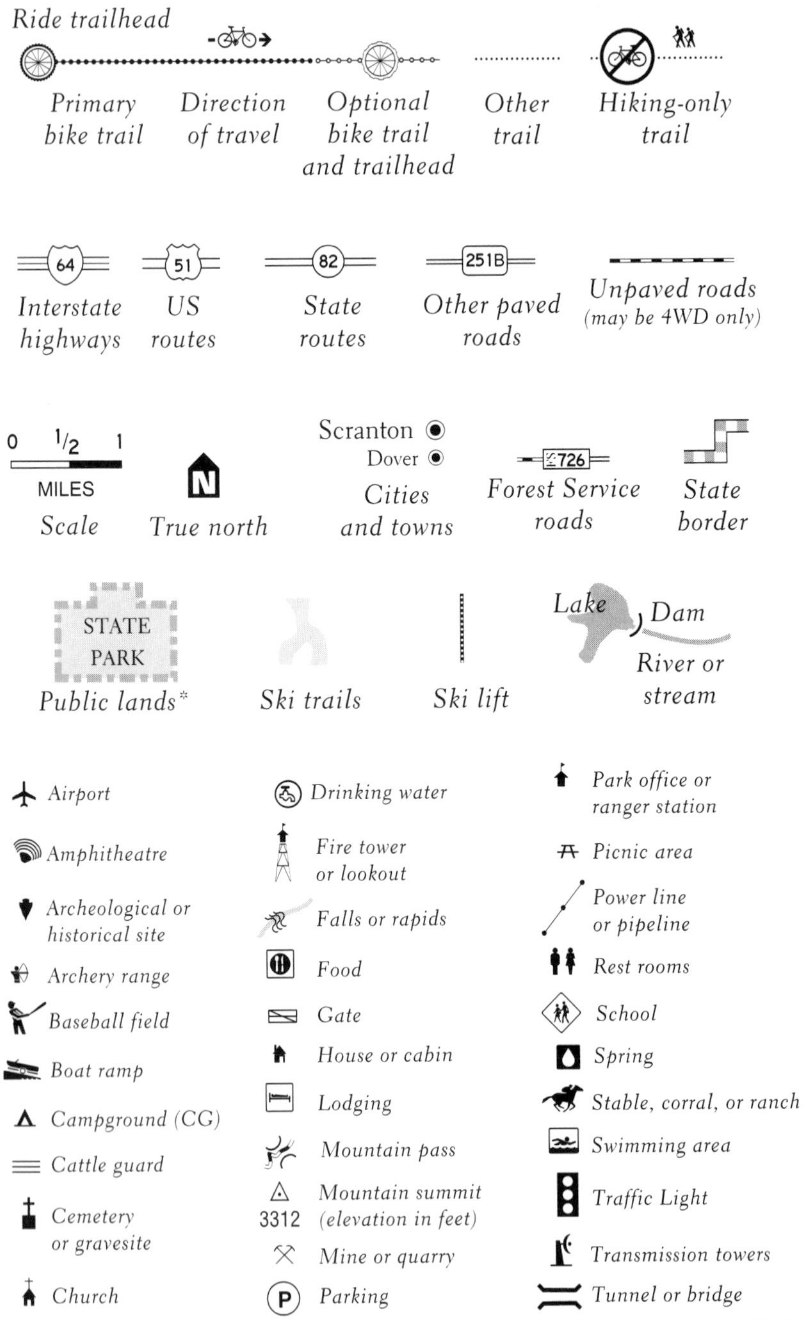

Ride trailhead

| Primary bike trail | Direction of travel | Optional bike trail and trailhead | Other trail | Hiking-only trail |

| Interstate highways | US routes | State routes | Other paved roads | Unpaved roads (may be 4WD only) |

64 · 51 · 82 · 251B

Scale — 0 1/2 1 MILES

True north — N

Scranton ◉
Dover ◉
Cities and towns

Forest Service roads — 726

State border

Public lands* — STATE PARK

Ski trails

Ski lift

Lake · Dam
River or stream

✈ Airport

☊ Amphitheatre

♥ Archeological or historical site

🏹 Archery range

Baseball field

Boat ramp

▲ Campground (CG)

≡ Cattle guard

✝ Cemetery or gravesite

♦ Church

🚰 Drinking water

Fire tower or lookout

Falls or rapids

🎰 Food

▭ Gate

House or cabin

▭ Lodging

Mountain pass

△ Mountain summit
3312 (elevation in feet)

✕ Mine or quarry

Ⓟ Parking

Park office or ranger station

┬ Picnic area

Power line or pipeline

👫 Rest rooms

School

■ Spring

🐎 Stable, corral, or ranch

Swimming area

Traffic Light

Transmission towers

Tunnel or bridge

Remember, private property exists in and around our national forests.

ACKNOWLEDGMENTS

Over the several years it took to put this book of rides together, I got a lot of help. Michael Margulis, author of *Mountain Biking New York* (1997, Falcon Press) loaned his expertise on several of his northern New Jersey rides. Dave Tambeaux and Dave Scull, two activists in the D.C./Baltimore trail advocacy scene and hopelessly addicted off-road fanatics, provided trail information for rides in Maryland. Other folks who helped by contributing information, listening to me bitch, or just coming along for the ride include Ann Lembo, Roger Bird, Steve Jones, Matt Marcus, Mike Hermann, Jes Stith, Jim Sota, Curt and Tawnya Finney, Mike Yozell, Neil Sandler, Jeremiah Bishop, Bruce and Robin Culver, Gil and Mary Willis, and Neal Palumbo.

FOREWORD

Welcome to *Mountain Bike!*, a series designed to provide all-terrain bikers with the information they need to find and ride the very best trails around. Whether you're new to the sport and don't know where to pedal, or an experienced mountain biker who wants to learn the classic trails in another region, this series is for you. Drop a few bucks for the book, spend an hour with the detailed maps and route descriptions, and you're prepared for the finest in off-road cycling.

My role as editor of this series was simple: First, find a mountain biker who knows the area and loves to ride. Second, ask that person to spend a year researching the most popular and very best rides around. And third, have that rider describe each trail in terms of difficulty, scenery, condition, elevation change, and all other categories of information that are important to trail riders. "Pretend you've just completed a ride and met up with fellow mountain bikers at the trailhead," I told each author. "Imagine their questions, be clear in your answers."

As I said, the *editorial* process—that of sending out riders and reading the submitted chapters—is a snap. But the work involved in finding, riding, and writing about each trail is enormous. In some instances our authors' tasks are made easier by the information contributed by local bike shops or cycling clubs, or even by the writers of local "where-to" guides. Credit for these contributions is provided, when appropriate, in each chapter, and our sincere thanks goes to all who have helped.

But the overwhelming majority of trails are discovered and pedaled by our authors themselves, then compared with dozens of other routes to determine if they qualify as "classic"—that area's best in scenery and cycling fun. If you've ever had the experience of pioneering a route from outdated topographic maps or entering a bike shop to request information from local riders who would much prefer to keep their favorite trails secret, or if you know how it is to double- and triple-check data to be positive your trail info is correct, then you have an idea of how each of our authors has labored to bring about these books. You and I, and all the mountain bikers of America, are the richer for their efforts.

You'll get more out of this book if you take a moment to read the Introduction, which explains how to read the trail listings. The Topographic Maps section will help you understand how useful topos will be on a ride, and will also tell you where to get them. And though this is a "where-to," not a "how-to" guide, those of you who have not traveled the backcountry might find Hitting the Trail of particular value.

In addition to the material above, newcomers to mountain biking might want to spend a minute with the glossary, page 343, so that terms like *hardpack*, *single-track*, and *waterbars* won't throw you when you come across them in the text.

Finally, the tips in the Afterword on mountain biking etiquette and the land-use controversy might help us all enjoy the trails a little more.

All the best.

Dennis Coello
St. Louis

PREFACE

Glance at a map of the east coast of the United States and two things jump out: First, a lot of cities are clustered along the Eastern Seaboard. And second, a substantial mountain range—the Appalachians—parallels the coast (and all those cities) from Georgia to New England.

The accident of geography that placed a major mountain range inland of the Atlantic Coast is a boon to mountain bikers who live in the populous East. Just consider: All you've got to do is load up the bikes, jump in the car, drive a few hours . . . and then plunge into off-road Nirvana on a nearly endless array of single-track trails and wooded roads that honeycomb the massive Appalachian Mountains.

Alas, there's only one problem. Often, there simply isn't enough time in the day to make this jaunt west to where mountain bikes were meant to be ridden—in the mountains. Even from Baltimore, Maryland, a city only an hour's drive from the closest mountain ridge, it's just not always convenient. Or, in the winter when the sun sets by five o'clock, it's not always *possible* to make the trek.

So what's an East Coast mountain biker to do when the urge strikes to hit the trail? This book has the answer—more than 100 of them, in fact. From the northern Mid-Atlantic states of Maryland, Pennsylvania, Delaware, and New Jersey, I've assembled a wide range of high-quality off-road riding destinations, most of which don't require a multihour drive west to the mountains. Here's why: Many state, county, and municipal parks, as well as city watersheds, are close to the region's major population centers and provide local riders with many convenient places to spin the cranks. There are also a few destinations close to large metropolitan areas that may surprise you—such as national wildlife refuges, government research centers, and even a few national parks that allow bikes. In other words, there's plenty of great riding right in your own backyard.

And what about when you've got the time to make the drive west to the mountains? You'll find those rides described here, too. We've got the best riding in the Allegheny range, including the Potomac and Laurel Highlands of West Virginia, Maryland, and Pennsylvania. You'll also find mountain trails a bit closer to major metropolitan areas, such as Maryland's Green Ridge and Savage River State Forests. And in Pennsylvania there are great rides around State College, Lewisburg, and the mountain bike mecca of Jim Thorpe.

Technical single-track, I discovered while researching this book, isn't found only in the mountains. Many trails close to metropolitan areas offer challenging riding to bikers who crave narrow trails, rocks, roots, and logs. And what about length? Alas, while many of the rides close to or in cities such as Baltimore and Philadelphia can't provide all-day escapes, they can be ridden in combination with other trails or retraced in the opposite direction (hey, the trail usually looks completely different on the way back), resulting in a jaunt a couple of hours long.

My survey of rides in the Mid-Atlantic North begins in the "Small Wonder" state of Delaware, heads south to Maryland (from its Kansas-flat eastern shore, through its rolling center, and west to the mountains), goes north to Pennsylvania (from the Laurel Highlands to Michaux State Forest in the south-central part of the state, and then east to York, State College, Jim Thorpe, and Philly), and on to New Jersey. I've also added three rides in the Catskills and Shawangunks of New York—only a few hours from New Jersey and one of the most scenic areas in the East. And that's not all. I've included some spectacular rides in eastern West Virginia, from Pocahontas County to Canaan Valley, the highest alpine valley this side of the Rockies.

In Delaware, about as mountainless a state as there is, mountain bikers needn't fret. Off-road cyclists can enjoy trails—not all of them flat—at several state and county parks. One of the best is Middle Run Valley Natural Area, 850 acres of forest and stream valleys that boast more than 15 miles of single-track trails. All of the Delaware trails I've included are convenient to the college town of Newark, home of the University of Delaware.

Maryland's Eastern Shore, a peninsula between the Atlantic Ocean and Chesapeake Bay, is renowned for its flat-as-Kansas topography. But if you think a self-powered vehicle with the word *mountain* in its name has no place in that kind of landscape, think again. I've included two rides that show off the shore's subtle beauty at its best. And while both rides are flat, the Eastern Shore's notorious headwinds almost guarantee you'll get a workout.

In southern Maryland, a state park, a state forest, and a wildlife refuge provide easy to moderate single-track trails on rolling terrain, along with two added bonuses: no rocks in the trails and plenty of chances to view aquatic waterfowl such as Canada geese and great blue herons. In central Maryland near the nation's capital, the 184-mile Chesapeake and Ohio Canal Towpath (the nation's most popular off-road trail) begins in trendy Georgetown. The C&O follows the Potomac River northwest to the western Maryland city of Cumberland. Along the way, off-road cyclists can enjoy equal amounts of scenic beauty, history, and—as you get away from the crowded Maryland suburbs of Washington—solitude. Last but not least, the wide towpath is virtually flat. If 184 miles is a bit too long, I've suggested places where you can start shorter rides along the path.

In Washington's Maryland suburbs, county and state parks are filling the growing need for legal mountain bike venues in the state's lush, rolling country-side. Montgomery County leads the way with Schaeffer Farm Trail in Seneca Creek State Park. Closer to Baltimore, two areas in Patapsco Valley State Park draw many D.C.-area riders to their challenging trail systems. North of Baltimore, mountain bikers like to play in the city's watersheds and on the flat North Central Railroad Trail, and on more challenging trails in Fair Hill Natural Resources Management Area and in Susquehanna State Park.

In Annapolis, the capital of Maryland, a paved rail-trail to Baltimore attracts throngs of cyclists on weekends. Only an hour or so away, northwest of D.C. near Frederick, single-track fanatics enjoy riding on real mountain trails in Gambrill and Greenbrier State Parks. Farther west, two state forests — Green Ridge and Savage River — draw mountain bikers attracted by equal doses of challenging trails and gorgeous scenery.

Pennsylvania is big, and so are its mountain-biking opportunities. In southwestern Pennsylvania, the Laurel Highlands boast the highest point in the state — Mount Davis at 3,213 feet. The Hidden Valley ski resort nearby is an excellent base for exploring some great trails in Forbes State Forest. Farther east — near Gettysburg, Waynesboro, and Chambersburg — Michaux State Forest is being hailed as one of the best mountain bike venues in the East, and it's only a couple of hours from Washington, Baltimore, and Philadelphia. Inside this book you'll discover some of the best rides at Michaux.

South-central Pennsylvania offers a surprising array of places to ride off-road, including Whitetail, a ski resort that keeps running its lifts after the slopes turn green. York is surrounded by county parks that are great riding destinations, while two flat trails around Harrisburg offer places for families to explore the countryside. State College also boasts great riding in and around the mountains just beyond the city limits — including a 30-mile, expert-only romp selected by the International Mountain Bicycling Association as a 1999 Epic Ride. To the east, outside Lewisburg, Bald Eagle State Forest offers more mountain biking over ridges and valleys near the state's geographical center. In the Poconos, Jim Thorpe (named for the Native American hero of the 1912 Olympics) offers scenic, easy trails on abandoned railroad grades and through a spectacular river gorge. The restored town on the Lehigh River, filled with bed-and-breakfasts and restaurants, is any mountain biker's reward for clean living.

Philadelphia and its environs also boast great off-road riding, from the flat and scenic Schuylkill Trail to the scenic spin through Fairmount Park (the largest municipal park in the United States), and in state and county parks in the suburbs. Among the best are French Creek State Park, Blue Marsh Lake (closer to Reading but still convenient to Philadelphia; its single-track trail has received numerous kudos in the national cycling press), and Valley Forge (where cyclists can cruise paved trails and get a history lesson at the same time).

Across the Delaware River in New Jersey, mountain bikers can explore a system of towpaths on the D&R Canal, ride excellent single-track in Wawayanda and Round Valley State Parks, and explore the vast nether regions of the Pine Barrens (bring a map and compass—it's easy to get lost in this huge wilderness). I've also included a few rides across the state line in New York because they're so close—well worth the drive for mountain bikers who enjoy spectacular mountain scenery.

West Virginia has earned the moniker "Colorado of the East" for a good reason: the 830,000-acre Monongahela National Forest. I've included some of the best off-road jaunts in and around this huge national forest, ranging from an easy but scenic ramble along the Greenbrier River to some of the toughest single-track in the country—Prop's Run in Slatyfork and Plantation Trail outside Davis. Each year, more and more mountain bikers in the populous East discover that West Virginia is well worth the drive. Try some of the trails in this book and you'll see why.

Armed with this guide and a fat-tired bike, you're ready to explore some of the best trails in the East. And if time doesn't allow, you can forgo the hassle of a multihour drive to the mountains. In other words, you're ready to start exploring the backcountry in your own backyard.

Joe Surkiewicz

Family

2 Lums Pond State Park
4 White Clay Creek State Park
5 White Clay Creek Trail
6 Assateague Island
7 Blackwater National Wildlife Refuge
14 C&O Canal Towpath
16 Capital Crescent Trail
20 Baltimore and Annapolis Trail Park
21 Patuxent Research Refuge North Tract
26 Northern Central Railroad Trail
39 North Woods Ramble
61 York Heritage Rail Trail
62 Stony Creek Wilderness Railroad Bed Trail
63 Conewago Recreational Trail
64 Lehigh Gorge State Park
69 Fairmount Park—Kelly and West River Drives
70 Schuylkill Trail
71 Valley Forge National Historical Park
72 Ridley Creek Park
80 Delaware and Raritan Canal State Park
86 Sussex Branch Trail
87 Paulinskill Valley Trail
93 Wallkill Valley Rail Trail
95 Greenbrier River Trail/Marlinton to Sharp's Tunnel
104 Camp 70 Road

Novice and Beginner (Trails, Not Roads)

2 Lums Pond State Park
8 Cedarville State Forest
10 St. Mary's River State Park
11 Black Hill Regional Park
29 Fair Hill Natural Resources Management Area
36 Poplar Lick/Elk Lick Loop
44 Caledonia Loop
46 Old Forge Loop
52 John Wert Path
56 Whitetail
65 Switchback Trail

73 Nottingham County Park
74 Hibernia County Park
84 Blue Mountain Lake Trail
99 Grant's Branch to Gandy Creek Loop

Intermediate and Advanced (Short Rides)

1 Iron Hill County Park
2 Middle Run Valley Natural Area
9 Jug Bay Natural Area
11 Schaeffer Farm Trail
15 Cabin John Trail
17 Cosca Regional Park
18 Gambrill State Park
19 Greenbrier State Park
23 Patapsco State Park—Avalon Area
24 Seminary Trail
25 Overshot Run Trail
27 Liberty Watershed
28 Susquehanna State Park
30 Hashawha Environmental Appreciation Center
31 Green Ridge MTB Trail
38 Race Loop
41 Slate Road, Piney Ridge Road to Pole Steeple Loop
42 ATV and Log Sled Trails via Piney Ridge Road
45 Mont Alto State Park Loop
54 Cowbell Hollow/Top Mountain Trail
55 Bear Gap Ride
58 Rocky Ridge County Park
59 Spring Valley County Park
60 Kain Park
66 Mauch Chunk Ridge
67 Weekend Warrior
68 Summer's Loop
75 French Creek State Park
76 Blue Marsh Lake
81 Round Valley Recreation Area
82 Allamuchy Mountain State Park
85 Kittatinny Valley State Park
88 Stokes State Forest
89 High Point State Park
90 Wawayanda State Park
91 Ringwood State Park

Intermediate and Advanced

- 92 Minnewaska State Park
- 96 Red Run
- 101 Allegheny Mountain/Seneca Creek Loop
- 106 Canaan Valley State Park

Intermediate and Advanced (Long Rides)

- 29 Fair Hill Natural Resources Management Area
- 37 Meadow Mountain/Monroe Run/Poplar Lick Loop
- 40 Kuhntown Loop
- 43 Long Pine Reservoir Loop
- 47 Tussey Mountain to Whipple Dam
- 48 Penn Roosevelt to Alan Seeger
- 49 State College to Alan Seeger
- 50 State College to Bear Meadows
- 51 Dirt Road Tour
- 53 The State College Epic Ride
- 56 Whitetail
- 75 French Creek State Park
- 76 Blue Marsh Lake
- 78 Wharton State Forest
- 79 Lebanon State Forest
- 81 Round Valley Recreation Area
- 92 Minnewaska State Park
- 94 Vernooy Kill Falls Trail
- 97 Prop's Run
- 98 Snowshoe
- 100 Big Run Loop
- 102 Plantation Trail
- 103 Canaan Loop Road (Forest Service Road 13)
- 107 Timberline

Lots of Loops

- 1 Iron Hill County Park
- 8 Cedarville State Forest
- 9 Jug Bay Natural Area
- 12 Schaeffer Farm Trail
- 13 Black Hill Regional Park
- 23 Patapsco Valley State Park—Avalon Area
- 29 Fair Hill Natural Resources Management Area
- 30 Hashawha Environmental Appreciation Center
- 33 Mertens Avenue

- 58 Rocky Ridge County Park
- 60 Kain Park
- 75 French Creek State Park
- 85 Kittatinny Valley State Park
- 98 Snowshoe
- 107 Timberline

Out-and-Backs

- 5 White Clay Creek Trail
- 6 Assateague Island
- 14 C&O Canal Towpath
- 15 Cabin John Trail
- 16 Capital Crescent Trail
- 20 Baltimore and Annapolis Trail Park
- 26 Northern Central Railroad Trail
- 47 Tussey Mountain to Whipple Dam
- 61 York County Heritage Rail Trail
- 62 Stony Creek Wilderness Railroad Bed Trail
- 63 Conewago Recreational Trail
- 64 Lehigh Gorge State Park
- 70 Schuylkill Trail
- 80 Delaware and Raritan Canal State Park
- 86 Sussex Branch Trail
- 87 Paulinskill Valley Trail
- 93 Wallkill Valley Rail Trail
- 95 Greenbrier River Trail/Marlinton to Sharp's Tunnel
- 104 Camp 70 Road
- 105 Olson Fire Tower

Shuttle Rides (When It's Nice to Have Two Cars)

- 14 C&O Canal Towpath
- 64 Lehigh Gorge State Park
- 70 Schuylkill Trail

Technical Heaven

- 1 Iron Hill County Park
- 11 Schaeffer Farm Trail
- 18 Gambrill State Park
- 23 Patapsco State Park—Avalon Area
- 28 Susquehanna State Park
- 29 Fair Hill Natural Resources Management Area
- 48 Penn Roosevelt to Alan Seeger
- 49 State College to Alan Seeger
- 56 Whitetail
- 58 Rocky Ridge County Park

Technical Heaven
(continued)

75 French Creek State Park
81 Round Valley Recreation Area
90 Wawayanda State Park
94 Vernooy Kill Falls Trail
96 Red Run
97 Prop's Run
98 Snowshoe
100 Big Run Loop
102 Plantation Trail
106 Canaan Valley State Park
107 Timberline

High-Speed Cruising

7 Blackwater National Wildlife Refuge
14 C&O Canal Towpath
21 Patuxent Research Refuge North Tract
26 Northern Central Railroad Trail
61 York County Heritage Rail Trail
62 Stony Creek Wilderness Railroad Bed Trail
63 Conewago Recreational Trail
64 Lehigh Gorge State Park
70 Schuylkill Trail
78 Wharton State Forest
79 Lebanon State Forest
80 Delaware and Raritan Canal State Park
83 Delaware Water Gap National Recreation Area
86 Sussex Branch Trail
87 Paulinskill Valley Trail
93 Wallkill Valley Rail Trail
95 Greenbrier River Trail/Marlinton to Sharp's Tunnel
104 Camp 70 Road
105 Olson Fire Tower

Wildlife Viewing

2 Lums Pond State Park
3 Middle Run Valley Natural Area
4 White Clay Creek State Park
5 White Clay Creek Trail
6 Assateague Island
7 Blackwater National Wildlife Refuge

9 Jug Bay Natural Area
14 C&O Canal Towpath
21 Patuxent Research Refuge North Tract
26 Northern Central Railroad Trail
30 Hashawha Environmental Appreciation Center
50 State College to Whipple Dam and Bear Meadows
52 John Wert Path
62 Stony Creek Wilderness Railroad Bed Trail
64 Lehigh Gorge State Park
65 Switchback Trail
78 Wharton State Forest
79 Lebanon State Forest
83 Delaware Water Gap National Recreation Area
92 Minnewaska State Park
95 Greenbrier River Trail/Marlinton to Sharp's Tunnel
96 Red Run
104 Camp 70 Road
106 Canaan Valley State Park

Great Scenery

7 Blackwater National Wildlife Refuge
14 C&O Canal Towpath
32 Stafford–East Valley Roads Loop
47 Tussey Mountain to Whipple Dam
53 The State College Epic Ride
56 Whitetail
64 Lehigh Gorge State Park
67 Weekend Warrior
69 Fairmount Park—Kelly and West River Drives
83 Delaware Water Gap National Recreation Area
89 High Point State Park
92 Minnewaska State Park
95 Greenbrier River Trail/Marlinton to Sharp's Tunnel
96 Red Run
97 Prop's Run
98 Snowshoe
99 Grant's Branch to Gandy Creek Loop

100 Big Run Loop
101 Allegheny Mountain/Seneca Creek
    Loop
104 Camp 70 Road
105 Olson Fire Tower
106 Canaan Valley State Park
107 Timberline

Historical Rides
14 C&O Canal Towpath
28 Susquehanna State Park
57 Gettysburg National Military Park
61 York County Heritage Rail Trail
69 Fairmount Park—Kelly and West
    River Drives
70 Schuylkill Trail
71 Valley Forge National Historical
    Park
72 Ridley Creek State Park
75 French Creek State Park
77 Tyler State Park
78 Wharton State Forest

79 Lebanon State Forest
80 Delaware and Raritan Canal State
    Park
91 Ringwood State Park
92 Minnewaska State Park

Most Difficult
(Technically *and* Aerobically)
18 Gambrill State Park
23 Patapsco Valley State Park—Avalon
    Area
48 Penn Roosevelt to Alan Seeger
53 The State College Epic Ride
56 Whitetail
81 Round Valley Recreation Area
94 Vernooy Kill Falls Trail
97 Prop's Run
98 Snowshoe
100 Big Run Loop
102 Plantation Trail
107 Timberline

INTRODUCTION

TRAIL DESCRIPTION OUTLINE

Each trail in this book begins with key information that includes length, configuration, aerobic and technical difficulty, trail conditions, scenery, and special comments. Additional description is contained in 11 individual categories. The following will help you to understand all of the information provided.

Trail name: Trail names are as designated on United States Geological Survey (USGS) or Forest Service or other maps, and/or by local custom.

At a Glance Information

Length/configuration: The overall length of a trail is described in miles, unless stated otherwise. The configuration is a description of the shape of each trail — whether the trail is a loop, out-and-back (that is, along the same route), figure eight, trapezoid, isosceles triangle, decahedron . . . (just kidding), or if it connects with another trail described in the book. See the Glossary for definitions of *point-to-point* and *combination*.

Aerobic difficulty: This provides a description of the degree of physical exertion required to complete the ride.

Technical difficulty: This provides a description of the technical skill required to pedal a ride. Trails are often described here in terms of being paved, unpaved, sandy, hard-packed, washboarded, two- or four-wheel-drive, single-track or double-track. All terms that might be unfamiliar to the first-time mountain biker are defined in the Glossary.

Note: For both the aerobic and technical difficulty categories, authors were asked to keep in mind the fact that all riders are not equal, and thus to gauge the trail in terms of how the middle-of-the-road rider — someone between the newcomer and Ned Overend — could handle the route. Comments about the trail's length, condition, and elevation change will also assist you in determining the difficulty of any trail relative to your own abilities.

Scenery: Here you will find a general description of the natural surroundings during the seasons most riders pedal the trail and a suggestion of what is to be found at special times (like great fall foliage or cactus in bloom).

Special comments: Unique elements of the ride are mentioned.

Category Information

General location: This category describes where the trail is located in reference to a nearby town or other landmark.

Elevation change: Unless stated otherwise, the figure provided is the total gain and loss of elevation along the trail. In regions where the elevation variation is not extreme, the route is simply described as flat, rolling, or possessing short steep climbs or descents.

Season: This is the best time of year to pedal the route, taking into account trail conditions (for example, when it will not be muddy), riding comfort (when the weather is too hot, cold, or wet), and local hunting seasons.

Note: Because the opening and closing dates of deer, elk, moose, and antelope seasons often change from year to year, riders should check with the local Fish and Game Department or call a sporting goods store (or any place that sells hunting licenses) in a nearby town before heading out. Wear bright clothes in the fall, and don't wear suede jackets while in the saddle. Hunter's-orange tape on the helmet is also a good idea.

Services: This category is of primary importance in guides for paved-road tourers and is far less crucial to most mountain bike trail descriptions because there are usually no services whatsoever to be found. Authors have noted when water is available on desert or long mountain routes and have listed the availability of food, lodging, campgrounds, and bike shops. If all these services are present, you will find only the words, "All services available in . . ."

Hazards: Special hazards like steep cliffs, great amounts of deadfall, or barbed-wire fences very close to the trail are noted here.

Rescue index: Determining how far one is from help on a particular trail can be difficult due to the backcountry nature of most mountain bike rides. Authors therefore state the proximity of homes or Forest Service outposts, nearby roads where one might hitch a ride, or the likelihood of other bikers being encountered on the trail. Phone numbers of local sheriff departments or hospitals have not been provided because phones are almost never available. If you are able to reach a phone, the local operator will connect you with emergency services.

Land status: This category provides information regarding whether the trail crosses land operated by the Forest Service, the Bureau of Land Management, or a city, state, or national park; whether it crosses private land whose owner (at the time the author did the research) has allowed mountain bikers right of passage; and so on.

Note: Authors have been extremely careful to offer only those routes that are open to bikers and are legal to ride. However, because land ownership changes over time, and because the land-use controversy created by mountain bikes still has not completely subsided, it is the duty of each cyclist to look for and to heed signs warning against trail use. Don't expect this book to get you off the hook when you're facing some small-town judge for pedaling past a "Biking Prohibited" sign erected the day before you arrived. Look for these signs, read them, and heed the advice. And remember, there's always another trail.

Maps: The maps in this book have been produced with great care, and, in conjunction with the trail-following suggestions, will help you stay on course. But as every experienced mountain biker knows, things can get tricky in the backcountry. It is therefore strongly suggested that you avail yourself of the detailed information found in the USGS (United States Geological Survey) 7.5 minute series topographic maps. In some cases, authors have found that specific Forest Service or other maps may be more useful than the USGS quads, and they tell how to obtain them.

Finding the trail: Detailed information on how to reach the trailhead and where to park your car is provided here.

Sources of additional information: Here you will find the address and/or phone number of a bike shop, governmental agency, or other source from which trail information can be obtained.

Notes on the trail: This is where you are guided carefully through any portions of the trail that are particularly difficult to follow. The author also may add information about the route that does not fit easily in the other categories. This category will not be present for those rides where the route is easy to follow.

ABBREVIATIONS

The following road-designation abbreviations are used in the *Mountain Bike!* series:

CR	County Road	I-	Interstate	
FR	Farm Route	IR	Indian Route	
FS	Forest Service road	US	United States highway	

State highways are designated with the appropriate two-letter state abbreviation, followed by the road number. Example: MD 417 = Maryland State Highway 417.

Postal Service two-letter state codes:

AL	Alabama	AZ	Arizona
AK	Alaska	AR	Arkansas

CA	California	NV	Nevada
CO	Colorado	NH	New Hampshire
CT	Connecticut	NJ	New Jersey
DE	Delaware	NM	New Mexico
DC	District of Columbia	NY	New York
FL	Florida	NC	North Carolina
GA	Georgia	ND	North Dakota
HI	Hawaii	OH	Ohio
ID	Idaho	OK	Oklahoma
IL	Illinois	OR	Oregon
IN	Indiana	PA	Pennsylvania
IA	Iowa	RI	Rhode Island
KS	Kansas	SC	South Carolina
KY	Kentucky	SD	South Dakota
LA	Louisiana	TN	Tennessee
ME	Maine	TX	Texas
MD	Maryland	UT	Utah
MA	Massachusetts	VT	Vermont
MI	Michigan	VA	Virginia
MN	Minnesota	WA	Washington
MS	Mississippi	WV	West Virginia
MO	Missouri	WI	Wisconsin
MT	Montana	WY	Wyoming
NE	Nebraska		

RIDE CONFIGURATIONS

Combination: This type of route may combine two or more configurations. For example, a point-to-point route may integrate a scenic loop or an out-and-back spur midway through the ride. Likewise, an out-and-back may have a loop at its farthest point (this configuration looks like a cherry with a stem attached; the stem is the out-and-back, the fruit is the terminus loop). Or a loop route may have multiple out-and-back spurs and/or loops to the side. Mileage for a combination route is for the total distance to complete the ride.

Loop: This route configuration is characterized by riding from the designated trailhead to a distant point, then returning to the trailhead via a different route (or simply continuing on the same in a circle route) without doubling back. You always move forward across new terrain but return to the starting point when finished. Mileage is for the entire loop from the trailhead back to trailhead.

Out-and-back: A ride where you will return on the same trail you pedaled out. While this might sound far more boring than a loop route, many trails look very different when pedaled in the opposite direction.

Point-to-point: A vehicle shuttle (or similar assistance) is required for this type of route, which is ridden from the designated trailhead to a distant location, or endpoint, where the route ends. Total mileage is for the one-way trip from the trailhead to endpoint.

Spur: A road or trail that intersects the main trail you're following.

Ride Configurations contributed by Gregg Bromka

TOPOGRAPHIC MAPS

The maps in this book, when used in conjunction with the route directions present in each chapter, will in most instances be sufficient to get you to the trail and keep you on it. However, you will find superior detail and valuable information in the USGS 7.5 minute series topographic maps. Recognizing how indispensable these are to bikers and hikers alike, many bike shops and sporting goods stores now carry topos of the local area.

If you're brand new to mountain biking you might be wondering, "What's a topographic map?" In short, these differ from standard "flat" maps in that they indicate not only linear distance but elevation as well. One glance at a topo will show you the difference, for contour lines are spread across the map like dozens of intricate spider webs. Each contour line represents a particular elevation, and at the base of each topo a particular contour interval designation is given. Yes, it sounds confusing if you're new to the lingo, but it truly is a simple and wonderfully helpful system. Keep reading.

Let's assume that the 7.5 minute series topo before us says "Contour Interval 40 feet," that the short trail we'll be pedaling is two inches in length on the map, and that it crosses five contour lines from its beginning to end. What do we know? Well, because the linear scale of this series is 2,000 feet to the inch (roughly 2¾ inches representing 1 mile), we know our trail is approximately ⅘ of a mile long (2 inches **X** 2,000 feet). But we also know we'll be climbing or descending 200 vertical feet (5 contour lines **X** 40 feet each) over that distance. And the elevation designations written on occasional contour lines will tell us if we're heading up or down.

The authors of this series warn their readers of upcoming terrain, but only a detailed topo gives you the information you need to pinpoint your position on a map, steer yourself toward optional trails and roads nearby, and to see at a glance if you'll be pedaling hard to take them. It's a lot of information for a very low cost. In fact, the only drawback with topos is their size—several feet square. I've tried rolling them into tubes, folding them carefully, even cutting them into blocks and photocopying the pieces. Any of these systems is a pain, but no matter how you pack the maps you'll be happy they're along. And you'll be even happier if you pack a compass as well.

In addition to local bike shops and sporting goods stores, you'll find topos at major universities and some public libraries, where you might try photocopying the ones you need to avoid the cost of buying them. But if you want your own and can't find them locally, contact:

USGS Map Sales
Box 25286
Denver, CO 80225
(800) HELP MAP (435-7627)

VISA and MasterCard are accepted. Ask for an index while you're at it, plus a price list and a copy of the booklet *Topographic Maps*. In minutes you'll be reading them like a pro.

A second excellent series of maps available to mountain bikers is that put out by the United States Forest Service. If your trail runs through an area designated as a national forest, look in the phone book (white pages) under the United States Government listings, find the Department of Agriculture heading, and run your finger down that section until you find the Forest Service. Give them a call and they'll provide the address of the regional Forest Service office, from which you can obtain the appropriate map.

TRAIL ETIQUETTE

Pick up almost any mountain bike magazine these days and you'll find articles and letters to the editor about trail conflict. For example, you'll find hikers' tales of being blindsided by speeding mountain bikers, complaints from mountain bikers about being blamed for trail damage that was really caused by horse or cattle traffic, and cries from bikers about those "kamikaze" riders who through their antics threaten to close even more trails to all of us.

The authors of this series have been very careful to guide you to only those trails that are open to mountain biking (or at least were open at the time of their research), and without exception have warned of the damage done to our sport through injudicious riding. We can all benefit from glancing over the following International Mountain Bicycling Association (IMBA) Rules of the Trail before saddling up.

1. *Ride on open trails only.* Respect trail and road closures (ask if not sure), avoid possible trespass on private land, obtain permits and authorization as may be required. Federal and state wilderness areas are closed to cycling.

2. *Leave no trace.* Be sensitive to the dirt beneath you. Even on open trails, you should not ride under conditions where you will leave evidence of your passing, such as on certain soils shortly after rain. Observe the different types of soils and trail construction; practice low-impact cycling. This also means staying on the trail and not creating any new ones. Be sure to pack out at least as much as you pack in.

3. *Control your bicycle!* Inattention for even a second can cause disaster. Excessive speed can maim and threaten people; there is no excuse for it!

4. *Always yield the trail.* Make known your approach well in advance. A friendly greeting (or a bell) is considerate and works well; startling someone may cause loss of trail access. Show your respect when passing others by slowing to a walk or even stopping. Anticipate that other trail users may be around corners or in blind spots.

5. *Never spook animals.* All animals are startled by an unannounced approach, a sudden movement, or a loud noise. This can be dangerous for you, for others, and for the animals. Give animals extra room and time to adjust to you. In passing, use special care and follow the directions of horseback riders (ask if uncertain). Running cattle and disturbing wild animals is a serious offense. Leave gates as you found them or as marked.

6. *Plan ahead.* Know your equipment, your ability, and the area in which you are riding—and prepare accordingly. Be self-sufficient at all times. Wear a helmet, keep your machine in good condition, and carry necessary supplies for changes in weather or other conditions. A well-executed trip is a satisfaction to you and not a burden or offense to others.

For more information, contact IMBA, P.O. Box 7578, Boulder, CO 80306, (303) 545-9011.

HITTING THE TRAIL

Once again, because this is a "where-to," not a "how-to" guide, the following will be brief. If you're a veteran trail rider, these suggestions might serve to remind you of something you've forgotten to pack. If you're a newcomer, they might convince you to think twice before hitting the backcountry unprepared.

Water: I've heard the questions dozens of times. "How much is enough? One bottle? Two? Three?! But think of all that extra weight!" Well, one simple physiological fact should convince you to err on the side of excess when it comes to deciding how much water to pack: A human working hard in 90-degree temperature needs approximately ten quarts of fluids every day. Ten quarts. That's two and a half gallons—12 large water bottles or 16 small ones. And, with water weighing in at approximately 8 pounds per gallon, a one-day supply comes to a whopping 20 pounds.

In other words, pack along two or three bottles even for short rides. And make sure you can purify the water found along the trail on longer routes. When writing of those routes where this could be of critical importance, each author has provided information on where water can be found near the trail—if it can be found at all. But drink it untreated and you run the risk of disease. (See *giardia* in the Glossary.)

One sure way to kill the protozoans, bacteria, and viruses in water is to boil it. Right. That's just how you want to spend your time on a bike ride. Besides, who wants to carry a stove or denude the countryside stoking bonfires to boil water?

Luckily, there is a better way. Many riders pack along the inexpensive and only slightly distasteful tetraglycine hydroperiodide tablets (sold under the names Potable Aqua, Globaline, and Coughlan's, among others). Some invest in portable, lightweight purifiers that filter out the crud. Unfortunately, both iodine *and* filtering are now required to be absolutely sure you've killed all the nasties you can't see. Tablets or iodine drops by themselves will knock off the well-known *giardia*, once called "beaver fever" for its transmission to the water through the feces of infected beavers. One to four weeks after ingestion, giardia will have you bloated, vomiting, shivering with chills, and living in the bathroom. (Though you won't care while you're suffering, beavers are getting a bum rap, for other animals are carriers also.)

But now there's another parasite we must worry about—*cryptosporidium*. "Crypto" brings on symptoms very similar to giardia, but unlike that fellow protozoan it's equipped with a shell sufficiently strong to protect it against the chemical killers that stop giardia cold. This means we're either back to boiling or on to using a water filter to screen out both giardia and crypto, plus the iodine to knock off viruses. All of which sounds like a time-consuming pain, but really isn't. Some water filters come equipped with an iodine chamber to guarantee full protection. Or you can simply add a pill or drops to the water you've just filtered (if you aren't allergic to iodine, of course). The pleasures of backcountry biking—and the displeasure of getting sick—make this relatively minor effort worth every one of the few minutes involved.

Tools: Ever since my first cross-country tour in 1965 I've been kidded about the number of tools I pack on the trail. And so I will exit entirely from this discussion by providing a list compiled by two mechanic (and mountain biker) friends of mine. After all, since they make their livings fixing bikes, and get their kicks by riding them, who could be a better source?

These two suggest the following as an absolute minimum:

tire levers
spare tube and patch kit
air pump
Allen wrenches (3, 4, 5, and 6 mm)
six-inch crescent (adjustable-end) wrench
small flat-blade screwdriver
chain rivet tool
spoke wrench

But, while they're on the trail, their personal tool pouches contain these additional items:

channel locks (small)
air gauge
tire valve cap (the metal kind, with a valve-stem remover)
baling wire (ten or so inches, for temporary repairs)
duct tape (small roll for temporary repairs or tire boot)
boot material (small piece of old tire or a large tube patch)
spare chain link
rear derailleur pulley
spare nuts and bolts
paper towel and tube of waterless hand cleaner

First-Aid kit: My personal kit contains the following, sealed inside double Ziploc bags:

sunscreen
aspirin
butterfly-closure bandages
Band-Aids
gauze compress pads (a half-dozen 4" X 4")
gauze (one roll)
ace bandages or Spenco joint wraps
Benadryl (an antihistamine, in case of allergic reactions)
water purification tablets/water filter (on long rides)
Moleskin/Spenco "Second Skin"
hydrogen peroxide, iodine, or Mercurochrome (some kind of antiseptic)
snakebite kit

Final considerations: The authors of this series have done a good job suggesting that specific items be packed for certain trails—rain gear in particular seasons, a hat and gloves for mountain passes, or shades for desert jaunts. Heed their warnings, and think ahead. Good luck.

Dennis Coello

AND NOW, A WORD ABOUT CELLULAR PHONES . . .

Thinking of bringing the Flip-Fone along on your next off-road ride? Before you do, ask yourself the following questions:

- Do I know where I'm going? Do I have an adequate map? Can I use a compass effectively? Do I know the shortest way to civilization if I need to bail out early and find some help?

- If I'm on the trail for longer than planned, am I ready for it? Do I have adequate water? Have I packed something to eat? Will I be warm enough if I'm still out there after dark?

- Am I prepared for possible injuries? Do I have a first-aid kit? Do I know what to do in case of a cut, fracture, snakebite, or heat exhaustion?

- Is my tool kit adequate for likely mechanical problems? Can I fix a flat? Can I untangle a chain? Am I prepared to walk out if the bike is unridable?

If you answered "yes" to *every* question above, you may pack the phone, but consider a good whistle instead. It's lighter, cheaper, and nearly as effective.

They start searching for you but dusk is only two hours away, and you have no signaling device and your throat is too dry to shout, and meanwhile you can't get the bleeding stopped, you are out of luck. I mean *really* out of luck.

And when the battery goes dead, you're on your own again. Enough said.

Jeff Faust
Author of Mountain Bike! New Hampshire

DELAWARE

Located halfway between New York and Washington, D.C., Delaware calls itself the Small Wonder. Though consisting of only a few counties jammed between the Delaware and Chesapeake Bays, Delaware offers a surprising amount of diversity between the rolling hills around the college town of Newark in the north and the beaches and flatlands to the south.

Delaware is mountainless, but that doesn't mean the state doesn't offer good places to ride mountain bikes. In my survey of the best riding in the state, I've concentrated on parks and nature preserves around Newark, which is conveniently close to Interstate 95 and home to the University of Delaware. They include Middle Run Valley Natural Area and its 20-mile system of challenging single-track; White Clay Creek and two easy but scenic rides, Lums Pond State Park and a 10-mile multipurpose trail near the Chesapeake and Delaware Canal; and Iron Hill County Park—a small park near I-95 with miles of fun, not-too-technical single-track that are a joy to ride.

Folks in Delaware aren't too far from great riding in nearby states, either. The most popular and closest is Fair Hill, just across the state line in Maryland.

You say there are no mountains in Delaware? Hey, no problem. This state offers plenty to explore on knobby tires.

RIDE 1 · Iron Hill County Park

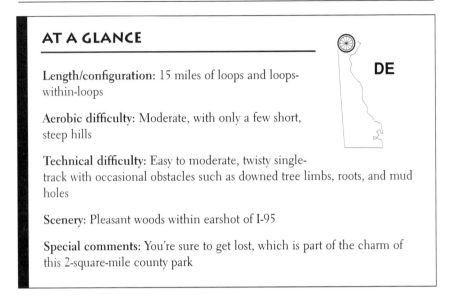

AT A GLANCE

DE

Length/configuration: 15 miles of loops and loops-within-loops

Aerobic difficulty: Moderate, with only a few short, steep hills

Technical difficulty: Easy to moderate, twisty single-track with occasional obstacles such as downed tree limbs, roots, and mud holes

Scenery: Pleasant woods within earshot of I-95

Special comments: You're sure to get lost, which is part of the charm of this 2-square-mile county park

As its name suggests, Iron Hill County Park is located at an old mining site. So it's no surprise that the 15 miles or so of single-track traverses several pits, bowls, and slag heaps. Sound a bit too industrial for a mountain bike venue? Not at all. Sooner or later you'll meet every mountain biker from this part of Delaware—and a lot of University of Delaware students from nearby Newark—in this popular county park. The trails are mostly flat, smooth dirt with a hard-packed clay base. The hilly spots are littered with a few rocks and roots, just to make sure you're paying attention.

Regulars sing the praises of the heart-stopping Mega-Dip, a 30-foot-deep trench with smooth, steep clay sides. It works like this: Once you drop in from one side of the trench, you're committed to making it up the other side—by pedaling furiously. Less experienced mountain bikers—or those who paint mental pictures of bandaged patients in traction at the thought of flying down steep embankments—may want to pass on the experience. As one frequent rider put it, "Only the gonzo survive!"

The Mega-Dip aside, riding at Iron Hill County Park is fairly sedate, with difficulty ranging from easy to moderate. The single-track is a joy to explore, and the trails are well maintained by local cyclists. It's twisty-turny stuff punctuated with lots of tree limbs and trunks to hop over.

General location: Newark.

Elevation change: Moderate. They didn't name this Iron Hill for nothing; but the climbs are generally long and easy, except around the trenches left from the mining era (they're easily avoided if white-knuckle descents aren't your thing).

RIDE 1 · Iron Hill County Park

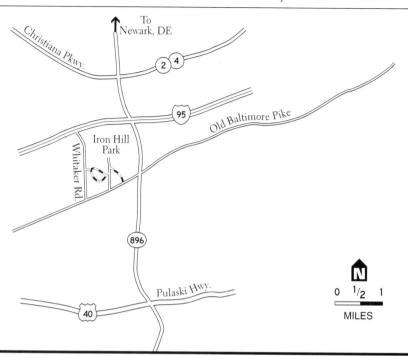

Season: Year-round.

Services: Picnic pavilions, barbecue pits in the woods, and grassy fields for playing frisbee round out the park's attractions. When you come, bring all you need; there's no phone, no ranger, and no water available in this two-square-mile park. All services are available in Newark.

Hazards: The clay-based trails get icy-slick when wet.

Rescue index: Good; access to phone and traffic is on nearby DE 896.

Land status: County park.

Maps: None available; none needed. See below.

Finding the trail: Take DE 896 south out of Newark. Turn right at the first traffic light after I-95, Old Baltimore Pike. Drive 1 mile to Whitaker Road, turn right, and go half a mile to the park entrance on the right. Park in the last (third) parking lot. All of the trails lead from the main fire road just beyond the yellow security bar. At the first intersection, turn right to reach the Mega-Dip and a labyrinth of single-track; turn left to explore a somewhat smaller maze of trails. The fire road continues for about a half-mile and ends at the first parking lot near the park entrance; more trails intersect the road on the way.

This easy fire road leads to a maze of fun single-track at Iron Hill Park.

Source of additional information:

Wooden Wheels Bike Shop
638 Newark Shopping Center
Newark, DE 19711
(302) 368-2453

Notes on the trail: Think of Iron Hill as the perfect backyard: hundreds of acres of woods honeycombed with narrow trails going every which way. Don't worry about getting lost—you will. Few of the trails are marked, and the ones that are blazed don't help because you don't know where they go. I rode here for about 2 hours with a friend; we got lost in 5 minutes and had a great time zooming around the single-track, oblivious to where the heck we were. When we decided we'd had enough, we chose trails that went uphill and eventually stumbled back into the parking lot. Great fun.

Final Note: For those driving on I-95, this is a great spot to stop and get a workout. It's about 2 minutes from the interstate.

RIDE 2 · Lums Pond State Park

AT A GLANCE

DE

Length/configuration: 10-mile loop

Aerobic difficulty: Easy

Technical difficulty: Easy

Scenery: Nice woods, fields, and glimpses of a lake

Special comments: Watch for horses on this multiuse trail

The 1,757-acre Lums Pond State Park is located on the north side of the Chesapeake and Delaware Canal, a major shipping link between Chesapeake and Delaware Bays. Lums Pond, the 200-acre lake that is the park's centerpiece, was created in the early 1800s to fill the locks of the canal and power a small mill. Today the park is an attractive recreational venue in this bustling corner of Delaware. Fishing, ball sports, picnicking, and boating are major draws, but mountain bikers aren't forgotten. They can ride a ten-mile multiuse trail that circumnavigates the lake. Though not particularly scenic—a hiker-only trail follows the lakeshore, while the bike/equestrian trail is mostly routed away from the water—it's a chance to spin the cranks through quiet woods without the hassles of traffic.

For most of its length, the trail is a wide, grassy fire road winding through high shrubbery and second-growth forest. Occasionally the trail leaves the woods, following the edge of corn fields and passing suburban houses. There isn't much in the way of hills—the few you'll encounter aren't long or steep—and the trail is technically very easy, with few rocks, roots, or fallen trees along the path. Except in late summer and fall, expect to get your feet wet in a few boggy spots that punctuate the ride.

And après-ride? In the summer, take a swim in the lake, rent a boat, or enjoy a picnic at one of many picnic areas scattered throughout this attractive park.

General location: Newark.

Elevation change: Nominal.

Season: Year-round. The trail has a few boggy spots that usually dry out by July and stay dry through the fall. In the spring and after extremely wet weather, much of the trail is submerged, making it not much fun to ride.

Services: Camping is available in the park April through October, and there's a food concession in the swimming/beach area. All other services are available in Newark.

RIDE 2 · Lums Pond State Park

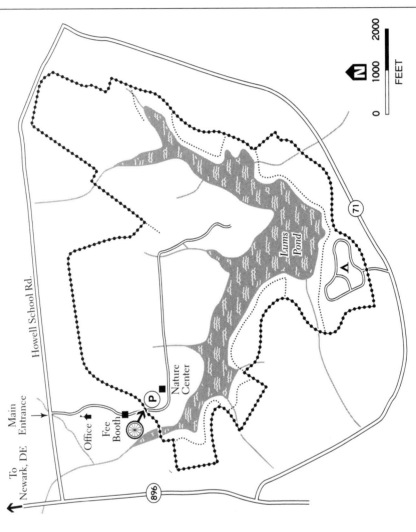

Hazards: Hunting is permitted in the park in the fall and winter; check at the park office.

Rescue index: Excellent. The trail passes paved roads and private residences. There's a pay phone at the entrance to the campground.

Land status: State park.

Maps: A trail map is available at the park office.

Finding the trail: Take DE 896 south from Newark and turn left on Howell School Road to the main entrance. Park at the nature center, just past the fee

Relax by the lake at
Lums Pond State Park
before or after a ride.

booth inside the park entrance. Ride your bike back toward the fee booth; the
multiuse trail crosses the road under the power lines. Turn left onto the trail
and ride counterclockwise around Lums Pond.

Source of additional information:

Lums Pond State Park
1068 Howell School Road
Bear, DE 19701
(302) 368-6989

Notes on the trail: The trail, which cyclists share with equestrians, is well
marked and easy to follow. Avoid riding after really wet weather, as much of the
trail is a quagmire of wheel-sucking Delaware clay punctuated with 4-inch-deep
horse-hoof holes. Ugh.

RIDE 3 · Middle Run Valley Natural Area

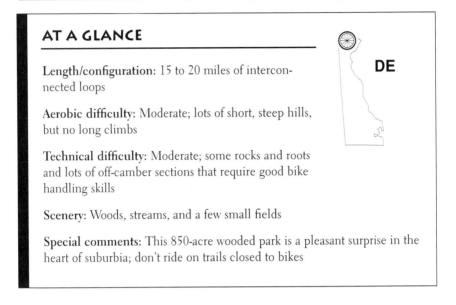

AT A GLANCE

DE

Length/configuration: 15 to 20 miles of interconnected loops

Aerobic difficulty: Moderate; lots of short, steep hills, but no long climbs

Technical difficulty: Moderate; some rocks and roots and lots of off-camber sections that require good bike handling skills

Scenery: Woods, streams, and a few small fields

Special comments: This 850-acre wooded park is a pleasant surprise in the heart of suburbia; don't ride on trails closed to bikes

Middle Run Valley Natural Area is a relatively new park located in suburban Newark—and it's a real boon to area mountain bikers. With close to 20 miles of single-track, Middle Run attracts a wide range of off-road enthusiasts who enjoy fun—but not overly buffed and maintained—wooded loop riding.

Among the best features of the park, aside from the trails, are the trees. Tall and abundant, the forests of Middle Run Valley represent a large sampling of species indigenous to Delaware: tulip tree/yellow poplar, American beech, oaks, American sycamore, green ash, maples, hickory, chestnut, black locust, and black cherry. Bird life is also abundant. The park is home to cardinals, woodpeckers, and chickadees, as well as such rare and uncommon birds as owls, hawks, and pheasants. Overall, Middle Run Valley supports more than 170 different types of birds. Other wildlife to look for include eastern gray and red squirrels, rabbits, woodchucks, moles, mice, voles, shrews, turtles, toads, salamanders, raccoons, opossum, and the occasional red fox and white-tailed deer.

General location: Newark.

Elevation change: Less than 500 feet on many short, steep hills.

Season: Year-round.

Services: All services are available in Newark.

Hazards: Watch for off-camber trail along steep stream banks. Three out of the four stream crossings don't have bridges; use care.

Rescue index: Excellent; the entire area is surrounded by paved roads and residences.

RIDE 3 · Middle Run Valley Natural Area

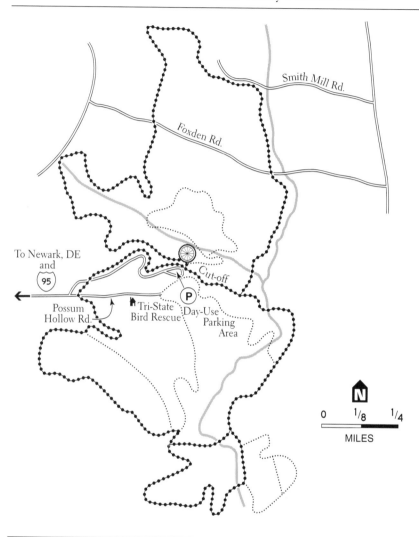

Land status: County park.

Maps: New Castle County Parks, (302) 323-6400; Wooden Wheels Bike Shop, (302) 368-2453.

Finding the trail: From I-95, take Exit 3 (DE 273) toward Newark. Turn right on South Chapel Street, which becomes Paper Mill Road. Next, turn right onto Possum Park Road and make an almost immediate left onto Possum Hollow Road and the park entrance. Look for a gravel road on the left that leads to the day-use parking area; park there. On your bike, look toward the opening in the woods, where there are two trailheads.

Source of additional information:

Wooden Wheels Bike Shop
638 Newark Shopping Center
Newark, DE 19711
(302) 368-2453

Notes on the trail: The park trails open to bikes are easy to follow and signed. For the easiest introduction to Middle Run Valley, try the 6.75-mile Lenape Trail, which starts and ends in the day-use parking area. It crosses paved roads, as well as Middle Run and its tributaries, several times and can be shortened by riding a cutoff and a shortcut.

RIDE 4 · White Clay Creek State Park

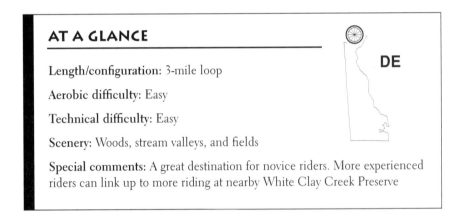

AT A GLANCE

DE

Length/configuration: 3-mile loop

Aerobic difficulty: Easy

Technical difficulty: Easy

Scenery: Woods, stream valleys, and fields

Special comments: A great destination for novice riders. More experienced riders can link up to more riding at nearby White Clay Creek Preserve

Tucked in a corner of Delaware near the curved Pennsylvania state line is White Clay Creek State Park, 707 acres of rolling fields and woods only three miles northwest of Newark on DE 896. This pleasant park, only minutes from I-95 where it crosses the Maryland-Delaware border, is an oasis for fat-tire cyclists in crowded New Castle County. And that includes a lot of students from nearby University of Delaware in Newark.

Not surprisingly, in mountainless Delaware you won't find steep hills on the park's system of multipurpose trails and paths. A three-mile multiuse trail open to mountain bikes is smooth and hard-packed, traversing woods and grassy fields. A few small creek crossings and a moderate hill climb are about the only hazards mountain bikers will encounter when exploring the park. What you will discover as you negotiate the trails is lush greenery, scenic vistas overlooking stream valleys, and impressive rock outcroppings.

Bring a fishing pole. The meandering White Clay Creek is stocked with rainbow and brown trout in the spring (opening day is the first Saturday in April), while Millstone and Cattail Ponds harbor bass, bluegill, and crappie. A large pic-

RIDE 4 · White Clay Creek State Park

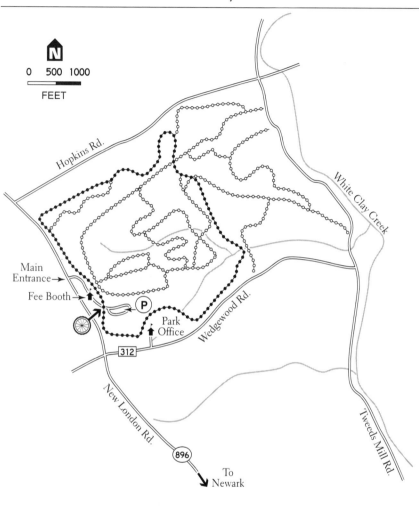

nic area and pavilion are perfect for a postride barbecue with family and friends.

Local riders say the best months to ride are April through December. Traffic on the trails gets heavy on the weekends, though, and cyclists and hikers should stay out of the woods during the deer-hunting seasons in November and January—except on Sundays, when no hunting is permitted.

Bathrooms, water, phones, a pavilion, a picnic area, and a horseshoe area are located near the park office. During the summer and on weekends and holidays in May, September, and October an entrance fee is charged. The park is open from 8 a.m. to sunset year-round.

General location: 3 miles northwest of Newark.

Elevation change: Nominal.

Season: Year-round.

Services: All services are available in Newark.

Hazards: Avoid riding during deer hunting season in the fall, or ride on Sundays when hunting isn't allowed.

Rescue index: Excellent. The park is small and surrounded by paved roads.

Maps: A trail map is available at the park office.

Finding the trail: To get to White Clay Creek State Park (formerly Walter S. Carpenter Jr. State Park) from Newark, follow DE 896 north approximately 3 miles to the entrance on the right. The multiuse trail begins behind the park office, near the entrance.

Source of additional information:

> White Clay Creek State Park
> 425 Wedgewood Road
> Newark, DE 19711
> (302) 368-6900

Notes on the trail: Cyclists looking for more mileage can explore adjacent White Clay Creek Preserve, 1,700 acres of woodlands donated to Pennsylvania and Delaware by the Dupont Company. In addition to cycling, visitors to the preserve can hike, fish, and bird-watch; a new visitor center hosts natural and cultural history programs. Another nearby riding option is Fair Hill Natural Resources Area a few miles west in Maryland.

RIDE 5 · White Clay Creek Trail

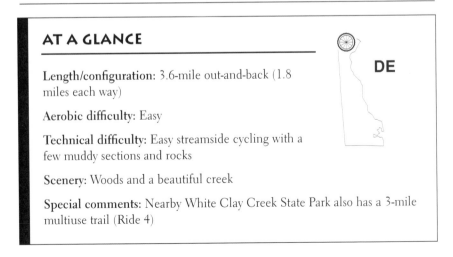

AT A GLANCE

DE

Length/configuration: 3.6-mile out-and-back (1.8 miles each way)

Aerobic difficulty: Easy

Technical difficulty: Easy streamside cycling with a few muddy sections and rocks

Scenery: Woods and a beautiful creek

Special comments: Nearby White Clay Creek State Park also has a 3-mile multiuse trail (Ride 4)

Although Delaware is
mountainless, good
single-track abounds.

White Clay Creek Preserve is part of a tract sold to William Penn in 1683 by Lenapi Chief Kekelappen. This Native American leader lived at the confluence of the middle and east branches of White Clay Creek, an area that's now a part of this bistate (Delaware and Pennsylvania) preserve. Located next to White Clay Creek State Park, the 1,253-acre tract of stream valley provides mountain bikers with an easy, 1.8-mile (one-way) out-and-back along a beautiful stretch of White Clay Creek. Starting at the Visitor Center off Hopkins Road, cyclists can ride north on the west side of the creek for an effortless, scenic, traffic-free trek.

Want to do more? Continue south across Hopkins Road and follow the dirt road along the creek to Newark. One drawback to this stretch is that you'll share the road with motorized traffic (usually very light). You can also ride to nearby White Clay Creek State Park, which has a three-mile multipurpose trail open to mountain bikes.

General location: Newark.

Elevation change: None.

Season: Year-round.

RIDE 5 · White Clay Creek Trail

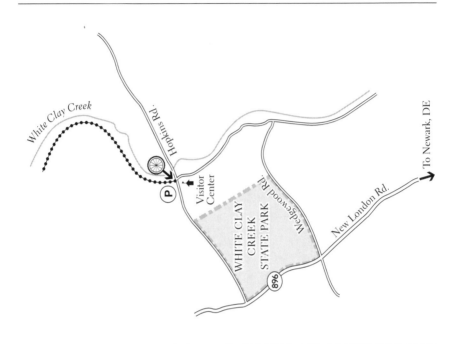

Services: All services are available in Newark.

Hazards: Hunting is allowed in the fall and winter; check at the preserve visitor center.

Rescue index: Excellent.

Land status: Pennsylvania Department of Conservation and Natural Resources.

Maps: None needed.

Finding the trail: Take DE 896 north out of Newark. Just past White Clay Creek State Park, turn right onto Hopkins Road (there's a sign). The dirt road to the visitor center is at the bottom of the hill on the left. Park at the preserve visitor center and ride your bike up the dirt road past the gate. At the sharp left turn, continue straight onto the single-track.

Source of additional information:

White Clay Creek Preserve
P.O. Box 172
Landenberg, PA 19350-0172
(610) 255-5415

Notes on the trail: The stone-walled cemetery outside the meetinghouse at the end of the trail contains the graves of many of the area's earliest settlers, including Dr. David Eaton. His home, across the street, is a classic example of a double-door Pennsylvania stone farmhouse. White Clay Creek is stocked with fish several times a year and is considered one of the area's best trout streams.

SOUTHERN MARYLAND AND
THE EASTERN SHORE

The 200-mile-long Chesapeake Bay, the largest estuary in the contiguous United States, bisects Maryland into the rural Eastern Shore, which includes Delaware and a bit of Virginia, and what is informally referred to as the Western Shore—the rest of the state.

Mountain bikers can explore the nearly Kansas-flat expanses of the Eastern Shore, bordered by the bay on the west and the Atlantic Ocean on the east. Sound boring? Admittedly, West Virginia it ain't. But there's lots to see and do on the Eastern Shore. And don't think that the flat-as-a-pancake landscape means you won't get a workout. The area is renowned for its ferocious headwinds.

Starting on the Atlantic coast, riders can take a cruise on Assateague Island, a 33-mile-long spit of sand below the summer tourist mecca of Ocean City. Mountain bikers can ride a paved bike path that features miles of undeveloped ocean beaches, maritime forests, astounding quantities of migratory birds, sun, salt air, and herds of wild horses made famous in the classic children's book *Misty of Chincoteague*.

Near Cambridge, fat-tire bikers can explore the unique landscape of Blackwater National Wildlife Refuge. Land and sky merge with the Chesapeake Bay, wildlife abounds, and you can explore back roads and the remains of a rural culture of Eastern Shore farmers and Chesapeake Bay watermen. There's nothing else like it in the United States.

Across the twin spans of the Chesapeake Bay bridges below Annapolis on the west side of the bay (which H. L. Mencken called "a great protein factory") lies rolling southern Maryland. Though still largely rural, much of this area between the Chesapeake Bay and the broad Potomac River is succumbing to sprawl as suburban Washington creeps farther south. Yet off the congested highways, several venues are attracting growing numbers of off-road cyclists. Attractions include large forests, rolling (and not intimidating) topography, and large numbers of wildlife, with heavy emphasis on waterfowl such as Canada geese and great blue herons.

Cedarville State Forest outside Waldorf offers a delightful system of single-track; it's a great place for novice riders to get a feel for the joys of riding a bike on narrow, twisting trails in deep forest. And though you and your bike may get muddy in this wet coastal forest, there are virtually no rocks on the paths.

Farther south, Jug Bay in Patuxent River Park provides more of the same, along with ample opportunities to view a wide array of bird life. Near the southern tip of the region is St. Mary's River State Park, with a fun, but not too challenging eight-mile single-track around a scenic lake.

RIDE 6 · Assateague Island

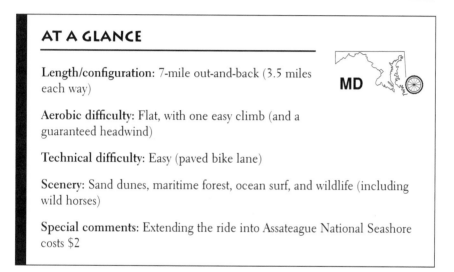

AT A GLANCE

Length/configuration: 7-mile out-and-back (3.5 miles each way)

MD

Aerobic difficulty: Flat, with one easy climb (and a guaranteed headwind)

Technical difficulty: Easy (paved bike lane)

Scenery: Sand dunes, maritime forest, ocean surf, and wildlife (including wild horses)

Special comments: Extending the ride into Assateague National Seashore costs $2

Assateague Island is a 37-mile barrier island south of Ocean City, Maryland— and it feels a world away from that wildly popular summer resort town. You won't find a boardwalk, traffic jams, or giant condominium high rises on this spit of sand, which separates Maryland and Virginia from the Atlantic. The southern (Virginia) portion of the island is the Chincoteague National Wildlife Refuge; most of the northern (Maryland) section is operated by the National Park Service as Assateague National Seashore. The state of Maryland also operates a park at the northern end of the island.

A three-and-a-half-mile paved bike lane through the state park offers a leisurely way to explore the island. This straight path parallels Bayberry Drive and isn't very exciting by itself. But it follows a dense maritime forest that offers sights of wildlife (songbirds, Sika deer), sand dunes, the pristine beach, and shrub thickets. Located along the Atlantic flyway, Assateague is visited by more than 275 species of birds, including snow geese, great blue herons, snowy egrets, peregrine falcons, and the endangered piping plover.

There's one more animal species that needs to be mentioned: wild horses. The island and its horses were immortalized in the classic children's book *Misty*

RIDE 6 • Assateague Island

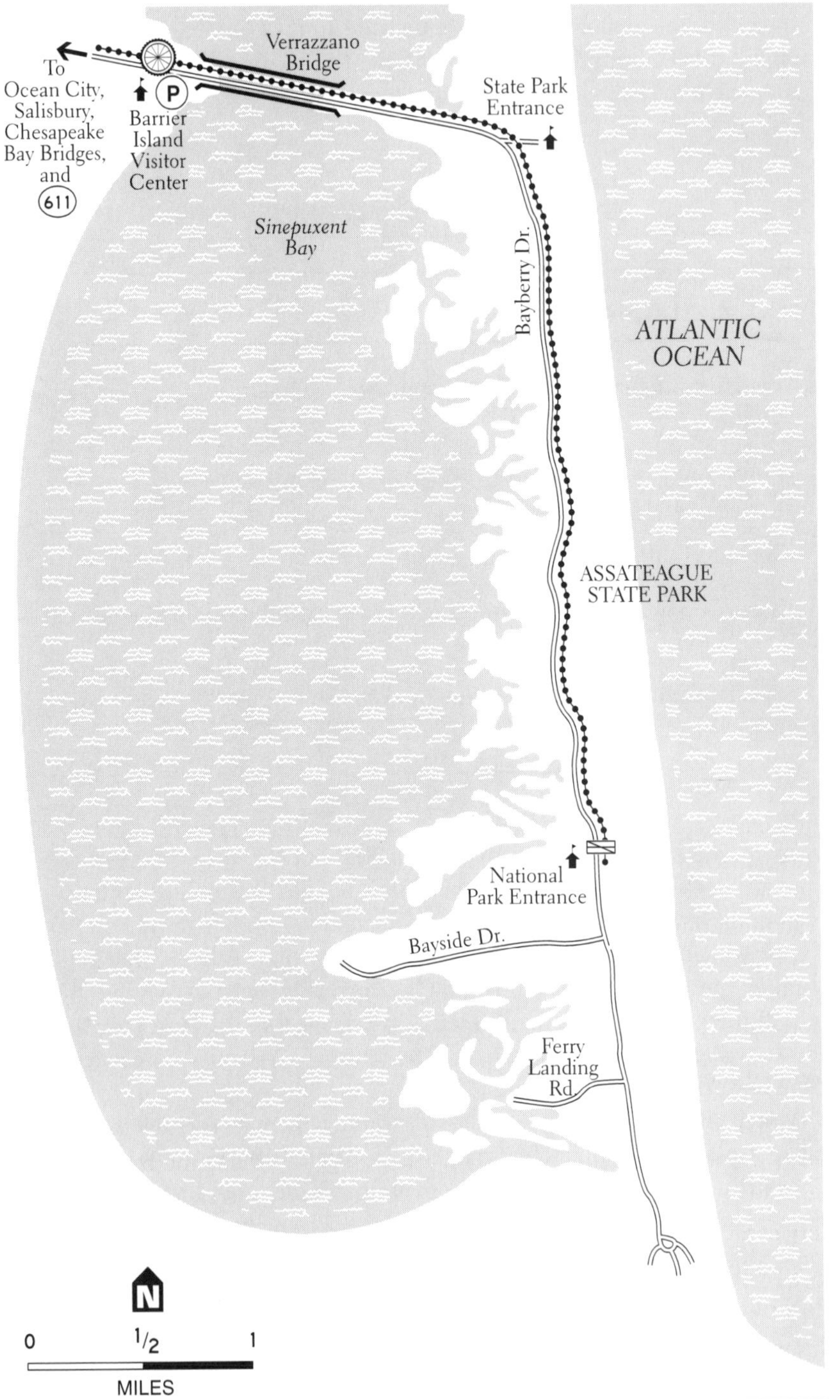

Verrazzano Bridge
To Ocean City, Salisbury, Chesapeake Bay Bridges, and 611
P
Barrier Island Visitor Center
State Park Entrance
Sinepuxent Bay
Bayberry Dr.
ATLANTIC OCEAN
ASSATEAGUE STATE PARK
National Park Entrance
Bayside Dr.
Ferry Landing Rd.
N
0
1/2
1
MILES

Wide, sandy beaches
are part of the charm
at Assateague Island.

of Chincoteague. On my visit the horses were everywhere—and causing small
traffic jams as tourists stopped to take pictures. Heed the signs. Wild horses kick
and bite, so keep your distance.

In the summer, bring a bike lock, a towel, and a change of clothes and frolic
in the surf at the state park. During the rest of the year (when biting insects are
less of a problem), pay the $2 entrance fee to the national seashore, ride a few
more miles of pavement, and explore some nature trails on foot.

General location: Ocean City.

Elevation change: None, except for an easy, 50-foot climb on Verrazzano Bridge.

Season: Spring and fall are best; summers are hot, humid, and buggy; winters
are cold and windy.

Services: Camping, rest rooms, a seasonal restaurant, and bike rentals are available on the island. All other services are available in Ocean City.

Hazards: Biting insects (late spring through early fall), traffic, and biting horses.

Rescue index: Excellent; the bike path follows a paved road.

Land status: State park.

Maps: A map is available at the Barrier Island Visitor Center on MD 611.

Finding the trail: From Annapolis and the Western Shore, take US 50 east across the twin Chesapeake Bay bridges (don't miss the US 50 turnoff just past Kent Island). Past Salisbury, take US 113 to Berlin, head east on MD 376, and go 4 miles to MD 611. Turn right and drive 5 miles to the Visitor Center on the right. From Ocean City, take MD 611 from its intersection with US 50 on the mainland just west of town. Park in the lot on the right side of the road just past the visitor center. The paved trail starts in the lot and has its own bridge over Sinepuxent Bay to Assateague Island. On the other side, bear right and follow the bike path along Bayberry Drive.

Sources of additional information:

> Assateague Island National Seashore
> 7206 National Seashore Lane
> Berlin, MD 21811-9742
> (410) 641-3030

> Assateague State Park
> 7307 Stephen Decatur Highway
> Berlin, MD 21811
> (410) 641-2120

Notes on the trail: The bike path ends at the entrance station to the national seashore; either turn back or pay $2 to ride a few more miles of paved trail and roads.

RIDE 7 · Blackwater National Wildlife Refuge

AT A GLANCE

Length/configuration: 5-mile loop (with a 25-mile loop option)

MD

Aerobic difficulty: Easy to moderate (if it's windy); the route is flat, but headwinds may not make it feel that way

Technical difficulty: Easy (paved roads)

Scenery: Low-key but unusual melding of land, tidal marsh, and water

Special comments: Best in fall and winter(especially November)

RIDE 7 · Blackwater National Wildlife Refuge

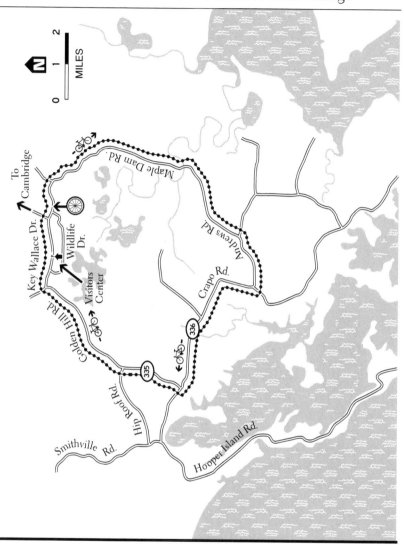

At the 17,000-acre Blackwater National Wildlife Refuge, cyclists can explore a unique topography and view a spectacular array of waterfowl and animal life. If that isn't enough reason to trek to this remote corner of Maryland's Eastern Shore, an optional bike ride on paved roads takes you through more unusual scenery and reveals a slice of rural Americana that evokes decades long past.

First, the lay of the land: At Blackwater, the Kansas-flat Eastern Shore melds into the waters of the Chesapeake Bay, revealing a broad landscape of water, forests, and tidal marsh. The rich nutrients from the abundant plant life in the

Bay, marsh, land, and wood meld into one at Blackwater National Wildlife Refuge.

vast marshes and bordering swamps are carried by the tide to the bay, creating one of the most fertile habitats on earth. In addition to a staggering number of waterfowl, the refuge supports a wide variety of other wildlife, including bald eagles, osprey, muskrats, the endangered Delmarva fox squirrel, white-tailed and Sika deer, turtles, lizards, skinks, snakes, salamanders, toads, and frogs. Don't forget your binoculars.

Wildlife Drive is a paved, five-mile auto and bicycle loop; observation points along the way are keyed to printed guides available at the entrance station, visitor center, or refuge headquarters. The one-way road is completely flat, so you can concentrate on viewing waterfowl, shorebirds, and other refuge denizens. Other attractions include two short hiking trails and an observation tower overlooking the junction of the Big and Little Blackwater Rivers and their marshlands. Along most of the route, the view is of wide marshes, distant stands of trees, soaring birds, and Blackwater River in the distance.

Most cyclists will probably find the ride too short. For more views of this vast landscape, try a 25-mile circuit on paved state roads through and around the refuge. You must share the road with cars, but traffic is usually light. A mountain bike is the preferred mode of two-wheeled transportation, as the narrow roads are so low they're often flooded by a few inches of water. The loop takes you past farms and old communities, collapsing barns and churches, abandoned gas stations, ramshackle houses, and fishing boats. Though the roads are utterly flat, don't assume pedaling will be effortless the whole way: No hills mean more headwinds, and the breezes can get quite blustery this close to the Chesapeake Bay.

General location: Cambridge.

Elevation change: None.

Season: Fall through spring. Summer heat, humidity, and biting insects are ferocious. Peak waterfowl migration is usually in November.

Services: All services are available in Cambridge and Salisbury.

Hazards: Light traffic. Biting insects are present from mid-April through September.

Rescue index: Excellent. Cars can be flagged down anywhere along the route, and farms and residences line the state roads.

Land status: National wildlife refuge and public highways.

Maps: A map of Wildlife Drive is available at the office. A Maryland state highway map shows the roads on the optional 25-mile loop.

Finding the trail: From Annapolis on the Western Shore, take US 50/US 301 east across the twin Chesapeake Bay bridges. Just past Kent Island, the two highways split; bear right onto US 50. In Cambridge, turn right onto Woods Road (look for the street sign), drive to MD 16, and turn right. Go about 1.5 miles and turn left onto Egypt Road, a narrow country lane that dead ends at Key Wallace Drive. Turn left for the start of Wildlife Drive or right to reach the Visitor Center. Wildlife Drive starts at the refuge headquarters, where you can park your car. You can also start from the Visitor Center, 1.5 miles west on Key Wallace Drive.

Source of additional information:

Refuge Manager
Blackwater National Wildlife Refuge
2145 Key Wallace Drive
Cambridge, MD 21613
(410) 228-2677

Notes on the trail: Wildlife Drive is a one-way paved lane starting at the refuge headquarters, located about 1.5 miles east of the Visitor Center on Key Wallace Drive. At the end of the drive, return to the start by turning right on MD 335 and right again onto Key Wallace Drive.

For the optional 25-mile loop ride through and around the refuge, start at the refuge headquarters and continue east on Key Wallace Drive across Little Blackwater River. A mile past the headquarters, turn right onto Maple Dam Road. After a stretch of ho-hum fields and woods, the scenery becomes spectacular as the road crosses the refuge's broad marshes. At the 6-mile point, cross a low bridge over a channel (the only climb on the ride). At mile 11, turn right onto

MD 336, which has a wide shoulder. At about mile 16, bear right onto MD 335 (or, if you're really strong and adventurous, continue straight for another 15 miles—one-way—to Hoopersville, an island community in the Chesapeake Bay). Once you're on MD 335—which doesn't have a shoulder—it's another 4.5 miles to Key Wallace Drive, where you turn right. Then ride 2.5 miles to the refuge headquarters to complete the loop.

RIDE 8 · Cedarville State Forest

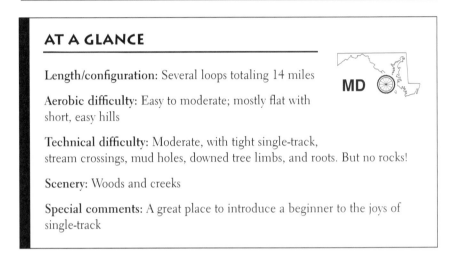

AT A GLANCE

Length/configuration: Several loops totaling 14 miles

MD

Aerobic difficulty: Easy to moderate; mostly flat with short, easy hills

Technical difficulty: Moderate, with tight single-track, stream crossings, mud holes, downed tree limbs, and roots. But no rocks!

Scenery: Woods and creeks

Special comments: A great place to introduce a beginner to the joys of single-track

The approximately 14 miles of single- and double-track in this 3,500-acre state forest in southern Maryland (about 20 miles southeast of Washington, D.C.) are mostly flat, with a few gentle rollers and the occasional steep but short pitch. The hallmark of these trails—and what makes this a favorite destination for many D.C.- and Baltimore-area riders—is the tight, twisty single-track. Because of its coastal location, there's nary a rock—a welcome relief to riders who must regularly do maintenance on their suspension forks after hammering the rock-strewn trails in the rest of the region. With only roots and the occasional soggy spot to get in your way, these trails are a joy to ride.

Cedarville is also an excellent destination for novices. With relatively nontechnical trails and no big climbs, the park provides easy riding for folks looking for undemanding off-road thrills. It's a great place to bring a friend or significant other for a relatively painless introduction to real trail riding.

While the scenery is nothing extraordinary on these forested trails, the woods are pretty any time of year, and frequent stream crossings (via footbridges) provide some visual variety. Caveat: Unless you arrive after a pro-

RIDE 8 · Cedarville State Forest

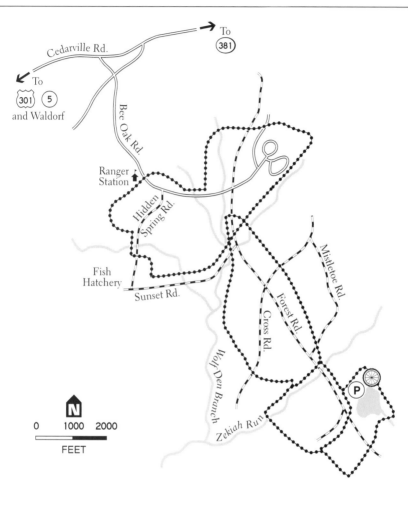

longed dry spell, expect to get wet. Many of the trails follow creeks, and you'll find yourself slogging through the occasional bog or mud hole. The Friends of Cedarville State Forest and the Mid-Atlantic Off-Road Enthusiasts (MORE) are working to reroute some of the trails away from low spots and to lay gravel on perennial wet spots; as you ride, keep your eyes peeled for changes in the direction of the trails up the slopes.

General location: Waldorf.

Elevation change: Nominal; mostly short, easy climbs on rolling trails.

Cedarville State Forest offers 14 miles of forested single-track that's perfect for novice riders.

Season: Year-round. Extremely wet in the spring, and hot and humid on summer afternoons.

Services: All services are available in Waldorf.

Hazards: Footbridges over creeks. Some of the trails pass through designated hunting areas, so during the late-fall hunting season, wear orange or ride only on Sundays, when hunting isn't permitted.

Rescue index: Good. The trails frequently intersect park roads, making it easy to flag down a car in an emergency.

Land status: State forest.

Maps: A trail map is available at the forest headquarters near the entrance.

Finding the trail: Drive south on US 301/MD 5 to Waldorf. Turn left onto Cedarville Road, drive 4 miles to Bee Oak Road, and turn right. After passing the park headquarters on the right (pick up a map), continue about half a mile to Forest Road and turn right. Go about 1 mile to Cedarville Pond on the left; park in the lot. On your bike, go back on Forest Road a few hundred feet, cross the bridge over Zekiah Run, and turn right onto Blue Trail on the right. The trail sign is hard to spot; if you miss it, continue a bit farther and turn right onto Mistletoe Road. Blue Trail crosses the road within 100 feet or so of Forest Road; turn left onto the trail.

Sources of additional information:

Southern Maryland Recreational Complex
11704 Fenno Road
Upper Marlboro, MD 20772
(800) 784-5380 or (301) 888-1410

Mid-Atlantic Off-Road Enthusiasts (MORE)
P.O. Box 2662
Fairfax, VA 22031
(703) 502-0359
Website: www.more-mtb.org

Notes on the trail: There's no one way to ride the numerous trails in Cedarville. The parking lot at the pond puts you near the trailheads of the Brown, Green, and Blue Trails. The Brown—a short, nontechnical, and mostly double-track trail that loops around the pond—is a good warm-up. The Blue, which is probably the best trail, is almost all single-track and can be strung together with the Orange to form a long loop. Don't follow any signs for the White Trail, which is an abandoned trail leading to some major bogs. If you feel like riding more, just reverse your direction of travel; everything will look completely different!

RIDE 9 · Jug Bay Natural Area

AT A GLANCE

Length/configuration: 8.5 miles of loops

MD

Aerobic difficulty: Moderate; mostly flat with a few long, easy hills and a couple of short, steep climbs out of stream valleys

Technical difficulty: Moderate; roots, rocks, and mud on tight single-track

Scenery: Woods, waterfowl, and glimpses of the wide Patuxent River

Special comments: You must register at the office and pay a day-use fee

RIDE 9 · Jug Bay Natural Area

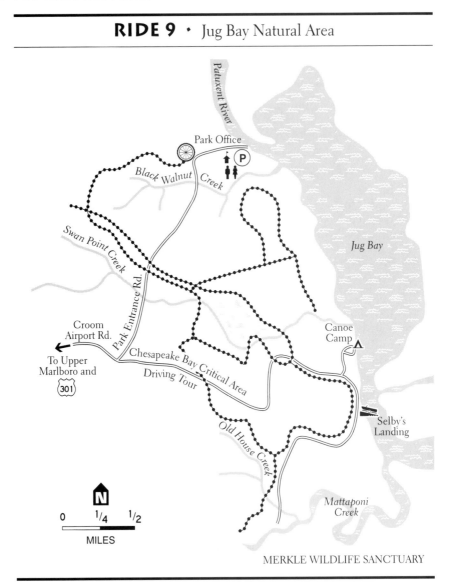

Park Office

P

Patuxent River

Black Walnut Creek

Swan Point Creek

Park Entrance Rd.

Jug Bay

Croom
Airport Rd.

Canoe
Camp

To Upper
Marlboro and
(301)

Chesapeake Bay Critical Area
Driving Tour

Selby's
Landing

Old House Creek

Mattaponi
Creek

N

0   1/4   1/2
MILES

MERKLE WILDLIFE SANCTUARY

This 2,000-acre tract of thick woodlands, hardwood swamps, and tidal wetlands in bustling Prince George's County provides a remarkable natural setting for mountain bikers to explore. An eight-and-a-half-mile system of trails along the shores of the Patuxent River, a major tributary of the Chesapeake Bay, winds through second-growth forests of ash, oak, dogwood, poplar, and pine. You'll catch frequent glimpses of the wide river, which supports an abundance of waterfowl such as Canada geese, ducks, and whistling swans.

The trails, which range from wide, grassy, wood lanes to twisting single-track littered with downed tree limbs and roots, occasionally plunge into narrow creek valleys, cross wooden footbridges, and ascend on short, steep climbs. The high clay content means that the soil holds water, and the paths are often wet long after it rains. In a few spots the trails cross bogs; except after prolonged periods of dry weather, expect both you and your bike to get muddy.

None of the trails are named or numbered, so it's easy to get disoriented. Yet because the park is surrounded by river and paved roads, it's not a problem; just don't start riding late in the day. Novice riders will find many of the trails challenging, while more experienced cyclists can find enough variety to make a visit worthwhile. Virtually all of the trails are loops that can be combined with other loops and ridden in two directions to create a full day of off-road riding.

General location: Upper Marlboro.

Elevation change: Moderate; gently rolling with a few short, steep climbs out of creek valleys.

Season: Year-round. Summer afternoons can be extremely hot, humid, and buggy. Large flocks of Canada geese winter here from October through early March.

Services: The nearest stores, restaurants, and gas stations are in Upper Marlboro, about 5 miles to the north. All other services are available in Washington and its Maryland suburbs.

Hazards: Watch for equestrians on the trails.

Rescue index: Excellent. The trails are short and the entire park is surrounded by paved roads and residences.

Land status: Maryland-National Capital Park and Planning Commission.

Maps: A trail map is available in the park office.

Finding the trail: Jug Bay is in Patuxent River Park, located east of US 301 about 5 miles south of Upper Marlboro. Heading south on US 301, turn left onto Croom Station Road, 1.5 miles south of the intersection with MD 4. Go 2.5 miles to Croom Road and turn left; then drive 1.3 miles to Croom Airport Road and turn left. Drive 2 miles to the park entrance on the left; it's another 1.5 miles to the park office. Hikers and riders must register at the office and pay a daily or annual fee for a permit to use the trails. Ride your bike back on the paved road from the park office past the gate on the right to the horseshoe symbol–marked equestrian trails that intersect the road on both sides. The trails on the right (the west side of the park) are mostly easy, wide lanes; the extensive trail system to the left is more technical single-track.

Source of additional information:

Patuxent River Park
16000 Croom Airport Road
Upper Marlboro, MD 20772
(301) 627-6074

Trails at Jug Bay Natural Area cross many small streams on wooden footbridges.

Notes on the trail: On Saturdays from April through October, you can extend any trip by riding a 4.5-mile (one-way) paved and dirt road to and through adjacent Merkle Wildlife Sanctuary. The highlight of this easy out-and-back is a 1,000-foot, S-shaped boardwalk across Mattaponi Creek and an observation tower for viewing the river. Bring binoculars to view a stunning array of birds and waterfowl. The road is also open on Sundays year-round, but cyclists must share it with traffic.

RIDE 10 · St. Mary's River State Park

AT A GLANCE

MD

Length/configuration: 8-mile single-track loop

Aerobic difficulty: Mostly flat and rolling with 7 or 8 moderate climbs

Technical difficulty: Enough roots, logs, and stream crossings to make it challenging for advanced beginners and interesting for more experienced riders

Scenery: Nice woods and views of a 250-acre lake

Special comments: Not just a spin around a lake; this is fun single-track. There's a $2 fee per car on weekends May through September

---

This 2,176-acre state park in once rural (but now booming) St. Mary's County features an eight-mile single-track around a lake popular with anglers and small boaters. Though the trail is mostly unblazed and occasionally splits into a maze of pathways, it's easy to follow: Just keep the lake to your left (or right, if you're riding the trail in a clockwise direction).

A fun, 8-mile single-track goes around the lake at St. Mary's River State Park.

RIDE 10 · St. Mary's River State Park

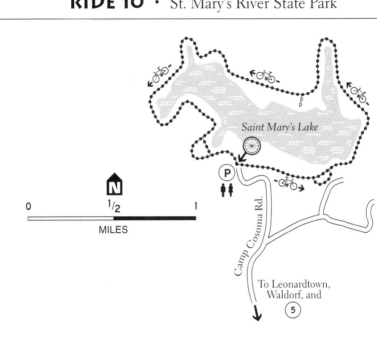

Saint Mary's Lake

N

0   1/2   1

MILES

P

Camp Cosoma Rd.

To Leonardtown,
Waldorf, and
5

This fun trail has just enough technical impediments (mostly roots and a few stream crossings) to keep things interesting. It passes through an attractive second-growth, mixed hardwood and pine forest and offers occasional glimpses of the lake. There are several wooden (plank) footbridges and sections of wooden planking and corduroy (small logs laid across the trail at right angles) over bogs. Except in extremely dry weather, expect to get at least a little wet.

General location: Leonardtown.

Elevation change: A couple of hundred feet.

Season: Year-round. The trail can be extremely muddy in the spring and after wet weather.

Services: Rest rooms, water, and a pay phone are located in the park. All other services are available in California, Leonardtown, and Lexington Park.

Hazards: Use care on the narrow wooden bridges; most don't have handrails, and those that do are too narrow to ride through. Avoid deer-hunting season in the late fall, except on Sundays, when hunting isn't permitted.

Rescue index: Good. Many trails shoot off from the lake toward surrounding private property and residences. Boaters can also be flagged down in an emergency.

Land status: State park.

Maps: Call or write Point Lookout State Park, Star Route Box 48, Scotland, MD 20687; (301) 872-5688. There is no ranger station at St. Mary's River State Park.

Finding the trail: Take MD 5 south from Waldorf and turn left on Camp Cosoma Road about 6.5 miles south of Leonardtown. Follow the road to the park entrance and park near the rest rooms at the end of the lot. If you're fac-ing the lake, the trail starts to the right (there's a sign) and finishes in the small, shaded parking lot to the left.

Source of additional information:

Point Lookout State Park
Star Route Box 48
Scotland, MD 20687
(301) 872-5688

Notes on the trail: Most bikers ride the trail counterclockwise. Just past the trailhead, the trail splits into a maze; you can take any path because they all link up again. When you reach the small fire road, turn left (toward the lake), go a short distance, and turn right and cross a field that leads to the dam. After crossing the dam, the trail becomes a narrow dirt road. Just before the road starts to go uphill, turn onto the single-track to the left (it's easy to miss). From this point the trail is easy to follow. Just keep the lake to your left, and when-ever you encounter a split in the trail, opt for the one to the left (although most of the trails converge).

THE MARYLAND SUBURBS OF WASHINGTON, D.C.

Three of Washington's sides are bordered by Maryland—a fact easily explained with a little history. George Washington chose the city's site where the Anacostia River flows into the Potomac upriver from his Mount Vernon plantation. Maryland and Virginia donated wedges of land from both sides of the Potomac to make the 100-square-mile diamond called the District of Columbia. In 1846, Virginia snatched its land back; today, Washington sits on the former Maryland acreage of the river's east bank. Maryland's Montgomery and Prince George's Counties surround Washington's northwestern and eastern borders.

Today, D.C. mountain bikers frequently go to the Maryland suburbs in search of places to get some mud between their knobbies. They won't find any mountains in the immediate area—you've got to drive an hour or two for that—but the closer 'burbs offer an array of off-road riding opportunities. In upscale Montgomery County (one of the most affluent suburbs in the country), mountain bikers flock to Schaeffer Farm, which offers ten miles of superb single-track just outside the town of Gaithersburg. In terms of high-quality, intense off-road riding on trails designed and built by mountain bikers, this is the place to go in suburban Maryland. Almost as nice (but farther afield) is Black Hills Regional Park. Rolling and scenic, it's the kind of local park anyone would be proud to call their own.

Cyclists also flock to the C&O Canal Towpath, a 184-mile trail that starts in Georgetown in Montgomery County and continues along the Potomac River and the remains of the old canal to Cumberland in western Maryland. Great Falls, just a few miles above Capital Beltway, is one of the most dramatic outdoor scenes in the eastern United States. Prince George's County boasts Cosca Regional Park, which is conveniently located just off Capital Beltway and has five miles of single-track.

Though they're at least an hour's drive from the Washington area, two popular western Maryland state parks have a draw that's hard to resist: real mountains. Located between Frederick and Hagerstown, Gambrill and Greenbrier State Parks attract the truly hard core who love brainstem-rattling single-track and long, steep climbs. Nice views, too.

RIDE 11 · Schaeffer Farm Trail

AT A GLANCE

Length/configuration: 3 interconnected loops totaling 10 miles

MD

Aerobic difficulty: Moderate; a great workout if ridden fast

Technical difficulty: Moderate to difficult single-track with lots of rocks, roots, logs, and stream crossings

Scenery: Pretty woods, rolling countryside, and farms

Special comments: Great single-track designed and built by single-track fanatics

Working hand in (cycling) glove with the Maryland Department of Natural Resources, Mid-Atlantic Off-Road Enthusiasts (MORE) has created one of the best mountain bike venues in the D.C.-Baltimore area: Schaeffer Farm Trail, a brand-spanking-new trail system in the heart of hectic Montgomery County. Schaeffer Farm features ten or so miles of mouth-watering single-track that will elevate the pulse of any intermediate to advanced mountain biker. With its new recreational mission, this state-owned, 2,000-acre tract of woods and fields bordering Seneca and Little Seneca Creeks is now safe from the clutches of housing developers. In the years to come, it will continue to be a beautiful patch of countryside serving mountain bikers, hikers, and equestrians — the recreational users who pitch in as volunteers to build and maintain the trail system.

Hop on your bike and ride just a few feet; it's clear that this trail was built by and for mountain bikers. The hard-packed dirt trail twists and turns as you barrel through a forest of second-growth mixed hardwood trees. Lots of dips and short climbs, some challenging creek crossings, plenty of downed tree limbs and trunks (most of them easy to hop), and occasional forays to the forest's edge add up to a delightful spin in the woods. Rocks and roots are minimal, and the single-track is totally dialed in. Yet the labyrinth of trails demands that you keep your eyes glued to the patch in front of your wheel as you rock 'n' roll along the single-track.

Occasionally you've got to stop and enjoy the scenery. Schaeffer Farm doesn't offer dramatic views, but the occasional stretches of trail that pop out of the woods provide glimpses across fields to the rolling countryside beyond the park. In the winter, when the leaves are off the trees, the views are better. Year-round,

RIDE 11 · Schaeffer Farm Trail

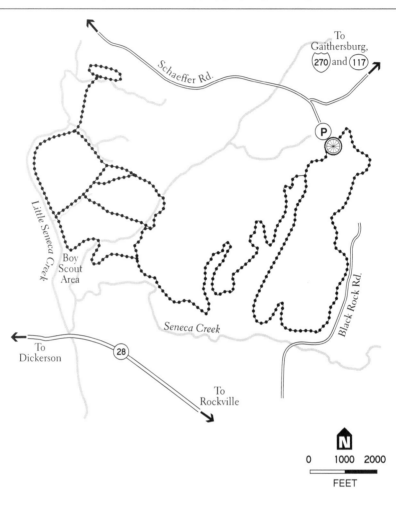

the forest and fields are beautiful and impart a sense of remoteness that belies the suburban setting.

Loop A, about three miles long, is a great warm-up trail that will take most riders about half an hour to finish. It intersects Loop B just beyond the parking lot; turn left to explore Loop B (actually a long out-and-back with a loop) and Loop C. You can reride any of the loops in both directions, including Loop A— a great way to end an exploration. Single-track fanatics who live well beyond the borders of Montgomery County—even hours away—can easily justify the drive to this terrific new off-road venue in the heart of suburban Washington. It's easy

Montgomery County bicycling activist Dave Scull shows fine single-track form on a trail he helped build at Schaeffer Farm.

to do a half-day of riding without getting bored. Hats off to MORE and Maryland DNR for a job well done.

General location: Gaithersburg.

Elevation change: Moderate. While located along a stream valley with ample opportunities for steep climbs, the trail is routed in an environmentally friendly way that avoids big elevation changes. Still, there are a handful of short, steep climbs, including one on Loop A that only very strong riders will be able to ride all the way.

Season: Year-round.

Services: Food stores, gas stations, and convenience stores are located on Clopper Road. All other services are available in Gaithersburg.

Hazards: A few tricky creek crossings.

Rescue index: Excellent. Sections of Loop A parallel a paved road.

Land status: State park.

Maps: A map is posted at the trailhead on a bulletin board. The trail system is well marked and easy to follow.

Finding the trail: From Interstate 270, take Exit 10 (Clopper Road/MD 117) west. Go about 5 miles; just past the intersection with MD 118, turn left on Schaeffer Road and go about 1.5 miles, past Burdette Lane on the left. The entrance, which has a sign, is on the left next to a house. The trailheads are at the end of the parking lot; go left to Loop A or right to Loops B and C (and the other end of Loop A).

Sources of additional information:

Seneca Creek State Park
11950 Clopper Road
Gaithersburg, MD 20878
(301) 924-2127

Mid-Atlantic Off-Road Enthusiasts (MORE)
P.O. Box 2662
Fairfax, VA 22031
(703) 502-0359
Website: www.more-mtb.org

Notes on the trail: Long-range plans for the trail system include adding footbridges over some creeks and building more miles of trails.

RIDE 12 · Seneca Creek State Park

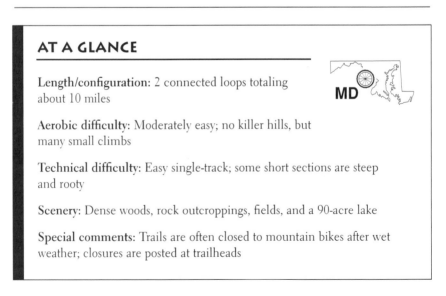

AT A GLANCE

Length/configuration: 2 connected loops totaling about 10 miles

MD

Aerobic difficulty: Moderately easy; no killer hills, but many small climbs

Technical difficulty: Easy single-track; some short sections are steep and rooty

Scenery: Dense woods, rock outcroppings, fields, and a 90-acre lake

Special comments: Trails are often closed to mountain bikes after wet weather; closures are posted at trailheads

Seneca Creek State Park is a typical stream valley park that stretches for 12 miles along Great Seneca Creek in western Montgomery County. From its headwaters north of Gaithersburg, the creek snakes through a narrow stream val-

RIDE 12 · Seneca Creek State Park

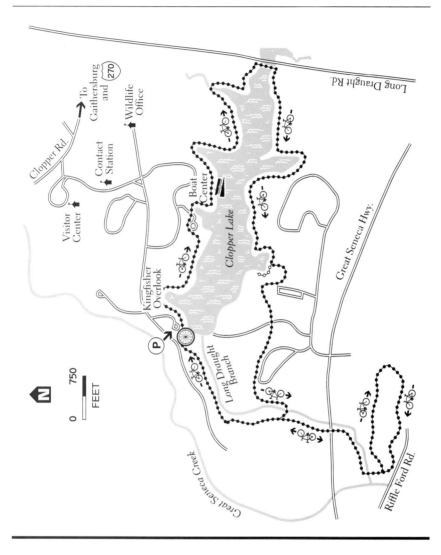

ley, passing through fields, dense woods, and rock outcroppings on its way south to the Potomac River. For D.C.-area mountain bikers, the park provides an excellent, scenic, and convenient destination with miles of moderately easy riding.

The only part of the 6,100-acre park developed for recreation is this day-use area west of Gaithersburg. Ninety-acre Clopper Lake provides water recreation and picnicking, disc golf (bring your own frisbee or buy one at the visitor center), and fishing. More than seven miles of trails are open to mountain bikes, including circular Lake Shore Trail and fun Long Draught Trail, which features many bridges across streams; fast, straight sections; and steep and rooty

Moderately easy single-track is the hallmark of Seneca Creek State Park.

switchbacks. With two loops and two connecting trails, the trails offer a wide range of riding configurations.

General location: Gaithersburg.

Elevation change: A couple hundred feet, but no long, steep climbs.

Season: Year-round, but wet weather often causes trail closings.

Services: All services are available in Gaithersburg.

Hazards: A few short, steep sections of trail.

Rescue index: Excellent; a car can be waved down on paved roads inside the park and on roads bordering the park. A pay phone is located at the road intersection above the boat center.

Land status: State park.

Maps: Trail maps are available at park headquarters.

Finding the trail: From I-270 in Gaithersburg, take MD 117 (Clopper Road) west. Look for the well-signed park entrance on the left. After entering the park, drive to the **T** intersection and turn right. Drive to Kingfisher Overlook (on the left) and park. Lake Shore Trail is on the left at the beginning of the parking lot.

Source of additional information:

Seneca Creek State Park
11950 Clopper Road
Gaithersburg, MD 20878
(301) 974-3683

Notes on the trail: From Kingfisher Overlook, ride the blue-blazed Lake Shore Trail clockwise (away from the dam). At the far end of the lake climb to Long Draught Road, go right, cross the bridge, and turn right again to get back onto the trail. About four-fifths of the way around the lake, go left on the white-blazed Mink Hollow Trail. Turn left on Long Draught Trail and pass under Great Seneca Highway soon after (stop and check out the wetlands observation booth); the trail eventually follows a jeep road. Just before the jeep road reaches Riffle Ford Road, the trail goes left, heads up and along a power line, and makes a 1.5-mile loop. After you ride the loop, go right on the jeep road and up the yellow-blazed Long Draught Trail to the road just below Kingfisher Overlook, the start of the ride.

Final Note: Don't cross Riffle Ford Road even though a trail on the other side heads downstream along Seneca Creek. This is Seneca Greenway Trail, one of the few trails on state land not open to mountain bikes. Why? It's part of a deal mountain biking advocates made with hikers and the state when Schaeffer Farm Trail was created in 1995. Do the local mountain biking community a favor and respect the restriction.

RIDE 13 · Black Hill Regional Park

AT A GLANCE

Length/configuration: 2-mile (one-way) out-and-back with a 5-mile loop (9 miles total)

MD

Aerobic difficulty: Moderate; some steep but short climbs

Technical difficulty: Easy single-track; some small stream crossings

Scenery: Woods, fields, and a lake nestled in the rolling Montgomery County countryside

Special comments: A good place for novices to experience single-track

RIDE 13 · Black Hill Regional Park

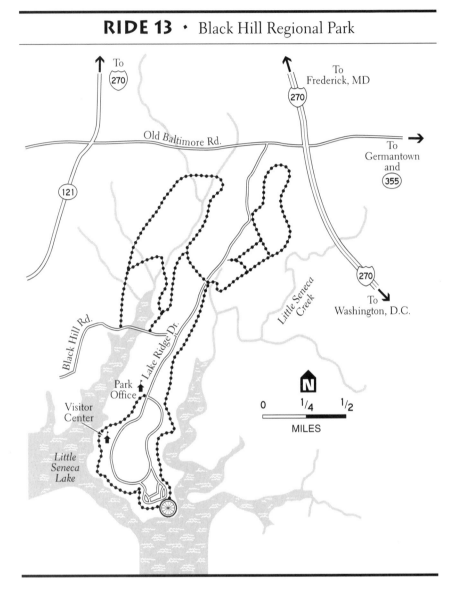

Located in northern Montgomery County on the fringe of Washington's ever-expanding suburbs, Black Hill Regional Park is a recreational mecca. Activities in this attractive, 1,800-acre park include picnicking, boating on 505-acre Little Seneca Lake, pontoon boat tours, hiking, birding, horseback riding, and mountain biking. The modern Visitor Center offers natural history educational programs, and the park hosts a variety of concert, stage, and outdoor activities year-round. It's exactly the kind of recreation complex you'd expect in affluent Montgomery County.

Neil Sandler, publisher of *Spokes* magazine, hits the trail at scenic Black Hill Regional Park.

A system of about ten miles of hiker-biker trails provides a well-needed venue for off-road cyclists in D.C.'s congested Maryland suburbs. The trails are kept in good shape, and, while not exactly easy, they can serve as an excellent introduction to riding on trails. Long stretches follow utility pipelines, providing a series of steep climbs and descents that mimic the kind of riding you'll find in the mountains. Because you're in rural Montgomery County, the climbs are relatively short, though the woods and surrounding countryside are pretty.

General location: Germantown.

Elevation change: A couple hundred feet of climbing on short, steep hills.

Season: Year-round, but the park is closed on Thanksgiving, Christmas, and New Year's Day.

Services: Rest rooms and water are located in the park. Camping is available at nearby Little Bennett Regional Park (call (301) 972-9222). All other services are available in Gaithersburg.

Hazards: Some descents on the utility cuts are very steep.

Rescue index: Excellent; the trails frequently cross or parallel paved roads.

Land status: Maryland-National Capital Park and Planning Commission.

Maps: A trail map is available at the Visitor Center.

Finding the trail: From Capital Beltway, take I-270 north to Exit 16 (MD 27 East). Then turn left on MD 355 and left again on Old Baltimore Road. Make a left turn into the park and drive straight to parking lot 5 (all the way to the end) and park. The paved hiker-biker trail starts near the rest rooms.

Source of additional information:

> Black Hill Regional Park
> 20930 Lake Ridge Drive
> Boyds, MD 20841
> (301) 972-9396

Notes on the trail: Ride your bike away from the lake and turn right at the fitness circuit. Turn left at the forest road, cross paved Lake Ridge Drive, and continue down Black Hill Road to the boat launch area. Cabin Branch Trail starts on the right just over the bridge. From this trail you can link to Hard Rock Trail, a loop you can ride to make your jaunt longer.

RIDE 14 · C&O Canal Towpath

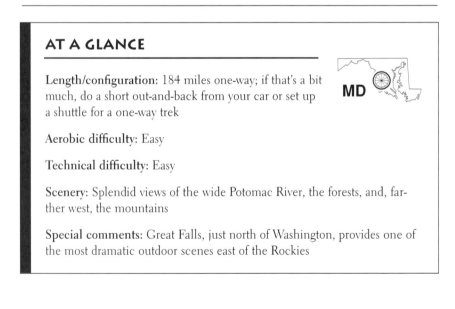

AT A GLANCE

Length/configuration: 184 miles one-way; if that's a bit much, do a short out-and-back from your car or set up a shuttle for a one-way trek

Aerobic difficulty: Easy

Technical difficulty: Easy

Scenery: Splendid views of the wide Potomac River, the forests, and, farther west, the mountains

Special comments: Great Falls, just north of Washington, provides one of the most dramatic outdoor scenes east of the Rockies

The C&O Canal Towpath, stretching 184 miles between Washington, D.C., and Cumberland, Maryland, is one of the nation's most historic and spectacularly scenic cycling trails. The 12-foot-wide path follows what remains of the Chesapeake and Ohio Canal, a dream of passage envisioned by George Washington that was built to link the nation's capital with its resources beyond the Appalachian Mountains.

President John Quincy Adams broke ground for the waterway on July 4, 1828. The canal, built with 74 lift locks designed to raise mule-pulled barges from nearly sea level to an elevation of 605 feet at Cumberland, reached that western Maryland city in 1850. Alas, the canal was doomed from the start. On the day it was dedicated, the Baltimore and Ohio Railroad began its push west. By the time the canal reached Cumberland, the railroad had been there for eight years, and thoughts of continuing the financially ailing waterway farther west were abandoned.

Operated as a conduit for eastern coal and continually battered by extensive flooding, the canal ceased operation in the 1930s. In 1971 the waterway was designated a national park and today serves as a recreational haven for Washingtonians who live both inside and outside Capital Beltway. Hikers, joggers, birders, anglers, mountain bikers, and anyone else in search of a bit of nature flock to the towpath year-round. They're rarely disappointed.

Exploring the towpath by mountain bike is a perfect way to enjoy the park. Two familiar companions are always with you—the wide Potomac River on one side and the canal (or what's left of it) on the other. Sometimes the canal is nothing more than a grassy ditch with trees growing out of it; along some stretches all that remains is a grassy slope where the mule-pulled barges used to float. Near Washington, though, sections are still operational, and in the summer you can take rides on mule-powered barges, just like when the canal was in its heyday 150 years ago. Though the towpath is nearly flat, a wide range of surfaces greets riders, including packed gravel, sand, wooden boards, and sections of dirt (or mud if it's rained recently) littered with rocks and roots. Flat, yes; always smooth, no.

A great deal of American history took place along this route, and the towpath provides curious cyclists with much to explore—especially those with the time and interest to venture away from the path. Great scenery greets you at nearly every subtle bend in the trail. The short list, starting in Washington: Georgetown, Great Falls Tavern (and a museum), Mather Gorge (where the wide Potomac River roars through spectacular Great Falls), Whites Ferry (the last regularly operating ferry on the Potomac), Harpers Ferry National Historical Park (the site of John Brown's raid, a precursor to the Civil War), Antietam National Battlefield (one of the bloodiest conflicts of the Civil War), Fort Frederick State Park (which dates from the French and Indian War), and the Paw Paw Tunnel (near milepost 165—a 3,118-foot, nineteenth-century engineering marvel built to avoid a series of loops in the Potomac River called the Paw Paw Bends; bring a flashlight). Forested islands in the Potomac, rock cliffs rising over the canal, wildlife, and fieldstone buildings, locks, and aqueducts are other sights to enjoy along the towpath.

Built during a time when four miles an hour was a blistering pace, the C&O Canal is a place to enjoy nature, soak up some history . . . and slow down. Pack a lunch, bring some friends, and savor one of the best off-road cycling destinations in the United States.

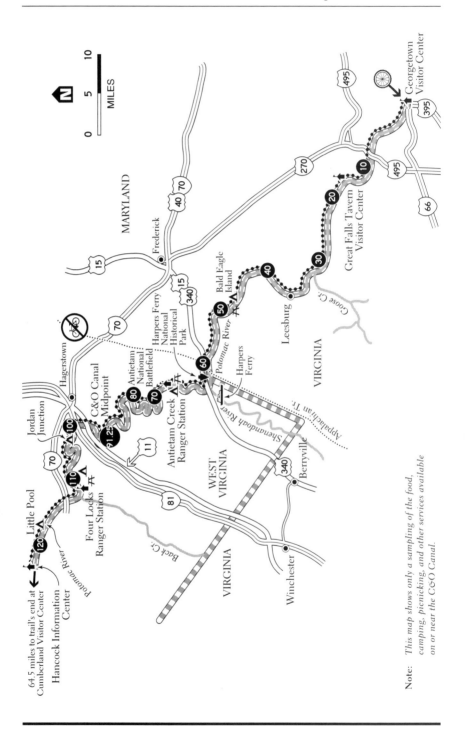

MARYLAND

Frederick

Hagerstown

Jordan Junction

C&O Canal Midpoint

Antietam National Battlefield

Harpers Ferry National Historical Park

Bald Eagle Island

Great Falls Tavern Visitor Center

Georgetown Visitor Center

Leesburg

VIRGINIA

Potomac River

Harpers Ferry

Goose Cr.

Antietam Creek Ranger Station

WEST VIRGINIA

Shenandoah River

Appalachian Tr.

Berryville

Back Cr.

Four Locks Ranger Station

Little Pool

64.5 miles to trail's end at Cumberland Visitor Center

Hancock Information Center

Potomac River

VIRGINIA

Winchester

MILES

N

0   5   10

Note: This map shows only a sampling of the food, camping, picnicking, and other services available on or near the C&O Canal.

General location: Along the Potomac River between Georgetown in Washington, D.C., and Cumberland, Maryland.

Elevation change: 600'; but because it's spread over 184 miles, the towpath is essentially flat.

Season: Year-round. Spring rains can turn sections into muddy quagmires. In the summer, mosquitoes will drive you crazy as soon as you roll to a stop; bring plenty of insect repellent. In July and August, the heat and humidity can be hellish. Mid- to late-October brings crisp, cool mornings, warm afternoons, and breathtaking fall colors.

Services: Restaurants, small stores, and bed-and-breakfasts are spread along the length of the towpath. Primitive hiker-biker campgrounds are located about every 5 miles; they're free and equipped with picnic tables, water pumps, and portable toilets. The town of Williamsport, at mile marker 100, is right on the canal and has all services, including a bike shop.

Hazards: None. But the towpath is prone to washouts after heavy winter and spring rains, so it's a good idea (and an absolute necessity for anyone riding the entire length) to call the park ahead of time and find out if any sections are damaged and closed to bikes.

Rescue index: Good. For most of its length, the canal and towpath are close to, and occasionally crossed by, roads. Many residences line or overlook the canal. The stretch from Paw Paw to Hancock is the most remote section.

Land status: National park.

Maps: Several publications are invaluable for folks trekking the entire distance. For a free list, call or write Parks and History Association, P.O. Box 40929, Washington, D.C. 20016; (202) 472-3083. The majority of visitors, however, only come for the day, and a map really isn't necessary (although a good road map is invaluable for finding the canal). For general information about the canal and a basic map, call or write Superintendent, C&O Canal National Historical Park, Box 4, Sharpsburg, MD 21782; (301) 739-4200.

Finding the trail: Most folks riding the entire 184 miles (which can be done in 5 or 6 days of easy pedaling) start in Cumberland and follow the Potomac River downstream. You can go the panniers-and-no-hot-shower-for-a-week route or stop at motels and bed-and-breakfasts along the way. Or do a combination. For transportation (for you and your bike) to the start of the ride—or any number of custom services that let you ride to your car or provide sag-wagon support for your gear as you pedal from inn to inn—call Catoctin Bike Tours in Mount Airy, Maryland, at (800) TOUR-CNO.

Daytrippers have virtually unlimited options for shorter explorations of the towpath. Popular starting points close to Washington for out-and-backs are Georgetown (milepost 0; terrible parking, but great bars and restaurants); Great Falls (milepost 14.3; park at Old Angler's Inn on MacArthur Boulevard or Swainn's Lock on River Road); Seneca Creek, where you can see 1 of 11 aqueducts that carried the canal over rivers and creeks (milepost 22.9; off MD 190);

The Paw Paw Tunnel is a 3,118-foot, 19th-century engineering marvel built to avoid a series of loops in the Potomac River called the Paw Paw Bends; don't forget your flashlight.

and Nolands Ferry, south of Frederick, Maryland (milepost 42; near Dickerson on MD 28).

Note: The farther you are from Washington, the better the scenery (with the exception of Great Falls, which is just north of Capital Beltway) and the thinner the crowds.

Sources of additional information:

Superintendent
C&O Canal National Historical Park
Box 4
Sharpsburg, MD 21782
(301) 739-4200

Parks and History Association
P.O. Box 40929
Washington, DC 20016
(202) 472-3083

184 Miles of Adventure/Hiker's Guide to the C&O Canal (48 pages, softcover, $4.95)
Mason-Dixon Council of the Boy Scouts of America
P.O. Box 2133
Hagerstown, MD 21742
One of the best guides to the towpath, it features more than 20 detailed maps and
the most accurate information for anyone interested in traveling the entire length by
mountain bike, foot, horse, llama. . . . The book can be ordered from the address
above, and it's widely available at bookstores and outdoor outfitters.

Notes on the trail: For all intents and purposes the towpath is flat, but why
make it more difficult than you have to? On any out-and-back, pedal the towpath upriver at the start, when you're fresh and bursting with energy; turn
around for the slightly downhill return. You could also set up a car shuttle so
that you only have to ride one way (downhill, right?). This takes a minimum of
two vehicles: Drive both vehicles to the end of your ride, park one of them, and
pile into the other car (the one with the bikes). Then drive to your starting
point, park, and begin the ride. At the finish, pile into the car you stashed ear-
lier and drive back to the start to retrieve the other car. (Note: Not everyone has
to go on the car-retrieval trip; if you've parked more than one car at the end of
the ride, others in your group can proceed to a predesignated eating establish-
ment and begin ordering food.) Does setting up a shuttle sound like an incredible waste of time, energy, and gasoline? It is. Never mind. Just do an out-and-
back; the scenery looks completely different on the return leg anyway.

RIDE 15 · Cabin John Trail

AT A GLANCE

Length/configuration: 10-mile out-and-back (5 miles
each way) with additional loops

MD

Aerobic difficulty: Easy to moderate; a few short, steep
climbs and descents that can be walked

Technical difficulty: Easy single-track, with a few sections of rocks, roots,
and sand

Scenery: Nice woods in a stream valley that cuts through congested
suburbs

Special comments: Suburban riding at its best; sometimes you don't even
hear the sounds of traffic

RIDE 15 · Cabin John Trail

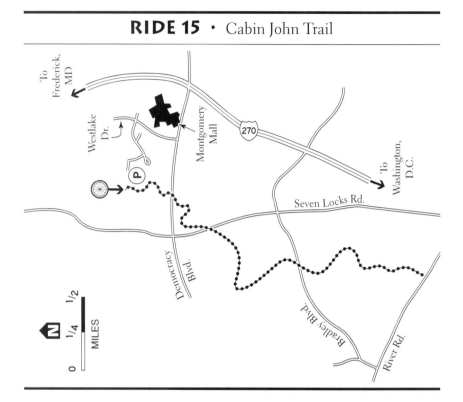

Who says there's no good riding in the suburbs? Amid the hustle and bustle of suburban Montgomery County, intrepid riders can explore Cabin John Trail, a narrow, five-mile (one-way), out-and-back single-track that follows a creek of the same name from Rockville to the Potomac River. The trail, though narrow, is mostly well buffed and easy to ride. A wilderness experience it's not. Riding the trail requires scrambling across hectic four-lane roadways that are usually clogged with traffic and constitute a major hazard, except on early weekend and holiday mornings. But your reward is fun riding along Cabin John Creek and through some attractive woods.

General location: Rockville.

Elevation change: Nominal, but there are a couple of steep climbs where the trail can't follow the stream as it flows south to the Potomac River.

Season: Year-round.

Services: Camping, water, and rest rooms are available in Cabin John Regional Park. All other services are available in Rockville.

Hazards: Watch for very heavy traffic where the trail crosses Democracy Boulevard and other major routes. Use care when riding narrow sections that skirt the high banks of Cabin John Creek.

Rescue index: Excellent. The trail frequently crosses paved roads.

The Cabin John Trail offers wooded seclusion — and excellent single-track — in hectic Montgomery County.

Land status: Maryland-National Capital Park and Planning Commission.

Maps: A trail map is available at the Cabin John Regional Park office and the Locust Grove Nature Center on Democracy Boulevard.

Finding the trail: If you're heading west on Capital Beltway (Interstate 495), take I-270 north to the Old Georgtown Road exit and go south. Then turn right onto Democracy Boulevard. If you're heading east on Capital Beltway from Virginia, take I-270 north, get off at the Democracy Boulevard exit, and go west. Now drive past Montgomery Mall on the right and turn right onto Westlake Drive. Then turn left into the parking lot for the Cabin John Regional Park skating rink and athletic area; park across from the rink. From the athletic area parking lot, pedal past the skating rink and take one of the trail entrances into the woods on the right.

Source of additional information:

Cabin John Regional Park
7400 Tuckerman Lane
Rockville, MD 20852
(301) 299-0024

Notes on the trail: After entering the woods, bear left and work your way down a maze of paths until you find the blue-blazed Cabin John Trail. (The trails in the woods near the athletic fields are good for zooming around if you've got extra energy after the main ride.) If you miss the trail, just follow any trail heading downstream along Cabin John Creek. Either way, you've got to cross Democracy Boulevard near its intersection with Seven Locks Road and many lanes of high-speed traffic. The trail resumes about a quarter-mile down Seven Locks Road, near where it narrows to one lane in each direction. Once you're back on the trail, keep your eyes peeled for blue blazes; it's easy to lose the trail. Next, there's a very steep climb followed by an insane descent; be careful. After the big climb, the trail is easy to follow. At River Road, many riders turn back; beyond this point the trail becomes mountain goat territory, with many steep hills. At the next major intersection, with the Capital Beltway, you must turn back. Bikes aren't allowed beyond this point (too steep, too dangerous).

RIDE 16 · Capital Crescent Trail

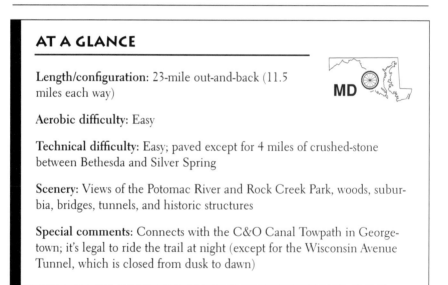

AT A GLANCE

Length/configuration: 23-mile out-and-back (11.5 miles each way)

MD

Aerobic difficulty: Easy

Technical difficulty: Easy; paved except for 4 miles of crushed-stone between Bethesda and Silver Spring

Scenery: Views of the Potomac River and Rock Creek Park, woods, suburbia, bridges, tunnels, and historic structures

Special comments: Connects with the C&O Canal Towpath in Georgetown; it's legal to ride the trail at night (except for the Wisconsin Avenue Tunnel, which is closed from dusk to dawn)

Capital Crescent Trail, the latest addition to a growing system of multiuser trails in and around the nation's capital, follows the route of the old Georgetown Branch, a B&O Railroad line completed in 1910 that ran between Georgetown and Silver Spring. The line carried coal and building supplies on a weekly train to Georgetown until service shut down in 1985. After several years of community efforts, the National Park Service purchased the right-of-way from Georgetown to the D.C. line. Montgomery County then bought the right-of-way from that point through Bethesda and Silver Spring.

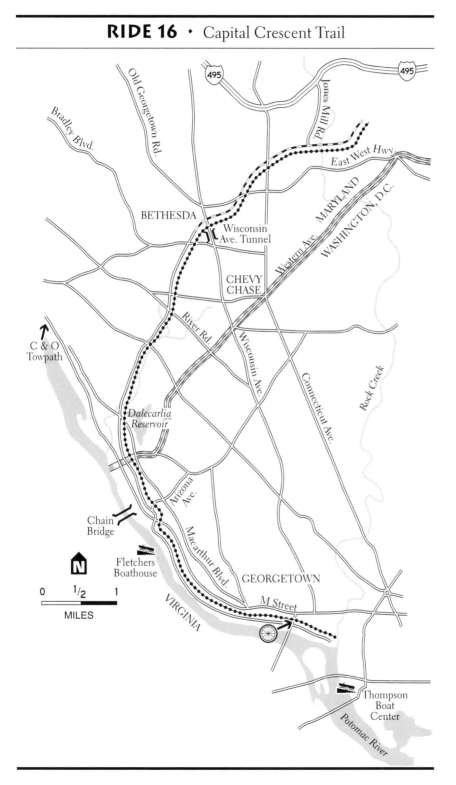

This popular 11.5-mile one-way trail, which opened in 1996, links parks, trails, and communities in the Washington metropolitan area and serves as a protected greenway for wildlife and outdoor recreation. A paved surface with gentle gradients runs from tony Georgetown along the Potomac River parallel to the C&O Towpath and curves into Bethesda, where users are diverted along a few blocks of streets in the center of town (the detour is well signed). In 1998, an old railroad tunnel beneath the streets was renovated and opened for trail users.

From central Bethesda to Silver Spring, the trail converts into a crushed-stone, interim hiker-biker trail temporarily named Georgetown Branch Trail. Trail users are also detoured around a trestle over Rock Creek Park onto side streets and a paved bike path (once again, the diversion is well signed). Plans are in the works to convert Georgetown Branch Trail into a combination bus or light-rail transitway with a paved trail alongside it. Once a decision is made to build the mass-transit route, this section will be renamed Capital Crescent Trail.

The new trail is a recreational boon to the crowded suburbs north of D.C., but it also benefits D.C. and Maryland bike and mass-transit commuters, providing a nonmotorized link between Washington's Metro subway stations at Bethesda and Silver Spring, and a fast (by bike, anyway) link from the Maryland suburbs to Metro-less Georgetown.

General location: The Maryland suburbs of Washington.

Elevation change: Negligible.

Season: Year-round.

Services: All services are available along the trail (including many bike shops). Public rest rooms are available at Fletchers Boat House on the C&O Canal.

Hazards: Traffic at many street crossings. The trail is usually crowded; cyclists should stay to the right and warn other users before passing (a handlebar-mounted bell works well).

Rescue index: Excellent; the trail is very popular and passes through congested suburbs with busy streets lined with residences and businesses.

Land status: C&O Canal National Historical Park (D.C.) and Maryland-National Capital Park and Planning Commission (Maryland).

Maps: Free trail maps are available along the trail. For a detailed 4-color map, send $1 and a stamped, self-addressed envelope to the Coalition for the Capital Crescent Trail (address below).

Finding the trail: The trail intersects or crosses many major traffic arteries in inner Montgomery County, including Connecticut Avenue, East West Highway, Wisconsin Avenue, Bradley Boulevard, River Road, Massachusetts Avenue, and MacArthur Boulevard. In Washington the trail follows the Potomac into Georgetown. Public parking is available on K Street near Key Bridge in Georgetown, at Fletchers Boat House on the C&O Canal, and in Bethesda. The trail is signed and easy to find as it curves through suburban Maryland; most cross-streets have trail signs, and street parking is ample near much of the trail.

When trails are muddy, fat-tire fanatic David Tambeaux opts for skinny tires and goes for a spin on the paved Capital Crescent Trail.

Source of additional information:

Coalition for the Capital Crescent Trail
Box 30703
Bethesda, MD 20824
For the latest trail conditions, call (202) 234-4874

Notes on the trail: The trail is easy to follow. Approximately 4 miles of trail from Bethesda to Silver Spring have a crushed-rock surface; long-term goals are to pave this section. The trail's connection to the 184-mile C&O Canal Towpath allows virtually unlimited cycling opportunities along the spectacularly scenic Potomac River. It's also easy to hook up with Mount Vernon Trail (in northern Virginia), which goes to George Washington's estate south of Alexandria, and to the W&OD Trail, which heads west toward the Blue Ridge Mountains of Virginia. For more on these Virginia trails, pick up a copy of *Mountain Bike! The Mid-Atlantic States: Charleston, SC to Washington, DC* ($15.95, Menasha Ridge Press, (800) 247-9437).

RIDE 17 · Cosca Regional Park

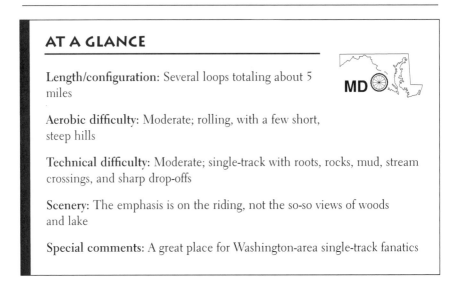

AT A GLANCE

Length/configuration: Several loops totaling about 5 miles

Aerobic difficulty: Moderate; rolling, with a few short, steep hills

Technical difficulty: Moderate; single-track with roots, rocks, mud, stream crossings, and sharp drop-offs

Scenery: The emphasis is on the riding, not the so-so views of woods and lake

Special comments: A great place for Washington-area single-track fanatics

If it's great scenery you're after around the nation's capital, go to the C&O Canal Towpath, a great cycling route close to Washington that offers splendid views of the Potomac River. Area riders who love single-track—a scarce commodity around D.C.—should consider a trip to Cosca Regional Park, 500 acres of woods outside suburban Clinton, Maryland, in Prince George's County. It's only minutes from Capital Beltway (near Andrews Air Force Base) and has more than five miles of trails to provide a few hours of fun.

Let's be frank. While Cosca is an attractive park that provides plenty of outdoor recreation for area residents—picnic sites, playgrounds, a lake with paddle boats, a nature center for youngsters—it's not very scenic. Power lines mar the modest views, chain-link fences border some of the trails, the paths look beat and worn, and, on my late-summer visit, the small lake was coated with scum. A well-used urban park, in other words, despite its suburban location. But, hey, the place welcomes off-road cyclists—and with the dearth of riding opportunities in the Washington area, it's definitely a place local riders should consider visiting.

General location: Clinton.

Elevation change: Nominal; a few short climbs.

Season: Year-round.

Services: Camping and a snack bar are available in the park. All other services are available in Clinton.

Hazards: Use care along narrow single-track that perches you precariously above the creek bed. Watch for traffic when you cross Thrift Road on Perimeter Trail.

Rescue index: Excellent; the park is small and surrounded by paved roads and residences.

RIDE 17 · Cosca Regional Park

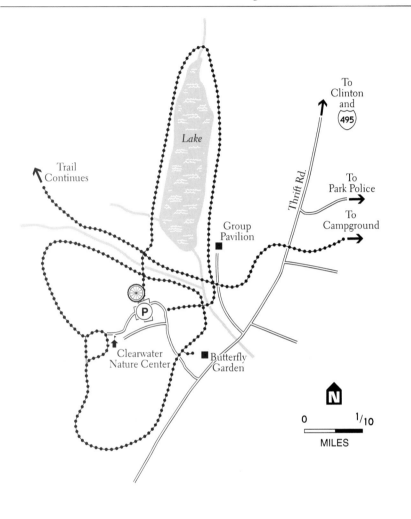

Land status: Maryland-National Capital Park and Planning Commission.

Maps: A trail map is available at the park office on Thrift Road.

Finding the trail: Take Exit 7 off Capital Beltway (I-495) to MD 5 (Branch Avenue) south toward Waldorf. Go about 4 miles to MD 223 (Woodyard Road) and turn right. Next, turn left on Brandywine Road. Go about three-fourths of a mile to Thrift Road (there's a traffic light) and turn right. Go about 2 miles to the third park entrance (marked "Clearwater Nature Center"), turn right, and park in the lot near the nature center. From the parking lot, walk down the steps

Located in the middle of congested Prince George's County, Cosca Regional Park has a nice system of single-track trails.

(or ride along the side), which lead to the 1.5-mile Lake Trail. This trail intersects with all the other main trails and a lot of other unmarked single-track. Lake Trail ends on the paved road leading to the nature center (and, of course, can be ridden in both directions).

Source of additional information:

> Cosca Regional Park
> 11000 Thrift Road
> Clinton, MD 20735
> (301) 297-4575

Notes on the trail: Other routes include the 4-mile Perimeter Trail, the 0.75-mile Graybark Trail, and the 0.25-mile Clearwater Trail (the last two begin behind the nature center). No specific directions are needed to ride this small park, but here's a suggestion: from the nature center, head down the steps toward the lake, go up the short steep hill, and follow the trail along the lake. Past the wooden bridges at the end of the lake, bear left and follow the small stream, where things start to get interesting (read: technical). Past the power lines, you can explore more trails in the section of the park that contains athletic fields.

RIDE 18 · Gambrill State Park

AT A GLANCE

Length/configuration: 6.5-mile loop

MD

Aerobic difficulty: Extreme; nearly 1,000 feet of climbing

Technical difficulty: Prime hammerhead territory; very tough, with barely rideable rock gardens, tight single-track, and a shifty shale surface

Scenery: Mostly scraggly second-growth forest; a few overlooks with nice views from the ridge

Special comments: A mountain ride that's nirvana for bikers who thrive on slow, technical riding

Gambrill State Park is another Maryland location that's high on the list of favorite places for hammerheads in search of anaerobic bliss. This 1,137-acre park abuts the Frederick watershed in the Catoctin Mountains and offers panoramic views of the City of Frederick Municipal Forest, Crampton's Gap, the Middletown and Monocacy Valleys, and South Mountain. It's the place to go when nothing else but a real ride in the mountains will do. Only the hard core need apply. This six-and-a-half-mile ride is technically and aerobically a killer, featuring steep climbs; narrow, twisty single-track on a tricky shale surface; rocks, limbs, tree trunks, and other obstacles littering the trail; and treacherously steep downhills. It's technical, slow riding at its best.

After a ride, enjoy the vistas from overlooks in the High Knob area and have a picnic. The Civilian Conservation Corps built many of the park structures with native timbers and stone in the 1930s and 1940s.

Strong riders armed with topo maps and compasses can use Gambrill as the start of an all-day, 25-mile-plus ride into adjacent Frederick watershed, a 6,000-acre forest offering great technical single-track, 17 miles of unpaved fire roads, thousands of feet of elevation gain—and virtually no trail blazes or signs (one reason I haven't included a Frederick watershed ride).

An easier option is to hook up with knowledgeable riders and follow their wheels. To latch onto an organized ride in the 'Shed, call the Mid-Atlantic Off Road Enthusiasts (MORE) at (703) 502-0359 or the Wheel Base (Frederick's pro bike shop, 229 North Market Street) at (301) 663-9288. Many local riders (myself included) say Frederick watershed offers the best technical riding this side of West Virginia.

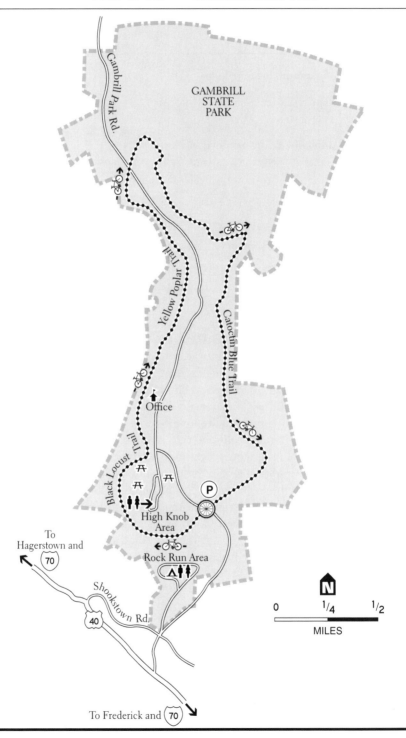

GAMBRILL
STATE
PARK

Gambrill Park Rd.

Yellow Poplar Trail

Catoctin Blue Trail

Office

Black Locust Trail

High Knob
Area

P

Rock Run Area

To
Hagerstown and
70

Shookstown Rd.

40

To Frederick and 70

N

0   1/4   1/2

MILES

The Yellow Trail at popular Gambrill State Park is maintained by volunteers from the Mid-Atlantic Off Road Enthusiasts.

General location: Frederick.

Elevation change: 1,000 feet.

Season: Year-round; due to the unusual soil composition and good drainage, the mountains are usually dry enough to ride when most places in Maryland are soaked.

Services: Camping is available in the Rock Run area of the park from Memorial Day through Labor Day. All other services are available in Frederick.

Hazards: Very steep downhills. In the fall hunting season (late November), wear orange or ride on Sundays, when hunting isn't permitted. Don't leave valuables visible in your car; thefts have occurred in this popular area. In an emergency, or to report suspicious behavior, call a park ranger at (800) 825-PARK. Pay phones are located at the bathhouse at Rock Run Campground and at Dan Dee Restaurant on US 40.

Rescue index: Poor; the trails go deep into the forest, away from paved roads and residences. A car could be waved down on unpaved Gambrill Park Road.

Land status: State park.

Maps: Trail maps are available at the trailhead parking lot. The USGS 7.5 minute quads are Myersville, Catoctin Furnace, Middletown, and Frederick.

Finding the trail: From US 40 and I-70, follow signs to the park entrance. Bear right, drive up the hill to the small trailhead parking lot on the right, and park. Ride your bike onto Black Locust Trail, which is signed.

Source of additional information:

> Cunningham Falls State Park
> 14039 Catoctin Hollow Road
> Thurmont, MD 21788
> (301) 271-7574

Notes on the trail: Black Locust Trail joins Yellow Poplar Trail. When the trails split, bear left onto Yellow Poplar Trail. After crossing Gambrill Park Road, turn right onto Catoctin Blue Trail, which takes you back to the parking lot. All park trails are open to mountain bikes except the 1-mile White Oak Trail.

RIDE 19 · Greenbrier State Park

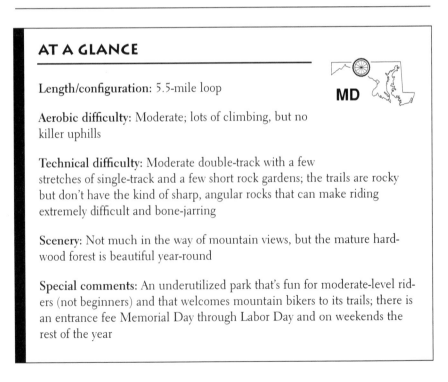

AT A GLANCE

Length/configuration: 5.5-mile loop

MD

Aerobic difficulty: Moderate; lots of climbing, but no killer uphills

Technical difficulty: Moderate double-track with a few stretches of single-track and a few short rock gardens; the trails are rocky but don't have the kind of sharp, angular rocks that can make riding extremely difficult and bone-jarring

Scenery: Not much in the way of mountain views, but the mature hardwood forest is beautiful year-round

Special comments: An underutilized park that's fun for moderate-level riders (not beginners) and that welcomes mountain bikers to its trails; there is an entrance fee Memorial Day through Labor Day and on weekends the rest of the year

RIDE 19 · Greenbrier State Park

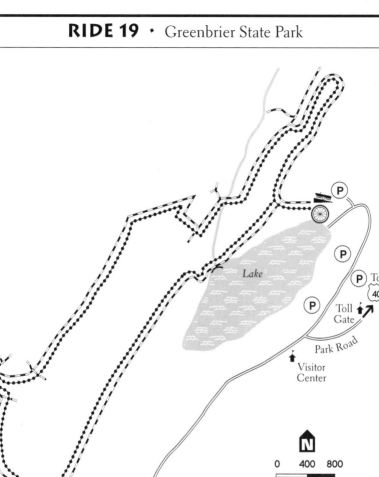

This 1,288-acre park on South Mountain between the western Maryland towns of Hagerstown and Frederick is an ideal destination for mountain bikers with moderate abilities. Unlike nearby Gambrill State Park (about ten miles east on US 40), this five-and-a-half-mile loop won't beat you to death on bone-jarring single-track, exhaust you on killer climbs, or tighten your sphincter on white-knuckle descents. Instead, Greenbrier offers well-groomed trails where you're continuously climbing or descending double-track winding through an attractive hardwood forest.

Wide double-track trails at Greenbrier State Park are perfect for intermediate riders.

The old roads (now double-track) follow routes laid out two centuries ago by pioneers who settled this corner of the Appalachian Mountains. Look closely and you can see the outlines and ruins of log cabins, massive stone fences, and iron furnaces. Also scattered throughout the park are great, flat, circular hearths, where charcoal was made to fuel furnaces. After the Civil War, the land became a series of wood lots, small parcels of land sold to nearby residents. In the 1960s, Maryland began purchasing the lots. The result is this park and its most popular feature, a 42-acre man-made lake.

While Greenbrier's lake draws big crowds in the summer, mountain bikers usually don't encounter much bicycle or foot traffic on the trails. "This is a really nice but underutilized park," says Dan Hudson of the Mid-Atlantic Off Road Enthusiasts, a Washington-area mountain bike club. "Once you get out on the trails, you won't see anyone. And the park is really bike-friendly." Dan's advice: After a ride, plan on swimming and sunning at the lake's sandy beach.

General location: Hagerstown.

Elevation change: A couple hundred feet.

Season: Year-round; the trails are hard and don't tend to get soggy from rain and snowmelt.

Services: Camping is available in the park. All other services are available in Hagerstown and Frederick.

Hazards: Hunting is permitted in some areas of the park, so it's a good idea not to ride during deer-hunting season in late November (except on Sundays, when hunting isn't permitted). If you do ride here during hunting season, wear bright clothes, make a lot of noise, and leave the furry white fanny pack at home.

Rescue index: Fair. The park is small and surrounded by roads where you could wave down a car in an emergency.

Land status: State park.

Maps: Trail maps are available at the Visitor Center. The USGS 7.5 minute quads are Funkstown and Myersville.

Finding the trail: From I-70 north of Frederick, take the Myersville exit to US 40 and follow signs to the park entrance. Drive past the entrance station, turn right at the next intersection, go to the boat ramp parking lot, and park. Ride your bike on the grassy area bordering the lake (on your left) toward the woods. Don't take Orienteering Trail, which you'll see straight ahead. Instead, follow the lake around to the left a short distance and take the next trailhead on the right into the woods.

Source of additional information:

South Mountain Recreation Area
21843 National Pike (US 40)
Boonsboro, MD 21713
(301) 791-4767

Notes on the trail: The trails are well marked and easy to follow, and the loop described here will get you started. You can easily spend half a day exploring. After finishing the loop, consider riding Orienteering Trail (it's dandy) and link up to some of the other trails in the park.

BALTIMORE, MARYLAND

Baltimore is a great mountain biking town, and I'm not just saying that because I live there. While you won't find many trails inside the city limits, you don't have to go very far to find a wide range of great places to ride off-road.

For starters, the city owns three watersheds in the suburbs that provide drinking water to the region. Thanks to new recreation guidelines developed by the Baltimore Department of Public Works, with input from the Maryland Association of Mountain Bike Operators (MAMBO), mountain bikers can legally ride more than 40 miles of great woods roads that wind through the Loch Raven, Liberty, and Prettyboy watersheds in the rolling hills of Baltimore County. Seminary Trail, which starts just a mile north of the Baltimore Beltway in Loch Raven watershed, is the area's most popular off-road riding spot. I've also included two less-visited trails in the watersheds: Overshot Run (also in Loch Raven) and a scenic trail at Liberty watershed, northwest of town. Ride these trails and discover why mountain bikers up and down the East Coast rave about the fun, scenic riding in Baltimore's watersheds.

Other top-notch venues nearby include the number-one destination for hammerheads in central Maryland: the Avalon Area of Patapsco Valley State Park. The trails are slow, steep, and technical—just what the doctor ordered for that full-suspension bike. For easier riding, try the trails at McKeldin, another Patapsco Valley State Park area west of the city (it's especially pretty in May, when the dogwoods bloom).

Baltimore also boasts two excellent rail-trails: the paved Baltimore and Annapolis Trail south of the city and the crushed-stone Northern Central Railroad Trail, which extends from Baltimore's northern suburbs to the Mason-Dixon Line. Both are excellent destinations for families—or when wet weather makes it too muddy to ride elsewhere.

A bit farther afield are Susquehanna State Park, featuring technical single-track and an easy river trail, and Fair Hills Natural Resources Management Area, a former Dupont family estate riddled with 30 miles of trails. Both parks are just off Interstate 95 northeast of the city. Last but not least is Hashawha, an environmental preserve near Westminster in Carroll County that boasts nearly 20 miles of trails.

RIDE 20 · Baltimore and Annapolis Trail Park

AT A GLANCE

Length/configuration: 28-mile out-and-back (14 miles each way)

MD

Aerobic difficulty: Easy; mostly flat

Technical difficulty: Easy; paved bike path

Scenery: Woods and suburbia

Special comments: A busy trail; watch for automobiles at intersections

---

One of the most popular rails-to-trails conversions in the Mid-Atlantic region is the 14-mile (one-way) Baltimore and Annapolis Trail Park, an easy paved path that connects Baltimore's southern suburbs to trendy Annapolis, Maryland's capital. The 112-acre linear park follows the railbed of the Old B&A Short Line Railroad and parallels busy MD 2. You're never far from the suburban sprawl that's the hallmark of northern Anne Arundel County, but you'll still get many glimpses of nature, especially along the southern end of the trail. The level path passes through hardwood forests and farmlands, as well as many suburban neighborhoods. The popular, well-used trail is often crowded on weekends with cyclists, inline skaters, hikers, and families out on a stroll, but because the path is 10 feet wide and follows a 66-foot-wide corridor, there's plenty of room for everyone.

The ride is easily extended. From the large parking lot at the southern end, it's four miles by bike into downtown Annapolis. If you park at the large lot and ride your bike into town, you can avoid the parking hassles in this popular tourist and yachting destination. The northern end of the trail links to the four-mile BWI (Baltimore-Washington International Airport) Trail, which goes to the Linthicum station of Baltimore's light-rail system. BWI Trail encircles Baltimore International Airport.

General location: Between Baltimore and Annapolis.

Elevation change: Nominal.

Season: Year-round.

Services: Most services, including bike shops, are located along the trail. All services are available in Baltimore, Glen Burnie, and Annapolis.

Hazards: The trail crosses many paved roads with heavy traffic.

Rescue index: Excellent; the trail is almost always in sight of paved roads.

Land status: County park.

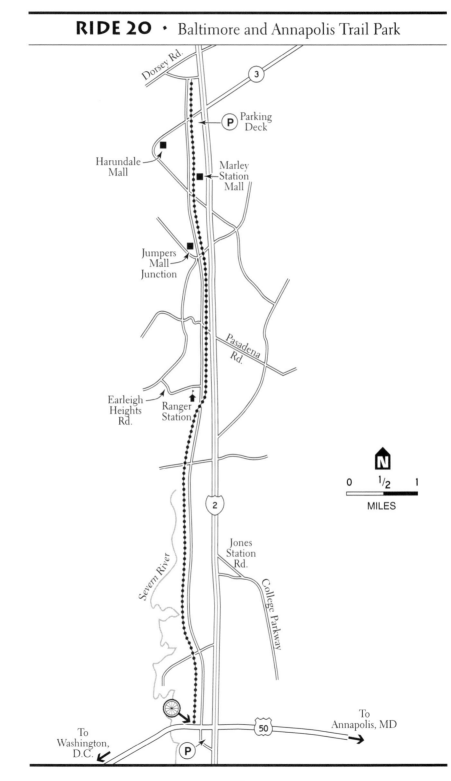

Maps: A map is available from B&A Trail Park, P.O. Box 1007, Severna Park, MD 21146; (410) 222-6244.

Finding the trail: To reach the southern terminus of the trail in Annapolis from the Baltimore Beltway (I-695), take Exit 4 to I-97 south and follow it to the end. Then take US 50 east for 3 miles to Exit 27 and get on MD 450 (get in the right lane). Parking for the trail is on the right, just past the flashing light. The notice board in the parking lot gives directions to the nearby trail.

To reach the northern end of the trail in Glen Burnie from the Baltimore Beltway, take Exit 4 to I-97 south and go 2 miles to Exit 16. Then turn left onto Baltimore-Annapolis Boulevard (MD 648) south. At Crain Highway (Business MD 3), turn right and make a left at the next light. Park in the parking garage; free low-clearance parking is on the left, and the trail is to the right.

Another option is to park 4.4 miles farther north at the light-rail station in Linthicum and, on your bike, ride BWI Trail south to the B&A Trail. You can also take a 1.3-mile spur trail to an aircraft observation area and watch planes take off and land at the huge airport.

Source of additional information:

B&A Trail Park
P.O. Box 1007
Severna Park, MD 21146
(410) 222-6244

Notes on the trail: To reach Annapolis from the B&A Trail, follow the wide shoulder of MD 450, cross the Severn River Bridge on the cycleway, and turn left at the second set of traffic lights onto King George Street. At the end of King George Street, turn right onto Randall Street, which leads to the city dock in downtown Annapolis; it's about 4 miles one-way from the B&A Trail.

RIDE 21 · Patuxent Research Refuge North Tract

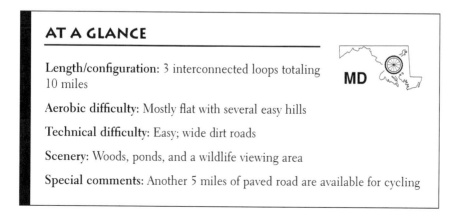

AT A GLANCE

Length/configuration: 3 interconnected loops totaling 10 miles

MD

Aerobic difficulty: Mostly flat with several easy hills

Technical difficulty: Easy; wide dirt roads

Scenery: Woods, ponds, and a wildlife viewing area

Special comments: Another 5 miles of paved road are available for cycling

This 8,100-acre tract of forest, open fields, and wetlands is located in the middle of the Baltimore-Washington suburban corridor, making it convenient for area cyclists who enjoy nature, quiet, and very easy riding. The refuge's mission is wildlife research, including surveying wildlife and monitoring their survival and growth rates. More than 200 bird species, as well as upland mammals such as eastern cottontail, white-tailed deer, red and gray fox, southern flying squirrel, gray squirrel, striped skunk, opossum, and bobcats live in the refuge. The vast expanse of woodlands, located next to the U.S. Army's Fort Meade, is also available for recreation. Ten-plus miles of dirt and gravel roads off-limits to motorized traffic are open for bicycles, hikers, and equestrians.

The roads are wide, mostly flat (except for a couple of easy hills), graded, and well marked with color-coded arrows, and they pass through a second-growth forest and by an occasional field. It's not a wilderness; signs are posted regularly and a large power line passes through the area. Yet this expanse of forest is quiet and offers miles of pleasant cycling without the worry or distraction of traffic. Four color-coded trails make up a system of three interconnected loops that can be ridden in a variety of ways to make a pleasant morning or afternoon of easy cycling.

You can extend your ride by pedaling out and back on the Wildlife Loop, a five-mile (one-way) paved road leading to ponds that offer additional opportunities to view wildlife. (Despite its name, it's not a loop, and you must share the road with light traffic.) The wildlife viewing area near the cluster of cycling trails features a 3.3-acre open pond to attract migratory and resident waterfowl, two nesting islands, and mud flats for wading birds and shore birds. The viewing area is surrounded by wetlands forested with red maple, river birch, green ash, sweet gum, black gum, and pin oak trees.

General location: Laurel.

Elevation change: Nominal.

Season: Year-round. Closed Thanksgiving, Christmas, and New Year's Day.

Services: Rest rooms and a soft drink machine are located at the visitor contact station. All other services are available in Laurel.

Hazards: Unexploded ammunition (!) left over from the refuge's former status as a U.S. Army firing range; don't venture off designated trails.

Rescue index: Good; the roads are patrolled by refuge personnel.

Land status: National wildlife refuge.

Maps: A trail map is available at the visitor contact station.

Finding the trail: From the Baltimore-Washington Parkway near Laurel, take MD 198 east 1.5 miles to Bald Eagle Drive and turn right (there's a sign). Follow signs to the visitor contact station and park. Visitors must sign in and, when leaving, sign out. The refuge is open daily from 8 a.m. to dusk. Park at the visitor contact station or in the lot at the wildlife viewing area half a mile away. Ride your bike on the paved Wildlife Loop to Green Trail, which leads to the system of dirt and gravel roads closed to motorized vehicles.

RIDE 21 · Patuxent Research Refuge North Tract

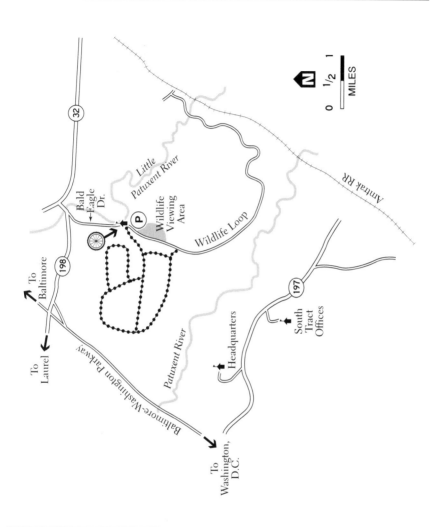

Source of additional information:

Patuxent Research Refuge
Visitor Contact Station
230 Bald Eagle Drive
Laurel, MD 20724-3000
(410) 674-3304

Notes on the trail: A nice place to stop on Yellow Trail (off Blue Trail) is a small fenced cemetery; some of the tombstones predate the Civil War.

RIDE 22 · Patapsco Valley State Park—McKeldin Area

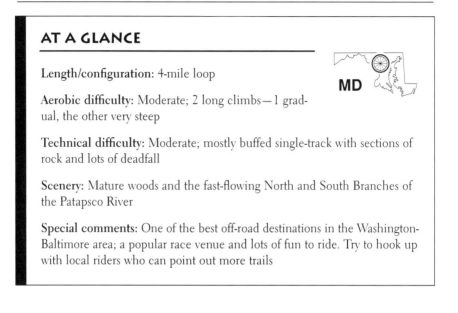

AT A GLANCE

Length/configuration: 4-mile loop

MD

Aerobic difficulty: Moderate; 2 long climbs—1 gradual, the other very steep

Technical difficulty: Moderate; mostly buffed single-track with sections of rock and lots of deadfall

Scenery: Mature woods and the fast-flowing North and South Branches of the Patapsco River

Special comments: One of the best off-road destinations in the Washington-Baltimore area; a popular race venue and lots of fun to ride. Try to hook up with local riders who can point out more trails

The 15,000-acre Patapsco River Valley on the fringe of the large Baltimore metropolitan area provides an escape for millions of people. The park sprawls along the Patapsco River from Liberty Dam (which forms Liberty Lake, one of three reservoirs that supply Baltimore's drinking water) to the river's mouth near Baltimore Harbor. The park, which has five recreation areas along the river valley west of Baltimore, is honeycombed with hiking and biking trails, equestrian trails, picnic shelters, and playing fields.

While not as popular with mountain bikers as the Avalon Area of Patapsco Valley State Park, the McKeldin Area is easier to ride and more scenic. This four-mile loop follows most (but not all) of the park's Switchback Trail, passing through pretty woods and offering views of the fast-flowing Patapsco River. Last but not least, it's a lot of fun to ride.

General location: Sykesville.

Elevation change: About 200', most of it in 2 long climbs out of the river valley.

Season: Year-round. It's particularly nice in May, when dogwood trees bloom.

Services: All services are available in Columbia, about 10 miles south of the park, and in Ellicott City, a few miles east on US 40.

Hazards: McKeldin is popular with equestrians, so watch for horses (and other users) on the trail.

Rescue index: Good; the trail is popular and crosses a paved park road near the halfway point. A pay phone is just past the entrance station.

RIDE 22 · Patapsco Valley State Park—McKeldin Area

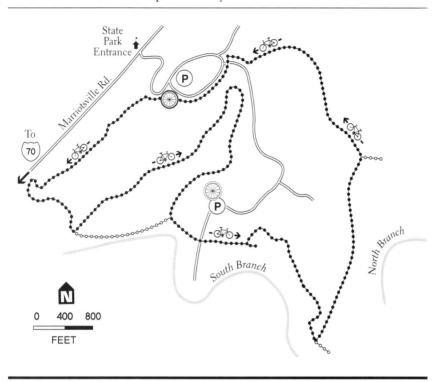

Land status: State park.

Maps: Trail maps are available at park headquarters in the Hollofield Area, off US 40 in Ellicott City (about 8 miles east of the park on US 40).

Finding the trail: From I-695 (the Baltimore Beltway) drive about 8 miles west on I-70 and exit onto Marriottsville Road north. (There is no northbound exit for Marriottsville Road for drivers going east on I-70.) From points west, take I-70 east to the US 40 exit for Ellicott City. Then turn left onto Marriottsville Road (there's a sign for the park). From Marriottsville Road drive about another 4 miles; the park entrance is on the right just past the river. Once you're in the park, drive up the hill and park in the lot just past the entrance station (there's a user fee on weekends and holidays from March 1 to October 31). On your bike, face the entrance station; Switchback Trail is signed and starts in the woods to the left of the paved road. An alternate starting point is the last parking lot at the end of the main park road (past C Field). Ride down the narrow paved road near the picnic pavilion; Switchback Trail crosses the road at the bottom of the hill just before the rest rooms on the right.

A small rock garden along the Switchback Trail offers technical challenges for riders at Patapsco Valley State Park's McKeldin Area.

Source of additional information:

Patapsco Valley State Park
8020 Baltimore National Pike
Ellicott City, MD 21043
(410) 461-5005

Notes on the trail: At the end of the downhill, the wide trail turns left back uphill; you can shorten the ride by going straight on the narrow trail and continuing along the river. Near the halfway point, the trail crosses a narrow paved park road that's closed to traffic. Rest rooms are on the right. (The paved road—to the left—leads to the last parking lot on the main park road, which is also the alternative starting point mentioned in Finding the Trail.)

Past the narrow paved road and rest rooms, the trail turns into narrow single-track and rolls (lots of small climbs) through deep woods before dropping back down to the river. Here, make the next left onto an unmarked trail (at this writing, anyway) that ends on a gravel road after a steep climb; turn right at the intersection with the paved main park road and return to your car. You can also cross the road and pick up a single-track that links with Switchback Trail at the top of the first big climb.

RIDE 23 · Patapsco Valley State Park—Avalon Area

AT A GLANCE

Length/configuration: 2 connected loops and a spur totaling 11 miles

MD

Aerobic difficulty: Brutal; lots of short, steep climbs

Technical difficulty: As hard as it gets; rock gardens, tricky stream crossings, roots, and logs

Scenery: All forest, except for a few rock outcroppings that provide views of the river valley

Special comments: The favorite destination for hammerheads in the Baltimore and Washington areas; not for beginners

The Avalon Area of Patapsco Valley State Park—one of five major areas in the 13,000-acre park that straddles the Patapsco River west of Baltimore—is rated by the local hard core as one of the top off-road destinations in the Baltimore-Washington area. And it's not for the scenery (although it's not bad). For mountain bikers who enjoy technical challenges and all-around difficulty, Avalon is the place to go.

And, boy, does this place get a lot of use. In fact, it's getting loved to death. Trail access groups such as MORE (Mid-Atlantic Off-Road Enthusiasts), MAMBO (Maryland Association of Mountain Bike Operators), and others are working with park officials to maintain the park trails, but it's an uphill battle. Riders come from all over to ride the 11 miles of trails here, and the heavy use is starting to show. Once-narrow single-tracks are widening as users dodge mud puddles and, as a result, increase the trails' width. (Hey, ride through water in the middle of the trail—you're on a mountain bike.) Only ride the trails when they're dry—or risk losing access to this premier off-road destination.

Avalon isn't just about mountain biking. The park features many historical sites, including Thomas Viaduct (the world's first multiarched stone railroad bridge), Patterson Viaduct, Gray's Cotton Mill, and Bloede's Dam (the world's first internally housed power plant). The Avalon Area also has fishing, picnicking facilities, and canoeing.

General location: Baltimore.

Elevation change: 500' to 600'.

Season: Late summer and fall, when the trails are usually driest, are best. Winter is good if it hasn't rained or snowed. In spring the trails can be muddy, and summer is usually hot and humid.

RIDE 23 · Patapsco Valley State Park—Avalon Area

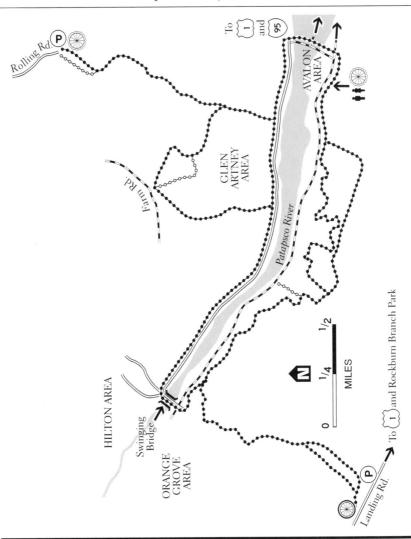

Services: All services are available in Baltimore.

Hazards: Sharp drop-offs, huge rocks, stream crossings, and big logs. Watch for horses (and yield if you see any).

Rescue index: Good; the trails are popular, especially on weekends. A pay phone is located in the Avalon Area, a developed section along the river with playgrounds, picnic pavilions, and rest rooms.

Land status: State park.

The calm before the storm: easy single-track at Patapsco Valley State Park's Avalon Area leads to some of the most technical off-road riding in the Washington-Baltimore area.

Maps: Trail maps are available at park headquarters in the Hollofield Area off US 40 in Ellicott City.

Finding the trail: From I-695 (Baltimore Beltway) near Arbutus, take I-95 south to US 1 south. Turn right on Montgomery Road west and cross over I-95. Drive past Old Landing Road and, about 200 yards later, turn right (north) at Landing Road. Drive 1 mile and turn left into Rockburn Branch Park and park your car. On your bike, continue on Landing Road about half a mile to the trail-head, which is just past Norris Lane; look for a waist-high Patapsco Valley State Park sign on your right.

The alternate start on the other side of the park is the park-and-ride lot on Rolling Road (MD 166), just off I-95 south of Baltimore Beltway. Park at the left side of the lot near the utility transformers, which are covered with bike stickers. On your bike, cross the "to I-95" entrance ramp and the 2-lane road behind the park-and-ride lot. The trailhead is a short distance to the left; look for a small state park boundary marker.

Both entrances are out-and-back spur trails that lead to 2 loops. You can also drive into the park and start your ride at the picnic grounds in the Avalon Area, the developed section along the river; the entrance to the park is on US 1 south of I-695.

Source of additional information:

Patapsco Valley State Park
8020 Baltimore National Pike
Ellicott City, MD 21043
(410) 461-5005

Notes on the trail: Don't overestimate your abilities. Lots of beginners find themselves in over their heads, and most get stuck (or worse) a long way from the trailhead. But if you're comfortable with highly technical single-track and steep climbing, you'll love Avalon.

RIDE 24 · Seminary Trail

AT A GLANCE

Length/configuration: 11-mile out-and-back (5.5 miles each way) and a 3-mile loop

MD

Aerobic difficulty: Moderate, with some long but not very steep climbs

Technical difficulty: Easy to moderate; a rough woods road with a few small stream crossings

Scenery: Woods and glimpses of a reservoir

Special comments: Baltimore's most popular off-road venue

With many long climbs and a few stream crossings, Seminary Trail (its formal name is Glen Ellen Trail, but no one calls it that) is best for advanced beginners and more experienced mountain bikers. The five-and-a-half-mile (one way) hard-packed double-track roller coasters through the numerous stream valleys feeding into Loch Raven Reservoir, one of three impoundments that supply drinking water to the Baltimore metro area. Then you can ride a three-mile loop on a rough woods road.

With 5,600 acres of woodland surrounding a huge reservoir, Loch Raven has a wilderness feel. In the summer and early fall, the riding seems largely a trip through tunnels of leaves with only an occasional glimpse of the reservoir, but in late fall and winter the views change dramatically. From the high ridges overlooking the huge body of water, it's easy to imagine you're riding in, say, upstate New York.

Located only a mile north of the Baltimore Beltway (I-695) near suburban Towson, Loch Raven Reservoir is the favorite riding place of local riders. In 1996, its popularity was almost the watershed's downfall, when the city of Baltimore (which owns the land in suburban Baltimore County) proposed new recreation guidelines that would prohibit mountain bikes on Loch Raven's many miles of woods roads. Local riders rallied, and after two years of negotiations the Maryland Association of Mountain Bike Operators (MAMBO) successfully worked out a plan that allows bikes on the unpaved roads in Loch Raven (and in Prettyboy and Liberty, the city's other two watersheds). In return for access, MAMBO (with more than 500 active members) pledged that mountain bikers would help maintain the trails, provide information on the new rules at trailheads, and patrol the trails at peak use periods. "That [was] the most significant achievement we made," said George Balog, Baltimore's director of public works, when the compromise was struck.

The regulations are posted at many trailheads. A quick summary: Don't ride when it's muddy (allow at least 48 hours after a soaking rain), stay off the single-track, and follow the International Mountain Bicycle Association's trail rules. Not hard—in fact, it's just common sense. Hats off to Baltimore and MAMBO for protecting a valuable venue for this popular sport. Help Baltimore-area riders maintain their access to the watershed by obeying the rules. If you're a local rider, you can help even more by joining MAMBO.

General location: Baltimore.

Elevation change: 800'.

Season: Spring rain can turn most of the fire roads into ankle-deep mud quagmires, making that a good time to explore the scenic paved roads of Baltimore County. Baltimore summers are infamous for heat and humidity, so plan to ride early in the day. Fall is the best season. The leaves turn brilliant colors, and as they fall, the views of the reservoir return. Winter, especially the mild ones the area has been experiencing in recent years, is a good time to experience the unrestricted views of the huge reservoir.

Services: All services are available in Baltimore. The closest bike shop is about 1.5 miles south on York Road in Towson.

Hazards: The second stream crossing, about a mile from Seminary Avenue, is lined with concrete and can be treacherously slick; a lot of folks, including me, always walk it (you won't even get your feet wet). Watch for other trail users; the trail is often crowded on nice weekends.

Rescue index: Excellent. Much of the ride skirts the boundaries of the watershed and the backyards of suburban homes. In addition, the ride crosses Loch Raven Drive twice, a popular destination for strollers and joggers that's closed to motor traffic 10 a.m. to 5 p.m. on weekends.

Land status: City of Baltimore watershed.

RIDE 24 · Seminary Trail
RIDE 25 · Overshot Run Trail

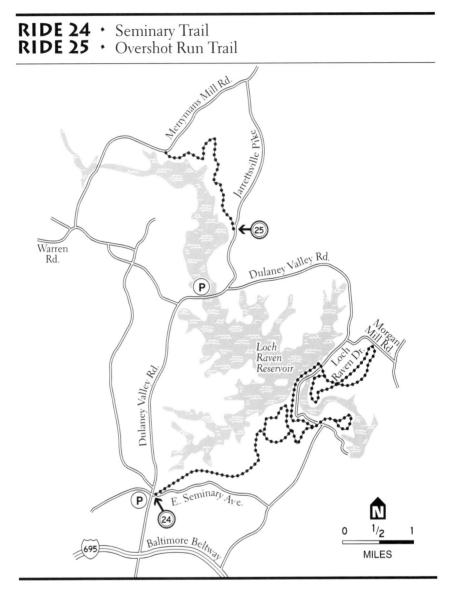

Maps: Trail maps are posted at the trailhead. The 7.5 minute USGS quad is Towson.

Finding the trail: From I-695 near Towson, take Dulaney Valley Road (Exit 27) north. At the second stop light, Seminary Avenue, turn left and immediately pull over and park (there's a wide shoulder and it's legal). On your bike, cross Dulaney Valley Road on Seminary Avenue and ride a few hundred yards to the trailhead on the left.

Source of additional information:

Maryland Association of Mountain Bike Operators (MAMBO)
1212 Kingsbury Road
Owings Mills, MD 21117
(410) 902-1295
Website: www.mambomaryland.com

Notes on the trail: At the start of the ride, keep bearing right to stay on the trail; the numerous trails to the left drop down to the reservoir shore. Almost immediately after the second stream crossing (the one lined with concrete), bear right again and continue along the fire road.

The fire road ends at the intersection of two paved roads, Providence Road and Loch Raven Drive. Turn left (past the gate, which is closed on weekends 10 a.m. to 5 p.m.) and descend on Loch Raven Drive. Cross the bridge and, after a couple hundred yards, look for a trailhead on the right. This 3-mile loop can be ridden in either direction. When you're finished, backtrack across the bridge to Seminary Trail and return to your car.

Note: At the intersection of Seminary Trail, Loch Raven Drive, and Providence Road (where there's a gate), look across the road and you'll see another trail that heads toward the reservoir. This is another short, steep loop you can add to lengthen the ride by a couple of miles. The loop actually begins down the trail at the first intersection (turn right). It's a pretty section of trail. Once you're back at the intersection, backtrack to Loch Raven Drive where you began.

RIDE 25 · Overshot Run Trail

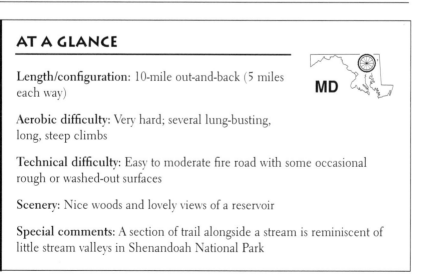

AT A GLANCE

Length/configuration: 10-mile out-and-back (5 miles each way)

MD

Aerobic difficulty: Very hard; several lung-busting, long, steep climbs

Technical difficulty: Easy to moderate fire road with some occasional rough or washed-out surfaces

Scenery: Nice woods and lovely views of a reservoir

Special comments: A section of trail alongside a stream is reminiscent of little stream valleys in Shenandoah National Park

Who says all mountain biking trails have to be technical single-track?

Overshot Run Trail, just north of Baltimore in Loch Raven watershed, is for strong riders. This five-mile (one-way) double-track fire road has some long, steep climbs through an attractive forest and offers fine views of Loch Raven Reservoir. The trail follows the northern end of the watershed, so views of the reservoir are frequent. The mixed hardwood and pine forest has a wilderness ambience; you may forget you're pedaling in the suburbs only a few miles from a major city. Deer sightings are common, and occasionally you'll startle a fox trotting down the trail.

Mountain biking was nearly banned in Baltimore's watersheds a few years back. But the Maryland Association of Mountain Bike Operators (MAMBO) and city officials worked out a compromise that allows bikes on the woods roads. Do yourself and fellow mountain bikers a favor by riding only when trails are dry and avoiding the single-track, which is closed to mountain bikes, equestrians, and hikers.

General location: Baltimore.

Elevation change: About 500'.

Season: In spring the trails are often wet and boggy, and summers in Baltimore are legendary for their heat and humidity. Fall and winter offer great fall foliage and, after the leaves are gone, expanded views of the reservoir.

Services: All services are available in Towson and Baltimore.

Hazards: Some very steep descents; be sure to keep your speed under control. Watch out for equestrians, especially when you're descending. Watch for traffic on the 2 miles of paved road that begin and end the ride.

Rescue index: Because the ride follows the boundary of the watershed, suburbia is just beyond the trees. Traffic could be flagged down on Warren Road (where you turn back).

Land status: City of Baltimore watershed.

Maps: The 7.5 minute USGS quad is Towson.

Finding the trail: From I-695 (Baltimore Beltway) take Exit 27 (Dulaney Valley Road) north approximately 4 miles. Park in the area on the left just before the bridge over the reservoir. To reach the trailhead, pedal out Dulaney Valley Road, cross the bridge (there's a wide shoulder), and bear left up the hill (watch for traffic). Look for a gate on the left side of the road about a mile past the bridge, where Overshot Run Trail begins. At the next paved road (Merrymans Mill Road), turn back.

Source of additional information:

Maryland Association of Mountain Bike Operators (MAMBO)
1212 Kingsbury Road
Owings Mills, MD 21117
(410) 902-1295
Website: www.mambomaryland.com

Notes on the trail: If you enjoy long, hard climbs, this is a great alternative to Seminary Trail (Ride 24). Plus, you'll see fewer people and it's more scenic.

RIDE 26 · Northern Central Railroad Trail

AT A GLANCE

Length/configuration: 40-mile out-and-back (20 miles each way)

MD

Aerobic difficulty: Easy

Technical difficulty: Easy

Scenery: Woods, farms, and a meandering river

Special comments: Connects with the York County Heritage Rail-Trail in Pennsylvania

Following the 160-year-old route of the Northern Central Railroad, this gentle, 20-mile (one-way) trail winds north from the Baltimore suburbs toward the Mason-Dixon Line through beautiful rural Maryland along Big Gunpowder Falls—and it's virtually flat. This greenway corridor lets cyclists explore a natural environment that's home to numerous mammals, reptiles, birds, and plants, including deer, beaver, and joe-pye weed. The ten-foot-wide, crushed-stone surface follows the right-of-way of the railroad, which transported Abraham Lincoln in 1863 to Gettysburg, where he gave his short but memorable speech.

The trail winds through forests, past farms and sumptuous estates, through small villages along Big Gunpowder Falls, and through the thoroughbred horse country near Monkton. Although the trail is never far from civilization, the route of the old railroad, which was put out of business by Hurricane Agnes in 1972, never parallels any roads. The result is tranquility and many picturesque views of the rural landscape.

The best direction to ride the trail is north (upstream) in an out-and-back configuration. Why? The trail isn't completely flat, and your return trip will be slightly downhill. At the Pennsylvania state line, the trail connects with the ten-mile York County Heritage Rail-Trail. So there's no need to stop.

General location: Baltimore.

Elevation change: Negligible.

Season: Year-round. But winters can be cold and wet with occasional snow, and summer afternoons are often hot and humid.

Services: Cold drinks, snacks, water, telephones, bike rentals, and minor bike repairs are available in Monkton, about 7 miles north of the southern terminus of the trail. Monkton Bike Rental rents bikes starting at $5 an hour; other services include repairs, canoe rental, and river float tube rentals; phone (410)

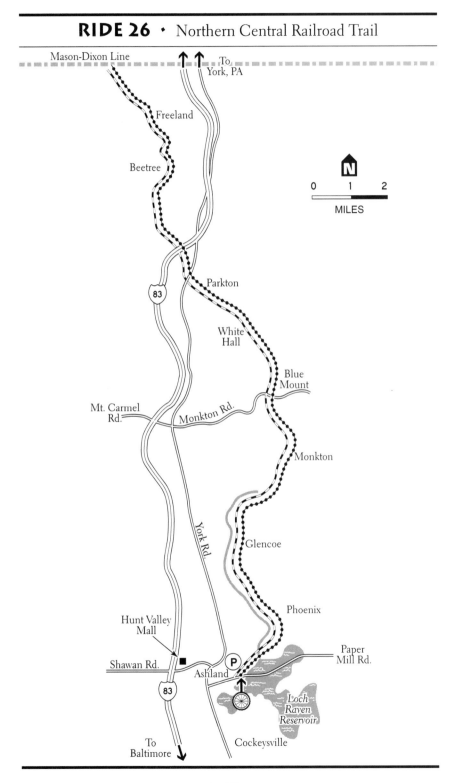

A small waterfall is one of the many attractions along the North Central Rail Trail.

771-4058. All other services are available in Cockeysville, a mile west of the southern end of the trail.

Hazards: None. Watch for traffic at road crossings, especially at busy Paper Mill Road and in Monkton.

Rescue index: Excellent. The trail passes private residences and crosses many small roads; pay phones are located at Paper Mill Road, Phoenix, Sparks, Monkton, White Hall, Bentley Springs, and Freeland.

Land status: State park.

Maps: Call Gunpowder Falls State Park for a current map (see below).

Finding the trail: From I-695 (Baltimore Beltway), take I-83 north about 5 miles to the Warren Road exit. At the second light (York Road), turn left and go 1 mile to Ashland Road and turn right. Here, you've got two options. Where Ashland Road meets Paper Mill Road (a half-mile from York Road), continue straight on Ashland Road and enter the residential community of Ashland. Go straight to the small public parking area (with about a dozen spaces) and park; the trail's southern terminus is at the north end of the lot. Or, continue on Paper

Mill Road past Ashland another half-mile to where the trail crosses the road (it's well marked). Pull over and park. Monkton is another popular starting place, but the lot fills up quickly on weekends and it's difficult to find; other small parking lots are located at major road crossings along the trail.

Source of additional information:

> Gunpowder Falls State Park
> P.O. Box 480
> Kingsville, MD 21087
> (410) 592-2897

Notes on the trail: Northern Central Railroad Trail is enormously popular, especially on weekends, and finding a place to park your car can be a problem. Rest rooms, picnic tables, benches, and exercise stations are located along the trail. Generally, the trail gets less crowded and more scenic the farther north you go.

RIDE 27 · Liberty Watershed

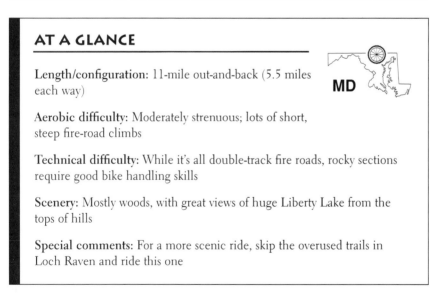

AT A GLANCE

Length/configuration: 11-mile out-and-back (5.5 miles each way)

MD

Aerobic difficulty: Moderately strenuous; lots of short, steep fire-road climbs

Technical difficulty: While it's all double-track fire roads, rocky sections require good bike handling skills

Scenery: Mostly woods, with great views of huge Liberty Lake from the tops of hills

Special comments: For a more scenic ride, skip the overused trails in Loch Raven and ride this one

Located northwest of Baltimore in Carroll County between Liberty Road and Westminster Pike, Liberty Lake is one of three drinking-water reservoirs serving Baltimore. Though not as popular as Loch Raven watershed (north of town), Liberty has many miles of unpaved fire roads open to exploration by mountain bike. Alas, the trails here don't get a lot of use, especially in

RIDE 27 · Liberty Watershed

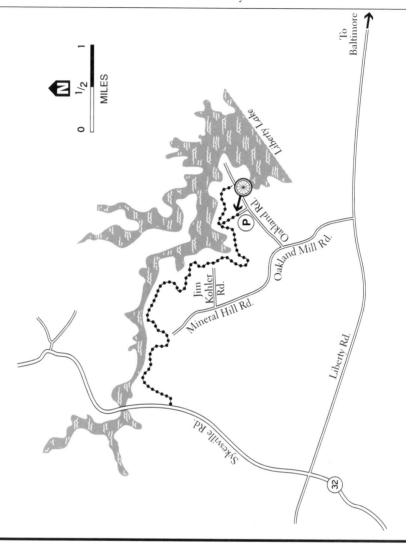

comparison to the overused Seminary Trail at Loch Raven. Baltimore-area hammerhead Jeremiah Bishop says more folks should get out of their Loch Raven rut and try this 11-mile trail. "The vistas of the lake are the great thing about this ride," he explains. "It's a really huge reservoir. Plus, I like the fact that it's got some fast, fun downhills. For Baltimore-area riders, Liberty is a breath of fresh air."

This breath of fresh air was almost lost by off-road cyclists. In 1996, the city of Baltimore, which owns this watershed, proposed new recreation guidelines that

Baltimore-area racer
Jeremiah Bishop
trains regularly at
Liberty Watershed.

would prohibit mountain bikes on the many miles of woods roads in the city's three watersheds: Liberty, Loch Raven, and Prettyboy. Local riders rallied, however, and after two years of negotiations, the Maryland Association of Mountain Bike Operators (MAMBO) successfully worked out a plan with the city that allows bikes on the unpaved roads in Liberty and in the city's other two watersheds. In return for access, MAMBO (with more than 500 active members) pledged that mountain bikers would help maintain the trails, provide information on the new rules at trailheads, and patrol the trails at peak use periods.

The regulations are posted at many trailheads. A quick summary: Don't ride when it's muddy (allow at least 48 hours after a soaking rain), stay off the single-track, and follow the International Mountain Bicycle Association's trail rules. Not hard—in fact, it's common sense. Hats off to Baltimore and MAMBO for protecting a valuable venue for this popular sport. Help Baltimore-area riders maintain their access to the watershed by obeying the rules. If you're a local rider, you can help even more by joining MAMBO.

General location: Eldersburg.

Elevation change: Around 800' to 900' (total).

Season: Year-round.

Services: A small shopping center at Liberty and Oakland Mill Roads can provide food and drink. All other services are available in Eldersburg and Baltimore.

Hazards: Loose rocks on descents, and hunters in the fall (except on Sundays, when hunting is not permitted).

Rescue index: Excellent.

Land status: City of Baltimore watershed.

Maps: The USGS 7.5 minute quad is Finksburg.

Finding the trail: From I-695 (Baltimore Beltway) drive out Liberty Road (northwest). Just past Wards Chapel Road, Liberty Road passes over Liberty Lake. After the bridge, turn right onto Oakland Mill Road. Coming from the other direction on Liberty Road, turn left onto Oakland Mill Road (again, after the first bridge; there are 2 bridges, and Oakland Mill Road is between them). Go 1 mile and turn right on Oakland Road (there's a church at the intersection). Drive a short distance and look for a Baltimore Public Works Department facility on the right; the trailhead is opposite, on the left. Keep driving, though, a short distance past the public works site and park on the left side of the road. Ride your bike back to the trailhead (the orange cable gate is easy to see).

Source of additional information:

Maryland Association of Mountain Bike Operators (MAMBO)
1212 Kingsbury Road
Owings Mills, MD 21117
(410) 902-1295
Website: www.mambomaryland.com

Notes on the trail: Less than a quarter-mile past the trailhead, the fire road splits; bear left. From this point on, just follow the main trail as it heads west along the lake's shoreline. About 2.5 miles into the ride, the trail passes through a very attractive pine forest. When you reach MD 32 (Sykesville Road), turn around.

Other riding options are nearby. At MD 32, turn right, follow the paved road (watch for traffic), cross the bridge, and look for trailheads on both sides of the road. The moral of the story: There's lots to explore at Liberty.

RIDE 28 · Susquehanna State Park

AT A GLANCE

Length/configuration: 11 miles of loops and a 4.4-mile out-and-back (2.2 miles each way) along the river

MD

Aerobic difficulty: Steep and anaerobic on the loops; easy on the river trail

Technical difficulty: Moderate to difficult on the loops; easy on the river trail

Scenery: Woods and fields, a working gristmill, historic buildings, and the Susquehanna River

Special comments: Moderately difficult single-track is made harder by too many waterbars; nice scenery of woods and fields

Located on the western shore of the Susquehanna River in Harford County, Susquehanna State Park features 2,639 acres of varying topography, including a wide river, heavy forest cover, massive rock outcroppings, and interesting historical buildings. Mountain bikers can choose between the 2.2-mile (one-way) Lower Susquehanna Heritage Greenway Trail (easy cruising along the river) or about 11 seriously challenging miles of interconnecting loops around the hills overlooking the river.

A good starting point is the picnic area on Stafford Road, which offers plenty of parking in the otherwise cramped Susquehanna River Valley. Deer Creek Trail (green blazes), a 2.1-mile loop, begins and ends near the parking lot. Two-mile Farm Road Trail (dark blue blazes) is an old dirt road that passes through woods and hay fields and connects to Rock Run Y Trail (yellow blazes) in the eastern end of the park; take this trail for a long exploration of the entire park. The three-mile Susquehanna Ridge Trail (red blazes) follows the western ridge of the Susquehanna River and ends at the Lapidum boat ramp area in the park's skinny eastern end. All of the trails feature plenty of steep climbs, occasional stream crossings, and way too many waterbars (railroad ties half-buried in the trail to prevent erosion—and to inadvertently frustrate off-road cyclists).

Mountain bikers in search of great scenery and easy riding should avoid the mostly single-track trails and instead ride Lower Susquehanna Heritage Greenways Trail, a rails-to-trails conversion that follows the river from Deer Creek (at the picnic area) to Conowingo Dam (where US 1 crosses the river on its way north into Cecil County and Pennsylvania).

Be sure to visit the park's historic area and see the Rock Run Grist Mill grind cornmeal by water power on weekends from spring through fall. Other historic

RIDE 28 · Susquehanna State Park

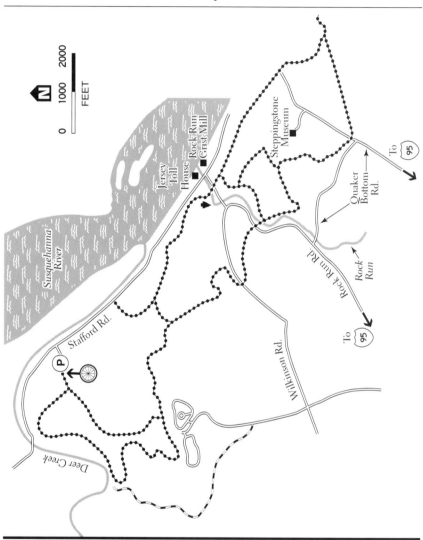

sites include the Jersey Toll House (a passing point for early settlers in the valley) and Archer Mansion, built in 1804. A nineteenth-century farm houses Steppingstone Museum, which displays and demonstrates late nineteenth- and early twentieth-century rural arts and crafts.

General location: Havre de Grace.

Elevation change: Several hundred feet on the loop trails; negligible on the river trail.

Season: Year-round.

Services: Camping is available in the park. The Bicycle Connection, a pro bike shop in Abingdon (near Bel Air), is about 20 miles away. All other services are available in Havre de Grace.

Hazards: Watch for horses along the trails. Be extra cautious when crossing the many waterbars, which can send daydreaming mountain bikers flying over the handlebars.

Rescue index: Excellent. The trails frequently parallel or follow paved roads.

Land status: State park.

Maps: A trail map is available at the office in the historic area.

Finding the trail: From I-95 take the MD 155 exit west (away from Havre de Grace); it's the first exit south of the Susquehanna River. Turn right onto Rock Run Road and follow signs to the park and picnic area. As you face the parking lot in the picnic area, the single-track starts in the woods on the right. The flat Lower Susquehanna Heritage Greenways Trail starts near the picnic area in the state park (across Deer Creek) or outside the park in the Conowingo Dam parking area.

Sources of additional information:

Susquehanna State Park
3318 Rocks Chrome Hill Road
Jarrettsville, MD 21804
(410) 557-7994

The Bicycle Connection
2906 Emmorton Road
Abingdon, MD 21009
(410) 515-3001

Notes on the trail: While all of the trails are open to bikes, some sections may be posted as danger areas. Follow posted signs for detours or, as the case may be, dismount and walk.

RIDE 29 · Fair Hill Natural Resources Management Area

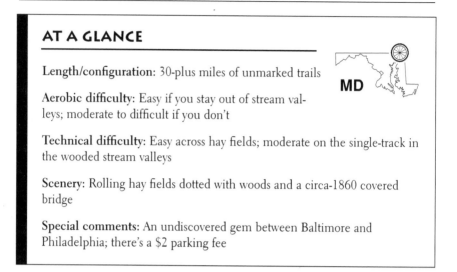

AT A GLANCE

Length/configuration: 30-plus miles of unmarked trails

MD

Aerobic difficulty: Easy if you stay out of stream valleys; moderate to difficult if you don't

Technical difficulty: Easy across hay fields; moderate on the single-track in the wooded stream valleys

Scenery: Rolling hay fields dotted with woods and a circa-1860 covered bridge

Special comments: An undiscovered gem between Baltimore and Philadelphia; there's a $2 parking fee

Fair Hill Natural Resources Management Area is the unwieldy name of a 5,600-acre former Dupont estate owned by the state of Maryland. One of the best-kept mountain biking secrets in the Mid-Atlantic region, it's conveniently located only minutes off I-95 between Philadelphia and Baltimore, bordering the Mason-Dixon Line that divides Pennsylvania and Maryland. It's a beautiful tract of rolling countryside in a pristine rural setting. William Dupont, one of the heirs to the huge Dupont chemical fortune, started developing Fair Hill in the 1920s for fox hunting. He died in 1965, and Maryland acquired the tract in 1975.

Not surprisingly, at Fair Hill the emphasis is on horses. Its rolling acres are home to Maryland's only steeplechase track, one of the few on the East Coast. The Fair Hill Training Center for race horses is also a training facility for Olympic equestrians. Yet in spite of Fair Hill's emphasis on things equine, mountain bikers are welcome to explore its more than 30 miles of single- and double-track. In addition to rolling fields and dense forests, off-road cyclists can enjoy a mazelike system of narrow trails and footbridges that cross Big Elk Creek, which bisects the property.

One of Fair Hill's attractions is its suitability for all levels of riders. Novices and folks in search of an easy spin can ride wide double-tracks through lush fields with little uphill climbing or technical challenges, while hammerheads can plunge down narrow wooded trails on twisting single-track on all-day rides. Or, riders can vary the ride by including any combination of the above.

Want an easy ride? Stick to the fields and don't take any single-track descents through the woods, which lead to the creek. Looking for something more ener-

RIDE 29 · Fair Hill Natural Resources Management Area

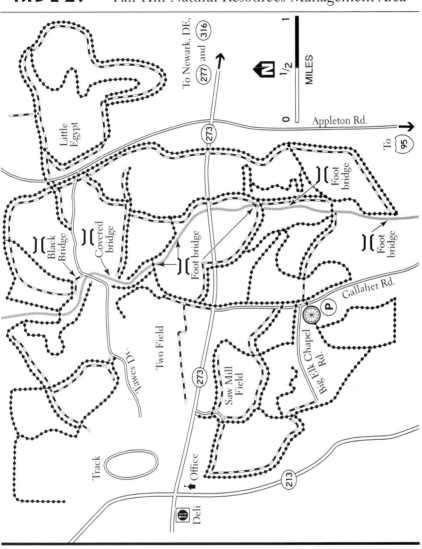

getic? Take the plunge down one of those paths and ride some exciting single-track littered with rocks, tree limbs, and the occasional muddy section. Just keep in mind that what goes down must eventually come back up.

General location: Elkton.

Elevation change: Most of the trails are gently rolling with no appreciable elevation change; optional steep but short descents lead to (and back up from) Big Elk Creek.

Ride through a covered bridge at Fair Hill, a former Dupont fox-hunting estate honey-combed with single-track and double-track trails.

Season: Year-round.

Services: There is a small deli in the shopping center across from the park office. All other services are available in Elkton and in Newark, Delaware.

Hazards: None, except yourself—you can be a danger to equestrians. Keep an eye out for horses.

Rescue index: Excellent. Fair Hill is bordered by roads and bisected by MD 273, so you're never far from a place where you can wave down a passing car.

Land status: State park.

Maps: A trail map is available from the park office. Write or call the Department of Natural Resources, Fair Hill, 376 Fair Hill Drive, Elkton, MD 21921; (410) 398-1246.

Finding the trail: Fair Hill is north of Elkton near the intersections of MD 273 and MD 213, in Cecil County. From I-95, take the first exit in Maryland (Exit 109B/MD 279) toward Newark, Delaware. Go 1 mile and turn left onto MD 277 (at Pat's Liquors); drive another mile to MD 316 and turn right. Go about 2.5 miles to MD 273 and turn left; now you're driving through Fair Hill. Turn left at Gallaher Road for the parking area and the ride that starts at Big Elk Chapel Road. The office is at the next intersection (MD 213) on the left, across from the small shopping center with the deli.

Source of additional information:

Department of Natural Resources, Fair Hill
376 Fair Hill Drive
Elkton, MD 21921
(410) 398-1246

Notes on the trail: You've got several options for starting a ride at Fair Hill. The easiest—and the one I recommend for first-time visitors—is to park across from the chapel at Gallaher Road and Big Elk Chapel Road. Turn south onto Gallaher Road (which intersects MD 273; the chapel is about a mile down on the left). On your bike, enter Fair Hill at the gate directly across from the parking lot and next to the small church. Continue straight for a descent to Big Elk Creek or bear left to get to trails leading to Saw Mill Field and the equestrian center.

Other options include parking near the barns and racetrack east of the Fair Hill office on MD 273 (rest rooms are in the white building). On your bike, follow the signs for the Cross Country Trail, which leads through Saw Mill Field and toward Gallaher Road. On the way, you'll pass horse jumps used by equestrians training for competition. Make a game out of your ride by searching for the tunnel and bridge that pass under and over Gallaher Road. You can also start a ride by parking at the lot on Tawes Drive (just past the nature center, north of MD 273). The highlight is the Big Elk Creek covered bridge, built in 1860 and reconstructed in 1992 at a cost of $152,000. It's one of five covered bridges in Maryland.

Most—maybe all—of the trails in Fair Hill are unmarked, so it's easy to get—well, not lost, the area's just too small for that—but disoriented. Just keep track of which side of Big Elk Creek you're on and stay inside Fair Hill's fenced boundaries. Bring plenty of food and water, and give yourself plenty of time so you're not racing a setting sun at the end of the day, and you'll be okay.

RIDE 30 · Hashawha Environmental Appreciation Center

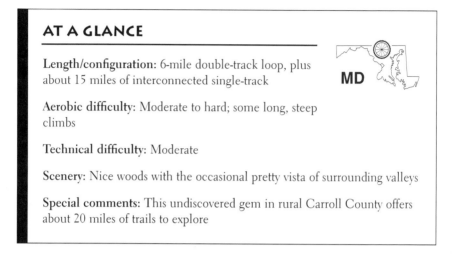

AT A GLANCE

Length/configuration: 6-mile double-track loop, plus about 15 miles of interconnected single-track

MD

Aerobic difficulty: Moderate to hard; some long, steep climbs

Technical difficulty: Moderate

Scenery: Nice woods with the occasional pretty vista of surrounding valleys

Special comments: This undiscovered gem in rural Carroll County offers about 20 miles of trails to explore

With more than 300 acres to explore—plus additional acreage from an adjacent watershed—Hashawha Environmental Appreciation Center offers mountain bikers a venue in the rolling hills of Carroll County, north of Washington and northwest of Baltimore. Since its opening in 1977, Hashawha has been providing environmental learning and outdoor recreation. On its 320 acres, the center manages diverse wildlife by providing a variety of habitats, from streams and ponds to wetlands, fields, coniferous forests, and hardwood stands.

Hashawha offers a conference building, a swimming pool, a sports recreation center, pavilions with picnic tables and grills, a two-acre lake, a wetlands boardwalk for wildlife observation, and a nature center with exhibits on insects, deer, Native Americans, reptiles and amphibians, raptors, recycling, and conservation. The environmental center also has a system of trails for hiking, horseback riding, and cycling. The main trail, a six-mile double-track loop around the center, passes through a hardwood forest. Leading off the main trail are many interconnected single-track trails, making a full day of riding possible.

General location: Westminster.

Elevation change: About 700'.

Season: Year-round.

Services: Rest rooms and soda machines are located in the Bear Branch Nature Center. All other services are available in Westminster.

Hazards: Watch for horses on the trails.

Rescue index: Excellent.

Land status: County park.

RIDE 30 · Hashawha Environmental Appreciation Center

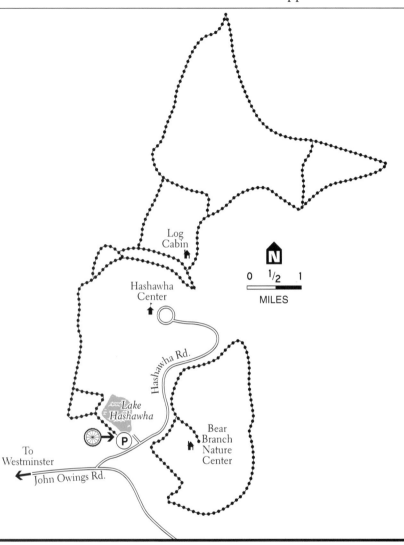

Log
Cabin

Hashawha
Center

N

0   1/2   1

MILES

Hashawha Rd.

Lake
Hashawha

To
Westminster

P

Bear
Branch
Nature
Center

John Owings Rd.

Maps: A map is available at the trailhead kiosk.

Finding the trail: In Westminster, take MD 97 north toward Gettysburg. Go 4.5 miles and turn right onto John Owings Road. Drive about 1.5 miles and turn left onto Hashawha Road (if John Owings Road has turned to dirt, you've missed it). Turn left and park in the lot with the sign for Lake Hashawha. Ride your bike around the left side of the pond, go up the hill, and turn right onto Loop 1/Yellow Trail (known informally to local riders as High Trail). After the rocky descent (probably the most technical section on the trail) follow the stream on the left. At the **T** intersection, go left and up the hill. Follow the yellow arrows to complete the loop. You can also ride the loop in the other direction.

Source of additional information:

Bear Branch Nature Center
300 John Owings Road
Westminster, MD 21158
(410) 848-2517

Notes on the trail: Look for a restored 1850s-era log cabin on the trail. You'll also see lots of single-track leaving the main trail as you ride the loop. These trails lead to the other 15-plus miles of trails at Hashawha. On weekends, follow the sounds of model airplanes for a stiff, one-way climb to the Carroll County Model Aerodrome. Local riders say the fun descent is worth the effort.

GREEN RIDGE STATE FOREST, MARYLAND

Mountain bikers in the Washington and Baltimore areas are lucky. When they get bored riding the same old trails over and over, relief is only two hours away. A half-hour west of Hancock, Maryland (where the state narrows down to a stone's throw between West Virginia and Pennsylvania), lies a series of mountain ridges running north and south. It's all state forest land, and it's one of Maryland's best-kept mountain biking secrets. Well off the beaten path, Green Ridge State Forest features 28,000 acres of mountain ridges and valleys. The forest is laced with dirt roads, jeep trails, and hiking trails. It's also a crazy quilt of campsites, private hunting shacks, vacation homes, overlooks, power-line cuts, and logging operations strewn over several low mountains that border the Paw Paw Bends of the Potomac River.

To be blunt, Colorado it ain't. These mountains have been heavily defor-ested, and the poor soil doesn't yield the lush kind of scenery you associate with, say, Shenandoah National Park in Virginia. Yet, in some respects, this is an advantage to mountain bikers; the area doesn't draw crowds or traffic, and on a mountain bike, the less scenic areas are quickly bypassed. There are plenty of beautiful views of mountains, forests, and the meandering Paw Paw Bends of the Potomac River.

Camping and mountain biking make a great combination at Green Ridge. Campsites are scattered throughout the forest, and many are secluded. Some are ideally located for the mountain biker bent on exploration, with easy access to many circuit rides so you don't have to move your car. The only inconve-nience is the lack of drinking water at campsites. Just bring lots of water jugs and a sun shower, and fill up at the park headquarters before you head out. Some campsites offer picnic tables (nice to have on a multiday visit), but other-wise they're primitive.

Getting to Green Ridge State Forest is easy because it's interstate all the way from Washington and Baltimore. Head out Interstate 70 (from Baltimore) or I-270 (from D.C.) to Hancock, and bear left onto I-68 (formerly US 40/48) toward Cumberland. From the top of Sideling Hill (where there is a Visitor Center and rest area), Green Ridge State Forest is visible to the left. Continue on I-68 over Town Hill to the next ridge, Green Ridge Mountain, and take Exit 64 (M. V. Smith Road) to the park headquarters. Pick up a free map and, if you're camping, register and pay for your campsite. Single-track fanatics won't want to miss Green Ridge's newest addition, the Green Ridge MTB Trail—11.5 miles of single-track bliss.

RIDE 31 · Green Ridge MTB Trail

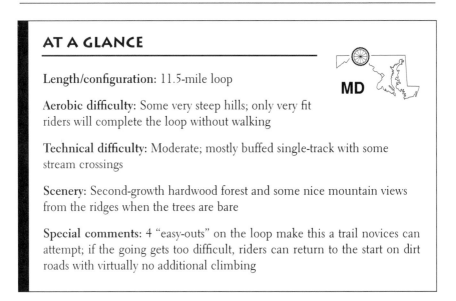

AT A GLANCE

MD

Length/configuration: 11.5-mile loop

Aerobic difficulty: Some very steep hills; only very fit riders will complete the loop without walking

Technical difficulty: Moderate; mostly buffed single-track with some stream crossings

Scenery: Second-growth hardwood forest and some nice mountain views from the ridges when the trees are bare

Special comments: 4 "easy-outs" on the loop make this a trail novices can attempt; if the going gets too difficult, riders can return to the start on dirt roads with virtually no additional climbing

With 40,000 acres of oak-hickory forest, Green Ridge State Forest is the second-largest state forest in Maryland. Located in the ridge and valley province of the Allegany Mountains, Green Ridge offers solitude, mountain views from the ridges, lots of places to camp, and opportunities to see wildlife such as white-tailed deer, wild turkey, squirrel, ruffed grouse, cottontail rabbit, quail, woodcock, red fox, and gray fox. Located only about two hours from Baltimore and Washington, Green Ridge had been growing a reputation for its steep jeep roads and seclusion. But something was missing: good single-track trails. No longer.

The new Green Ridge MTB Trail, built for mountain bikers, opened in 1998. The 11.5-mile loop gives cyclists even more reasons to visit this western Maryland destination. "We wanted to promote ecotourism, so we thought about building a trail specifically for mountain bikers," says Harry Cage, a Green Ridge forest ranger. "We had some old jeep roads that weren't maintained, so we did an environmental review and built the trail to get more people to come out here."

RIDE 31 · Green Ridge MTB Trail

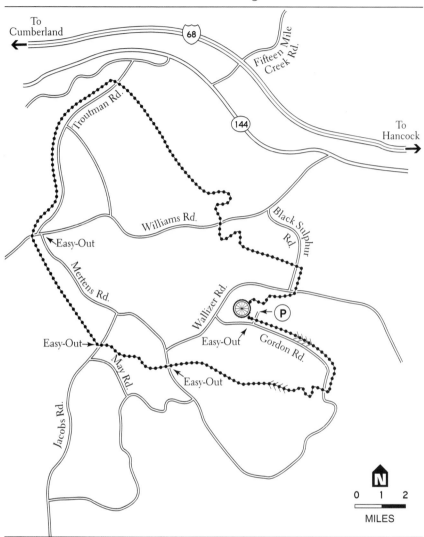

Build it and they will come. Cage says usage of the new trail has surpassed expectations, and there's a good chance the trail will be expanded.

General location: Green Ridge State Forest.

Elevation change: About 1,000'.

Season: Year-round; avoid deer-hunting season in the late fall (or ride on Sundays, when hunting isn't permitted).

The new MTB Trail
at Green Ridge State
Forest is attracting
riders from throughout
the mid-Atlantic area.

Services: Primitive camping is permitted at the parking area and at nearby campsites ($6 a night). All other services are available in Cumberland and Hancock.

Hazards: 3 stream crossings (1 comes up suddenly on a blind turn, but it's signed).

Rescue index: Good; the trail crosses unpaved roads carrying light traffic at several points.

Land status: State forest.

Maps: Pick up a map at the forest headquarters on M. V. Smith Road. The USGS 7.5 minute quad is Flintstone.

Finding the trail: From I-68, take Exit 62 (Fifteen Mile Creek Road). At the top of the ramp, turn right, take the next left onto MD 144, and go 1.6 miles. Turn left onto Williams Road and follow paved roads for a total of 2.5 miles (important: stay on paved roads). Turn left onto Black Sulphur Road and right onto Wallizer Road. Park in the field on the left (there's a sign). Ride your bike to the end of the field and the trailhead, which is signed.

Source of additional information:

Green Ridge State Forest
28700 Headquarters Drive, N.E.
Flintstone, MD 21530
(301) 478-3124

Notes on the trail: The trail is very well signed in the clockwise (recommended) direction. Decreasing-increment signs at half-mile intervals let you know how much farther you have. If you decide to bail, the 4 easy-outs are also well marked.

RIDE 32 · Stafford–East Valley Roads Loop

AT A GLANCE

MD

Length/configuration: 9-mile loop

Aerobic difficulty: Very demanding

Technical difficulty: Easy double-track

Scenery: Second-growth forest, mountains, and great views of the Potomac

Special comments: Great views of the Paw Paw Bends; the place to come for a great workout

The demands of this nine-mile loop in Green Ridge State Forest are strictly cardiovascular, not technical. The ride starts with a stiff climb up Stafford Road to the ridge of Town Hill Mountain and ends with another steep climb just before you return to your car. Only very well-conditioned cyclists will be able to ride up these hills; lesser mortals will have to push their bikes up the steep (but relatively short) climbs. Stafford Road is a well-maintained dirt road; East Valley Road is an old jeep road—essentially, a double-track—closed to motor traffic.

The rewards of this ride? No Name Overlook on Stafford Road and Banner's Overlook (at the intersection of Stafford Road and Mertens Avenue) offer grand views of the Paw Paw Bends, the Potomac River's meandering course between Maryland and West Virginia. The C&O Canal, stretching from Cumberland to Washington, follows the river on the Maryland side. Both Stafford and East Valley Roads are roller-coaster romps through hardwood forests.

RIDE 32 · Stafford–East Valley Roads Loop

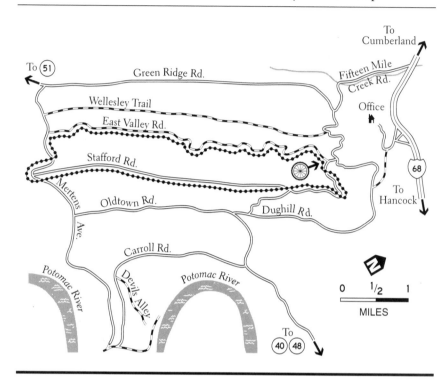

General location: Green Ridge State Forest.

Elevation change: About 1,500'.

Season: Good year-round (with the exception of deer-hunting season, which starts the Monday after Thanksgiving). Summers are usually hot, humid, and buggy, so plan your rides to start and finish early in the day. Green Ridge usually doesn't get much snow, so winter riding is good. Spring and fall are the best seasons. Spring offers relatively mud-free riding on these hard-pack roads, and fall offers cool weather and beautiful foliage when the leaves are changing.

Services: There are small grocery stores on Orleans Road north of I-68 and in Flintstone. The nearest bike shop is in Cumberland. All other services are available in Hancock and Cumberland.

Hazards: The descent from Banner's Overlook on Mertens Avenue is very steep; be on the lookout for traffic.

Rescue index: Good. With the exception of East Valley Road, the loop carries light traffic.

Land status: State forest.

Green Ridge State Forest
offers views of mountains
and valleys stretching
into the distance.

Maps: Trail maps are available at Green Ridge State Forest headquarters on M. V. Smith Road (Exit 64 from I-68).

Finding the trail: From I-68, take Exit 62 (Fifteen Mile Creek Road). Turn left at the stop sign, cross back over the highway, and follow the road about 2 miles. After crossing Fifteen Mile Creek, the road ascends Green Ridge Mountain. Just before the top, turn left at the intersection (straight is Green Ridge Road). Continue past the parking area for Wellesley Trail and turn right onto Stafford Road. Park at the intersection with East Valley Road (look for the gate on the right). Ride your bike up (and I mean up) Stafford Road. You'll finish at the trail beyond the gate at the intersection of Stafford and East Valley Roads on the right.

Source of additional information:

Green Ridge State Forest
28700 Headquarters Drive, N.E.
Flintstone, MD 21530
(301) 478-3124

Notes on the trail: This part of Green Ridge State Forest has spectacular views of the Potomac River as it snakes between Maryland and West Virginia. Also, Stafford and East Valley Roads are a blast to ride—a series of undulating hills that let momentum do most of the hard work. The intersection with East Valley Road comes up very fast. Be alert; it's easy to blow past it.

RIDE 33 · Mertens Avenue Area

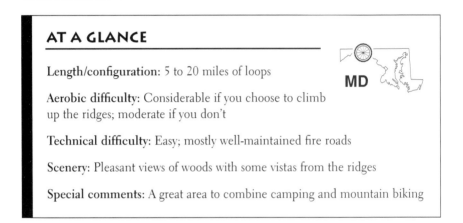

AT A GLANCE

Length/configuration: 5 to 20 miles of loops

MD

Aerobic difficulty: Considerable if you choose to climb up the ridges; moderate if you don't

Technical difficulty: Easy; mostly well-maintained fire roads

Scenery: Pleasant views of woods with some vistas from the ridges

Special comments: A great area to combine camping and mountain biking

The attractions of this area are low-key: miles and miles of roads twisting through mountain hollows and second-growth forest, the luxury of camping in one spot for days while mountain biking different trails every day, and solitude. The maze of small roads and trails is great for exploration by mountain bike; rides lasting from an hour to all day are possible. The roads are well maintained, but watch out for the steep climbs that go up to the ridges; switchbacks are rare.

Loop rides are easy to design. Here's some help: The easiest roads are Gordon, Railroad Hollow (an old railroad right-of-way), and Mertens Avenue (heading west, away from Green Ridge Mountain). More challenging roads are Jacobs, Twigg, Piclic, and Sugar Bottom. You can link to the area north of I-68 (which bisects the forest) by going out Fifteen Mile Creek Road. (Piclic Road is a good choice to reach it.) To get to the Stafford–East Valley Roads Loop (Ride 32), take Fifteen Mile Creek Road over Green Ridge Mountain to Stafford Road.

The roads are well maintained because of county residents who live on private land inside state forest boundaries. Railroad Hollow is a single-track that requires some scrambling over small streams, but it is virtually flat. Piclic Road has a steep and rocky drop as it approaches Fifteen Mile Creek Road, but it also

RIDE 33 · Mertens Avenue Area

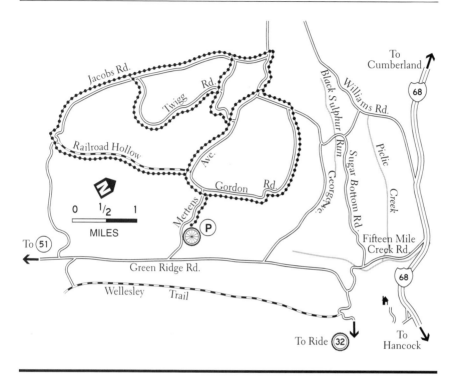

has the best descent (fast and verging on the technical). Gordon Road is the prettiest ride in the area. If you pedal Railroad Hollow in the late afternoon, you may see a flock of wild turkeys.

Look for signs to the new Green Ridge MTB Trail (Ride 31), where you can enjoy some genuine single-track riding.

General location: Green Ridge State Forest.

Elevation change: Up to 500'.

Season: Summers here are as hot, humid, and buggy as in the nearby cities, so try to start your ride early in the day and beat the worst heat. Spring, the wettest season, is a good time to visit Green Ridge because the well-maintained roads are usually less muddy than the forest trails at home. Winter is good, too, if you like cold-weather riding (snow is rare). Fall is probably the best time to ride because of the cool weather and fall foliage.

Services: There are small grocery stores on Orleans Road north of I-68 and in Flintstone. The nearest bike shop is in Cumberland. All other services are available in Hancock and Cumberland.

Most riding at Green
Ridge State Forest is
along wide—but often
steep—fire roads

Hazards: Water is scarce in these mountains, so be sure to carry enough. Watch for automobile traffic on the steep descents.

Rescue index: Good. Farms and private residences are scattered throughout the forest.

Land status: State forest.

Maps: Available at Green Ridge State Forest headquarters on M. V. Smith Road (Exit 64 from I-68).

Finding the trail: From I-68 get off at Exit 62, Fifteen Mile Creek Road (1 mile west of M. V. Smith Road). Turn left at the stop sign, cross back over the highway, and follow the road about 1 mile (it runs alongside its namesake on the left). After crossing Fifteen Mile Creek, the road begins climbing up Green Ridge Mountain. Just before the top there's an intersection; continue straight (the road's name changes to Green Ridge Road). Go about 2 miles to the second right (Mertens Avenue) and turn. You'll begin to see campsites (where you can park your car) after the descent from the ridge.

Source of additional information:

Green Ridge State Forest
28700 Headquarters Drive, N.E.
Flintstone, MD 21530
(301) 478-3124

Notes on the trail: Though Green Ridge State Forest has its drawbacks—it's a weird mix of forests, hunting shacks, power-line cuts, logging operations, and even a juvenile detention center—the area's pluses far outweigh its minuses. It's close to major population centers, but it's located in a sparsely populated area and is largely ignored by everyone but hunters (and you'll only see them in the fall).

Stake out a campsite, set up a tent, and do a loop ride before lunch and another one after. Or start with your lunch in the morning and ride all day, returning to your campsite before dinner. Come to Green Ridge for the kind of riding usually associated with the western United States—long treks over mountain ridges. The scenery isn't the same, but your quads won't know the difference.

RIDE 34 · North of Interstate 68

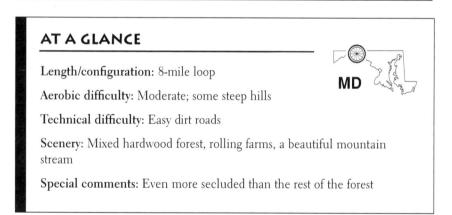

AT A GLANCE

Length/configuration: 8-mile loop

Aerobic difficulty: Moderate; some steep hills

MD

Technical difficulty: Easy dirt roads

Scenery: Mixed hardwood forest, rolling farms, a beautiful mountain stream

Special comments: Even more secluded than the rest of the forest

This section of Green Ridge State Forest is less popular than the areas below I-68, so it's even more secluded. With fewer campsites and private cabins (none on Treasure Road), it has more of a wilderness feel. The scenery? Low mountains and mixed hardwood forests, and some rolling farmland on old Cumberland Road. The ride along Fifteen Mile Creek—a narrow dirt road that follows the falling mountain stream—is beautiful.

Except for a short, steep, rocky descent on Treasure Road, this eight-mile loop follows well-maintained dirt roads and requires no technical skills. The challenges are on the long climbs, especially on Old Cumberland Road. To connect with other rides in the area, take Fifteen Mile Creek Road south into

RIDE 34 · North of Interstate 68

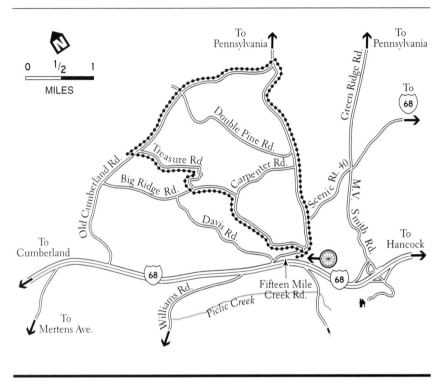

the main body of the forest. Go left on Sugar Bottom Road for the easiest way into the Mertens Avenue area. To get to Stafford and East Valley Roads, stay on Fifteen Mile Creek Road, turning left as you approach the ridge on Green Ridge Mountain; then, after you pass the Wellesley Trail parking area, turn right on Stafford Road.

General location: Green Ridge State Forest.

Elevation change: About 400'.

Season: Good year-round (with the exception of deer-hunting season, which starts the Monday after Thanksgiving). Summers are usually hot, humid, and buggy, so plan your rides to start and finish early in the day. The area usually doesn't get much snow, so winter riding is good. Spring and fall are the best seasons; spring offers relatively mud-free riding on these hard-pack roads, and fall offers cool weather and beautiful foliage when the leaves are changing.

Services: There are small grocery stores on Orleans Road north of I-68 and in Flintstone. The nearest bike shop is in Cumberland. All other services are available in Hancock and Cumberland.

With its wide fire roads, Green Ridge State Forest makes it easy for groups to ride together.

Rescue index: Good; the roads pass private residences and farms.

Land status: State forest.

Maps: Available at Green Ridge State Forest headquarters off Exit 64 (M. V. Smith Road) on I-68.

Finding the trail: From I-68 take Exit 62 (Fifteen Mile Creek Road). Turn right at the stop sign and park your car at the pulloff a quarter-mile on the right. Start the ride on Big Ridge Road, the paved road on the left from where you park (it turns to dirt at the top of the hill).

Source of additional information:

Green Ridge State Forest
28700 Headquarters Drive, N.E.
Flintstone, MD 21530
(301) 478-3124

Notes on the trail: Although this area isn't easy to link with other rides in Green Ridge (you must cross over I-68 on Fifteen Mile Creek Road—hardly a wilderness experience), it's worth a visit on its own. The highway isolates the area from the rest of the forest, and once you start your ride you probably won't see anyone else.

SAVAGE RIVER STATE FOREST, MARYLAND

If you drive from the east, dramatic changes occur about half an hour west of Cumberland as you crest Big Savage Mountain on Interstate 68. In summer the temperature drops, and in winter the weather can turn near-Arctic in intensity. Wide, rolling valleys dominated by hemlock forests separate the mountains. The character of the mountains changes, too. They're higher, wetter, and not as steep as the ridges to the east. You've reached the Appalachian Plateau.

Welcome to Garrett County, Maryland's most isolated county. Located entirely on the Appalachian Plateau, Garrett County averages 2,300 feet in elevation. Although farming, coal mining, and timbering dominate the county's economy, outdoor recreation is big business. Because of cool, bug-free summers and dependable snow (or at least snow-making) conditions for skiing, the county draws vacationers from Pittsburgh, Washington, and Baltimore.

Deep Creek Lake, a 3,900-acre reservoir, is the major tourist hub, and many vacation homes litter its 65-mile shoreline. The county also has two major white-water attractions, the Youghiogheny (YOCK-uh-ganey) and Savage Rivers, which draw paddlers and rafters from around the world. In 1989 the World Whitewater Canoe/Kayak Championships were held on the rapids of the Savage River.

Befitting an isolated corner of the Appalachian Mountains, Garrett County has 70,000 acres of state forests and parks, creating a mecca for mountain bikers. The largest and most accessible tract of state-owned land is 53,000-acre Savage River State Forest, which straddles Big Savage Mountain to the east and Meadow Mountain to the west. It contains two state parks (New Germany and Big Run), the 350-acre Savage River Reservoir, and many lakes, rivers, and streams. Camping, swimming, fishing, and rental cabins make the forest an attractive destination for mountain bikers, and there are many miles of forest trails and woods roads to explore.

New Germany State Park is a great place to set up a base camp. The park is easy to reach (only five miles from I-68, the county's major highway), and all the rides that follow start there. New Germany has the basic amenities: camping, hot showers, and a lake for swimming (perfect after a ride). Aprés-ride, the nearby college town of Frostburg has restaurants ranging from French and Italian to Greek. For breakfast, drive to Grantsville and stoke up on buckwheat pancakes at the Casselman Restaurant (circa 1824). For details about camping, call New Germany State Park at (301) 895-5453.

RIDE 35 · Meadow Mountain O.R.V. Trail

AT A GLANCE

MD

Length/configuration: 10-mile out-and-back (5 miles each way)

Aerobic difficulty: Moderate

Technical difficulty: Easy woods road

Scenery: Beautiful mature woods and some mountain vistas

Special comments: A good beginner's ride

Meadow Mountain Off-Road Vehicle Trail, a five-mile (one-way) out-and-back, follows the ridge of Meadow Mountain through beautiful mature hemlock and hardwood forest interspersed with views of Big Savage Mountain, surrounding valleys, and small farms. This ride requires almost no technical skill because most of the trail is along a well-maintained woods road. Yet the dirt road is punctuated by climbs, bogs, and rough sections that make the ride challenging. Flatlanders will breathe a little harder—and may do some pushing—on the half-mile climb up Meadow Mountain at the start. The rest of the trail follows the ridge.

If you start from parking lot 5 in New Germany State Park, the first half-mile is along paved road to the trailhead in the park maintenance area. (You can also park in front of the park office and skip the paved road.) The trail is a well-maintained, ten-foot-wide forest road, but plenty of boggy and rocky sections will keep your attention riveted to the 100 square inches in front of your wheel. The optional trail to Meadow Mountain Overlook at the end of the O.R.V. trail is narrower and littered with deadfall. The reward for your efforts is a spectacular, down-the-throat view of Monroe Run with Big Savage Mountain in the background.

Stay alert for wildlife. The mountains are home to a great diversity of animal species, ranging from black bear to brook trout, and great-horned owls to long-tailed salamanders. Mammals include deer, bobcat, raccoon, squirrel, beaver, and bats. There are more than 100 species of birds, including hawks, owls,

RIDE 35 • Meadow Mountain O.R.V. Trail

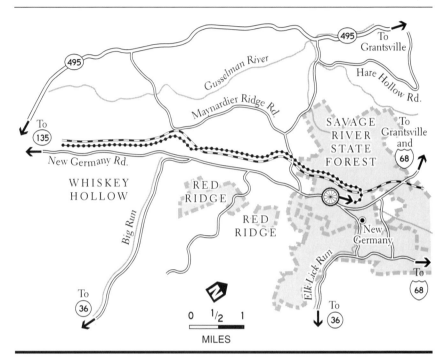

turkey, grouse, and warblers. Snakes, turtles, salamanders, frogs, and fish complete the long list of animals you may encounter.

General location: Grantsville.

Elevation change: About 500'.

Season: The best riding conditions are from June through October. Summer on the Appalachian Plateau is much cooler than in big cities to the east, and there are no mosquitoes or ticks. In mid-June the mountain laurel along the ridge blooms. Early spring can be very muddy. Snow is possible from October through April. Avoid riding during deer-hunting season (after Thanksgiving). The spectacular fall foliage is at its best in late September and early October.

Services: The nearest restaurants, lodging, and grocery stores are in Grantsville, north of I-68. Frostburg, a college town about a half-hour drive east of New Germany, has a selection of restaurants and lodging. The nearest bike shop is in Cumberland.

Hazards: The woods road is well maintained, but watch for downed trees. Use caution at all road crossings. You may come across timber rattlesnakes, especially on the ridge—keep your eyes open and give the snakes plenty of room.

Rescue index: Good. The O.R.V. trail parallels New Germany Road, which carries light traffic. Residences can be reached from Otto Lane, Maynardier Ridge Road, and Frank Brenneman roads.

Land status: State forest and park; county roads.

Maps: Trail maps are available at the State Forest Administrative Office on New Germany Road. The Grantsville and Bittinger USGS 7.5 minute quads and the Garrett County topo map (available at the administrative office) are also good.

Finding the trail: Take Exit 24 from I-68 and follow signs to New Germany State Park/Savage River State Forest. The administrative office and the trail-head are on the right side of New Germany Road, where you can park. Or turn left into New Germany State Park and park in lot 5 across from the lake (there's no overnight parking). From lot 5, ride back to the park entrance and cross New Germany Road to the trailhead, which is just past the park office.

Source of additional information:

Savage River State Forest
Route 2, Box 63-A
Grantsville, MD 21536
(301) 895-5759

Notes on the trail: The ride starts with a 0.7-mile climb to a T intersection, where you turn left. (To the right, the O.R.V. trail continues 4.5 miles north toward I-68.) After a couple of miles, the trail reaches another T intersection. Turn left and ride a short distance to the intersection of 2 dirt roads (Otto Lane and West Shale Roads). From here you can see the O.R.V. trail to the right.

When the trail ends at Frank Brenneman Road (the trail to Meadow Mountain Overlook is across the road), you have the option of creating a loop ride by returning to the park on New Germany Road (paved with a wide shoulder). To ride the loop, turn left and descend to the intersection. Then turn left again for the 5-mile spin back to the park.

RIDE 36 · Poplar Lick/Elk Lick Loop

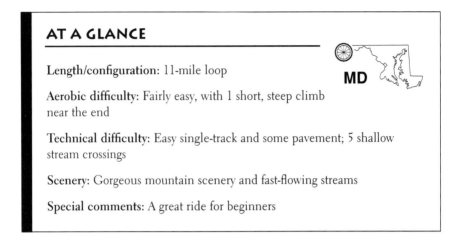

AT A GLANCE

MD

Length/configuration: 11-mile loop

Aerobic difficulty: Fairly easy, with 1 short, steep climb near the end

Technical difficulty: Easy single-track and some pavement; 5 shallow stream crossings

Scenery: Gorgeous mountain scenery and fast-flowing streams

Special comments: A great ride for beginners

This fun ride starts with five miles of gentle downhill through a gorgeous forest beside a fast-flowing mountain stream. Though it lacks spectacular views of the surrounding mountains, this ride shows off the intrinsic beauty of the Appalachian Plateau. Be on the lookout for wildlife; bear, deer, bobcat, raccoon, great-horned owls, beaver, and bats are abundant. The rhododendron along the streams blooms in early July, and the fall foliage peaks in late September or early October.

The 11-mile loop begins in a hemlock forest and follows Poplar Lick Run, a beautiful mountain stream. The forest changes to second-growth hardwood as you descend. Then the O.R.V. trail ends in a wide, grassy meadow where Poplar Lick Run flows into the Savage River. There are a few, short stretches of easy single-track. The return trip, on paved road, follows Elk Lick Run. (A note to purists: Don't let the paved road put you off. This is a very pretty ride.)

The trail requires no technical skill except for the five stream crossings along Poplar Lick, which can be walked. In the spring or after rain, expect to get your feet wet; you may have to carry your bike and wade through calf-deep water. Last but not least, there's a stiff climb on McAndrew Hill Road just before the finish.

General location: Grantsville.

Elevation change: Around 900'.

Season: The best biking conditions are from June through October. Early in the spring the dirt roads and trails can be extremely muddy, and the stream crossings are deep. This may not be the best choice for a cold-weather ride, either, as snow is possible from October through April. Avoid riding in deer-hunting season (late fall).

RIDE 36 • Poplar Lick/Elk Lick Loop

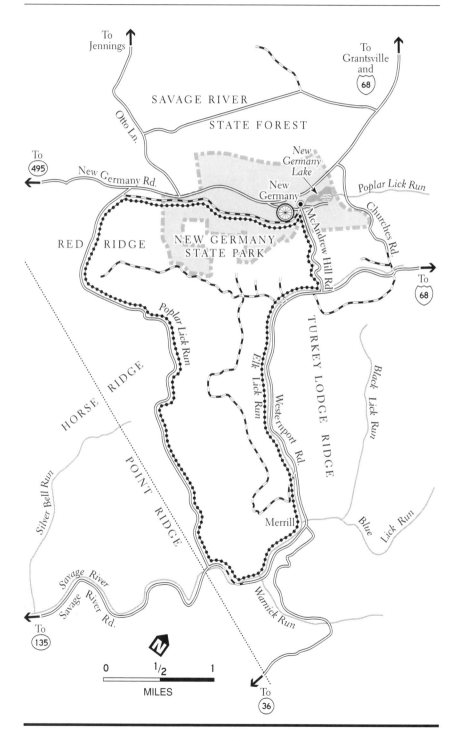

The Poplar Lick/
Elk Lick Loop
features 11 miles of
easy riding through
a beautiful forest.

Services: The nearest restaurants, lodging, and grocery stores are in Grantsville, north of I-68. Frostburg, a college town about a half-hour drive away, has a selection of restaurants and lodging. The nearest bike shop is in Cumberland.

Hazards: Watch for traffic on county roads and the off-road vehicle trail; traffic is minimal, but stay alert. Slippery rocks can make stream crossings hazardous; use extreme care during periods of high water (usually in the spring).

Rescue index: Excellent. You can flag down motorists on New Germany Road (follow the O.R.V. trail uphill from the intersection with Three Bridges Trail) and other roads along the loop. There are residences along the paved and unpaved roads on the second half of the ride.

Land status: State forest and park; county roads.

Maps: Ask for a map of Poplar Lick O.R.V. Trail and the New Germany Hiking Trails at the park office, across from the park entrance on New Germany Road. You can also purchase a Garrett County topo map there.

Finding the trail: Take Exit 24 (Grantsville exit) from I-68 and follow the signs for New Germany State Park/Savage River State Forest. Park in lot 5 at New Germany State Park. The trailhead is near the end of the lot.

Source of additional information:

Savage River State Forest
Route 2, Box 63-A
Grantsville, MD 21536
(301) 895-5759

Notes on the trail: The key to reaching Poplar Lick O.R.V. Trail is to stay with the stream. (Don't climb any hills.) Look for the gate that marks the entrance to the O.R.V. trail (on Three Bridges Trail) and follow it downstream for about 5 miles. The trail ends at the intersection with Savage River Road; turn left and go 1.5 miles to the stop sign. Turn left onto paved Westernport Road, where you cross a rail and concrete bridge over the Savage River. Follow this county road (traffic is light) for almost 3 miles along Elk Lick Run. After you cross the third wooden bridge, turn left onto the second road (McAndrew Hill Road). Follow this unpaved road back to New Germany State Park.

RIDE 37 · Monroe Run Loop

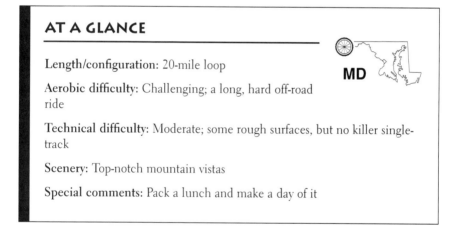

AT A GLANCE

Length/configuration: 20-mile loop

MD

Aerobic difficulty: Challenging; a long, hard off-road ride

Technical difficulty: Moderate; some rough surfaces, but no killer single-track

Scenery: Top-notch mountain vistas

Special comments: Pack a lunch and make a day of it

This is a ride for, as they say, the well-conditioned cyclist. It's a long and strenuous 20-mile loop. Expect to encounter rough riding surfaces (mud, rocks, gravel, logs) and many stream crossings, but no gnarly single-track. Start early in the day and pack a lunch. Though the trails are well marked, it's a good idea to carry a topo map and a compass.

The ride along Meadow Mountain is on a woods road featuring views of the surrounding mountains. The fast descent on Big Run Road, through beautiful forests, ends at Big Run State Park with views of Savage River Reservoir, an uncluttered jewel ringed by cliffs and forested hills. Poplar Lick O.R.V. Trail is a five-mile woods road with five stream crossings. Three Bridges Trail is a single-track that connects with Green Trail, an easy woods road that returns you to

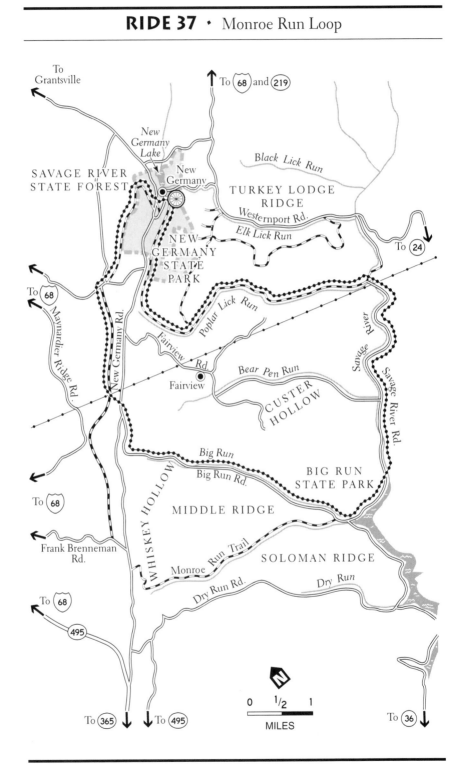

New Germany State Park. Warning: This ride could induce sensory overload during peak fall foliage in late September or early October.

General location: Grantsville.

Elevation change: About 1,400'.

Season: June through October offers the best riding conditions. The summer climate is very pleasant, and Garrett County is famous for its lack of mosquitoes and ticks. Early spring can be extremely muddy. From October through April, snow is possible. Avoid riding in deer-hunting season (late fall). Mountain laurel blooms peak along the ridges in mid-June, and rhododendron blooms along the streams in early July.

Services: The nearest restaurants, lodging, and grocery stores are in Grantsville, north of I-68. Frostburg, about a half-hour drive, has a good selection of restaurants and lodging. The nearest bike shop is in Cumberland.

Hazards: Watch for motorized vehicles on county roads and the O.R.V. trail; traffic is usually light, but stay alert. Slippery rocks make stream crossings hazardous — use care during periods of high water (usually in the spring). Keep an eye out for rattlesnakes, especially along the ridges.

Rescue index: Good. Meadow Mountain O.R.V. Trail parallels New Germany Road, which carries a lot of traffic. There is a phone at B.J.'s Store, a small grocery store on Savage River Road 1 mile upstream from Big Run State Park.

Land status: State forest and park; county roads.

Maps: A hiking map of the loop is available at the New Germany park office. You can also pick up a topo map of Garrett County there.

Finding the trail: Take Exit 24 off I-68 and follow the signs to New Germany State Park/Savage River State Forest. Turn left into the park and park in lot 5, or turn right and park at the administrative office. The trailhead (Meadow Mountain O.R.V. Trail) is on the right just past the administrative office.

Source of additional information:

Savage River State Forest
Route 2, Box 63-A
Grantsville, MD 21536
(301) 895-5759

Notes on the trail: On Meadow Mountain O.R.V. Trail, which starts this loop, look for an old woods road that makes a sharp left immediately before the power lines. This trail is marked with a "No snowmobiling" sign. Follow the steep road to a yellow-pole gate on New Germany Road and turn right; go a quarter-mile and turn left onto Big Run Road, which descends to Big Run State Park. Turn left onto Savage River Road, which parallels its namesake, to Poplar Lick O.R.V. Trail on the left (there's a sign). Follow this trail to the gate and pick up the blue-blazed Three Bridges Trail, which continues upstream along Poplar Lick Run. Turn left at the end and follow Green Trail (a woods road) back to New Germany State Park.

THE LAUREL HIGHLANDS OF
PENNSYLVANIA

Two hundred and fifty miles west of Philadelphia, the Laurel Highlands of southwestern Pennsylvania stretch over a five-county region dominated by two large mountain ridges, the Laurel and the Chestnut, carved by the Youghiogheny (YOCK-uh-ganey) River and the Conemaugh Gorges. These mountains offer virtually unlimited possibilities for rugged, scenic mountain biking.

A lot has happened in the Laurel Highlands' hills, valleys, and deep forests. Major skirmishes in the French and Indian War were fought here, and George Washington suffered his only military defeat at Fort Necessity. The Whiskey Rebellion, the country's first constitutional crisis, was crushed by Federal troops under the command of General "Mad" Anthony Wayne. We've been paying taxes ever since. The nineteenth century brought coal mining, steel making, and coke production to the area, and railroads and canals linked the region with Pittsburgh to the west and Cumberland, Maryland, to the south. Following the decline of the steel industry, tourism became increasingly important. The hills and mountains attract hikers, skiers, and white-water enthusiasts. The Youghiogheny River, which defines the southwest corner of the highlands, is considered the best whitewater river east of the Mississippi.

Hikers can trek Laurel Highlands Hiking Trail, which stretches for 70 miles between Ohiopyle and Youngstown. Connellsville-Cumberland Trail, a proposed 70-mile hiking and biking route along the old Western Maryland Railroad right-of-way, will eventually link up with the C&O Canal (see Ride 14), which extends to Washington, D.C.

The Laurel Highlands are characterized by beautiful vistas, tidy farms, and tens of thousands of acres of forests. Because of its relatively high altitude (Mount Davis, the state's highest point at 3,213 feet, is nearby), the region's climate is significantly colder (and snowier) in winter and cooler in the summer than in the cities to the west and east.

The following rides start from Hidden Valley Resort, 12 miles west of Somerset, Pennsylvania. Hidden Valley is a vacation-home resort and ski area (downhill and cross-country). To take advantage of its beautiful setting (it's surrounded by 25,000 acres of state wilderness lands), the resort began renting mountain bikes in the mid-1980s. Hidden Valley made a financial commitment to mountain biking largely because of Jim Sota, a former employee. "I suggested we look into offering mountain bikes after I got my first bike 15 years ago," recalled Sota, who managed the bike shop in the summer and the cross-country skiing facilities in the winter. "We started small, with only ten rental bikes, but it's proven popular. Now Hidden Valley has a rental stable of bikes and a bike shop, and sponsors a race every fall."

All of the trails from Hidden Valley lead to state forests. Where they cross private land, Hidden Valley has permission for users to pass. Mountain bikers may park at the ski lodge or at the lake house/bike rental shop. Sota suggests that bikers stop at the shop to check on trail conditions and pick up a map, and to let employees know when you will be returning.

RIDE 38 · Race Loop

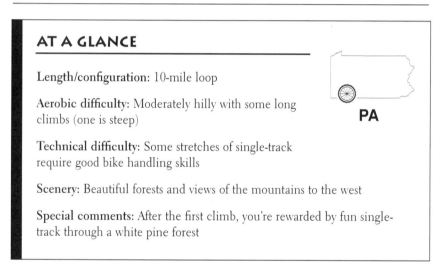

AT A GLANCE

Length/configuration: 10-mile loop

Aerobic difficulty: Moderately hilly with some long climbs (one is steep)

PA

Technical difficulty: Some stretches of single-track require good bike handling skills

Scenery: Beautiful forests and views of the mountains to the west

Special comments: After the first climb, you're rewarded by fun single-track through a white pine forest

Race Loop at Hidden Valley Resort is a moderately hilly, ten-mile loop that will give experienced mountain bikers a good workout. The ride requires some technical skill due to short sections of rocky single-track. The first climb is long and steep, but the rest of the climbs are easier. Trail surfaces vary from mud to paved road, but most are packed dirt. The higher elevations offer excellent views of the mountains to the west and of Jones Mill Run Valley. The foliage in mid-October is spectacular. This area contains abundant wildlife (white-tailed deer, bear, rabbit, pheasant, turkey, squirrel, grouse) and a variety of plant species. The clear mountain streams and beautiful western Pennsylvania scenery attract visitors from all over the country.

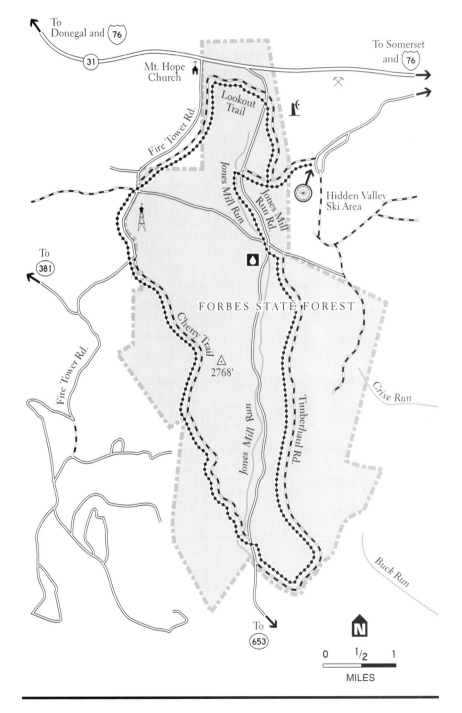

To Donegal and (76)

To Somerset and (76)

(31)

Mt. Hope Church

Lookout Trail

Fire Tower Rd.

Jones Mill Run

Jones Mill Run Rd.

Hidden Valley Ski Area

To (381)

FORBES STATE FOREST

Cherry Trail

2768'

Fire Tower Rd.

Jones Mill Run

Timberhaul Rd.

Crise Run

Buck Run

To (653)

N

0   1/2   1

MILES

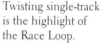
Twisting single-track
is the highlight of
the Race Loop.

The first part of the loop is paved road leading to a dirt and grass trail. Roots and rocks make for a bumpy ride on Lookout Trail. The pipeline adjacent to Fire Tower Road is smooth dirt with some muddy sections, and Cherry Trail has some rocky and muddy sections. Timberhaul Road is a hard-pack and gravel double-track. After the first climb, you're rewarded with a delightful single-track through a mature white pine forest. What's more, the rest of the loop is almost as enjoyable. Vistas of the mountains to the west are visible as you ride through settings ranging from deciduous hardwood and coniferous forests to open meadows.

General location: Somerset.

Elevation change: About 1,000'.

Season: Late spring through fall.

Services: Lodging, food, and bike rentals are available at Hidden Valley, and camping is available at Kooser State Park, 2 miles east of Hidden Valley on PA 31. All other services are available in Somerset.

Hazards: Rocky sections come up fast on descents, so look ahead. Watch out for a sharp left turn on Cherry Trail that has a surface of large loose gravel.

Rescue index: Good. Jones Hills Run Road carries light traffic that can be flagged down.

Land status: Private (Hidden Valley Resort) and state forest.

Maps: Pick up a trail map at the bike rental shop in Hidden Valley. The USGS 7.5 minute quad is Bakersville.

Finding the trail: Hidden Valley Resort is located off PA 31 between Somerset and Donegal. From points north and west, take the Pennsylvania Turnpike to Exit 9/Donegal. Continue 8 miles east on PA 31 to Hidden Valley. From Washington, D.C., and points south and east, take the Pennsylvania Turnpike to Exit 10/Somerset. Continue 12 miles west on PA 31 to Hidden Valley. Follow the signs to the lodge. Start the ride in the ski area parking lot at Hidden Valley Resort. Exit the parking lot and make a left up Parke Drive.

Sources of additional information:

Mountain Bike Shop, Hidden Valley Resort
One Craighead Drive
Somerset, PA 15501
(800) 458-0175, ext. 473

District Forester, Forbes State Forest
P.O. Box 519
Laughlintown, PA 15655
(814) 238-9533

Notes on the trail: Head up Parke Drive to Valley View Drive just above the upper parking lot. You can either continue up Parke Drive, which is easier, or turn right onto Valley View Drive; Valley View Trail, which is very steep, is 40 feet up the road on the left. For the easier—and longer—climb, continue up Parke Drive, make a left on Gardner Road at the stop sign, and take the next right onto Lookout Trail (there's a sign). Follow the trail 100 yards and make the next right; continue following Lookout Trail, which parallels Gardner Road. Either way, the loop starts on Lookout Trail at the intersection of Valley View and Gardner Roads.

RIDE 39 · North Woods Ramble

AT A GLANCE

Length/configuration: 3-mile loop

Aerobic difficulty: Easy; the trail's not flat, but it's close

Technical difficulty: Easy; some rocky sections

Scenery: Mountain views, forests, and meadows

Special comments: A great introductory ride to the Laurel Highlands for novice riders

PA

This three-mile loop features excellent views of the mountains of western Pennsylvania. Little technical skill is required, though there is one short section of loose rock. The first quarter-mile is hard-packed; the next mile is a gradual climb on a grass trail. There are no steep hills. The top of the climb is a two-wheel-drive road, and the return trail is all grass. "Ramble" is a good name for this easy ride.

Somerset County is visible from the top of the trail, and there's a good view of Laurel Ridge looking north into the forest regeneration area. This region is typical of Pennsylvania forests and meadows. In addition to enjoying the views and excellent pedaling, you can visit a stone spring house on the return.

General location: Somerset.

Elevation change: About 300'.

Season: Late spring through fall.

Services: Lodging, food, and bike rentals are available at Hidden Valley. Camping is available at Kooser State Park, 2 miles east of Hidden Valley on PA 31. All other services are available in Somerset.

Hazards: Watch for rocks while you're riding through the forest regeneration area on North Woods Trail, and look out for groundhog holes (which can devour front wheels, causing the dreaded face-plant) in the fields at the end of the ride.

Rescue index: Excellent; you're always close to a paved road.

Land status: Private and state forest land.

Maps: Pick up Hidden Valley Resort trail maps and the Department of Forestry snowmobile trail map from the bike rental shop at Hidden Valley Resort.

Finding the trail: Hidden Valley Resort is located off PA 31 between Somerset and Donegal. From points north and west, take the Pennsylvania Turnpike to Exit 9/Donegal. Continue 8 miles east on PA 31 to Hidden Valley. From Washington, D.C., and points south and east, take the Pennsylvania Turnpike to Exit

RIDE 39 · North Woods Ramble

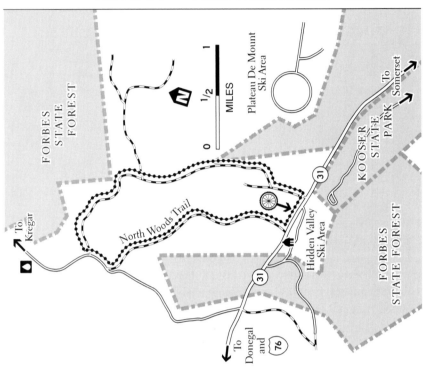

10/Somerset. Continue 12 miles west on PA 31 to Hidden Valley. Turn left to enter the resort and drive to the lake house/bike rental shop to start the ride. Pedal back out to the entrance, cross PA 31 (watch for traffic), ride just past the stone spring house, and stay left. Then follow the North Woods Trail signs.

Sources of additional information:

Mountain Bike Shop, Hidden Valley Resort
One Craighead Drive
Somerset, PA 15501
(800) 458-0175, ext. 473

District Forester, Forbes State Forest
P.O. Box 519
Laughlintown, PA 15655
(814) 238-9533

Notes on the trail: On the return, you can either take the dirt road back to PA 31 or take the trail through the field on the left (an apple tree marks the beginning of the trail). This trail passes through a short section of woods followed by a view of orchards. A note to allergy sufferers: in late summer, the fields can become overgrown with goldenrod.

RIDE 40 · Kuhntown Loop

AT A GLANCE

Length/configuration: 15-mile loop

Aerobic difficulty: Moderate to hard; requires good stamina

PA

Technical difficulty: Moderate; cross-country ski trails and woods roads

Scenery: Woods and fields with views of surrounding mountains

Special comments: A ride into the heart of the Laurel Ridge area on old dirt roads used by early settlers

The trails and roads on this 15-mile loop are a good introduction to the history of the Laurel Highlands. North Woods and Schaffer Trails were once railroad lines that hauled logs out from logging operations. The dirt roads provided access for early settlers who have long since moved on. The smooth sections of road near the Pennsylvania Turnpike are used by modern-day logging operations. Toward the end of the ride, there's a stone spring house along the dirt road.

This ride, designed for experienced and well-conditioned cyclists, takes you to the heart of the Laurel Ridge area. The trails and roads are typical of many others found in the region. The top of the ridge provides several views of the surrounding mountains. Most of the ride passes through woods and, with the rise and fall of elevation, is representative of the region's topography.

General location: Somerset.

Elevation change: About 800'.

Season: Late spring through fall.

Services: Lodging, food, and bike rentals are available at Hidden Valley. Camping is available at Kooser State Park, 2 miles east of Hidden Valley on PA 31. All other services are available in Somerset.

RIDE 40 · Kuhntown Loop

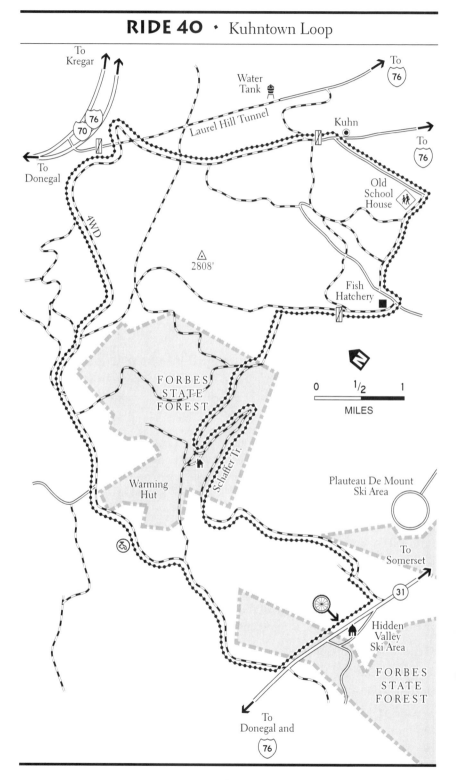

To Kregar

To 76

Water Tank

76 70

Laurel Hill Tunnel

Kuhn

To 76

To Donegal

4WD

Old School House

2808'

Fish Hatchery

0   1/2   1

MILES

FORBES STATE FOREST

Schaffer Tr.

Warming Hut

Plauteau De Mount Ski Area

To Somerset

31

Hidden Valley Ski Area

FORBES STATE FOREST

To Donegal and

76

Hazards: Watch for rocky sections and four-wheel-drive traffic on some of the roads. There is a sharp left turn with loose gravel on the descent into the turnpike area.

Rescue index: Good. There are a number of residences near the fish hatchery and along the dirt road after the steep climb. After you climb the dirt trail past the Pennsylvania Turnpike, help is best reached at Hidden Valley Resort.

Land status: State forest, public roads, and private property.

Maps: Pick up a map at the bike rental shop in Hidden Valley. The USGS 7.5 minute quads are Bakersville and Seven Springs.

Finding the trail: Hidden Valley Resort is located off PA 31 between Somerset and Donegal. From points north and west, take the Pennsylvania Turnpike to Exit 9/Donegal. Continue 8 miles east on PA 31 to Hidden Valley. From Washington, D.C., and points south and east, take the Pennsylvania Turnpike to Exit 10/Somerset. Continue 12 miles west on PA 31 to Hidden Valley. Turn left to enter the resort and drive to the lake house/bike rental shop to start the ride. On your bike, pedal back out to the entrance, cross PA 31 (watch for traffic), ride just past the stone spring house, and stay left. Then follow the North Woods Trail signs to begin the ride.

Sources of additional information:

Mountain Bike Shop, Hidden Valley Resort
One Craighead Drive
Somerset, PA 15501
(800) 458-0175, ext. 473

District Forester, Forbes State Forest
P.O. Box 519
Laughlintown, PA 15655
(814) 238-9533

Notes on the trail: The first 2.5 miles are on grassy ski trails. After you pass the warming hut at the bottom of Schaffer Trail, the surface is mostly dirt and gravel. Some sections are rutted and washed-out dirt road, and there is a steep, long climb over loose rock after the fish hatchery. The climb out of the valley near the Pennsylvania Turnpike is mostly packed dirt. Once you reach the road at the top, it's dirt road for the remainder of the ride.

MICHAUX STATE FOREST, PENNSYLVANIA

Located between Gettysburg to the east and Chambersburg to the west, Michaux State Forest encompasses more than 82,000 acres of Pennsylvania forests and mountains. With a well-defined system of roads, snowmobile trails, and foot trails, Michaux (me-SHOW) is an increasingly popular destination for mountain bikers. Only a few hours from large metropolitan areas such as Baltimore, Washington, and Philadelphia, Michaux is convenient to many bikers hankering for a weekend of exploration. With its extensive trail and road system, the forest offers a wide variety of interesting, scenic rides for all ability levels.

The forest's prominent geographic feature is South Mountain, a long ridge that runs north out of nearby Maryland into Pennsylvania. Forty miles of the Appalachian Trail, the 2,000-mile foot trail running from Maine to Georgia, follows South Mountain ridge for the length of the forest. The Appalachian Trail is closed to mountain bikes, as are most trails in the state parks in the forest. Yet that leaves hundreds of miles of legal trails open to mountain bikers.

Jes Stith, owner of Gettysburg Bicycles & Fitness, has raced mountain bikes for ten years and trains in Michaux regularly. He says the forest offers hard-core riders and racers looking for difficult training rides lots of technical single-track and numerous long climbs, and offers nonexpert riders moderate trails and roads. "Plus," he says, "it's so darned beautiful up there." With a knowledgeable staff dedicated to mountain biking, Gettysburg Bicycles & Fitness is headquarters for off-road enthusiasts in south-central Pennsylvania. Be sure to stop by for information on other great places to ride in Michaux.

Folks in search of more help exploring Michaux now have it: Appalachian Excursions, an off-road outfitter in south-central Pennsylvania, specializes in guided tours of the forest. From May through October, the outfitter offers guided mountain bike tours for riders of all abilities. Owners Curt and Tawnya Finney provide half-day, all-day, and overnight tours of Michaux starting at various locations within a 30-minute drive of Chambersburg. For more information and current rates, call Appalachian Excursions at (717) 749-2074.

RIDE 41 · Pole Steeple Loop

AT A GLANCE

Length/configuration: 11-mile loop

Aerobic difficulty: A hard ride with long, steep climbs

Technical difficulty: Loose scree on the roads requires good bike handling skills

Scenery: Great views from the ridges

Special comments: Stash your bikes and hike to Pole Steeple for more great views

PA

Located in south-central Pennsylvania between Gettysburg and Chambersburg, Michaux State Forest encompasses 82,000 acres of mountains, lakes, and valleys. With a well-defined mix of rugged dirt roads, the forest is a favorite destination of mountain bikers throughout the Mid-Atlantic.

The forest roads make for challenging riding, and this 11-mile loop, which starts in Pine Grove Furnace State Park, is no exception. It follows Slate Road and Piney Mountain Ridge Road to scenic Pole Steeple, an 80-foot-high rock formation atop a ridge; the views are great. At the side trail leading to the cliffs, stash your bike and hike down.

This difficult ride will challenge intermediate riders and give advanced riders a good workout. Plentiful steep climbing and some technical descents on woods roads covered with loose scree make good bike handling skills a must. Attractions include dense forests, great views of mountains and valleys, and plenty of opportunities to glimpse wildlife. The state park, where the ride begins and ends, features hiking and nature trails, interesting historical features, and two lakes for swimming after the ride.

General location: Gettysburg.

Elevation change: The initial grunt up Slate Road to the top of the ridge on Pine Ridge Road has about a 500' elevation gain in less than 3 miles. Piney Ridge Road to Pole Steeple undulates with 100' gains and losses. After Pole Steeple, it's all downhill.

Season: Year-round. Late spring and fall are usually the most comfortable seasons; July and August can be hot, muggy, and buggy.

Services: Water, rest rooms, a general store, and camping are available in Pine Grove Furnace State Park. All other services are available in Gettysburg and Chambersburg.

RIDE 41 • Pole Steeple Loop

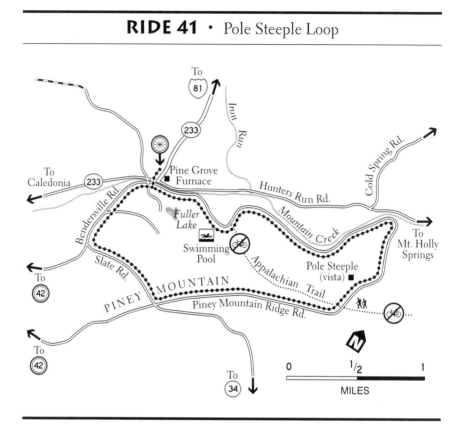

Hazards: Hunting is permitted in the forest in the fall. Either wear orange or ride on Sundays, when hunting isn't permitted. Watch out for motorized all-terrain vehicles.

Rescue index: Good. Bendersville Road is paved and carries traffic.

Land status: State forest and park.

Maps: Pick up a trail map at Pine Grove Furnace State Park. The USGS 7.5 minute quad is Dickinson.

Finding the trail: From Interstate 81 take US 30 or Route 94 to PA 233 and Pine Grove Furnace State Park. Park near the stone furnace. Pedal south on Bendersville Road about a half-mile to Slate Road and turn left.

Sources of additional information:

District Forester, Michaux State Forest
10099 Lincoln Way East
Fayetteville, PA 17222
(717) 352-2211

Gettysburg Bicycle & Fitness
100A Buford Avenue
Gettysburg, PA 17325
(717) 334-7791

Notes on the trail: Climb Slate Road to Piney Ridge Road and turn left. Cross the Appalachian Trail (remember, the AT is closed to mountain bikes) and pick up the blue-blazed trail to Pole Steeple. (The dead-end spur on the left leads to a cliff overlook.) Some sections on Piney Ridge Road are fast descents on loose, irregular surfaces. The final descent is a deeply rutted road that frequently has water running on it. Near the end you'll drop down the ravine to Laurel Forge Pond and follow the cinder path back to Pine Grove Furnace.

RIDE 42 · ATV and Log Sled Trails via Piney Ridge Road

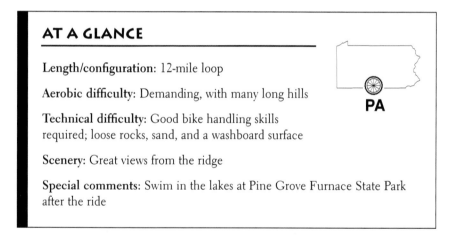

AT A GLANCE

Length/configuration: 12-mile loop

Aerobic difficulty: Demanding, with many long hills

Technical difficulty: Good bike handling skills required; loose rocks, sand, and a washboard surface

Scenery: Great views from the ridge

Special comments: Swim in the lakes at Pine Grove Furnace State Park after the ride

PA

This 12-mile loop in 82,000-acre Michaux State Forest follows a combination of paved roads, two-wheel-drive roads, hard-packed dirt roads, all-terrain-vehicle trails, and multiuse trails. You'll encounter a few steep spots, but the ride isn't very technical. With lots of elevation gain and screaming descents on loose rock and dirt, it requires a good level of fitness and good bike handling skills.

The loop takes you through a mix of second-growth hardwood and conifer forest; the views of the surrounding mountains and valleys are especially good along Piney Ridge Road. The descent on Log Sled Trail passes through a beautiful wooded hollow that follows a mountain stream. Pine Grove Furnace State Park features hiking and nature trails, and, in the summer, two lakes for swimming.

General location: Gettysburg.

RIDE 42 • ATV and Log Sled Trails via Piney Ridge Road

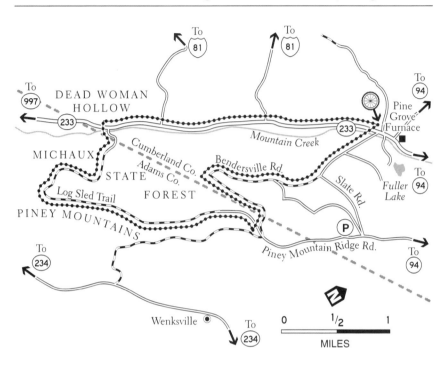

Elevation change: About 900'.

Season: Year-round. The best time to ride is late spring and fall. July and August can be hot, humid, and buggy.

Services: Pine Grove Furnace State Park has a general store, camping, rest rooms, and water. All other services are available in Chambersburg, Carlisle, and Gettysburg.

Hazards: Watch for motorized all-terrain vehicles on the woods roads. Hunting is permitted in the state forest in the fall. Either wear orange or ride on Sundays, when hunting isn't permitted.

Rescue index: Good. Traffic can be waved down on paved PA 233.

Land status: State forest and park.

Maps: A trail map is available in the park office. The USGS 7.5 minute quads are Pine Grove Furnace and Arentsville.

Finding the trail: From I-81, take US 30 or Route 94 to PA 233 and Pine Grove Furnace State Park. Park near the furnace. Pedal out Bendersville Road past Slate Road to the orange-signed all-terrain-vehicle trail on the left.

Sources of additional information:

District Forester, Michaux State Forest
10099 Lincoln Way East
Fatetteville, PA 17222
(717) 352-2211

Gettysburg Bicycles & Fitness
100A Buford Avenue
Gettysburg, PA 17325
(717) 334-7791

Notes on the trail: At the end of the climb up the all-terrain-vehicle trail, turn right onto Piney Ridge Road. Ride for 4 miles to Log Sled Trail on the right. Descend to PA 233, turn right, and return to Pine Grove Furnace.

RIDE 43 · Long Pine Reservoir Loop

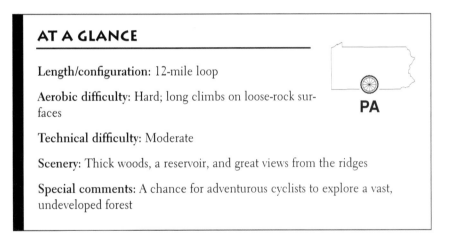

AT A GLANCE

Length/configuration: 12-mile loop

Aerobic difficulty: Hard; long climbs on loose-rock surfaces

Technical difficulty: Moderate

Scenery: Thick woods, a reservoir, and great views from the ridges

Special comments: A chance for adventurous cyclists to explore a vast, undeveloped forest

PA

The major attraction to this 12-mile loop is the chance to explore a vast, undeveloped forest. The geography features long ridges, called "flats" because of their flat-top profiles. Another nice aspect of this ride is Long Pine Reservoir, a large, beautiful lake nestled in the hills that's a popular destination for anglers. The hollows and valleys between the flats are heavily wooded, mostly with conifers. Views of the surrounding valleys and mountains from the ridges are striking in any season.

Steep climbs on loose rock and dirt require good fitness and bike handling skills. Aside from that, this ride isn't very technical. The trail follows hard-pack dirt roads (some sections are washboarded), rough double-track covered with loose rock, and single-track that varies from packed dirt with a pine-humus surface to football-sized rock scree.

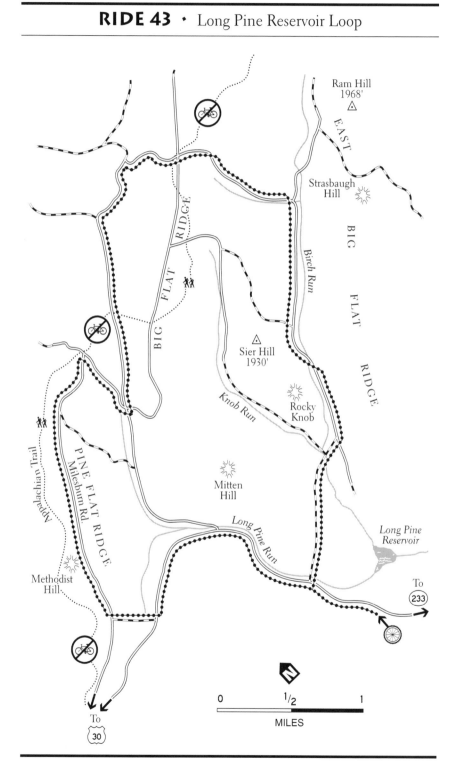

Ram Hill
1968'

EAST

Strasbaugh
Hill

BIG

Birch Run

FLAT

Sier Hill
1930'

Knob Run

Rocky
Knob

RIDGE

FLAT RIDGE

BIG

RIDGE

Appalachian Trail

PINE FLAT RIDGE

Milesburn Rd.

Mitten
Hill

Long Pine Run

Long Pine
Reservoir

Methodist
Hill

To
233

To
30

0   1/2   1

MILES

General location: Chambersburg.

Elevation change: Around 1,500'.

Season: The best riding is between late spring and fall. Early spring can be wet, and summer can be hot, humid, and buggy. Autumn is the best season, but avoid riding in deer-hunting season, which starts in the late fall.

Services: Water, rest rooms, and camping are available in Caledonia State Park on PA 233. All other services are available in Chambersburg.

Hazards: Aside from all-terrain vehicles and blind curves on single-track descents, the biggest hazard is getting lost. There are many roads, unmarked trails, and a sameness to the topography, so it's easy to get confused. Carry a map and compass.

Rescue index: Fair. The area is closed to motorized vehicles; the closest help is traffic on PA 233.

Land status: State forest.

Maps: The USGS 7.5 minute quad is Caledonia Park.

Finding the trail: From I-81, take US 30 or PA 94 to PA 233. Look for a dirt road on the north side of PA 233 at the Chambersburg Reservoir pull-out. Take this road approximately 3 miles to Long Pine Reservoir and park in the parking area. Pedal north from the parking area on the dirt road.

Sources of additional information:

District Forester, Michaux State Forest
10099 Lincoln Way East
Fatetteville, PA 17222
(717) 352-2211

Gettysburg Bicycles & Fitness
100A Buford Avenue
Gettysburg, PA 17325
(717) 334-7791

Notes on the trail: From the parking area, ride north on the dirt road past the first road on the right of the fork. At the next fork, bear left and climb to the top of Big Pine Flat. Turn right along the power-line right-of-way and right again onto the dirt road. After 2 miles or so, take the fourth trail on the right. (All 4 trails drop down the south side of the mountain to a road in the valley.) Turn right onto the road at the bottom of the descent and go straight at the next inter-section. About a mile later, take the rough dirt road and climb to a partially clear-cut meadow. Bear right at the next trail intersection. Continue climbing to the top of Big Flat. Cross the road and take the trail for the descent. At the dirt road, turn right toward the reservoir. Bear right at the fork, turn left at the dirt road, and return to the parking area.

Confused? Even mountain bikers who ride the area regularly get disoriented on occasion. Carry a map and compass, and give yourself enough time so that you're not racing against a setting sun.

RIDE 44 · Caledonia Loop

AT A GLANCE

Length/configuration: 4-mile loop

Aerobic difficulty: Moderate; long, gradual climbs and descents

Technical difficulty: Moderately easy, with wide, grassy trails

Scenery: Tall pines, fern beds, and mountains

Special comments: Caledonia State Park has a swimming pool, picnic tables, and refreshments

PA

Curt Finney of Appalachian Excursions says this is a great ride for a family outing and for novice riders in search of an easy, fun mountain trail that's not too challenging. The loop, which follows wide, grassy, cross-country ski trails, offers plenty of places to pull off and enjoy the scenery, and it's located in an area noted for abundant wildlife: white-tailed deer, red fox, squirrels, owls, and ruffed grouse—the Pennsylvania state bird.

General location: Chambersburg.

Elevation change: About 100'.

Season: Spring through fall.

Services: Rest rooms, camping, and showers are available at Caledonia State Park. All other services are available in Chambersburg and Gettysburg.

Hazards: Watch for trail runners. Deer-hunting season begins in late fall; wear bright colors or ride on Sundays, when hunting isn't permitted.

Rescue index: Good. Traffic on New Baltimore Road can be flagged down in an emergency.

Land status: State park and forest.

Maps: The USGS 7.5 minute quad is Caledonia.

Finding the trail: From I-70 in Maryland take MD 66 (Exit 35) to Smithsburg. Turn right onto PA 64 and go to Waynesboro, Pennsylvania. At the square in town, turn right onto PA 997 north and continue to US 30. At the stoplight, turn right onto US 30 and continue to Caledonia State Park. Turn right onto PA 233 south, cross the bridge, and turn left onto Golf Course Road. Go 0.4 mile, turn right onto New Baltimore Road, and continue 0.8 mile to the parking area. The trailhead is on the right.

RIDE 44 · Caledonia Loop

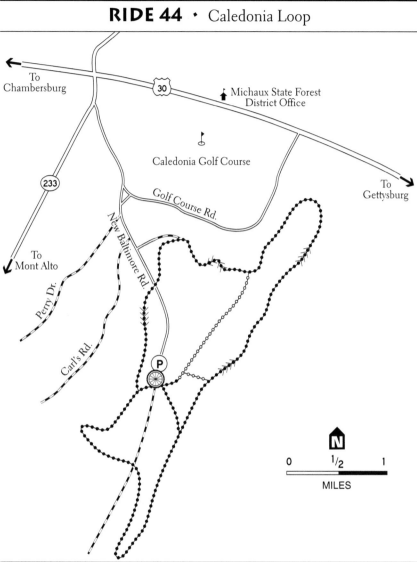

Sources of additional information:

Caledonia State Park
40 Rocky Mountain Road
Fayetteville, PA 17222
(717) 352-2161

Appalachian Excursions
306 Park Street
Mont Alto, PA 17237
(717) 749-2074
Email: appexcur@innernet.net

The 4-mile Caledonia Loop boasts easy, wide, grassy trails. *(Photo by Curt Finney)*

Notes on the trail: The trail is well signed and easy to follow.

RIDE 45 · Mont Alto State Park Loop

AT A GLANCE

Length/configuration: 13-mile loop

Aerobic difficulty: Intermediate, with long, steep climbs

Technical difficulty: Intermediate to advanced, with steep descents on loose rocks that require good bike handling skills

Scenery: Stream crossings, ponds, and large groves of pine trees

Special comments: Stop and check out the sand quarry as you ride by

PA

RIDE 45 • Mont Alto State Park Loop

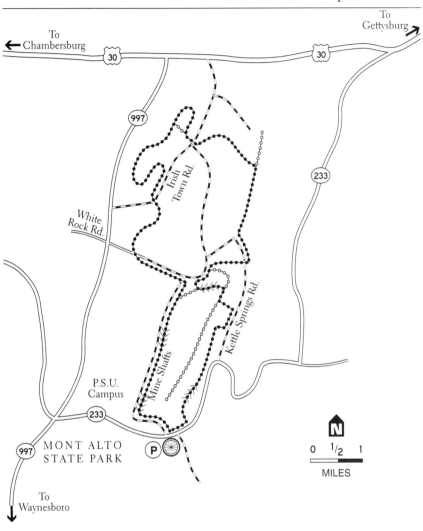

This 13-mile loop through Michaux State Forest is a challenging off-road romp for intermediate and advanced cyclists. It starts with a long, steep climb followed by some really cool single-track descents. The final two miles pass through Meeting of the Pines Natural Area, home to five species of pines: white, pitch, table mountain, shortleaf, and Virginia. Attractions include glimpses of old mine shafts, dense forest, stands of mountain laurel, and plenty of chances to see wildlife. Mont Alto State Park, a 24-acre picnic area where the ride begins and ends, has picnic tables, rest rooms, and a gentle flowing stream that's great for cooling off after a summer ride.

Good bike-handling
skills are required at
Mont Alto State Park.
(Photo by Curt Finney)

General location: Waynesboro.

Elevation change: 300'.

Season: All year, but late spring through fall are best.

Services: Water and rest rooms are available in Mont Alto State Park. All other services are available in Waynesboro and Chambersburg.

Hazards: Hunting season begins in the fall. Either wear bright colors or ride on Sundays, when hunting isn't permitted.

Rescue index: Good. Traffic can be waved down on paved PA 233 and PA 997. Kettle Spring Road (a dirt road) intersects with PA 233. White Rock Road and Irish Town Road (both dirt roads) intersect with PA 997.

Land status: State park and forest.

Maps: The USGS 7.5 minute quad is Waynesboro.

Finding the trail: From I-70 in Maryland, take Route 66 (Exit 35) to Smithsburg. Turn right onto MD 64 and continue to Waynesboro, Pennsylvania. Turn right at the square onto PA 997 north and follow it to the square in Mont Alto. Turn right onto PA 233 north and go 1 mile to Mont Alto State Park. The parking lot is on the right. On your bike, pedal north on PA 233 for about 0.7 mile (go past Staley Road, the first dirt road on the right). Turn left onto a steep logging road to begin the loop.

Sources of additional information:

Caledonia State Park
40 Rocky Mountain Road
Fayetteville, PA 17222
(717) 352-2161

Appalachian Excursions
306 Park Street
Mont Alto, PA 17237
(717) 749-2074
Email: appexcur@innernet.net

Notes on the trail: After turning left on the steep logging road, go around the gate, make a right, and follow the grassy double-track for about a mile. Turn right onto a single-track trail and follow it to a dirt road. Turn left onto the road and go about half a mile. Turn left through a rock gate and follow the trail to a dirt road. Turn right onto the next road, go about half a mile, turn right onto a trail, and follow it to a dirt road. Turn left onto this road and follow it to a yellow gate. Turn right, go around the yellow gate, follow it to a double-track, and take that to the next gate. Next, turn right onto a dirt road and follow for it for 0.1 mile. The trail is straight ahead. Take it to a dirt road, turn right, and go about half a mile. Turn left and follow the trail to a paved road; turn left again. After the road changes to dirt, turn to the right and follow a double-track to Meeting of the Pines Natural Area. Stay on the double-track to the Pennsylvania State University campus. Then follow the dirt road on the left back to Mont Alto State Park and your car.

RIDE 46 · Old Forge Loop

AT A GLANCE

Length/configuration: 8-mile loop

Aerobic difficulty: Moderate, with gradual climbs and descents

PA

Technical difficulty: Moderately easy to intermediate; mostly double-track trails punctuated with rocks and log crossings

Scenery: Thick, lush fern beds line the sides of the trail

Special comments: The trails on this ride are more than 100 years old

This eight-mile loop is ideal for advanced-beginner and intermediate riders looking for an easy but fun introduction to 84,000-acre Michaux State Forest. Novice riders with a bit of riding experience will be challenged by the log crossings and rocky areas along the trail, while intermediate riders will find this ride is just a whole lot of fun.

But not so fast. Along the way, stop and take in the beauty of the forest. Old Forge picnic area, where the ride begins and ends, has picnic tables, rest rooms, and water. Camp Penn, just across the road from the park, was a Civilian Conservation Corps camp during the 1930s. Though a paranormal experience on the ride isn't likely, it's certainly possible. The trails were first blazed in the late 1800s during the Industrial Revolution by horse-drawn wagons loaded with charcoal for the iron furnace at Old Forge State Park. Rumor has it that at night local riders have seen ghosts of the old men tending the charcoal pits. Now, there's an excuse to get into nighttime riding.

General location: Waynesboro.

Elevation change: 100'.

Season: Year-round.

Services: Water, rest rooms, and picnic tables are available at the Old Forge picnic area. All other services are available in Waynesboro.

Hazards: Deer-hunting season begins in late fall. Wear bright colors or ride on Sundays, when hunting isn't permitted.

Rescue index: Good. Traffic can be waved down on paved Old Forge Road.

Land status: State forest.

Maps: The USGS minute quad is Waynesboro.

RIDE 46 · Old Forge Loop

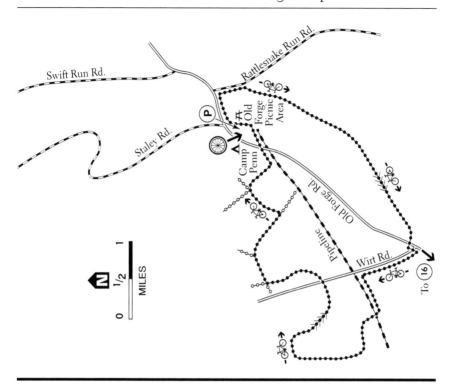

Finding the trail: From I-70 in Maryland, take MD 66 (Exit 35) to Smithsburg. Turn right onto MD 64 and continue to the flashing red light; turn right onto MD 418. Follow it across the state line to PA 16 and turn left. Take the next right onto Old Forge Road and follow it to the Old Forge picnic area. Park in the lot on the right and pedal north on Old Forge Road for about 0.1 mile. Turn right onto Rattlesnake Run Road.

Sources of additional information:

Pennsylvania Bureau of Forestry
10099 Lincoln Way East
Fayetteville, PA 17222
(717) 352-2211

Appalachian Excursions
306 Park Street
Mont Alto, PA 17237
(717) 749-2074
Email: appexcur@innernet.net

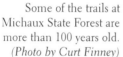

Some of the trails at
Michaux State Forest are
more than 100 years old.
(Photo by Curt Finney)

Notes on the trail: After turning right on Rattlesnake Run Road, ride across a bridge and go around a yellow gate on the right. Follow the trail to a paved road, cross the road, and continue on the dirt road. Next, turn left onto a water line and right onto the trail. Follow the trail to a dirt road, cross the road, and follow the trail to another water line. Turn left and follow the water line back to the picnic area where you parked.

STATE COLLEGE, PENNSYLVANIA

State College, located near the geographical center of Pennsylvania, is aptly named. The 36,000-student campus of Pennsylvania State University dominates the town. To a mountain biker's eye, however, the major attractions are the surrounding mountains and neat-as-a-pin farmland. Not only is pedaling a mountain bike right out of town feasible, it's the best way to reach the nearby hills. With recent growth causing downtown congestion, mountain bikes are now the preferred way to get around. These days it seems as if every Penn State student rides a mountain bike around campus.

To support this kind of activity, State College boasts several bike shops. The biggest, the Bicycle Shop on West College Avenue, is impressive. Its large showroom is dominated by high-quality, big-ticket bikes, including road and mountain tandems. The secret to the shop's large selection is sales volume. "Bikes are the favorite form of transportation in State College," says Mike Hermann, former sales manager. "Every year, we get a big rush of kids who spend between $300 and $500 for a bike. It's a bargain for them when you consider the cost of parking and car insurance." And every four years, there's a complete turnover of students, guaranteeing continued sales.

The Bicycle Shop actively supports mountain biking by sponsoring several races throughout the year. On Sundays, there's usually an informal ride led from the shop. The large staff is knowledgeable and willing to give visitors maps and directions to trailheads.

RIDE 47 · Tussey Mountain to Whipple Dam

AT A GLANCE

Length/configuration: 18-mile out-and-back (9 miles each way)

Aerobic difficulty: Moderate; requires good stamina for the 2 climbs

PA

Technical difficulty: Easy

Scenery: Classic Appalachian mountains and valleys

Special comments: An especially nice ride in the spring and fall

---

This easy nine-mile (one-way) out-and-back features classic Appalachian scenery. The woods, rocks, and mountain streams are reminiscent of New England. The verdant green foliage in the spring and blazing colors in the fall are spectacular. Most of the ride is through thick woods on well-maintained woods roads that pass several springs. The lookout tower provides spectacular views of the surrounding ridges and valleys. Though this ride is nontechnical, the climb to the fire tower and the return climb from Whipple Dam require good stamina.

The rewards are worth it. In the summer you can swim at Whipple Dam. Look for a large field of blueberries surrounding the lookout tower—another reason to do this ride in late summer. Keep an eye open for the abundant wildlife in the area, including black bears.

General location: State College.

Elevation change: Approximately 1,600'; the first 800' are steep, gained over 3 miles. On the return from Whipple Dam, the same elevation gain is spread over 7 miles.

Season: Spring and fall are the best times for mountain biking in central Pennsylvania. Summer is hot, humid, and buggy, and snow is possible between November and March. However, since the final destination of this ride is a public swimming area, this is a popular summer ride. Avoid riding in deer-hunting season (after Thanksgiving).

Services: Whipple Dam has water (turned off in winter) and rest rooms (year-round). A snack bar operates between Memorial Day and Labor Day. All other services are available in State College.

Hazards: Watch for traffic on Laurel Run Road.

RIDE 47 · Tussey Mountain to Whipple Dam

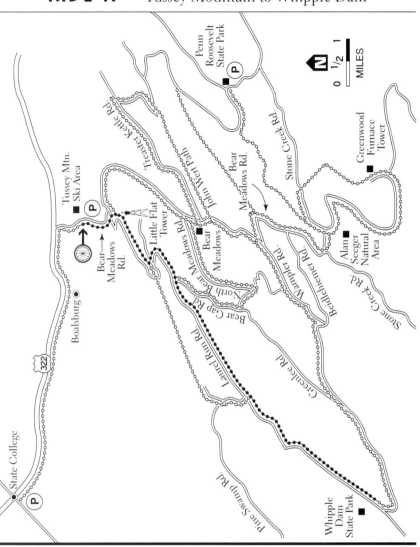

Rescue index: Good. This is a well-traveled road, so you should have no problem flagging down a vehicle, but the spur to the tower is closed to motor vehicles.

Land status: State forest and park.

Maps: The USGS 7.5 minute quads are State College and McAlevys Fort. Purple Lizard Recreational Map, the best local trail map, is available locally or at www.purplelizard.com.

Finding the trail: From State College, take Business US 322 south to Tussey Mountain Ski Area. Continue into Rothrock State Forest and the parking area immediately on the left. You can park in the ski area lot, but the state has built a new lot to take pressure off private ski lot use. After parking, get on your bike and turn right at the first intersection onto a dirt road; from here climb to the lookout tower.

Source of additional information:

The Bicycle Shop
441 West College Avenue
State College, PA 16801
(814) 238-9422
Website: www.thebicycleshopinc.com

Notes on the trail: The turnoff to the lookout tower is not marked, but it's simple to get to; it's the only left-hand turn within 100 yards of the top of the climb. Look for a gate. After you visit the tower, retrace the route to Laurel Run Road and continue downhill. The stretch from the ski area to the fire tower is all uphill, and from the fire tower to Whipple Dam it's all downhill. Stay on Laurel Run Road to reach Whipple Dam. To return, retrace the route to the parking lot at Tussey Mountain.

RIDE 48 · Penn Roosevelt to Alan Seeger and Back

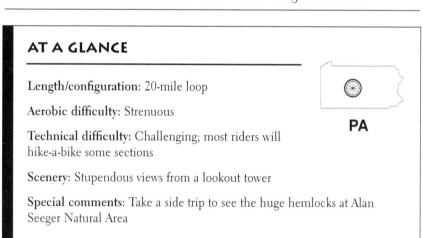

AT A GLANCE

Length/configuration: 20-mile loop

Aerobic difficulty: Strenuous

Technical difficulty: Challenging; most riders will hike-a-bike some sections

Scenery: Stupendous views from a lookout tower

Special comments: Take a side trip to see the huge hemlocks at Alan Seeger Natural Area

PA

This rigorous, 20-mile loop offers a special treat: a stop in the virgin forest at Alan Seeger Natural Area. Hike down the trail (no bikes allowed) to view the huge pine trees. Rumor has it these are the largest pine trees in North America. A large mountain stream flows through the area, which is thick with

RIDE 48 · Penn Roosevelt to Alan Seeger and Back
RIDE 51 · Dirt Road Tour
RIDE 52 · John Wert Path

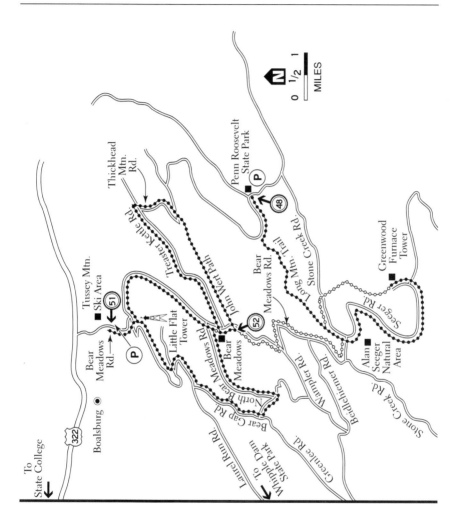

rhododendron. The lookout tower, on one of the area's highest points, provides great views of surrounding ridges and valleys.

The ride features steep climbing and challenging terrain over ridges and through valleys covered with second-growth hardwood forests. Expect to shoulder your bike for about 300 yards as you climb Grass Mountain out of Penn Roosevelt picnic area. Long Mountain Trail, a twisting single-track over terrain that changes on almost every turn, demands total concentration. Next is a hard-packed dirt road that climbs steeply to the lookout tower.

All of the roads on the loop are either hard-packed dirt or paved. The single-track eventually turns into a jeep trail. The big climbing starts at the intersection of Seeger and Stone Creek Roads.

General location: State College.

Elevation change: Around 2,000'.

Season: The roads are rideable from April through October. Spring can be muddy, and snow is possible from November through March. Avoid riding in deer-hunting season (after Thanksgiving).

Services: Water, rest rooms, and camping are available at the Penn Roosevelt picnic area. All other services are available in State College.

Hazards: The descent on the single-track above Penn Roosevelt picnic area (Long Mountain Trail) is very fast, and the terrain changes at every corner. Watch for snakes on the ridges in warm weather.

Rescue index: Fair. Except for the single-track and jeep trails, the ride is on public roads. However, this remote area doesn't carry a lot of traffic, especially in late fall and early spring.

Land status: State forest.

Maps: The USGS 7.5 minute quads are State College and McAlevys Fort. The best trail map is the Purple Lizard Recreational Map, available locally or at www.purplelizard.com.

Finding the trail: From State College, take US 322 south toward Lewistown. Turn right near the bottom of the Seven Mountains descent (at the reservoir) and follow the paved road through Rothrock State Forest to the Penn Roosevelt State Forest picnic area. Park near the lake.

Source of additional information:

> The Bicycle Shop
> 441 West College Avenue
> State College, PA 16801
> (814) 238-9422
> Website: www.thebicycleshopinc.com

Notes on the trail: The turnoff to the lookout is the only left-hand option available, so you can't miss it. There are several options for returning to Penn Roosevelt picnic area from the lookout tower. They're all fun!

RIDE 49 · State College to Alan Seeger and Back

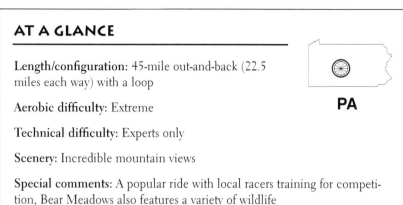

AT A GLANCE

Length/configuration: 45-mile out-and-back (22.5 miles each way) with a loop

Aerobic difficulty: Extreme

Technical difficulty: Experts only

Scenery: Incredible mountain views

Special comments: A popular ride with local racers training for competition, Bear Meadows also features a variety of wildlife

PA

This 45-mile out-and-back, popular with racers training for competition, features three major ascents of 800 to 1,000 feet each. Overall, this ride is for experienced, hard-core mountain bikers. Forest roads provide frequent views of the surrounding ridges and valleys.

Though the dirt roads have several steep ascents and descents, watch out for the extremely technical Ross Trail, which drops from the Greenwood Furnace lookout tower to Stone Creek Road and Alan Seeger Natural Area. The trail is at the end of the clearing on the right after the tower, and though not posted, it's obvious. (Skip the Johnson Trail, a very rocky hiking trail.) Ross Trail is a ridge-top single-track with technical and extremely steep sections. It was built and maintained by mountain bikers, but it still has a double black diamond rating. Most riders should backtrack down the dirt road, which is one of the steepest, fastest drops in the region.

Other features on the ride include the lookout tower above Alan Seeger Natural Area, which has excellent views. There's also a short hiking trail (no bikes allowed) in Alan Seeger Natural Area that shouldn't be missed. Bear Meadows Natural Area is a bog with a variety of wildlife.

General location: State College.

Elevation change: There are 3 major climbs: Tussey Mountain to Bear Meadows Natural Area, Alan Seeger Natural Area to the lookout tower, and, on the return, Alan Seeger to Bear Meadows. Then the ride drops for the return to State College. Total elevation gain is about 3,000'.

Season: Rideable between April and November, although midsummer can be hot and humid. Expect snow after November and through March. Spring can be muddy. Avoid riding in deer-hunting season (after Thanksgiving).

Services: All services are available in State College.

RIDE 49 · State College to Alan Seeger and Back

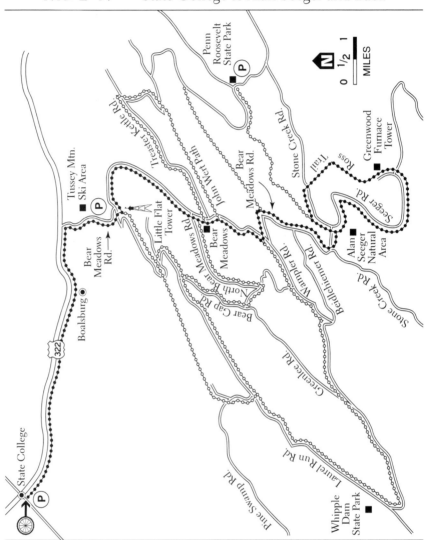

Hazards: The descent from the lookout tower on Ross Trail to Stone Creek Road into Alan Seeger Natural Area is very difficult and should only be attempted by expert riders.

Rescue index: Good. Most of the ride is along traffic-bearing roads. However, traffic gets lighter as the ride moves away from US 322.

Land status: State forest; state and county roads.

Maps: The USGS 7.5 minute quads are State College and McAlevys Fort. The

Experienced off-road cyclists find plenty of challenging riding around State College.

best trail map is the Purple Lizard Recreational Map, available locally or at www.purplelizard.com.

Finding the trail: From State College, pedal out Business US 322 south to the turnoff for Tussey Mountain Ski Area (at Bear Meadows Road, on the right). Follow Bear Meadows Road to Stone Creek Road and turn left into Alan Seeger Natural Area. Take Seeger Road to the tower and drop down Ross Trail to complete the loop.

Source of additional information:

The Bicycle Shop
441 West College Avenue
State College, PA 16801
(814) 238-9422
Website: www.thebicycleshopinc.com

Notes on the trail: The ride starts in State College, goes through Bear Meadows Natural Area to Alan Seeger Natural Area, climbs to Greenwood Furnace lookout tower, and returns to State College. Ross Trail, just past the tower, replaces an old route that descended into and through part of the natural area, a no-no for bikes. Local riders rebuilt an older trail to produce Ross Trail, which is more fun and avoids the natural area.

RIDE 50 · State College to Whipple Dam and Bear Meadows

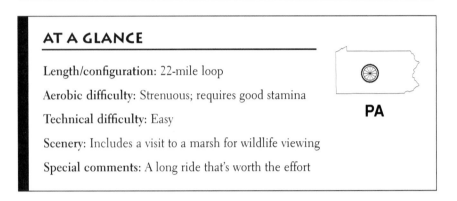

AT A GLANCE

Length/configuration: 22-mile loop

Aerobic difficulty: Strenuous; requires good stamina

Technical difficulty: Easy

Scenery: Includes a visit to a marsh for wildlife viewing

Special comments: A long ride that's worth the effort

PA

Bear Meadows is a pristine area that's well worth the long ride. Visitors can view birds and fish from an observation platform over the marsh. This is even a nice place to visit on a rainy day, since it's so rich in fauna and wildlife. The wet, swamplike environment attracts many birds. And they don't call it Bear Meadows for nothin'—keep an eye peeled for deer and bear. More fun things to do on this ride include climbing the lookout tower at Tussey Mountain and, in the summer, swimming at Whipple Dam State Park.

Most of this 22-mile loop follows hard-packed dirt roads. The Little Shingletown Road descent is a rocky jeep trail. The trail around Bear Meadows Natural Area is closed to bikes, but it's a great hike. Lock your bike at the parking area and explore on foot; the observation tower is less than a five-minute hike and the trail is well marked. Beware: This ride requires good stamina, as it has two long climbs with 800- to 1,000-foot elevation gains each.

General location: State College.

Elevation change: More than 1,600'. There's a steep 800' climb to the lookout tower at Tussey Mountain, and then the loop descends and climbs about 800' to Bear Meadows Natural Area.

Season: Rideable between April and November, although midsummer can be hot and humid. Spring can be muddy, and expect snow from November through March. Avoid riding in deer-hunting season (after Thanksgiving).

Services: Whipple Dam has water and rest rooms; a snack bar is open between Memorial Day and Labor Day. All other services are available in State College.

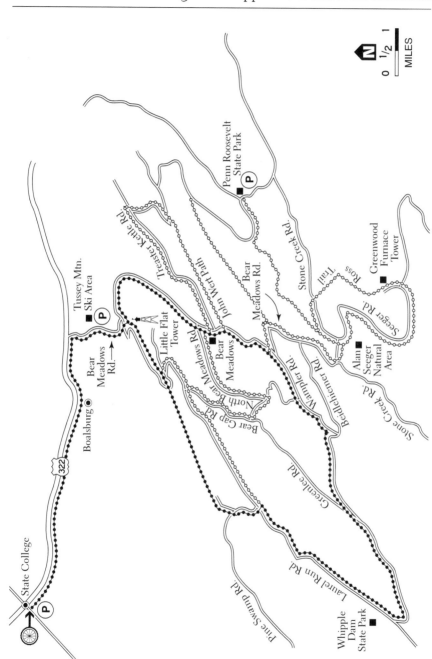

Hazards: Watch for snakes on the ridges in warm weather. Be alert for traffic on the dirt roads.

Rescue index: Good to fair. Whipple Dam and Bear Meadows are popular areas, but there are no residences or farms along the dirt roads.

Land status: State forest and parks.

Maps: The USGS 7.5 minute quads are State College and McAlevys Fort. The best trail map is the Purple Lizard Recreational Map, available locally or at www.purplelizard.com.

Finding the trail: From State College, ride out PA 322 south to Tussey Mountain Ski Area. Follow Bear Meadows Road into Rothrock State Forest. Take the first right, Laurel Run Road, to the mountaintop. A gate (but no trail sign) on the right marks Little Shingletown Road Trail. Head out on this trail, which follows Mid-State Trail at this point and shares its right-of-way. Mid-State Trail branches to the right in a few hundred yards (no bikes). Keep left.

Source of additional information:

> The Bicycle Shop
> 441 West College Avenue
> State College, PA 16801
> (814) 238-9422
> Website: www.thebicycleshopinc.com

Notes on the trail: Bear Meadows Natural Area is a day-use area in pristine condition because no fishing or boating is allowed. The large, flat bog, punctuated by a slow-moving stream, changes appearance with the seasons, making it a popular destination year-round.

RIDE 51 · Dirt Road Tour

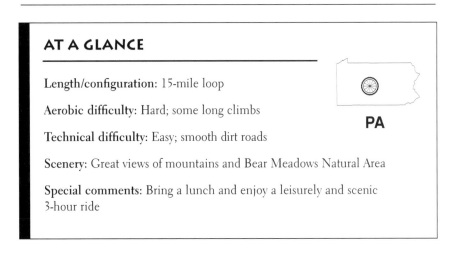

AT A GLANCE

Length/configuration: 15-mile loop

Aerobic difficulty: Hard; some long climbs

Technical difficulty: Easy; smooth dirt roads

Scenery: Great views of mountains and Bear Meadows Natural Area

Special comments: Bring a lunch and enjoy a leisurely and scenic 3-hour ride

PA

This dirt-road cruise is a favorite of Mike Hermann, a State College mountain biker of long standing and a professional cartographer. Hermann says this ride makes a perfect starting point to explore Rothrock State Forest and enjoy some beautiful overlooks. Plan on riding for two or three hours at an easy pace from Tussey Mountain Ski Area. Strong riders can do the loop in less than an hour if they don't stop to enjoy the views. While aerobically demanding, the route follows relatively smooth dirt roads.

General location: State College.

Elevation change: 800'.

Season: Spring through fall.

Services: All services are available in State College.

Hazards: Watch for light traffic on the dirt roads.

Rescue index: Excellent.

Land status: County and state forest roads.

Maps: The best trail map is the Purple Lizard Recreational Map, available locally or at www.purplelizard.com.

Finding the trail: From State College, ride out PA 322 south to Tussey Mountain Ski Area. Follow Bear Meadows Road into Rothrock State Forest. Most folks use the ski area parking lot, although there is a state forest parking area a few hundred yards into the forest. On your bike, look for Laurel Run Road (dirt) on the right and take it to the top of the mountain. Just over the top is a gated road on the left; follow it 1 mile to the end, where you'll find a huge blueberry patch, a lookout tower, and great views of Mount Nittany and Penns Valley. This is called Little Flat.

Source of additional information:

The Bicycle Shop
441 West College Avenue
State College, PA 16801
(814) 238-9422
Website: www.thebicycleshopinc.com

Notes on the trail: From Little Flat, return to Laurel Run Road and turn left; cruise downhill for a mile and look for Gettis Ridge Road on the left. This road is payback for the 2 miles of carefree downhill coasting you just enjoyed. Take Gettis Ridge Road and climb . . . and climb . . . and climb. It's only about 2 miles long, but the grade is steep. Your reward is a great vista near the summit. If you need water, there's Keith Spring, where you can drink from a pipe by the road. The water is safe and cold and runs almost year-round. Continue climbing until you get to Greenlee Road. This area is called Big Flat because, well, it's big and flat. The soil is sandy, and pine trees are abundant. Turn left and continue on Gettis Ridge Road to North Bear Meadows Road on the left. It's all downhill from here.

RIDE 48 • Penn Roosevelt to Alan Seeger and Back
RIDE 51 • Dirt Road Tour
RIDE 52 • John Wert Path

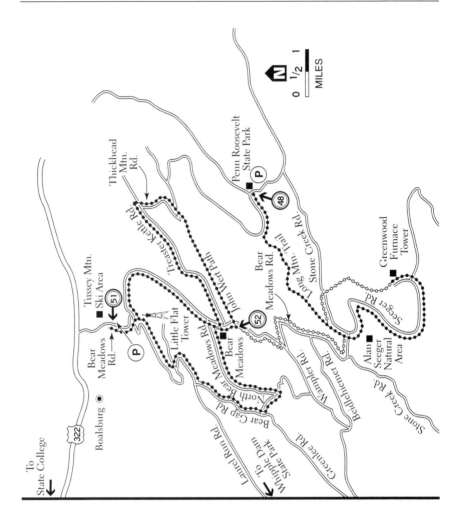

Don't go so fast that you miss the view about a half-mile down: a beautiful overlook of Bear Meadows Natural Area. Two miles of downhill cruising take you to Bear Meadows Road. Turn left and cruise a few more miles downhill to the ski area.

RIDE 52 · John Wert Path

AT A GLANCE

Length/configuration: 6-mile loop

Aerobic difficulty: Easy, with one long climb

Technical difficulty: Moderate, with stretches of rocky single-track

Scenery: Rhododendron thickets and giant hemlock stands

Special comments: A cross-country ski trail that's a fun, moderately difficult mountain bike jaunt

PA

Technical trails are difficult to categorize because everyone has their own definition of what is and what isn't difficult. John Wert Path helps beginners establish a baseline. The trail is relatively safe, too. While flat and continuously rocky, it doesn't have any dangerous drop-offs and doesn't skirt along cliff edges. The short sections of single-track, however, connect rock fields that may appear unrideable to the novice. There is always a way through, though you may have to try several times before you clean the trail. Remember to bring extra tubes; pinch flats are common on rocky trails like this. When you can aggressively ride this trail, you'll be confident on any technical ride.

This ride has more to offer than the technical challenges of finding your way through a rock garden. It's scenic, too. It winds through rhododendron thickets and explores giant hemlock stands. A hundred yards from the start, you'll think you're a hundred miles from a road, a car, your job, and civilization.

Bear Meadows Natural Area, where the trail begins and ends, is a day-use area in pristine condition because no fishing or boating is allowed. The large, flat bog, punctuated by a slow-moving stream, changes appearance with the seasons, making it a popular destination year-round.

General location: State College.

Elevation change: 400'.

Season: Late spring through fall.

Services: All services are available in State College.

Hazards: None.

Rescue index: Good.

Land status: State forest.

Maps: The best trail map is the Purple Lizard Recreational Map, available locally or at www.purplelizard.com.

Finding the trail: From State College, ride out PA 322 south to Tussey Mountain Ski Area. Follow Bear Meadows Road into Rothrock State Forest. John Wert Path begins after the parking area at Bear Meadows Natural Area; there is a trailhead sign, and the trail is marked with blue blazes. You'll find the marker on the left after the bridge.

Source of additional information:

> The Bicycle Shop
> 441 West College Avenue
> State College, PA 16801
> (814) 238-9422
> Website: www.thebicycleshopinc.com

Notes on the trail: John Wert Path ends at an opening of a gas-line cut. To complete the loop continue across the cut and past some camps to reach Thickhead Mountain Road. Coast downhill and turn left onto Treaster Kettle Road, continuing to Bear Meadows Road. There is a healthy climb in the middle of this section, but then it's all downhill to Bear Meadows.

RIDE 53 · The State College Epic Ride

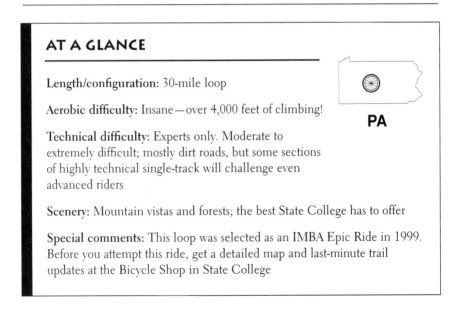

AT A GLANCE

Length/configuration: 30-mile loop

Aerobic difficulty: Insane—over 4,000 feet of climbing!

Technical difficulty: Experts only. Moderate to extremely difficult; mostly dirt roads, but some sections of highly technical single-track will challenge even advanced riders

Scenery: Mountain vistas and forests; the best State College has to offer

Special comments: This loop was selected as an IMBA Epic Ride in 1999. Before you attempt this ride, get a detailed map and last-minute trail updates at the Bicycle Shop in State College

PA

To celebrate the spirit of epic mountain bike rides, the International Mountain Bicycling Association (IMBA) joined with two major sponsors to create IMBA Epics. In 1999, four demanding rides made the grade, including trails in

RIDE 53 · The State College Epic Ride

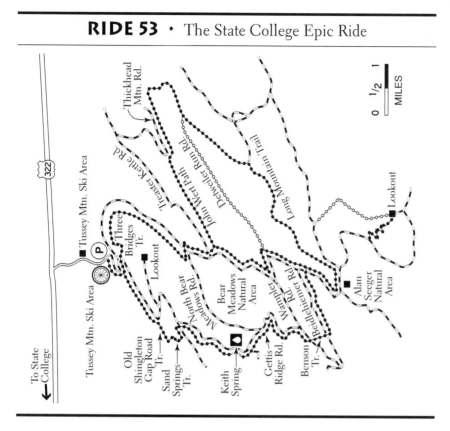

Downieville, California; Fruita, Colorado; Slatyfork, West Virginia; and State College, Pennsylvania. If an epic ride is your idea of a good time, find out why this part of central Pennsylvania got the nod from IMBA. This 30-mile loop features excellent vistas as it traverses classic central Pennsylvania ridge and valley topography. The route passes through Bear Meadows and Alan Seeger Natural Areas; Bear Meadows is a prehistoric nonglaciated bog, and Alan Seeger is home to some of the oldest and largest giant hemlocks in the country.

The Sphincter Phactor: The scariest parts of the loop are Sand Springs and the Benson Trail, technical single-tracks that follow old logging chutes and have steep, loose sections. Double-track on Long Mountain Trail features extreme high-speed potential combined with changing trail surfaces, downed trees, and loose rock. You've been warned.

John Wert Path is two miles of single-track and rock fields on level terrain. Lonberger Trail has rocky sections but becomes smoother and faster toward end. Overall, this epic ride has it all: a mix of old logging roads and railroad grades, technical single-track, steep descents, and loose rock on many stretches. Combine all that with 4,500 feet of climbing and it all adds up to one word: epic.

Bone-rattling
rock gardens are just
part of the fun on the
State College Epic Ride.

General location: State College.

Elevation change: 4,500'.

Season: Year-round.

Services: All services are available in State College.

Hazards: Light traffic on the dirt roads.

Rescue index: Fair to poor. Dirt roads are well traveled, but the single-track leads to remote terrain with potentially dangerous conditions. No phones. No one to hear you scream.

Land status: County roads and state forest.

Maps: The Purple Lizard Recreational Map is available locally or on the web at www.purplelizard.com.

Finding the trail: The ride starts in Rothrock State Forest, 6 miles south of State College and Pennsylvania State University. Take PA 322 to Tussey Mountain Ski Area and park at the trailhead parking lot on Bear Meadows Road a half-mile from the ski area.

Source of additional information:

The Bicycle Shop
441 West College Avenue
State College, PA 16801
(814) 238-9422
Website: www.thebicycleshopinc.com

Notes on the trail: From the state forest parking lot, head into the forest and take the first right on Laurel Run Road. Look for the Lonberger Path trailhead on the left within 100 yards. Pedal up this steep single-track to the next Lonberger trailhead sign. Take the unmarked, uphill trail on the right, and within 50 yards you'll see another trail on the right. Follow it to Laurel Run Road.

Continue uphill on Laurel Run Road to the summit and turn right on gated Old Shingletown Gap Road. Look for a blue-blazed trail on the left in a half-mile (Sand Springs Trail). From there, descend to Laurel Run Road. Turn left and continue to Bear Gap Road, where you turn right and climb to the top. Make a left on Gettis Ridge Road and follow it to the intersection with Wampler Road. Then turn right and look for Benson trailhead on the left. Next, descend to Beidleheimer Road, turn left on Bear Meadows Road, and turn left to Bear Meadows Natural Area. Just before the bridge at the natural area is a signpost for John Wert Path on right; take it. Follow this trail until it ends and continue uphill on Thickhead Mountain Road to the summit. Descend, bearing left to Long Mountain Trail. This trail is hard to find because you're descending fast; the sign is on the big corner on the right. (If you reach the state park lake, you've gone too far.)

Hike-a-bike up Long Mountain Trail to the single-track on top and ride it to the gas-line clearing. Then continue on double-track into the woods. Descend to Alan Seeger Natural Area, climb to Bear Meadows Natural Area (again), and continue to North Bear Meadows Road. Turn left and look for Lonberger trailhead on the right. Follow this single-track back to your car.

BALD EAGLE STATE FOREST, PENNSYLVANIA

Bald Eagle State Forest, near the geographical center of Pennsylvania, lies midway between State College to the west and the Susquehanna River to the east. Named after a Native American chief, the forest comprises 191,858 acres in the ridge and valley region of the state, and that means there's a lot to explore. The dominant features are sandstone ridges that rise as much as 2,100 feet above sea level. The many streams in the area originate in the forested ridges and drain southeasterly toward the Susquehanna River. With more than 340 miles of roads, just as many miles of foot trails, and 300 miles of designated snowmobile trails, Bald Eagle State Forest draws mountain bikers from throughout Pennsylvania and the Northeast.

Be sure to stop by R. B. Winter State Park, located in the forest, and pick up a copy of the *Mountain Bike Trail Guide to the Bald Eagle State Forest Central Region*. This one-page guide features 25 off-road trails (totaling 48 miles) in the forest, all near R. B. Winter State Park. That's not all—the area has another 100 miles of connecting forestry roads. Like I said, there's a lot to explore in Bald Eagle State Forest.

RIDE 54 · Cowbell Hollow/Top Mountain Trail

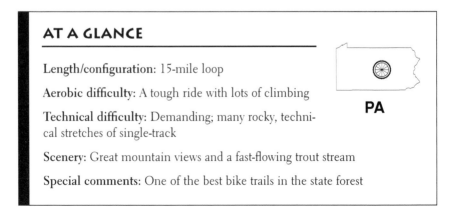

AT A GLANCE

Length/configuration: 15-mile loop

Aerobic difficulty: A tough ride with lots of climbing

Technical difficulty: Demanding; many rocky, technical stretches of single-track

Scenery: Great mountain views and a fast-flowing trout stream

Special comments: One of the best bike trails in the state forest

PA

RIDE 54 · Cowbell Hollow/Top Mountain Trail

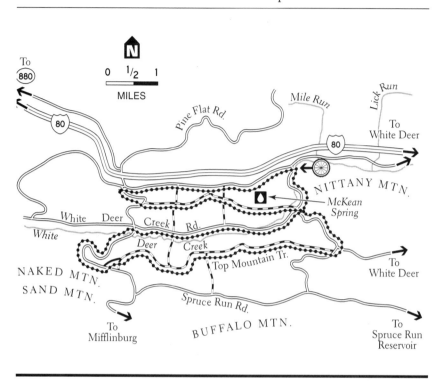

This 15-mile loop, a typical north-central Pennsylvania combination of forest roads and trails, features Top Mountain Trail, one of the best mountain bike rides in Bald Eagle State Forest. This abandoned jeep trail, which varies from smooth to very rocky, is fast and challenging, with lots of turns, short climbs, and descents. It also has excellent views of the surrounding mountains. Sugar Valley Narrows Road is a hard-packed dirt road, and the other forest roads on this ride are hard-packed dirt covered with loose stones. Cowbell Hollow Trail is one of the most rideable single-tracks in the area, but watch out for deadfalls.

With steep climbs and rocky, technical single-track, this trail is for experienced riders. Less experienced riders will find large parts of the loop rideable, but they should have good stamina and be ready to push their bikes over the rocky sections. White Deer Creek, which riders cross twice, is one of the area's larger creeks. This rocky, fast-flowing trout stream has some excellent camping spots along it. Mook's Spring on Running Gap Road, 100 yards south of the Top Mountain Trail intersection, is a dependable water source.

General location: Lewisburg.

Elevation change: Around 1,500'.

Season: The best time to ride this loop is between April and October. Spring can be very muddy. The best views can be had after the leaves are off the trees, but don't ride in deer-hunting season, usually after Thanksgiving. Winter months are risky; expect snow after November. The forest roads are often covered in ice, even after long spells of warm weather.

Services: Camping is available at R. B. Winter State Park, about 12 miles southwest of this loop. All other services are available in Lewisburg.

Hazards: Sections of Top Mountain Trail are extremely rocky. In winter and early spring, expect parts of the trails to be ice-covered.

Rescue index: Good. There's light traffic along White Deer Creek Road. I-80 parallels most of this ride.

Land status: State forest.

Maps: USGS 7.5 minute quads are Carroll and Williamsport S.E.

Finding the trail: Take Exit 29 from Interstate 80 (10 miles west of PA 15). From the exit ramp, go down the hill a few hundred yards to the dirt road and park near the intersection with Sugar Valley Narrows Road.

Sources of additional information:

Department of Environmental Resources
Bureau of Forestry
P.O. Box 147
Laurelton, PA 17835-0147
(570) 922-3344

Campus Cycle & Fly Fishing Center
223 Market Street
Lewisburg, PA 17837
(570) 524-2998

Notes on the trail: The ride starts from an interstate exit that inexplicably leads directly to a desolate state forest road. Ride your bike west on Sugar Valley Narrows Road and bear left onto Garden Hollow Road, followed by an almost immediate left onto Cooper Mill Road. There's a steep climb to the top. On the downhill, turn left onto Cowbell Hollow Trail at the first 180-degree hairpin turn (look for a sign). This up-and-down jeep trail turns into a brushy singletrack that descends to White Deer Creek. Cross the creek at the small bridge and turn right onto White Deer Creek Road.

Almost immediately, make a sharp left onto Running Gap Road and climb to the top. Turn right on Top Mountain Trail. This single-track is self-evident, but if you're in doubt, follow the blue blazes and bear left. Regardless of the branch you end up riding, it will eventually intersect with Cooper Mill Road (the first forest road). Turn right onto Cooper Mill Road and head downhill (you may have a short climb first, depending on which branch of Top Mountain Trail you finished on) to White Deer Creek Road. Turn right and ride to the end. Turn right again and ride back to your car.

RIDE 55 · Bear Gap Ride

AT A GLANCE

Length/configuration: 12-mile (total) figure eight

Aerobic difficulty: Moderate to difficult

Technical difficulty: Stretches of rocky surface, but less experienced bikers can walk the tough stuff

Scenery: Second-growth forests and vistas of surrounding ridges and valleys

Special comments: In the summer, you can swim at the state park

PA

This 12-mile figure eight is a challenging ride designed for experienced mountain bikers. Intermediate riders with good stamina and the willingness to walk some sections should also be able to complete the ride without suffering permanent damage. Most of the trail is through second-growth hardwood forests, with many vistas of the surrounding ridges and valleys. Stop at Sand Mountain Tower and climb to the top for breathtaking views that are especially spectacular on a clear day at dusk or during a full moon. You can also swim at the state park.

These forest roads are mostly hard-packed dirt covered with loose stones. Spring Mountain Trail is relatively flat and rideable by novice mountain bikers. Parts of Bear Gap are expert only, but they're short enough to walk. Old Tram Trail is moderately rocky.

General location: Lewisburg.

Elevation change: About 1,400'.

Season: Generally rideable between April and November. Spring can be very muddy; fall, after the leaves are off the trees, offers the best views. The trails and roads can be icy in winter, even after prolonged warm spells. Expect snow from November through March.

Services: All services are available in Lewisburg, 18 miles east of R. B. Winter State Park.

Hazards: Bear Gap Trail is very rocky and in wet weather can be filled with flowing water. Avoid riding in deer-hunting season (after Thanksgiving).

Rescue index: Good; R. B. Winter State Park is usually staffed. Also, traffic can be flagged down on PA 192.

Land status: State forest.

Maps: The USGS 7.5 minute quads are Carroll, Williamsport S.E., and Hartleton. You can pick up a copy of the Bald Eagle State Forest mountain bike map at the state park office.

RIDE 55 · Bear Gap Ride

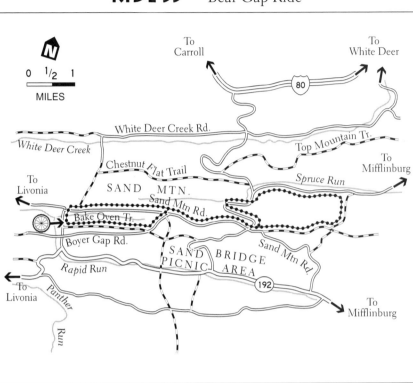

Finding the trail: R. B. Winter State Park, where the ride begins, is 18 miles west of Lewisburg on PA 192. After you reach the park, follow the signs to the camping area and park in the lot between the lake and the camping area. From the parking lot, ride your bike north on the paved park road half a mile uphill to the first intersection with a dirt forest road and turn right onto Sand Mountain Road.

Sources of additional information:

Department of Environmental Resources
Bureau of Forestry
P.O. Box 147
Laurelton, PA 17835-0147
(570) 922-3344

Campus Cycle & Fly Fishing Center
223 Market Street
Lewisburg, PA 17837
(570) 524-2998

Notes on the trail: On Sand Mountain Road, ride to the first intersection (Boyer Gap Road is to the right) and take Cracker Bridge Trail to the left. At the bottom of the hill, turn right, follow Old Tram Trail east to Cooper Hill Road, and turn right. At the top after the long climb, turn left. Very soon you'll reach a fork; bear left (which is almost straight) and continue to Bear Gap Trail (no trail sign). Here's how to verify that you're on Bear Gap: The trail goes slightly downhill at first, with a grassy meadow on the left, followed by a steep downhill through trees and across a small stream.

Take the trail downhill to Spruce Run Road and turn left. At the next intersection, go left onto Cooper Hill Road. Repeat the climb and, at the top, turn right onto Sand Mountain Road. After a short climb to the top, you'll see the fire tower. Continue downhill on Sand Mountain Road. Turn left at Boyer Gap and right onto Bake Over Trail; head back to the park.

SOUTH-CENTRAL PENNSYLVANIA

From the historic village of Gettysburg to the state capital of Harrisburg, south-central Pennsylvania offers a surprising range of off-road riding. In addition to scenic mountain trails, easy rail-to-trail conversions, and excellent county parks that welcome mountain bikers, Whitetail—a system of trails at the nation's newest downhill ski center—awaits off-road cyclists. You can eliminate the climb to the mountaintop by riding the ski lift (yes, you can load your bike on, too).

Gettysburg, of course, is where the Union turned back the Confederacy for the second time in 1863 during the Civil War and clinched victory for the North. Riding the rolling, gentle park roads by mountain bike is the perfect way to explore the battleground, the site of the largest military engagement in the Western Hemisphere. To the west is Whitetail, where mountain bikers play when the slopes are green. You've got to pay to play, but the resort provides lift service to the summit of Two Top Mountain, as well as bike rentals, instruction, guided tours, food, drink, and—last but not least—hot showers for patrons (bring your own towel) and cold showers for their bikes.

York has great places to ride, including several county parks outside town. (At the appropriately named Rocky Ridge, you get a bird's-eye view of the Three Mile Island nuclear power plant.) South of town, York Heritage Rail Trail provides flat, easy, scenic riding, and the old railroad grade—still in use—offers a history lesson as it leads cyclists through old industrial towns. An added bonus: The trail connects with the Northern Central Railroad Trail in Maryland (Ride 26), adding more miles of level trail to explore.

More easy riding is found outside Harrisburg. Stony Creek Wilderness Trail is an easy ride through a 44,000-acre wilderness. Conewago Recreation Trail, another rails-to-trails conversion, takes riders through scenic farmland in Lancaster County.

RIDE 56 · Whitetail Mountain Biking Center

AT A GLANCE

Length/configuration: 26 miles of interconnected loops

Aerobic difficulty: Moderate to very difficult, including a 1,000-foot vertical gain to the top of the mountain (optional if the ski lift is running)

PA

Technical difficulty: Moderate to difficult; fire roads and very technical single-track

Scenery: Spectacular views from the ridges; nice fields and forests below the ridges

Special comments: There's a fee; the chair lift operates on weekends and major holidays May through October

The view is dramatic from the 1,800-foot summit of Two Top Mountain, the highest point at Whitetail Ski Resort. Ridges such as Clay Lick and Casis Knob undulate in the distance, fleecy clouds dot a deep blue sky, and a hawk soars at eye level. All that's missing is the snow. In summer, the Bear Pond Mountains of south-central Pennsylvania are carpeted in a forest of green. The uniform for the day is a T-shirt and shorts, not insulated ski pants, a jacket, and mittens.

The mode of transportation to the mountaintop is the same one used in the winter—a chair lift—but the way down is via a steel-framed, fat-tired mountain bike, not a metal-edged set of fiberglass skis. Mountain bikes have moved to the ski slopes, tempting an increasing number of paying customers to carve down the mountains on two wheels and enticing many ski resorts to open for a second season that starts in May and lasts through the fall. Cyclists flock to Whitetail to explore a new dimension that removes some—but not all—of the exertion from off-road riding. The ski resort also gives novices and folks who only ride on paved roads and bike paths a chance to try their mountain bikes where they were meant to be ridden—on a mountain.

At the top of Whitetail's chair lift, riders can choose from several routes to explore the ridge. Trails range from twisting technical paths through the forest to a nontechnical but steep dirt road down the mountain. The resort boasts more than 26 miles of well-marked, maintained trails. The narrow trails, with names such as High Road, Breakdown Boulevard, Bear Pond Loops, and the

RIDE 56 · Whitetail Mountain Biking Center

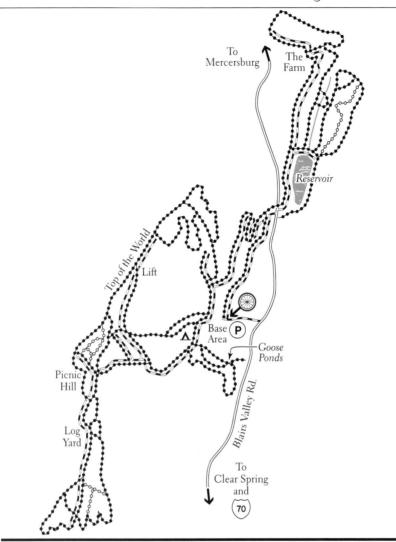

Glades, introduce novice mountain bikers to a world without cars, traffic lights, or joggers. Two-wheeled explorers pedal through a mix of pine and deciduous trees and glens full of waist-high mountain laurel. Short, often steep ups and downs punctuate the trails that honeycomb the mountaintop.

Along the way, breaks in the trees reveal valleys and neighboring ridges to the south. Wildlife is abundant, and a sharp eye often glimpses white-tailed deer, flocks of wild turkeys, and a variety of bird life. The only sounds are the rustle of wind in the trees, birds (grouse make a sound like someone beating a drum faster and faster), and the occasional high-pitched squeal of brakes from other mountain bikers exploring the ridge. Though the trails are well marked, they're often rugged, rocky, and wet. Routes interspersed with rock outcroppings, fallen branches, steep uphills, and sudden descents require off-road cyclists to keep their eyes focused on the upcoming terrain. Yet successfully negotiating these hazards is part of the thrill of riding a mountain bike on a mountain. Whitetail makes it easy for novices to obtain basics that, when mastered, make the sport a pleasurable and popular way of exploring the outdoors.

"My advice for beginners is to get with an instructor," says Dave DePeters, a Whitetail trail guide. "Because the terrain is different on a mountain, you'll be more comfortable on the first ride or two if you're with someone experienced." Hooking up with an instructor is easy. Whitetail offers a two-hour workshop on weekends at $20 per person or group lessons at $10 per person. Afterward, explore Dowling Farm Loop by the reservoir and other easy trails at the foot of the mountain. As your skills develop, come back to Whitetail and take the chair lift to the summit of Two Top Mountain to explore a system of trails for intermediate and advanced riders.

A trail pass to ride all of Whitetail's trails is $6. The chair lift is open on weekends. An all-day trail and lift pass is $23; an afternoon trail and lift pass is $15. A season pass (including lift) is $99. Bike rentals are $55 on weekends (including trail and lift pass, helmet, and a water bottle you can keep) and $40 on weekdays.

General location: Mercersburg, which is 15 miles northwest of Hagerstown, Maryland.

Elevation change: As much as you want. It's approximately a 1,000' climb to the top of Two Top Mountain, though most visitors opt for the chair lift (weekends and holidays only). Easier trails at the foot of the mountain offer much less elevation gain, but they're not flat.

Season: Friday through Monday, mid-May through October, from 9 a.m. to 6 p.m.; closed Tuesday through Thursday (except for groups, by reservation only). The chair lift operates on weekends and major holidays.

Services: Camping, bike rentals and repairs, and food are available at Whitetail. All other services are available in Mercersburg and Hagerstown.

Hazards: Most trails coming off the mountain are long and steep with waterbars that can send unsuspecting riders flying over the handlebars. Mountain weather can change with very little warning. In a thunderstorm, avoid open areas on the summit and get to lower ground.

Rescue index: Excellent; though not regularly patrolled, the trails are ridden by Whitetail personnel with radios.

Land status: Private.

Maps: A trail map is included with a trail pass.

Finding the trail: To get to Whitetail from Washington, D.C., Baltimore, and points west, take Interstate 70 to Exit 18 (Clear Spring) and MD 68 north to the intersection with US 40. Cross US 40 onto Mill Street and drive north to the stop sign; turn right on Broadfording Road and drive half a mile. Then turn left on Blairs Valley Road and go 5 miles to the resort entrance. From Harrisburg and points north, take I-81 south to Exit 3 (PA 16 west) and drive 10 miles to Mercersburg. Turn left at the stop light, go 3 miles, turn left on Blairs Valley Road, and drive 3.7 miles to the resort. Whitetail employees at the mountain bike center can provide trail directions and advice.

Source of additional information:

> Whitetail Ski Resort and Mountain Biking Center
> 13805 Blairs Valley Road
> Mercersburg, PA 17236
> (717) 328-9400

Notes on the trail: The trails at Whitetail are designed to please cyclists ranging from novice to expert, but keep in mind that these are mountains, and even the easiest trails include short uphills, rocks, small stream crossings, mud holes, and the occasional bog. Complimentary hot showers and a bike wash are available after a ride; just remember to bring a towel.

RIDE 57 · Gettysburg National Military Park

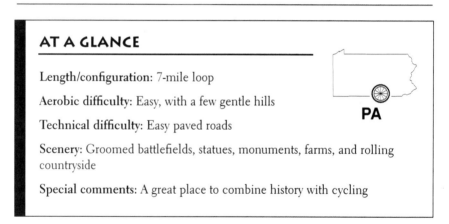

AT A GLANCE

Length/configuration: 7-mile loop

Aerobic difficulty: Easy, with a few gentle hills

Technical difficulty: Easy paved roads

Scenery: Groomed battlefields, statues, monuments, farms, and rolling countryside

Special comments: A great place to combine history with cycling

PA

What happened in the fields and woods outside this Pennsylvania hamlet in the summer of 1863? Simply put, the Confederate tide was pushed back for the second time by a wall of determined men who made up the Union forces. In effect, the Southern cause was lost on these fields. The cost in human life and suffering was enormous. When the fighting ended on July 3, 1863, casualties from both armies totaled more than 50,000. It was the largest armed conflict ever fought in the Western Hemisphere.

RIDE 57 · Gettysburg National Military Park

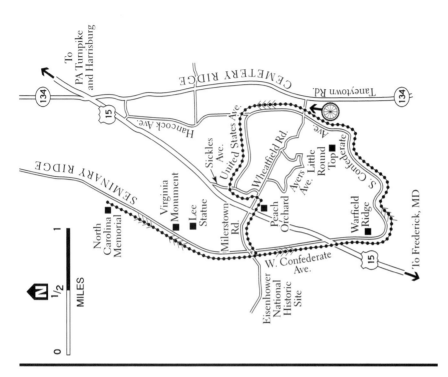

Touring Gettysburg National Military Park on a mountain bike is the best way to understand the human dimension of this crucial battle. Unlike the millions who view the park through the windshield of the family car or a tour bus window, cyclists have a distinct advantage. For one thing, pedaling makes you feel wonderfully alive, a heartening contrast to the grim events of the Civil War. Furthermore, markers and monuments are much more accessible on a fat-tired bike. You're not as likely to drive by an intriguing spot as when you're touring by car, with the endless hassle of parking, getting out, and getting back in. The wind is in your hair, you smell the fields and woods in the rolling countryside, and riding up the easy hills is invigorating; all this contributes to the experience. And it's easy to peel off across the flat, stony fields to examine monuments and markers that look too far away to walk to.

On this easy, seven-mile ride along a mostly paved bike route, you'll see monuments, gun emplacements, markers, fences, and old stone walls. Modest vistas of the surrounding fields, woods, and, in the spring, clusters of forget-me-nots make for a low-key but memorable experience for most cyclists. Most notable: The Virginia Memorial, with its huge statue of General Robert E. Lee astride his horse, commemorates Pickett's Charge, the last Confederate assault of the battle. From this spot, Lee watched 12,000 of his troops march across a mile of open field toward the Federal line. After the ill-fated attack, 8,000 dead littered the field. Little Round Top, with its commanding view of the battlefield, saw some of the fiercest fighting on the second day of battle. In the National Cemetery, north of the visitor center, you can see where Abraham Lincoln read his Gettysburg Address at the cemetery's dedication on November 19, 1863.

Your visit to Gettysburg will give you a greater understanding of the historic events that took place here and impart rich insights into the huge scale of human suffering that occurred here in 1863—all because you toured the battlefield on a mountain bike.

General location: Gettysburg.

Elevation change: Negligible.

Season: Year-round. In the spring and summer the park is often jammed with visitors. Also, July and August can be very hot and humid, so plan to visit early in the day to avoid the worst of it.

Services: All services are available in Gettysburg.

Hazards: None. Watch for traffic (especially tour buses) on the paved roads.

Rescue index: Excellent.

Land status: National park.

Maps: A map of the bike route is available at the visitor center.

Finding the trail: Gettysburg is located on US 30 in south-central Pennsylvania between York and Chambersburg; it's about a 2.5-hour drive from Philadelphia and a 2-hour drive from Baltimore or Washington. From the Visitor Center in the national park (easy to find; just follow the signs), pedal south on Taneytown Road (PA 134) to Wheatfield Road and turn right. You can also drive to this point in your car.

Sources of additional information:

Gettysburg National Military Park
Gettysburg, PA 17325
(717) 334-1124

Gettysburg Convention and Visitors Bureau
35 Carlisle Street
Gettysburg, PA 17325
(717) 334-6274

Notes on the trail: It's easy to extend your ride beyond the bicycle tour recommended by the park; just follow the signs for the auto tour.

RIDE 58 · Rocky Ridge County Park

AT A GLANCE

Length/configuration: 12 miles of loops

Aerobic difficulty: Moderate

Technical difficulty: Moderate to difficult; lots of rocks and waterbars

Scenery: Mostly woods with glimpses of the Susquehanna River Valley

Special comments: Rocky Ridge is appropriately named; you and your suspension fork will get a workout. Yes, that's Three Mile Island in the distance

PA

York County mountain bikers are fortunate to have 750-acre Rocky Ridge County Park, a wooded hilltop with about 12 miles of mostly single-track. Most of the nine trails in the park intersect, making it easy for intrepid off-roaders to devise multiple loop rides that can easily keep them rolling through a full day's riding. And they don't call it Rocky Ridge for nothing; long stretches of rock-infested single-track will give your bike's suspension a real workout.

The small forested park's trails are extremely well marked, so getting lost shouldn't be a problem. You don't really even need a trail map if you've got the time and energy to explore. The paved main road serves as a link between many of the trails, making it easy to connect all the trails for a long ride. In addition, numerous short single-tracks connect the main trails (and aren't shown on the map). Local riders say Rocky Ridge offers the best single-track riding in York County. It's a terrific park for intermediate and advanced riders.

General location: York.

Elevation change: No major elevation gains (none of the trails drop to the valley floor), but expect to climb a few hundred feet on most loops.

Season: Year-round.

Services: Rest rooms, water, pay phones, and a soft-drink vending machine are available in the park. All other services are available in York.

Hazards: Use caution on the long stretches of rocky trail and on steep descents. Avoid riding in deer-hunting season (late fall), except on Sundays, when hunting isn't permitted.

Rescue index: Excellent.

Land status: County park.

RIDE 58 · Rocky Ridge County Park

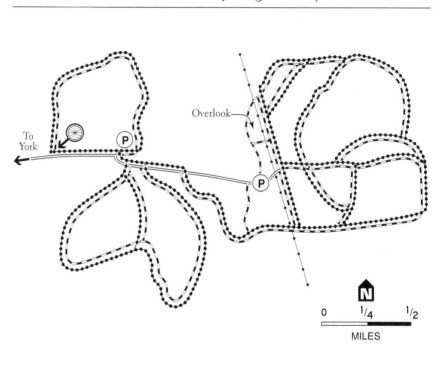

Maps: Call the park office at (717) 840-7440.

Finding the trail: To reach Rocky Ridge, take US 30 east of York to Mt. Zion Road (PA 24). Drive north for 1 mile, turn right onto Deininger Road, and go 1 mile to the park entrance. For the widest variety of trail options, park in the second lot, near the power lines. Trail 8 is on the north end of the lot and Trail 1 is on the east end.

Source of additional information:

York County Parks
400 Mundis Race Road
York, PA 17402
(717) 840-7440

Notes on the trail: For a good introductory ride, take Trail 1 (a gravel fire road) east out of the second parking lot (near the power lines) and continue straight onto Trail 2, a single-track that loops around and merges into Trail 1. At the picnic table and overlook, you can either continue on Trail 1 back to the lot or take Trail 4, a rock-strewn path that ends at the main paved park road. Turn right to

Views at Rocky Ridge
County Park include
the Three Mile Island
nuclear power plant.

return to your car. To do another loop, turn left and continue past Trail 6 on the left to Trail 5. Bear right at the fork and continue onto Trail 6; there's a long, steep descent (careful on the waterbars) followed by—you guessed it—a long climb back to the main road.

A wide gravel path—Trail 8—heads north from the second parking lot and leads to an overlook. That's the infamous Three Mile Island nuclear power plant in the distance. Alas, the dramatic view of the surrounding countryside and the Susquehanna River is marred by power lines.

RIDE 59 · Spring Valley County Park

AT A GLANCE

Length/configuration: 5-mile loop

Aerobic difficulty: Moderate to difficult; the climbs aren't long, but they're steep

Technical difficulty: Moderate; mostly buffed single-track with some rocks and roots along the creek

Scenery: A pretty wooded valley with views of farms and fields from the ridge

Special comments: Look for old hand-built stone walls while you ride. Codorus Creek is a stocked trout stream

PA

Spring Valley County Park is 868 acres of woods, fields, and a stream tucked in the rolling farmland of south-central Pennsylvania. Located in a small valley along the east branch of Codorus Creek, the park features a catch-and-release fishing pond, a trout stream, picnic tables and pavilions, and a small system of hiking trails that mountain bikers are invited to explore. It sounds like a perfect venue for beginning off-road cyclists, and it is—for novices who don't mind sections of rocky trail and short, steep climbs. Most intermediate and advanced riders will enjoy the combination of tight single-track and challenging riding. Though the five-mile trail system isn't long, riders can reconfigure loops by riding the trails in the opposite direction. Ride fast and hard, and you'll definitely get a good workout.

General location: York.

Elevation change: Up to several hundred feet, depending on how many times you make the climb to the ridge.

Season: Year-round.

Services: Rest rooms are located in the park. All other services are available in York.

Hazards: Use caution during deer-hunting season (late fall) or ride on Sundays, when hunting isn't allowed. Watch for horses on the trails.

Rescue index: Excellent; the park is small and surrounded by residences and farms.

Land status: County park.

Maps: Call or write York County Parks for a map (see below).

RIDE 59 · Spring Valley County Park

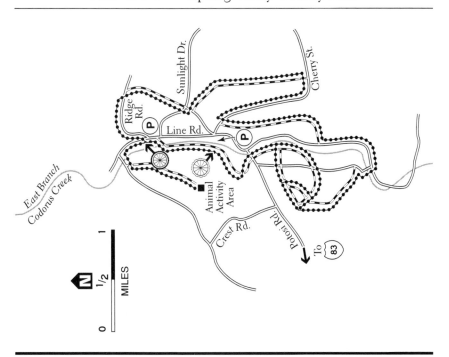

Finding the trail: To reach the park, take Exit 2 off I-81 (PA 216/Glen Rock) about 10 miles south of York. Go east 0.1 mile and turn right onto Potosi Road, drive 2.1 miles to Crest Road, and turn left to enter the park. Continue straight down the hill and turn left at the stop sign; park at the first lot (unshaded) or turn left onto the dirt road just past the lot and park in the next lot (shaded) next to Sunlight Drive. The main trail, across the creek from the parking areas, is accessible by footbridges.

Source of additional information:

York County Parks
400 Mundis Race Road
York, PA 17402
(717) 840-7440

Notes on the trail: Take the main trail north to where it crosses Potosi Road and then ride the road a short distance uphill; pick up the trail on the other side. There's a steep climb up the ridge (you'll cross Line Road); the reward is a small maze of single-track that can be ridden in several directions. The park trails, which get a lot more use from equestrians than mountain bikers, are well maintained and easy to follow.

Spring Valley
County Park features
a maze of single-track.

RIDE 60 · Kain Park

AT A GLANCE

Length/configuration: 12 miles of trails on 6 interconnected loops

Aerobic difficulty: Hard; many long hills, some of
which are steep

PA

Technical difficulty: Everything from wide, grassy fire roads to technical
single-track

Scenery: Woods, rolling countryside, and big lakes

Special comments: Tall pines along the lakes evoke the North Woods of
Maine; Trails may be closed to bikes after wet weather

Kain Park, better known to York riders as Lake Redman and Lake Williams, offers 12 miles of unpaved trails on 1,675 acres of woodlands surrounding the two lakes. Trails run the gamut from wide, grassy fire roads to twisty single-track loaded with tree roots and rocks. The combination of occasionally challenging trail conditions and very long, steep climbs puts this park in the intermediate category. First-time riders and folks looking for a place to do a relaxing, easy spin should go elsewhere.

That said, experienced off-road riders will love this place. The heavy traffic on South George Street and the sound of cars and trucks roaring by on I-83 disappear as you head into the woods. The tall pines that border most of the two drinking-water impoundments (Lake Redman is the upper lake; Lake Williams the lower) evoke a feeling of the Adirondacks or the North Woods of Maine.

Six trails, varying in length from 1.4 to 2.7 miles, can be ridden in a number of combinations. If you add them together and ride in both directions, you'll have no trouble devising a full day of riding. From the parking lot below the dam on South George Street, you can ride a five-mile loop around Lake Williams (Trails 2 and 4), ride Trail 1 (a two-mile loop), or ride them both. If you've got something left in your legs after that, find Trail 3 (1.4 miles), which leads to Trail 5 (1.8 miles) and Trail 6 (1.6 miles).

All of the trails feature good water views from the lake shore or through the trees. The upper part of Trail 3 passes through some high, wide fields, while Trails 2 and 4 offer a more remote feel. For even better views of the surrounding area, visit the observation towers, which are accessible from the parking lot on South George Street and on Trail 6, east of I-83. One thing is certain: York County mountain bikers are fortunate to have this excellent system of trails at their doorstep.

General location: York.

Elevation change: The woodlands surrounding the 2 lakes are quite hilly, so no matter what configuration you ride, expect to climb at least a few hundred feet.

Season: Year-round. Trails are often closed during and after wet weather; check the signs in the parking lots or call ahead.

Services: Fast-food restaurants and a motel are located a mile north of the park on Leader Heights Road. Rest rooms and a soft-drink vending machine are available at the Lake Redman boat-launch area (where Trails 3 and 5 start). All other services are available in York.

Hazards: Trail 1 is best ridden counterclockwise, but doing so makes the single-track descent extremely steep. Hunting is allowed in certain areas of the park after Labor Day; wear orange or ride on Sundays, when hunting isn't permitted. Traffic is very heavy on South George Street, which bisects the park. Watch out for horses, which are allowed on all the trails.

Rescue index: Excellent. The park is surrounded by suburbs, busy roads, and farms; many of the trails come close to or cross paved roads.

Land status: County park.

RIDE 60 · Kain Park

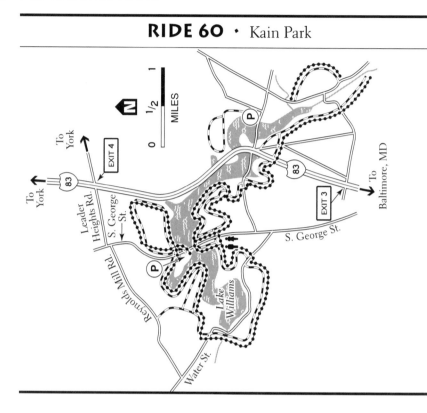

Maps: To get a trail map, call York County Parks at (717) 771-9440.

Finding the trail: The central place to begin a ride is the parking lot on South George Street, a mile south of Leader Heights Road on the right (Exit 4 west off I-83 just south of York) and directly below the dam. On your bike, backtrack north on South George Street a short distance past the bridge to the start of Trail 2 on the left (a gated fire road.) Across busy South George Street is the start of Trail 1; at this point it's a narrow single-track. Another option is to ride your bike south from the parking lot and up the hill to Trail 4 on the right and Trail 3 on the left (at the top of the steep set of railroad-tie steps). Trail 3 leads to Trails 5 and 6. If the lot on South George Street is full, drive south to the small town of Jacobus and turn left onto Church Street; it's 0.6 miles to the Lake Redman boat-launch area. From here you can get on Trail 3, which starts along the lake shore, to the left of the boat launch and rest rooms. You can reach Trails 5 and 6 by riding in the other direction (toward I-83).

Source of additional information:

York County Parks
400 Mundis Race Road
York, PA 17402
(717) 771-9440

Late-afternoon light
illuminates a ridge
at Kain Park.

Notes on the trail: All trails are marked. Trail 1, as noted above, should be ridden counterclockwise. That way you go down, not up, an extremely steep and technical single-track (built in 1996 by a local BMX club with members who no doubt think the trail is anything but steep and technical). The section of Trail 4 that parallels Water Street is best ridden in an east-west direction (that is, away from South George Street). If you're riding a counterclockwise loop around Lake Williams, you can ride on paved Water Street to avoid the steep hills on Trail 4; it's a very scenic, low-traffic section of blacktop. Then pick up Trail 4 just past the entrance to the boat-launch area (both are on the left) to continue the lake loop ride.

All of the trails have long and steep sections, as well as muddy spots near the lake shore (and everywhere after wet weather).

RIDE 61 · York County Heritage Rail Trail

AT A GLANCE

Length/configuration: 20-mile out-and-back (10 miles each way)

Aerobic difficulty: Easy

Technical difficulty: Easy

Scenery: Woods, fields, small Pennsylvania villages, and old mills

Special comments: Connects with the Northern Central Railroad Trail in Maryland (Ride 26)

PA

Meandering north from the Mason-Dixon Line, which separates Pennsylvania and Maryland, the York County Heritage Rail Trail follows ten miles of tracks belonging to the recently revived Northern Central Railway. While the virtually flat, ten-foot-wide, crushed-stone trail is adjacent to the railroad bed, cyclists needn't worry about getting run down by a train. Today the railway only runs scenic excursions, and the diesel trains chug by at a modest ten miles an hour.

And the scenery? Unlike the contiguous Northern Central Railroad Trail to the south—which rarely parallels any paved roads and has more of a wilderness ambience—this trail passes through a landscape that shows the handiwork of hundreds of years of human habitation: farms, old mills, stone walls, foundations of long-forgotten factories, and other relics of nineteenth- and twentieth-century America. The trail also follows the South Branch of Codorus Creek, so there are ample views of woods and water.

In addition, the trail passes through a few small villages that dot the rolling piedmont of Pennsylvania. New Freedom is a former manufacturing center and railroad town, and Glen Rock was a center for the milling industry at the turn of the century and the site of a carriage works and a distillery. Today, cyclists can stop by Mamma's Pizza and Subs, at the trail's intersection with Main Street, for a soft ice cream or cold drink. The old Glen Rock Flour Mill, a bit farther north along the trail, is now an inn and restaurant.

Hanover Junction, the northern terminus of the trail (which is scheduled to be continued north another 12 miles to York), once had two hotels and a small rail yard. Abraham Lincoln, on his way to Gettysburg in 1863 to deliver his famous address, changed trains at the depot, which still stands and will eventually be restored. In 1865 the Lincoln funeral train passed this way en route north.

RIDE 61 · York County Heritage Rail Trail

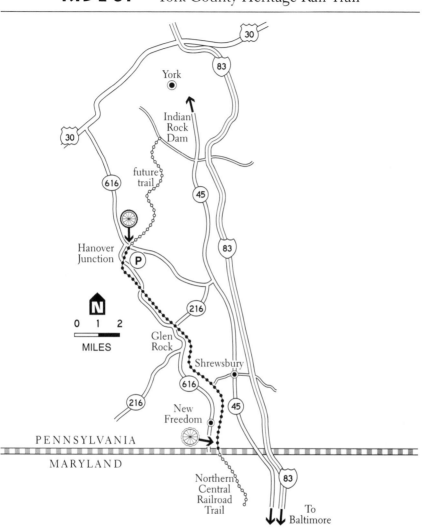

General location: York.

Elevation change: Negligible.

Season: Year-round.

Services: Food and drink are available at small towns along the trail. All other services are available in York.

Hazards: Watch for traffic at street crossings.

Rescue index: Excellent. The trail passes towns, private residences, farms, and paved roads.

The York County
Heritage Rail Trail is
flat, wide, easy, and scenic.

Land status: County park.

Maps: For a trail map, call York County Parks at (717) 840-7440.

Finding the trail: From I-83 south of York, take Exit 3 (PA 214 West/Logan-ville). Turn left on Main Street, go half a mile to PA 214, and turn right. Follow serpentine PA 214 (it's well marked) for about 5 miles and turn left on PA 616 south. The parking lot for the trail's northern terminus is about a half-mile on the left.

Other parking lots are located in Shrewsbury (take Exit 1 from I-83 and go west on PA 851 for 2 miles) and New Freedom (take Exit 1 from I-83 and go west on PA 851 to Railroad Borough; then turn left onto PA 616 south and continue for 1.5 miles to New Freedom; park at Front and Franklin Streets, at the old train station).

Sources of additional information:

York County Heritage Rail Trail
RD 8, Box 438A
York, PA 17403
(717) 428-2586

York County Parks
400 Mundis Race Road
York, PA 17402
(717) 840-7440

Notes on the trail: Rest rooms are located at Hanover Junction, Railroad (west of Shrewsbury), and New Freedom. At the Maryland state line, the trail becomes the Northern Central Railroad Trail and continues south for another 20 miles to Cockeysville, a suburb north of Baltimore.

RIDE 62 · Stony Creek Wilderness Railroad Bed Trail

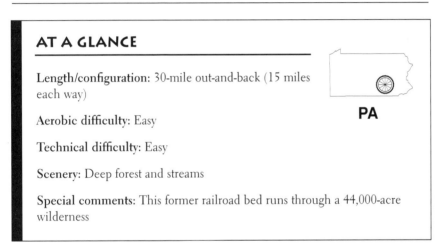

AT A GLANCE

Length/configuration: 30-mile out-and-back (15 miles each way)

Aerobic difficulty: Easy

Technical difficulty: Easy

Scenery: Deep forest and streams

Special comments: This former railroad bed runs through a 44,000-acre wilderness

PA

Stony Creek flows through an uninhabited, 24-mile forested valley only a few miles north of thriving Harrisburg, the capital of Pennsylvania. It's the largest roadless track in southern Pennsylvania. With the exception of small grassy openings maintained to provide food for deer and turkey, the entire valley is forested.

Running through the heart of the valley is a 15-mile former railroad bed that has been transformed into a well-maintained, ten-foot-wide, dirt and gravel path for hikers, mountain bikers, equestrians, and, in winter, cross-country skiers and snowmobilers. It's flat and follows a straight-line route through the valley. The old railroad right-of-way is extremely popular, especially on weekends in warm weather. The trail provides glimpses of fast-flowing Stony Creek and wildlife such as deer, turkey, ruffed grouse, pileated woodpeckers, scarlet tanagers, rose-breasted grosbeaks, ravens, broad-winged hawks, and great horned owls. Black bears have also returned to the valley; the best time to spot one is midsummer, when the wild blueberries in the clearings are ripe. In June, the oak and hemlock forest comes alive with mountain laurel blossoms.

RIDE 62 · Stony Creek Wilderness Railroad Bed Trail

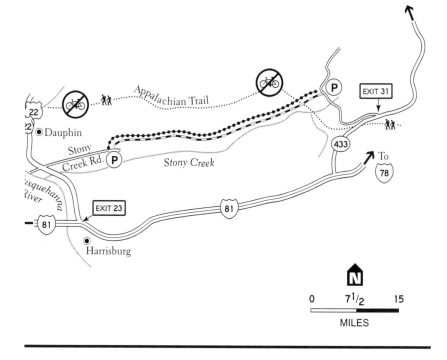

The ideal place to begin an out-and-back along the creek is at the western terminus. That way you can ride as far as you like—up to 15 miles to the eastern end of the trail. Turn around for the return trip, which is slightly downhill.

General location: Harrisburg.

Elevation change: Negligible.

Season: Spring, summer, and fall.

Services: Gas and food are available in Dauphin. All other services are available in Harrisburg.

Hazards: This trail is located in a popular hunting area. From early October through January and in May, wear fluorescent orange or ride on Sundays, when hunting isn't permitted.

Rescue index: Not good; this is a 44,000-acre wilderness. But it's also a popular trail, so except in extremely cold or inclement weather, other trail users can be flagged down if necessary.

Land status: Pennsylvania Game Commission.

Stony Creek Wilderness Railroad Bed Trail leads mountain bikers into a 44,000-acre wilderness.

Maps: Indiantown Gap, Grantville, Enders, Halifax, and Tower City USGS 7.5 minute quads cover the majority of the Stony Creek Wilderness.

Finding the trail: The western end of the wilderness is the most accessible. Take I-81 to Harrisburg and get off at Exit 23, US 22/322 North. At the village of Dauphin (where the four-lane road ends), take PA 225 north into Dauphin. Turn right onto Stony Creek Road, drive 6.5 miles to the gate, and park in the area on the right. The trail starts beyond the gate.

Source of additional information:

Pennsylvania Game Commission
2001 Elmerton Avenue
Harrisburg, PA 17110-9797
(717) 787-4250

Notes on the trail: Most visitors—many of whom are families out for a stroll or a pleasant spin on their bikes—stick within a few miles of the trail at either end of the valley. No fires or overnight camping are allowed in the wilderness, except for primitive camping within 200 feet of the Appalachian Trail (1-night limit per site). The Appalachian Trail crosses the railroad grade near its eastern terminus. (Remember, it does not allow bikes.)

RIDE 63 · Conewago Recreational Trail

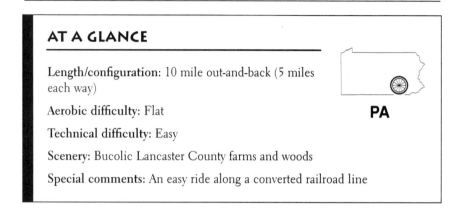

AT A GLANCE

Length/configuration: 10 mile out-and-back (5 miles each way)

Aerobic difficulty: Flat

Technical difficulty: Easy

Scenery: Bucolic Lancaster County farms and woods

Special comments: An easy ride along a converted railroad line

PA

This former stretch of the Cornwall & Lebanon Railroad along Conewago Creek has been converted to a linear park that's perfect for biking, hiking, horseback riding, and cross-country skiing. Located between PA 230 and the

RIDE 63 · Conewago Recreational Trail

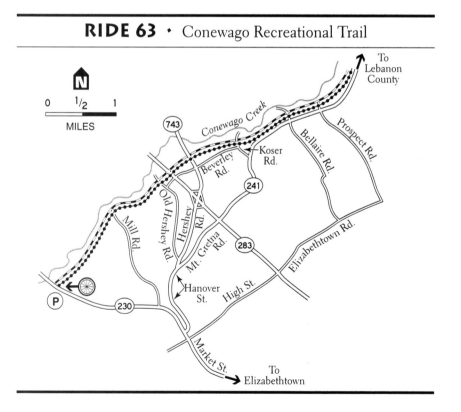

The Conewago Recreational Trail is an easy 5-mile (one-way) ride along a converted railroad line in Lancaster County.

Lebanon County line, the five-mile trail passes through scenic woods, farms, and fields. If there's a problem with the trail, it's that it's too short. (Then again, maybe not; see Notes on the Trail.)

Before Lancaster County purchased it in 1979, the route had been operated by the Cornwall & Lebanon Railroad since 1883. By 1910, eight passenger trains a day used the route. Passengers could make connections to anywhere in the country; in fact, a customer boarding a train at 10:50 a.m. could be in New York City before 5 p.m. As the interstate highway system expanded after World War II, train service along the rails steadily declined. After Hurricane Agnes struck in 1972, the tracks were abandoned. Now the old right-of-way is a valuable recreational resource for this part of southern Pennsylvania.

General location: Harrisburg.

Elevation change: None.

Season: Year-round.

Services: Restaurants, gas, camping, and motels are available in Elizabethtown. All other services are available in Harrisburg.

Hazards: Although not permitted on the long, narrow park, hunting may be permitted on private property adjacent to the trail; use caution in the late fall and winter. Watch for traffic where the trail crosses paved roads.

Rescue index: Excellent.

Land status: County park.

Maps: A map is available at the trailhead on PA 230.

Finding the trail: The best place to start a ride along the old right-of-way is 1 mile northwest of Elizabethtown along PA 230. A parking lot, rest rooms, and a pay phone are at the trailhead. The 66-foot-wide route is easy to follow, and each half-mile is clearly marked.

Source of additional information:

Lancaster County Department of Parks and Recreation
1050 Rockford Road
Lancaster, PA 17602
(717) 299-8215

Notes on the trail: Don't wander off the path; it's private property on both sides. The trail gets a bit more scenic and narrows to single-track above the twin overpasses of US 283, about halfway through the ride. The trail officially ends at the county line, though the old railroad right-of-way continues east past it—and gets lots of use, as the many knobby-tire tracks attest. Although there weren't any "no trespassing" signs posted when I rode the trail (hmm . . .), the adventurous biker should be cautious since much of the land surrounding this rail-trail is private property (and hunting grounds).

JIM THORPE, PENNSYLVANIA

In the western Pocono Mountains of Pennsylvania, the Lehigh River cuts a spectacular 1,000-foot-deep gorge through tabletop mountains and thousands of acres of state park and game lands. To take advantage of 30 miles of abandoned railroad grade along the river, Pennsylvania created Lehigh Gorge State Park, 6,000 acres of spectacular parkland that stretches south from an Army Corps of Engineers dam near Wilkes Barre to a town with the unlikely name of Jim Thorpe. This combination of a scenic river gorge, state game lands, and a restored Victorian-era village results in one of the best mountain biking destinations in the East.

The area's rich history is also an attraction, especially to mountain bikers. This is coal country, and many of the rail lines used to haul coal from mines to river ports are now converted trails that make for easy pedaling. In the mid-nineteenth century, industry was booming and, as the transportation hub of the region, so were the towns of Mauch Chunk and East Mauch Chunk (today's Jim Thorpe). Canal, railroad, and river traffic converged in the towns. Millionaires built mansions, hotels, an opera house, and churches in fine Victorian style on the hillsides overlooking the Lehigh River. When the boom ended later in the century, the towns and the mountainous region around them became a popular summer resort known as the Switzerland of America.

The Great Depression of the 1930s clinched the area's decline. Towns fell into disrepair, unemployment took its toll, and young people fled the region. In the early 1950s, the local newspaper started an economic development fund and urged citizens to contribute a nickel a week. In 1954, the communities were rewarded for their spunk when the widow of Jim Thorpe, the hero of the 1912 Stockholm Olympic Games (who died a pauper in a Philadelphia hospital in 1953), agreed to let the two towns merge under the great athlete's name and build a monument and mausoleum for him.

The 1980s marked the beginning of an era of prosperity and restoration for the handsome town. Tourism is now big business. Shops, restaurants, bed-and-breakfasts, and lots of late-model cars line the streets of Jim Thorpe. There are also plenty of mountain bikes, and no wonder. With Lehigh Gorge State Park at its doorstep and miles of hiking trails winding through the town to the overlooks nearby, Jim Thorpe was made for fat-tired bikes. The trails, converted from old railroad rights-of-way, follow two percent grades, making for nearly effortless riding. Thousands of acres of state game lands extend the variety of mountain biking from the town.

Since 1986, Jim Thorpe has hosted Mountain Bike Weekend, held every June in nearby Mauch Chunk Lake Park. Bill Drumbore and Galen Van Dine, local riders who help organize the event, discovered mountain biking when it was virtually unheard of in the East. (Drumbore built his first mountain bike in a garage using old ten-speed and BMX parts. It's now stored in the basement of Hotel Switzerland in Jim Thorpe and displayed in the bar during Mountain Bike Weekend.) Every year Drumbore and Van Dine help organize rides for the hundreds of mountain bikers who converge on the town for camaraderie and great cycling. They also helped with the rides that follow.

Jim Thorpe is between Allentown and Scranton, off the Northeast Extension of the Pennsylvania Turnpike (about an hour-and-a-half drive from Philadelphia). From New York City, take Interstate 80 east to PA 209 south, about a three-hour drive.

RIDE 64 · Lehigh Gorge State Park

AT A GLANCE

Length/configuration: 60-mile out-and-back (30 miles each way)

Aerobic difficulty: Easy

Technical difficulty: Easy

Scenery: Spectacular, bottom-up view of a huge river gorge

Special comments: Check out the abandoned railroad tunnel near the first bridge that crosses the river

PA

Located 100 miles northwest of Philadelphia, Jim Thorpe is one of the most popular mountain bike venues in the East. Nestled among the slopes of the western Pocono Mountains, this scenic village of restored Victorian-era townhouses, Italianate mansions, and an opera house offers excellent off-road trails by day and the creature comforts of bed-and-breakfasts, chi-chi restaurants, and trendy shops at night. It's any biker's reward for clean living.

In addition to playing host to Mountain Bike Weekend each June, Jim Thorpe is the southern gateway to Lehigh Gorge State Park, which hugs the Lehigh River for 30 meandering miles of fast-flowing river, dramatic cliffs, woods, and

RIDE 64 • Lehigh Gorge State Park

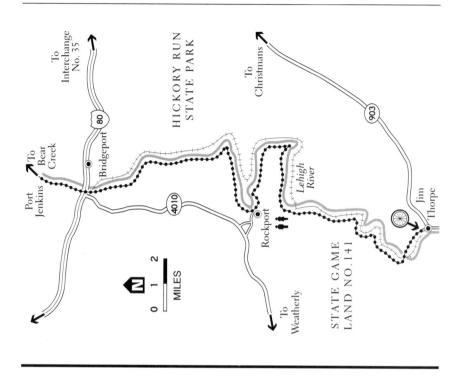

the ruins of nineteenth-century industry. A flat, easy trail follows the remains of the Lehigh Canal towpath and abandoned railroad grades. Cyclists are treated to views of ruined bridges, old tunnels, spectacular rock outcroppings, waterfalls, and kayakers and rafters coming around a broad bend in the river. The river is almost always in sight, coursing over rocks and rapids.

This ride emphasizes scenery, not bike handling skills or endurance. As you ride north, check out the abandoned railroad tunnel adjacent to the first bridge crossing over the river. At many points along the way you can see the remains of the old canal that parallels the river. Look up and you'll be treated to the sight of waterfalls plunging into the river through siltstone and sandstone rock formations.

General location: Jim Thorpe.

Elevation change: Negligible.

Season: Year-round.

Services: Mountain bikes can be rented at Blue Mountain Sports & Wear. All other services are available in Jim Thorpe.

Hazards: Hunting is allowed in the park in late fall, so wear orange or ride on Sundays, when hunting isn't permitted. Watch for trains at rail crossings.

Rescue index: Poor. The trail follows a deep gorge surrounded by state game lands, so access is limited to park entrances.

Land status: State park.

Maps: Available at Blue Mountain Sports & Wear and the tourist bureau in Jim Thorpe.

Finding the trail: Jim Thorpe, located between Allentown and Scranton, is about a 90-minute drive from Philadelphia. Take the Northeast Extension of the Pennsylvania Turnpike to Exit 34 and follow US 209 south to Jim Thorpe. In town, turn right onto PA 903, which crosses the Lehigh River. Go three blocks to the stop sign, continue straight across PA 903, and go down the hill to Coalport Road and the park entrance. The trail starts on Coalport Road on the left at the Glen Onoko access area. Rest rooms are located along the trail at Glen Onoko and Rockport (about 7 miles).

Sources of additional information:

Lehigh Gorge State Park
RD 2, Box 56
Weatherly, PA 18255-9512
(717) 427-5000

Carbon County Tourist Promotion Agency
P.O. Box 90, Railroad Station
Jim Thorpe, PA 18229
(717) 325-3673 or (888) JIM-THORPE

Blue Mountain Sports & Wear
34 Susquehanna Street
Jim Thorpe, PA 18229
(800) 599-4421

Notes on the trail: While most folks start an out-and-back from Jim Thorpe, consider these options. Set up a shuttle by leaving a car in Rockport, about 7 miles upriver. Or contact Blue Mountain Sports & Wear, Jim Thorpe's mountain bike outfitter, for information on the shuttle service to Rockport and White Haven that lets you ride downhill to Jim Thorpe.

RIDE 65 · Switchback Trail

AT A GLANCE

Length/configuration: 11-mile loop

Aerobic difficulty: Easy to moderate

PA

Technical difficulty: Moderate single-track and a steep descent on the Back Track; the rest is easy

Scenery: Woods, views of Lehigh River Gorge, a babbling brook, and an old house in Jim Thorpe

Special comments: Ride the Back Track into Jim Thorpe to avoid a huge climb

Switchback Trail is the old right-of-way of one of America's first railroads, the gravity railway between old Mauch Chunk (part of Jim Thorpe today) and the coal mines of Summit Hill. Cars full of coal rolled to waiting barges in Jim Thorpe (the Down Track), and mules pulled the empty cars up a steep incline where they rolled back to the mines (the Back Track). Later, steam power replaced the mules. The gravity railroad began operation in 1828 and ran until 1933. After the Civil War and the decline of the canal system the railroad fed, the system was converted into a passenger ride, foreshadowing the development of the roller coaster. It was a major national tourist attraction in the last half of the nineteenth century.

Today this venerable route is best enjoyed on a mountain bike, which lets fat-tired cyclists with a yen for adventurous riding explore the hills surrounding Jim Thorpe. The 11-mile loop for intermediate mountain bikers (and adventurous beginners who don't mind a little walking) features forest trails, great views of Lehigh River Gorge, a ramble through old Jim Thorpe, and a spin through a thick rhododendron and hemlock forest along a fast-flowing mountain brook. Sound too good to be true? That's not all. With only two percent grades along most of the ride, there are no steep climbs.

General location: Jim Thorpe.

Elevation change: About 600'.

Season: Year-round.

Services: Camping is available at Mauch Chunk Lake Park. Mountain bikes can be rented at Blue Mountain Sports & Wear. All other services are available in Jim Thorpe.

RIDE 65 · The Switchback Trail

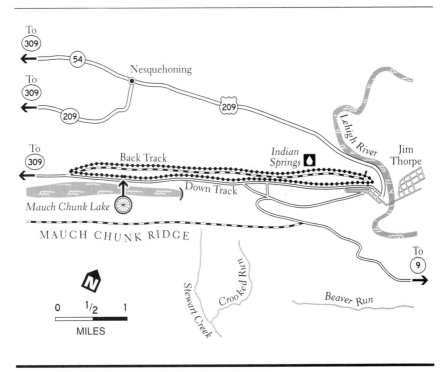

Hazards: Novice riders may want to walk the steep, rocky descent from the Back Track into Jim Thorpe.

Rescue index: Good. The Back Track follows a ridge away from roads. The rest of the loop is either in town or parallels a paved road.

Land status: County park.

Maps: Blue Mountain Sports & Wear and the tourist bureau in town carry maps.

Finding the trail: Jim Thorpe, between Allentown and Scranton, is about a 90-minute drive from Philadelphia. Take the Northeast Extension of the Pennsylvania Turnpike to Exit 34 and follow US 209 south to Jim Thorpe. Mauch Chunk Lake Park, a good starting place for this ride, is 3 miles west of Jim Thorpe on US 209 (the Lentz Trail Highway). Park at the office or any other parking lot in Mauch Chunk Lake Park. Pedal out the main entrance of the park, turn left on US 209, and go a half-mile to where the Back Track intersects the road on the right. The narrow trail follows a wooded ridge that will test your bike handling skills as you encounter downed tree limbs, rocks, old railroad ties, and the other impediments mountain bikers love to overcome.

Sources of additional information:

Mauch Chunk Lake Park
P.O. Box 7
Jim Thorpe, PA 18229
(717) 325-3669

Carbon County Tourist Promotion Agency
P.O. Box 90, Railroad Station
Jim Thorpe, PA 18229
(717) 325-3673 or (888) JIM-THORPE

Blue Mountain Sports & Wear
34 Susquehanna Street
Jim Thorpe, PA 18229
(800) 599-4421

Notes on the trail: On the Back Track, keep an eye out for a short turnoff on the left that leads to the Point, a rock outcropping with an unobstructed view north of Lehigh River Gorge where hawks soar at eye level. Next, get ready for the steep, rocky descent into town that marks the final section of the Back Track. The return to the park along the Down Track is an easy, 2% uphill grade along a scenic stream in the woods. Watch out for wildlife, like the young black bear I spotted (very briefly) rambling along the path around dusk.

To start the loop in Jim Thorpe, ride your bike up Broadway, turn right at the opera house, and bear left at the top of the hill onto a wooded trail — the Down Track of the Switchback Trail leading to Mauch Chunk Lake Park. A half-mile past the park entrance, the Down Track intersects with the Back Track; turn right for the return leg to Jim Thorpe.

RIDE 66 · Mauch Chunk Ridge

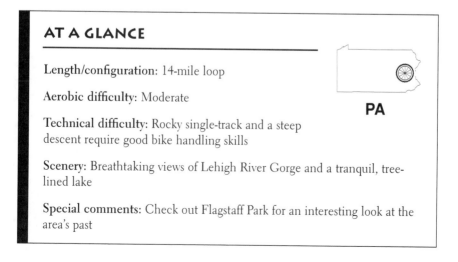

AT A GLANCE

Length/configuration: 14-mile loop

Aerobic difficulty: Moderate

PA

Technical difficulty: Rocky single-track and a steep descent require good bike handling skills

Scenery: Breathtaking views of Lehigh River Gorge and a tranquil, tree-lined lake

Special comments: Check out Flagstaff Park for an interesting look at the area's past

RIDE 66 · Mauch Chunk Ridge

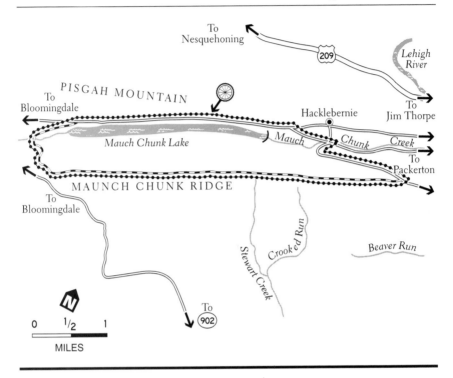

To
Nesquehoning

209

Lehigh
River

PISGAH MOUNTAIN

To
Bloomingdale

Hacklebernie

To
Jim Thorpe

Mauch Chunk Lake

Mauch *Chunk* *Creek*

To
Packerton

MAUNCH CHUNK RIDGE

To
Bloomingdale

Stewart Creek

Crooked Run

Beaver Run

To
902

0   1/2   1

MILES

This 14-mile loop is a great example of the tremendous diversity of off-road riding Jim Thorpe offers. For example, the view of Lehigh River Gorge and Jim Thorpe from Flagstaff Park spans a whopping 65 miles. The park, containing a restaurant, a nightclub, and a view to die for, was known as the Ballroom of the Clouds during the swing era of the 1930s and 1940s and was home base for the Dorsey Brothers Band. Sound too civilized for a mountain bike ride? Relax—the next section of trail on the ride features bone-jarring single-track followed by fast double-track along a ridge and a steep descent to a huge lake.

The ride starts with an easy cruise on Switchback Trail (Ride 65) and climbs one and a half miles to the top of Mauch Chunk Ridge and Flagstaff Park. Next is two miles of rough single-track on a narrow, rocky trail. Then you follow the ridge on an old dirt road and make a right for a steep descent along a powerline cut to Shoreline Trail. Most of the ride on the ridge is through second-growth hardwood forest. After the descent, follow the wooded shoreline of Mauch Chunk Lake. This trail twists through evergreen forests and has views of the lake and Mauch Chunk Ridge. Look for the bird sanctuary and observer's shack on the marshy lake shore. In addition to being good shelter in a storm, the shack offers an excellent view of the lake, and the wetlands teem with birds. Keep an eye peeled for wildlife (including black bear) while you're riding.

General location: Jim Thorpe.

Elevation change: About 450'.

Season: In the summer you can swim at the lake after the ride. In the fall, the spectacular foliage is mirrored on the lake. Spring can be very muddy, especially along the lake. Expect snow between November and March. Avoid riding in hunting season (late fall), except on Sundays, when hunting is not permitted.

Services: Seasonal camping is available at Mauch Chunk Lake Park. Mountain bikes can be rented at Blue Mountain Sports & Wear. All other services are available in Jim Thorpe.

Hazards: Watch for cars on the paved road up to Mauch Chunk Ridge. The drop off the ridge at the power lines is very steep and rocky.

Rescue index: Good. The trail is never more than a couple of miles from paved roads. Mauch Chunk Lake Park is staffed from April through October.

Land status: The trail along Mauch Chunk Ridge is on private property; obtain permission to ride from Flagstaff Park (just past the turnoff for the single-track). Mauch Chunk Lake Park is owned by the Carbon County Parks and Recreation Commission.

Maps: Maps are available at Blue Mountain Sports & Wear in Jim Thorpe. The USGS 7.5 minute quad is Nesquehoning.

Finding the trail: Jim Thorpe, between Allentown and Scranton, is about a 90-minute drive from Philadelphia. Take the Northeast Extension of the Pennsylvania Turnpike to Exit 34 and follow US 209 south to Jim Thorpe. Mauch Chunk Lake Park is 3 miles from Jim Thorpe on PA 209 (the Lentz Trail Highway). Park at the office or at any of the other parking lots. Switchback Trail is located at the park entrance.

Sources of additional information:

Mauch Chunk Lake Park
P.O. Box 7
Jim Thorpe, PA 18229
(717) 325-3669

Blue Mountain Sports & Wear
34 Susquehanna Street
Jim Thorpe, PA 18229
(717) 325-4421 or (800) 599-4421

Notes on the trail: The ride starts on Switchback Trail, which crosses PA 209 at the entrance to Mauch Chunk Lake Park. Follow the trail past the dam, where it bears left. At the intersection with the paved road, turn right and climb 1.5 miles to the ridge top; the trailhead is on the right. Continue a short distance on the road to Flagstaff Park, catch the view, and get permission to ride the ridge trail.

Double back to the single-track (now on the left). After about 2 miles, the trail becomes a grassy road for another 3 miles. Turn right at the T intersection. At the power line, turn right and descend. Look for the single-track to the left that goes into the woods (about two-thirds of the way down). In the woods, follow the path over two wooden bridges and emerge in a field. Turn right and keep the woods to your right as you head toward the lake. Return to the start on Shoreline Trail. Once you arrive at the lake, Shoreline Trail is easy to find.

RIDE 67 · Weekend Warrior

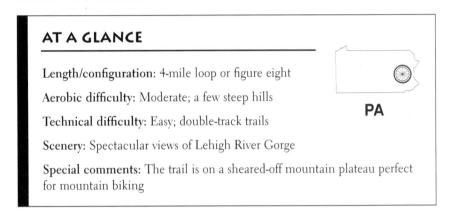

AT A GLANCE

Length/configuration: 4-mile loop or figure eight

Aerobic difficulty: Moderate; a few steep hills

Technical difficulty: Easy; double-track trails

Scenery: Spectacular views of Lehigh River Gorge

Special comments: The trail is on a sheared-off mountain plateau perfect for mountain biking

PA

The western Poconos were sheared by glaciers, making the tops smooth and rolling—perfect for mountain biking. This four-mile ride, which can be ridden as a loop or a figure eight, follows double-track on top of Broad Mountain. The road passes through mixed hardwood forests (mostly oak with some maple and gray birch) interspersed with open fields. The mountain borders Lehigh River Gorge, providing different views of the river and mountains, as well as hawks soaring at eye level.

The optional ride to the first overlook goes down a rocky power-line cut; the view of the gorge (almost 1,000 feet deep) makes it worth the return climb. The second overlook is even better: Jim Thorpe, with Flagstaff Park towering over it, straddles both sides of the river flowing deep inside the gorge below.

General location: Jim Thorpe.

Elevation change: About 600'. The optional, out-and-back drop down the power line to the first overlook adds about 350'.

Season: Summer and fall are the best seasons to ride this loop. The mountaintop is relatively cool in the summer, and the fall colors are spectacular (early and mid-October). Spring can be very muddy, and snow is possible from November through March. These are state game lands, so avoid riding during fall hunting season (or ride on Sundays when hunting is not permitted).

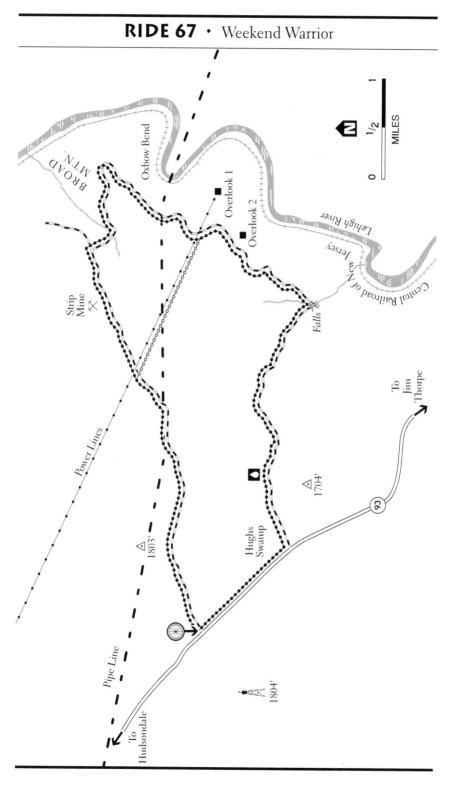

Services: Mountain bikes can be rented at Blue Mountain Sports & Wear. All other services are available in Jim Thorpe.

Hazards: The descent to the first (optional) overlook is steep and rocky. Watch for heavy truck and car traffic on PA 93 on the last mile of the ride.

Rescue index: Poor. PA 93 is the loop's only traffic-bearing road. There are no residences on the ride. The trail's farthest distance from PA 93 is about 5 miles.

Land status: State game lands.

Maps: Available at Blue Mountain Sports & Wear in Jim Thorpe. The USGS 7.5 minute quads are Christmans and Weatherly.

Finding the trail: Jim Thorpe, between Allentown and Scranton, is about a 90-minute drive from Philadelphia. Take the Northeast Extension of the Pennsylvania Turnpike to Exit 34 and follow US 209 south to Jim Thorpe. Drive north on PA 209 for 2 miles to the first traffic light (PA 93) and turn right. Go approximately 3 miles and park in the second lot on the right near the gate. The fire road beyond the gate starts the ride.

Sources of additional information:

Carbon County Tourist Promotion Agency
P.O. Box 90, Railroad Station
Jim Thorpe, PA 18229
(717) 325-3673

Blue Mountain Sports & Wear
34 Susquehanna Street
Jim Thorpe, PA 18229
(717) 325-4421 and (800) 599-4421

Notes on the trail: The recommended way to ride this loop is in a figure eight. From the second pulloff on PA 93, ride beyond the gate on the fire road. After 2.5 miles, turn right and follow the power lines. At the intersection a mile later, go straight for the descent to the first overlook. Return to this intersection from the overlook and turn right. (It will be a left if you come down the power lines.) Follow this loop for 2.5 miles back to the first intersection. Turn left and retrace the ride along the power lines; at the intersection where you went straight to the overlook, turn right.

 After a half-mile there is a **T** intersection; turn left to reach the second overlook. Double back to the **T** intersection and go straight. Follow the road for 3 miles (through 2 stream crossings and a steep climb) to the next intersection; continue straight. At the gate in the parking lot on PA 93, turn right and ride 1 mile along the road to your car.

RIDE 68 · Summer's Loop

AT A GLANCE

Length/configuration: 15-mile loop

Aerobic difficulty: Moderate, with a few short, steep climbs

Technical difficulty: Creek crossings and rough surfaces require good bike handling skills

Scenery: Deep forests and views of Lehigh River Gorge

Special comments: Come here for views most visitors to the area never see

PA

This 15-mile loop on state game land is characterized by deep forests, making it a nice ride on hot days. Great views of Lehigh River Gorge, especially in the fall, are an added attraction. During mid-June, the mountain laurel is in full bloom. Watch for wildlife, including deer, black bear, and birds.

While this ride is entirely on forest roads, sections of steep descents and climbs on rutted surfaces make it challenging, especially if they're ridden fast. After starting on pavement, the trail changes to dirt with some stretches of coarse gravel. On the return leg, a creek crossing is followed by a hard-pack uphill. Midway through the ride, the trail passes over Rockport Tunnel, an active railroad tunnel through the mountain. The view of Lehigh River Gorge is one of the best—and one few visitors to the area ever see. A series of steep, short climbs ends the ride.

General location: Jim Thorpe.

Elevation change: About 600'.

Season: Summer and fall are best. The mountain is usually covered with snow in winter and deep mud from melting snow in early spring.

Services: All services are available in Jim Thorpe. Mountain bikes can be rented at Blue Mountain Sports & Wear.

Hazards: The biggest danger is running out of water. Watch for snakes in warm weather and avoid riding during fall hunting season (or ride on Sundays when hunting is permitted).Use care on the long descents.

Rescue index: Poor. The small private community of Christmansville is near the start of the ride. If you've begun the descent toward Drake's Creek and need help, keep going in that direction toward your car.

Land status: State game lands.

RIDE 68 · Summer's Loop

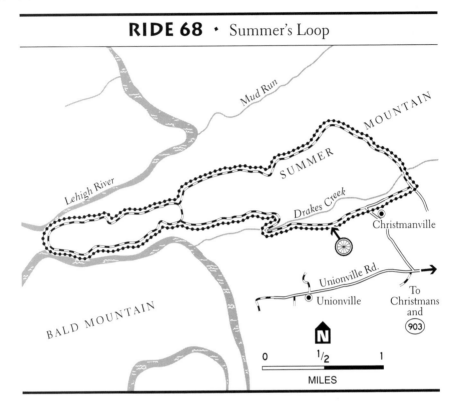

Maps: The USGS 7.5 minute quad is Christmans.

Finding the trail: Jim Thorpe, between Allentown and Scranton, is about a 90-minute drive from Philadelphia. Take the Northeast Extension of the Pennsylvania Turnpike to Exit 34 and follow US 209 south to Jim Thorpe. Drive north from Jim Thorpe on PA 903 for 10.5 miles. At the sign for Penn Forest Garage (directly across from Smith's Hardware Store), turn left onto Unionville Road. Follow this road (don't turn off on side roads) for 2.5 miles to a power line and turn right onto Schoolhouse Road. Continue to the Y intersection and take the dirt road to the left. After about a half-mile, look for a small open area by the power line; park there. To start the ride, pedal back out the dirt road to the Y intersection and go straight. Follow the road to another Y intersection. Look for a house on the corner and a gate across the road to the left. Take the left past the gate and ride uphill. Go straight until the road turns to dirt at a Y intersection. Turn right to begin the loop.

Source of additional information:

Blue Mountain Sports & Wear
34 Susquehanna Street
Jim Thorpe, PA 18229
(717) 325-4421 or (800) 599-4421

Notes on the trail: Pennsylvania state game lands provide a lifetime of mountain biking opportunities, but they offer nothing in the way of road signs, trail signs, blazes, or anything else to help riders find their way around. Carry a topo map and a compass, and give yourself enough time to explore. Don't forget your spirit of adventure.

PHILADELPHIA, PENNSYLVANIA

The City of Brotherly Love isn't just home to the Liberty Bell and great cheese steak subs. It also offers plenty for fat-tire fanatics. My survey of great Philly riding starts in Fairmount Park, the largest municipal park in the country. An easy, eight-mile ramble starts behind the Philadelphia Museum of Art (immortalized in the *Rocky* movies) and features river views, a statue by Frederic Remington, Boathouse Row, and acres of manicured park. The trails in Fairmount Park also link to Schuylkill Trail, an easy, 21.5-mile river trail that follows the eponymous river to another great mountain bike destination, Valley Forge. Get a history lesson as you pedal your bike past the aging industrial towns of Manayunk, Conshohocken, and Norristown along the Schuylkill River.

At Valley Forge, where George Washington and his army wintered in 1777–78, fat-tired cyclists come to ride a rolling, 6.5-mile paved trail and get another history lesson. The ragtag American army was transformed into a real fighting force here, emerging in June 1778 to pursue British General Howe's forces into New Jersey. Today, Valley Forge is an oasis of green fields and woods surrounded by superhighways, high rises, and suburban sprawl.

More great trails can be found in state and county parks. Ridley Creek State Park has an easy, five-mile paved trail, and Tyler State Park (north of town) boasts a system of hilly paved trails, rolling fields and woods, and a covered bridge. To the south, Nottingham County Park has a system of easy dirt trails that wind through outcroppings of serpentine stone.

West of Philadelphia, hammerheads like getting hammered on 40 miles of technical single-track at French Creek State Park, while more sedate riding is the hallmark of the easy multiuse trails in Hibernia County Park. Outside Reading, Blue Marsh Lake has earned a national reputation for its fun and scenic single-track, which follows the shoreline of the huge lake.

RIDE 69 · Fairmount Park—Kelly and West River Drives

AT A GLANCE

Length/configuration: 8-mile loop

Aerobic difficulty: Easy

Technical difficulty: Mostly flat, paved bike path

Scenery: River, well-manicured park lands, mansions, and statues

Special comments: On weekends and holidays, combine this ride with a tour of Philadelphia's most historic square mile

PA

Boasting 8,900 acres of winding creeks, rustic trails, and lush green meadows, and 100 miles of jogging, bicycling, and bridal paths, Philadelphia's Fairmount Park is the largest landscaped city park in the world. This easy eight-mile loop starts behind the Philadelphia Museum of Art and is an excellent introduction to this most unusual urban getaway. Natural beauty, proximity to some of America's richest historical sites, and an adjacent world-class art palace are all excellent reasons to explore the park.

The paved bike path winds past a seemingly never-ending profusion of visual delights. The wide Schuylkill River is always in sight, and you'll often spot scullers and racing eights on the river training for a race. In the spring, the azalea gardens behind Boathouse Row, a group of classic Tudor structures, are ablaze in brilliant reds and oranges. Guarding nearby Fairmount Waterworks are six Revolutionary War heroes that are among 200 pieces of sculpture dotting the park. Boathouse Row is home to the "Schuylkill Navy," Philadelphia's famous rowing clubs.

General location: Philadelphia.

Elevation change: Negligible.

Season: Year-round.

Services: All services are available in Philadelphia.

Hazards: Traffic where the bike path crosses parking lot entrances.

Rescue index: Excellent.

Land status: City park.

Maps: Get a downtown map of Philadelphia or call the Philadelphia Visitors Center at (800) 537-7676 or (215) 636-1666.

RIDE 69 · Fairmont Park–Kelly and West River Drives

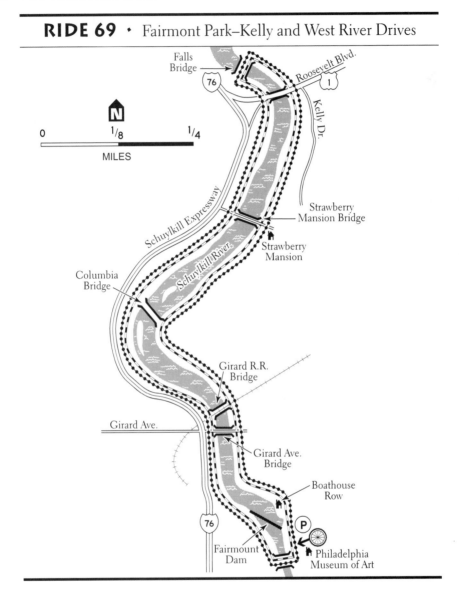

Finding the trail: From I-95, take the Vine Street Expressway west and get on Ben Franklin Parkway, which ends at the Philadelphia Museum of Art. From Schuylkill Expressway (Interstate 76), exit at 30th Street and follow signs to the museum. Park in the lot behind the Philadelphia Museum of Art. The paved bike path follows the river upstream and parallels Kelly Drive.

Source of additional information:

Philadelphia Visitors Center
(800) 537-7676 or (215) 636-1666

An easy ramble through Fairmount Park offers views of the wide Schuylkill River in downtown Philadelphia.

Notes on the trail: Riding north along the east side of the river on the bike path that follows Kelly Drive (named after John Kelly, Olympic rowing champion and brother of Grace), fat-tired cyclists are treated to views of the river, manicured lawns, and more statues and monuments. Plenty of benches and picnic tables will tempt you to pull over, stop, and soak up the scenery.

Above Girard Street Bridge and across Kelly Drive, look for Frederic Remington's *Cowboy*, the sculptor's only large-scale work. Three sculpture plazas along the river depict the nation's founding and development. Farther north, away from the center of the city, the popular park gets a little wider and generally less crowded. At Falls Bridge halfway through the ride, turn left to cross the river for the return leg south along the west bank of the river. Traffic is lighter along West River Drive, but the ride is a bit bumpier where tree roots push up the asphalt.

As you continue south, views of Philly's skyline unfold. Look for Boelsen Cottage, circa 1660, across West River Drive. You'll also see exercise stations where you can hop off your bike for an upper-body workout. After passing the low dam in the river across from the classically styled Waterworks, swing across the river on Spring Garden Bridge, bear left, ride around the huge art museum (immortalized in the *Rocky* films), and return to your car.

Combine this easy ramble along Schuylkill River with a bike tour of center-city Philadelphia's "most historic square mile." You'll ride past Independence Hall (where the Declaration of Independence was adopted and the U.S. Constitution was written), the Liberty Bell Pavilion, Declaration House (where Thomas Jefferson drafted the Declaration of Independence), and Christ Church (an active parish since 1695). To avoid car and truck traffic, go early in the morning on a weekend or holiday. Head down Benjamin Franklin Parkway (the broad boulevard in front of the Philadelphia Museum of Art) to City Hall and go east on Market Street.

RIDE 70 · Schuylkill Trail

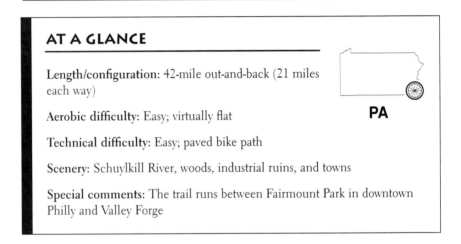

AT A GLANCE

Length/configuration: 42-mile out-and-back (21 miles each way)

Aerobic difficulty: Easy; virtually flat

Technical difficulty: Easy; paved bike path

Scenery: Schuylkill River, woods, industrial ruins, and towns

Special comments: The trail runs between Fairmount Park in downtown Philly and Valley Forge

PA

Schuylkill Trail, which follows the river of the same name from center-city Philadelphia to Valley Forge, is a flat, 21-mile (one-way) bikeway that runs northwest of the city. The trail offers cyclists plenty of river views, chances to see wildlife, sections of rural countryside, and glimpses into America's industrial past, which has been preserved throughout the ancient river valley for two-wheeled travelers who take the time to explore this fascinating stretch of paved trail.

Along the way you'll see several centuries of human development: the remains of river and canal navigation, evidence of limestone and iron-ore quarrying, iron and steel production, and railroad transportation. More recent development along the route includes high-rise urban renewal in the boroughs of Conshohocken and Norristown. Like an archaeologist on an urban dig, you'll discover layer after layer of human activity on a leisurely ramble along Schuylkill Trail.

General location: Philadelphia.

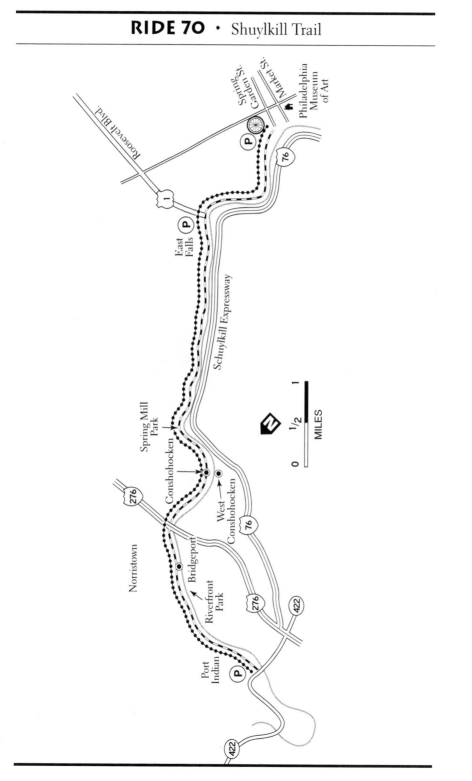

The paved Schuylkill Trail connects Valley Forge and downtown Philadelphia along the river of the same name.

Elevation change: Negligible.

Season: Year-round.

Services: All services are available in Philadelphia.

Hazards: None.

Rescue index: Excellent. The trail passes through a highly populated and industrial area and crosses many roads.

Land status: The rail-trail bikeway is a cooperative project of Montgomery County, the city of Philadelphia, and the municipalities of Conshohocken, Norristown, Plymouth, Upper Merion, West Norriton, and Whitemarsh.

Maps: Call the Montgomery County Planning Commission at (610) 278-3736.

Finding the trail: To get to the eastern terminus (Fairmount Park): From I-95, take the Vine Street Expressway west and get on Ben Franklin Parkway, which ends at the Philadelphia Museum of Art. From Schuylkill Expressway (I-76), exit at 30th Street and follow the signs to the museum. Park behind the art palace (instantly recognizable to *Rocky* fans). Pedal north along the paved path that follows Kelly Drive and the Schuylkill River through Fairmount Park (Ride 69). The path links up with the Manayunk Canal Towpath and Schuylkill Trail.

To get to the western terminus (Betzwood): Drive past the entrance to Valley Forge National Historic Park (18 miles northwest of Philadelphia at the intersection of I-76 and US 422) to the parking area on the other side of the Schuylkill River. Additional parking along the trail can be found at Riverfront Park in Norristown and near the trail in Conshohocken, Spring Mill, and Manayunk.

Source of additional information:

> Montgomery County Planning Commission
> Montgomery County Courthouse
> P.O. Box 311
> Norristown, PA 19404-0311
> (610) 278-3736

Notes on the trail: Both ends of the trail offer additional areas ripe for exploration. Valley Forge National Historic Park features a 6.5-mile paved bike path through the rolling countryside where George Washington and the Grand Army wintered in 1777–78 (Ride 71). A scenic, 2.5-mile riverside walking trail extending beyond the western terminus of the trail connects to Pawlings Road. In downtown Philadelphia, Fairmount Park offers grand views of the Schuylkill River, the city's striking skyline, numerous outdoor sculptures, and stately mansions as you pedal along West River and Kelly Drives (Ride 69). The imposing Philadelphia Museum of Art marks the eastern end of Schuylkill Trail.

RIDE 71 · Valley Forge National Historical Park

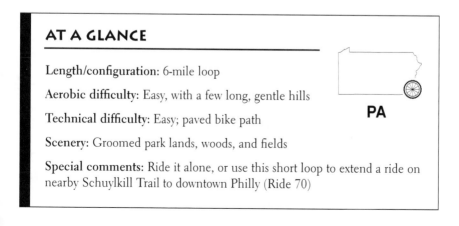

AT A GLANCE

Length/configuration: 6-mile loop

Aerobic difficulty: Easy, with a few long, gentle hills

Technical difficulty: Easy; paved bike path

Scenery: Groomed park lands, woods, and fields

Special comments: Ride it alone, or use this short loop to extend a ride on nearby Schuylkill Trail to downtown Philly (Ride 70)

PA

RIDE 71 · Valley Forge National Historical Park

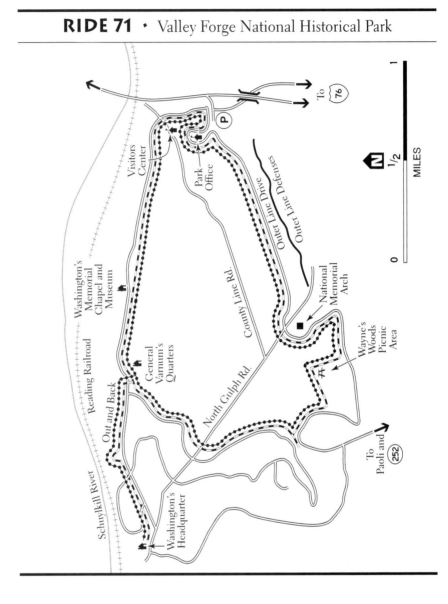

It's an American icon: Valley Forge, where General George Washington and 12,000 men of the Grand Army encamped along the Schuylkill River during the harsh winter of 1777–78. Despite inadequate supplies such as food, blankets, and clothing and disease sweeping the camp (killing 2,000 troops), a new fighting force was created here. Friedrich von Steuben, a former member of the elite general staff of Frederick the Great of Prussia, volunteered his military skills to the patriot cause, setting up an effective training program that transformed the ragtag army into a real fighting force. It emerged in June 1778 to pursue British forces into New Jersey as they marched on New York.

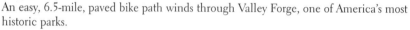

An easy, 6.5-mile, paved bike path winds through Valley Forge, one of America's most historic parks.

Today, Valley Forge's green fields and woods are surrounded by highways, high rises, and suburban congestion. Cyclists, joggers, and tourists flock year-round to the beautiful park, where a six-mile paved bicycle path allows cyclists to tour the park at a leisurely pace. You'll get a feel for the rolling terrain as you pedal up and down the gentle hills past reconstructed log huts where General Peter Muhlenberg's brigade anchored the camp's outer line of defense. The imposing National Memorial Arch, Artillery Park, and General Varnum's Quarters are other sights you'll see.

General location: Philadelphia.

Elevation change: Nominal; one short, easy climb.

Season: Year-round.

Services: All services are available in Philadelphia and its suburbs.

Hazards: None.

Rescue index: Excellent.

Land status: National park.

Maps: A trail map is available at the Visitor Center.

Finding the trail: Valley Forge is at the intersection of the Pennsylvania Turnpike (I-76) and US 422, 18 miles northwest of Philadelphia. Follow signs to the park entrance and park your car in the lot past the Visitor Center, where the trail starts and ends.

Source of additional information:

> Valley Forge National Historical Park
> Valley Forge, PA 19481
> (610) 783-1077

Notes on the trail: Ride the loop in a clockwise direction. Rest rooms are located at the Visitor Center, Wayne's Woods picnic area, and Artillery Park. A short out-and-back section leads to Washington's headquarters.

RIDE 72 · Ridley Creek State Park

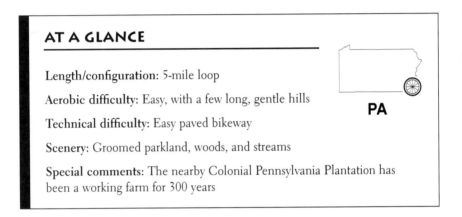

AT A GLANCE

Length/configuration: 5-mile loop

Aerobic difficulty: Easy, with a few long, gentle hills

Technical difficulty: Easy paved bikeway

Scenery: Groomed parkland, woods, and streams

Special comments: The nearby Colonial Pennsylvania Plantation has been a working farm for 300 years

PA

Ridley Creek State Park is a mecca for Philly-area cyclists in search of leisurely riding. A five-mile paved bike trail that makes a loop through the 2,606-acre park is a perfect destination for those whose legs—and maybe their rear ends—cry out for relief from the relentlessly flat riding on the paved Fairmount Park and Schuylkill Trails. The wide path offers some variety as it rolls over gentle hills, passing through diverse habitats, woods, and fields and along Ridley Creek, a popular trout stream. You'll see the remains of many old stone buildings in the woods.

There's more to this park than just the bike trail. It's located on the site of a small eighteenth-century village known as Sycamore Mill. Visitors can see the miller's house, the office and library, and several small mill-workers' dwellings. Don't miss Hunting Hill, the impressive mansion that serves as the park office. Built in 1914, this stone structure sits on well-manicured grounds.

Another site worth seeing is the Colonial Pennsylvania Plantation, a working farm for nearly 300 years. Spring through fall, historical interpreters give visitors an accurate picture of farm life on a 1776 Quaker farm, as do a variety of farm animals and an authentic landscape. An admission fee (around $5) is charged.

RIDE 72 • Ridley Creek State Park

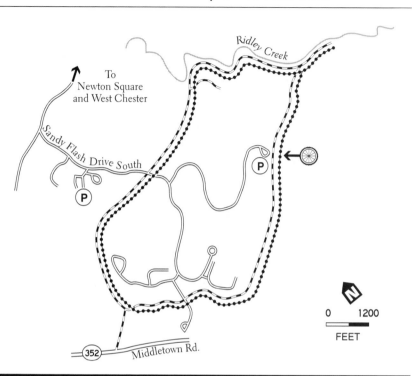

General location: Philadelphia.

Elevation change: Nominal; gently rolling terrain.

Season: Year-round.

Services: All services are available in Newtown and Philadelphia.

Hazards: The bike path can get very crowded on weekends with walkers, in-line skaters, and families with young children, so use caution when riding.

Rescue index: Excellent.

Land status: State park.

Maps: A trail map is available at the park office.

Finding the trail: The main entrance to Ridley Creek State Park is on PA 3, 2.5 miles west of Newtown Square. You can also enter the park from Gradyville Road east of PA 352 or west of PA 252. Follow signs inside the park to picnic area 17 and the exercise court. Park your car in the cul-de-sac and begin riding on the 20-foot-wide path visible through a line of trees.

Hunting Hill, built in 1914, is a stone structure situated on the well-manicured grounds of Ridley Creek State Park.

Source of additional information:

Ridley Creek State Park
Sycamore Mills Road
Media, PA 19063
(610) 892-3900

Notes on the trail: Mountain bikes are not allowed on the park's 17 miles of hiking and equestrian trails. You can, however, extend the ride by exploring the low-traffic, low-speed paved roads throughout the park. Rest rooms are located at the start of the ride, at the park office, and at picnic areas along the route.

RIDE 73 · Nottingham County Park

AT A GLANCE

Length/configuration: 8 miles of trails in several loops

Aerobic difficulty: Moderate

Technical difficulty: Easy to moderate

Scenery: Woods, fields, and a unique barrens environment

Special comments: Look for signs of mining activity while you ride

PA

With a unique topography and eight miles of unpaved multiuse trails perfect for casual mountain biking, Nottingham County Park is an excellent destination for off-road cyclists looking for something different. The trails traverse a delicate ecosystem that's home to all kinds of wildlife, including 17 species of warblers, whippoorwills, barred owls, bobwhite quails, and wild turkeys. The 651-acre park sits atop an outcropping of serpentine stone nearly six miles long and two miles wide. The result is a unique natural area of rare flora and fauna; half the park is pitch pine forest called barrens (the stunted growth of the trees results from the dry, acidic soil). From the mid-1800s until 1930, the area was the center of a feldspar and chromium quarrying industry. Mine openings and sinkholes throughout the park give evidence to the mining activity.

For mountain bikers, the park's greatest attraction is the system of trails. Two primitive campsites and two scenic overlooks await exploration by intrepid cyclists, who can ride trails with names such as Buck, Mystery Hole, Lonesome Pine, Doe, Chrome, and Fawn. Watch for five species of rare plants, including maidenhair fern and moss pink, that are found exclusively in the barrens. Judging from some of the trail names, don't be surprised if you spot a few white-tailed deer as you pedal these easy trails.

General location: Oxford.

Elevation change: Nominal.

Season: Year-round.

Services: All services are available in Oxford, about 5 miles north.

Hazards: None.

Rescue index: Good. This is a small park, and the trails are frequently bisected by park roads.

Land status: County park.

RIDE 73 · Nottingham County Park

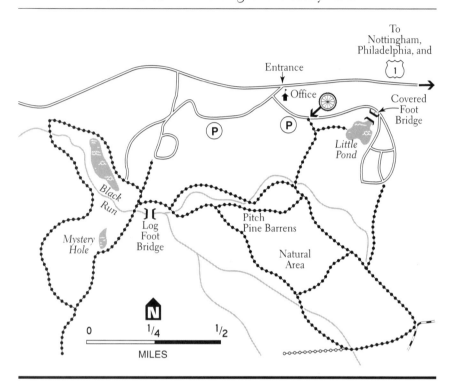

Maps: A trail map is available at the park office and at a kiosk near the entrance.

Finding the trail: From the US 1 Bypass, take the PA 272 Nottingham exit, turn left at the top of the ramp, and drive a quarter-mile to Herr Drive. Turn right and continue to the stop sign; turn right and follow signs to the park entrance.

Source of additional information:

Nottingham County Park
150 Park Road
Nottingham, PA 19362
(610) 932-9195

Notes on the trail: No specific directions are needed to ride the short trails in the park. It's a good idea, though, to check with the park office for the latest trail conditions.

Small covered footbridges and easy trails lend charm to Nottingham County Park.

RIDE 74 · Hibernia County Park

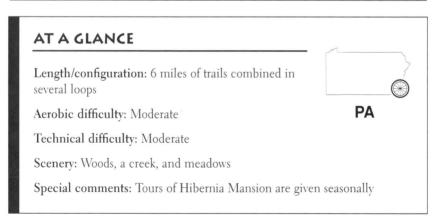

AT A GLANCE

Length/configuration: 6 miles of trails combined in several loops

Aerobic difficulty: Moderate

Technical difficulty: Moderate

Scenery: Woods, a creek, and meadows

Special comments: Tours of Hibernia Mansion are given seasonally

PA

Located just beyond the hustle and bustle of suburban Philadelphia, this 800-acre park of woodlands and meadows features miles of trails, open fields, and picnic areas. Its two and a half miles of paved road and six miles of unpaved multiuse trails are ideal for fat-tired bikes. The paths lead cyclists through forests and fields where they can observe wildlife, fish in Brandywine Creek, or stop for a picnic lunch.

RIDE 74 · Hibernia County Park

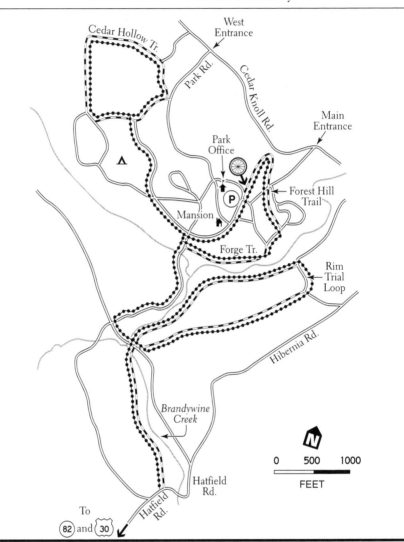

The grounds also feature Hibernia Mansion, the home of an early ironmaster. Seasonal tours are given of the large house and grounds. The entire site is listed on the National Register of Historic Places.

General location: Downingtown.

Elevation change: Nominal.

Season: Year-round.

Services: Primitive camping is available in the park. Rest rooms are located at

Hibernia County Park has 6 miles of trails near Hibernia Mansion, the home of an early ironmaster.

the park office and at picnic areas throughout the park. All other services are available in Downingtown.

Hazards: Watch for cars on the paved roads.

Rescue index: Good. The small park is surrounded by roads, and the trails are intersected by roads inside its boundaries.

Land status: County park.

Maps: A trail map is available at the park office.

Finding the trail: The park is located approximately 30 miles west of Philadelphia and 2 miles north of PA 82 where it intersects US 30. From PA 82, turn left on Cedar Knoll Road and drive 1.25 miles to the park entrance. Forest Hill Trail starts at the park office.

Sources of additional information:

Hibernia County Park
Box 429, RD 6
Martin's Corner/Wagontown Road
Coatesville, PA 19320
(610) 384-0290

Chester County Parks and Recreation Department
235 West Market Street
West Chester, PA 19382
(610) 344-6415

Notes on the trail: Ride as much or as little as you like at this compact park. Cedar Hollow Trail is a 1-mile loop near the group camping area, while Forest Hill Trail can be ridden in a loop or connected with Rim Trial Loop and a path along Brandywine Creek. All of the loops are connected by paved park roads.

RIDE 75 · French Creek State Park

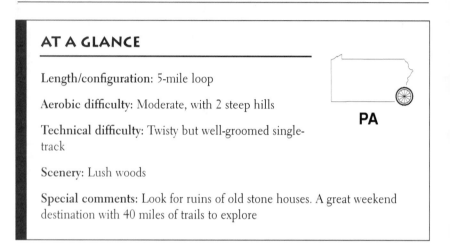

AT A GLANCE

Length/configuration: 5-mile loop

Aerobic difficulty: Moderate, with 2 steep hills

Technical difficulty: Twisty but well-groomed single-track

Scenery: Lush woods

Special comments: Look for ruins of old stone houses. A great weekend destination with 40 miles of trails to explore

PA

With 7,300 acres of woodlands, open fields, lakes, and streams, and 40 miles of trails, French Creek State Park has all the makings of a great mountain biking destination in populous southeastern Pennsylvania. And guess what? The park delivers on its potential as an excellent venue to spin the cranks off-road. There is a problem, though. Which trails should you ride? Here's a suggestion: try the system of trails on the east end of the park near the campground. It features several single-track paths that aren't too difficult for intermediate riders and in-shape novices.

Start on the green-blazed Lenape (Len-a-pay) Trail for a five-mile circuit through a mature maple and elm forest that's so neat it almost looks manicured. Sections of the trail are rocky; intermediate-level riders should find it doable — in fact, it's a lot of fun. Along the way, keep your eyes peeled for the remains of a stone cabin and a spring house in the woods; lots of deadfall and intense, fast-turning single-track; and two steep climbs — one on a washout on Raccoon Trail and the other up to Millers Point (a 30-foot rock formation). The last half of the loop has some double-track and emerges back at Lenape Trail close to PA 345.

While the ride doesn't have any real views to speak of, the winding single-track through the woods will delight most riders. Because this loop represents only a small fraction of the trails at French Creek, why not explore some others and make a weekend of it? Brush Hill Campground has four camping loops,

RIDE 75 • French Creek State Park

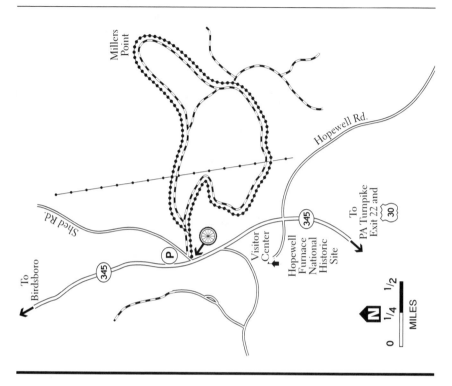

a modern bathhouse, and wooded campsites. And its central location puts it close to many trailheads.

After a ride, you can also visit adjacent Hopewell Furnace National Historic Park, a restored early American iron-making community where costumed historical interpreters demonstrate and recount the story of Hopewell's iron-making years. Another option is the Daniel Boone Homestead about eight miles to the north. The legendary frontiersman was born here in 1734. The historic site interprets the early life of the Boones (his parents settled the place in 1730) and shows the lifestyles of the cultures that settled eighteenth-century rural Pennsylvania.

General location: Reading.

Elevation change: 2 steep climbs make up the majority of the approximately 600' elevation gain on the 5-mile loop. If you link this loop with other trails in the park, it's easy to climb 1,000 feet or more.

Season: Year-round.

Services: All services are available in Reading. Brush Hill Campground inside the park has 201 campsites and access to showers.

The Lenape Trail offers 5 miles of twisting, buffed single-track in French Creek State Park.

Hazards: Hunting is permitted in the park from fall through March. Wear orange or ride on Sundays, when hunting isn't permitted. Watch for railroad-tie waterbars on some single-track trails.

Rescue index: Good. Many roads bisect the trails inside the park.

Land status: State park.

Maps: Available at the park office.

Finding the trail: The park is located about 7 miles northeast of the Pennsylvania Turnpike's Morgantown exchange (Exit 22) on PA 345. The green-blazed Lenape Trail crosses the parking lot near the Brush Hill Campground contact station. There's also trailhead parking near the intersection of PA 345 and Shed Road, where you can start the ride.

Source of additional information:

French Creek State Park
843 Park Road
Elverson, PA 19520-9523
(610) 582-1514

Notes on the trail: Ride the circuit counterclockwise to avoid a treacherously steep descent from Millers Point. Then again, if you like steep descents—or hate pushing your bike up a ridiculously steep hill that gains nearly 200 feet in elevation—ride the loop in a clockwise direction.

RIDE 76 · Blue Marsh Lake

AT A GLANCE

Length/configuration: 24-mile loop

Aerobic difficulty: Moderate; many long, though not very steep, climbs

Technical difficulty: Moderate; well-groomed single-track

Scenery: Woods, fields, and a big lake

Special comments: Hot showers are available at the Dry Brooks Day Use Area

PA

This 6,200-acre U.S. Army Corps of Engineers project is a recreational gold mine in the Reading area. Mountain bikers flock to Blue Marsh Lake year-round to enjoy this excellent, 24-mile single-track that traces the lake's shoreline. It's a testimonial that good trail riding doesn't always require tall mountains or dramatic elevation changes.

While the terrain is rolling, most riders will find that many of the climbs can be made in the saddle (read: no standing on the pedals required, at least if you've got low enough gears). The trail starts off wide and easy but soon narrows to proper single-track width. Surprisingly, the path remains relatively nontechnical and doesn't blindside you with complications such as rock gardens and tangles of roots. This trail, which runs from Stilling Basin to the Dry Brooks Day Use Area, can be ridden in a loop and completed with a short section of pavement on Palisades Drive.

Starting at Stilling Basin, the trail follows the edge of the lake through forests and crosses the occasional gravel road. Almost the entire trail offers pleasant vistas of the 1,200-acre lake. The climbs get bigger as you go, with a few steep uphills and descents in the Catalpa Trees area. You'll pass through thick forest interspersed with a few sections of open pasture. There's also an occasional wooden bridge. This is a well-maintained trail suitable for fit riders of all abilities.

General location: Reading.

Elevation change: Some climbs gain about a hundred feet.

Season: Year-round.

Services: Rest rooms, showers, telephones, and food are available at the Dry Brooks Day Use Area. All other services are available in Reading.

RIDE 76 • Blue Marsh Lake

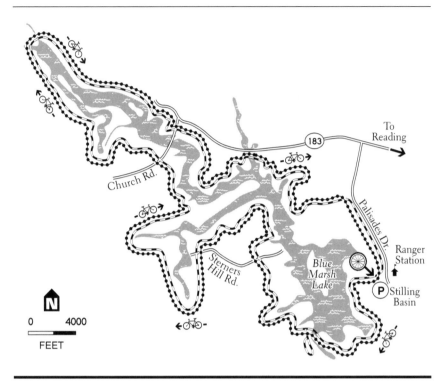

Hazards: Hunting is allowed, so wear orange in the fall or only ride on Sundays, when hunting isn't permitted.

Rescue index: Excellent. The trail is popular and crosses many roads.

Land status: U.S. Army Corps of Engineers.

Maps: A trail map is available at the ranger station.

Finding the trail: Blue Marsh Lake is located off PA 183, about 6 miles northwest of Reading. Turn left onto Palisades Road and go past the Dry Brooks Day Use Area. Then drive past the ranger station and administration building (where you can get a trail map) and take the next left. Park at the lot near Stilling Basin, below the dam. Then pedal up the hill toward the dam to start the ride in a clockwise direction. You can also ride counterclockwise by starting at the Dry Brooks Day Use Area.

Source of additional information:

Blue Marsh Lake Project
U.S. Army Corps of Engineers, Philadelphia District

Blue Marsh Lake is renowned for its 24 miles of well-groomed single-track.

RD 1, Box 1239
Leesport, PA 19533
(215) 376-6337

Notes on the trail: Blue Marsh Lake frequently gets hyped in the bicycling press as one of the 10 best bike rides in the United States. Puh-leeze. Like I said, it's a great trail for folks who live in the area, but don't cancel your plans to ride in Colorado or West Virginia. It would be easy to name 10 other rides in Pennsylvania alone that top this trail—at least, if mountain scenery is part of the criteria.

If a 24-mile ride is a bit much, you can create a shorter loop by starting at Stilling Basin and returning on any number of back roads the trail crosses on the south side of the lake. Finally, in the summer you can take a postride dip at the lake's swimming beach, located at the Dry Brooks Day Use Area; there's a $1 per person fee.

RIDE 77 · Tyler State Park

AT A GLANCE

Length/configuration: 10-mile loop

Aerobic difficulty: Moderate; a few long, but not very steep, climbs

PA

Technical difficulty: Easy; paved bike paths

Scenery: Woods, a covered bridge, a fast-moving stream, and fields

Special comments: Bikes aren't allowed on unpaved trails

Tyler State Park, an island of greenery only 20 miles northeast of Philadelphia, is an oasis of forests, streams, rolling fields, and pre-Revolutionary Americana amid the suburban sprawl of Bucks County. The park comprises 1,711 acres of woodlands and fields that have been carefully preserved in their pristine glory. Original stone buildings, some dating back to the early 1700s, have also been preserved and are maintained by individuals who lease them.

Neshaminy Creek winds through the park, separating the forests from the parking and commercial areas. Things to see as you explore the ten miles of paved, eight-foot-wide trails (bikes, alas, aren't allowed on the unpaved hiking trails) include the 1775 Thompson Dairy House, a covered bridge, a youth hostel, cultivated fields, and the Pennsylvania Guild of Craftsmen Craft Center.

The paved trails are easy to ride. No specific route is recommended; just bring your bike and explore. Picnic tables and water are in key locations throughout the park.

General location: Philadelphia.

Elevation change: A few hundred feet up one long but generally easy hill.

Season: Year-round.

Services: All services are available in Newtown. Rest rooms are located near the boat concession area and the pedestrian causeway over the creek.

Hazards: None.

Rescue index: Excellent; the park is small and popular, so getting help is easy.

Land status: State park.

Maps: A trail map is available at the ranger office near the entrance.

Finding the trail: Tyler State Park is easy to reach from Exits 27 and 28 of the Pennsylvania Turnpike. From Exit 27 follow PA 322 east from Willow Grove through Richboro to the park entrance. From Exit 28 take US 1 north to I-95.

RIDE 77 · Tyler State Park

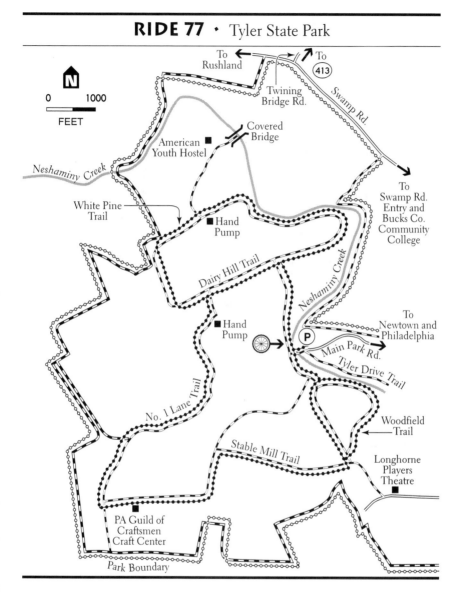

Follow I-95 north to the Newtown-Yardley exit. Drive west through Newtown to the park entrance on PA 322.

After entering the park, drive to the first parking area past the ranger office. Park your car and ride your bike to Quarry Trail (it's marked), which winds through the picnic grove and connects with Tyler Drive Trail. Follow this trail to the pedestrian causeway, cross Neshaminy Creek, and turn right onto Mill Dairy Trail. From here it's easy to devise a loop that takes in most of the park's bike trails.

Easy riding along Neshaminy Creek is one option at Tyler State Park.

Source of additional information:

Tyler State Park
Department of Environmental Resources
Newtown, PA 18940
(215) 968-2021

Notes on the trail: The bike trails are all named and well marked. It's easy to create a loop ride in either a clockwise or a counterclockwise direction that will take in most of the 10 miles of paved trails. Not enough riding? Reverse your direction and ride it again. It will look completely different.

NEW JERSEY

Joisey. Just say the word and the mind floods with unsavory images: tank farms along the New Jersey Turnpike, crowded suburbia in the nation's most densely populated state, and plumes of orange-tinted smoke as corporations release more toxic waste per square mile into the air than anywhere else in the country. New Jersey, some say, is the armpit of the nation. I say it's a bad rap, especially when it comes to mountain biking.

Here's a new set of impressions for people in search of off-road adventure in the Garden State (don't sneer—drive through bucolic south Jersey and you'll understand how it got the name). Allamuchy, Ringwood, Round Valley, and Wawayanda will change forever any negative vibes about the state tucked between New York, Pennsylvania, the Atlantic Ocean, and Delaware Bay. These places and many more offer great opportunities to ride and feature a wide range of off-road experiences, including grueling forest routes, glimpses of wildlife (even bears, if you're lucky), and scenic towpaths. And let's not forget about what may be New Jersey's most unique mountain bike venue: the mysterious Pine Barrens. John McPhee, a New Jersey resident, writes in his nonfiction classic, *The Pine Barrens* (Noonday Press, ISBN 0-37451-442-9, $11):

> From the fire tower on Bear Swamp Hill, in Washington Township, Burlington County, New Jersey, the view usually extends about twelve miles. To the north, forest land reaches to the horizon. The trees are mainly oaks and pines, and the pines predominate. Occasionally, there are long, dark serrated stands of Atlantic white cedars, so tall and so closely set that they seem to be spread against the sky on the ridges of hills, when in fact they grow along streams that flow through the forest. To the east, the view is similar, and few people who are not native to the region can discern essential differences from the high cabin of the fire tower, even though one difference is that huge areas out in this direction are covered with dwarf forests, where a man can stand among the trees and see for miles over their uppermost branches. To the south, the view is twice broken slightly—by a lake and by a cranberry bog—but otherwise

it, too, goes to the horizon in forest. To the west, pines, oaks, and cedars continue all the way, and the western horizon includes the summit of another hill—Apple Pie Hill—and the outline of another fire tower, from which the view three hundred and sixty degrees around is virtually the same as the view from Bear Swamp Hill, where, in a moment's sweeping glance, a person can see hundreds of square miles of wilderness. The picture of New Jersey that most people hold in their minds is so different from this one that, considered beside it, the Pine Barrens, as they are called, become as incongruous as they are beautiful. West and north of the Pine Barrens is New Jersey's central transportation corridor, where traffic of freight and people is more concentrated than it is anywhere else in the world. The corridor is one great compression of industrial shapes, industrial sounds, industrial air, and thousands and thousands of houses webbing over the spaces between the factories. . . . In the central area of the Pine Barrens—the forest land that is still so undeveloped that it can be called wilderness—there are only fifteen people per square mile. This area, which includes about six hundred and fifty thousand acres, is nearly as large as Yosemite National Park. It is almost identical in size with Grand Canyon National Park, and it is much larger than Sequoia National Park, Great Smoky Mountains National Park or, for that matter, most of the national parks in the United States. . . .

The Pine Barrens, honeycombed with roads and trails ripe for exploration on two wheels, is just the tip of the iceberg of great riding opportunities you'll find in New Jersey. From easy woods roads in Stokes State Forest and the state's highest peak in High Point State Park (1,803 feet) to double-track loops around Blue Mountain Lake at Delaware Water Gap National Recreation Area, New Jersey offers off-road riding that can satisfy all levels of mountain bikers, including hammerheads in search of anaerobic bliss. At Round Valley, you can climb nearly 2,000 feet on an 18-mile out-and-back that's plenty technical.

Forget all the bad things you ever heard about New Jersey. The riding is great.

RIDE 78 · Wharton State Forest

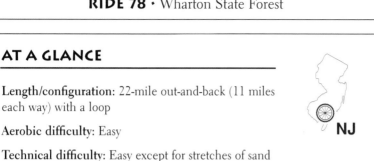

AT A GLANCE

Length/configuration: 22-mile out-and-back (11 miles each way) with a loop

Aerobic difficulty: Easy

NJ

Technical difficulty: Easy except for stretches of sand

Scenery: Dense woods and slow-moving rivers

Special comments: Explore Batsto Village and its 33 historic buildings

This huge chunk of the Pine Barrens—109,000 acres, most of which were once the property of Philadelphia industrialist Joseph Wharton—is the largest tract in the New Jersey state park system. Most of it is undeveloped forest laced with rivers and hundreds of miles of sand roads that comprise a unique habitat and a region rich in cultural and industrial history. An iron industry flourished in the Pine Barrens during the Revolutionary War and the War of 1812 and attracted a large population to the now nearly deserted region. Iron used to make munitions and supplies came from bog ore found along the streams and in the swamps, and supplied local furnaces and forges that flourished throughout the barrens. The industry declined in the later years of the century, as did the glass and paper industries that followed. Eventually the towns and villages disappeared, and this may account for the Pine Barrens' undefinable spookiness. Batsto Village, the site of a former bog-iron and glass-making industrial center, shows what things were like at the end of the nineteenth century. Its 33 historic buildings include a gristmill, sawmill, general store, mansion, and Visitor Center. Crafts are demonstrated in the village during the summer months. It's definitely worth a visit.

The natural history of the region is also rich. The pinelands habitats, southern swamps, and flood plains are home to many rare plant and animal species. The Pine Barrens sit atop a massive freshwater aquifer, and four rivers flow through Wharton. As a result, the forest is a very popular canoeing destination, with four established canoe trails. Some advice: For more insight into this fascinating region, read John McPhee's *The Pine Barrens*, a classic nonfiction book that will pique your curiosity to explore the barrens by bike.

This 22-mile (total), combination out-and-back with a loop begins in Atsion and follows the slow-moving Mullica and Batsto Rivers for 11 miles to Batsto. It starts and finishes on Quaker Bridge Road. At Quaker Bridge, bear right and follow the river on the west bank. At Batsto, cross the river on a paved road and

RIDE 78 · Wharton State Forest

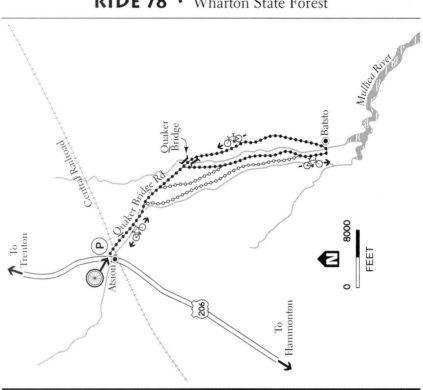

begin the return leg on the opposite bank. At Quaker Bridge begin retracing your route back to Atsion.

The wide, flat road is sandy, so expect to get a workout on the ride. The forest is low and dense, and innumerable double-tracks shoot off into them. Resist the urge to explore. To avoid getting lost, stick to Quaker Bridge Road and the rivers, and you'll be okay. On most of the ride, the Mullica River or the Batsto River is in sight.

General location: The Pine Barrens, approximately 40 miles southeast of Philadelphia.

Elevation change: None.

Season: Year-round. Bugs can make exploration uncomfortable from April through October. Wear long sleeves even if it's hot. Locals say the best days for riding are the occasional warm days in January and February.

Services: Camping and hot showers are available in the forest at Atsion. All other services are available in Vineland.

Explore thick forests
and sandy roads in
the Pine Barrens of
southern New Jersey.

Hazards: It's easy to get lost; everything looks the same, and with more than 109,000 acres, getting lost is something you want to avoid. Hunting is allowed in the forest, so in the fall wear orange or only ride on Sundays, when hunting isn't permitted.

Rescue index: Fair. The forest is laced with 500 miles of lightly trafficked paved and unpaved roads and has private residences scattered throughout. Still, you can ride for hours without spotting another person.

Land status: State forest.

Maps: A trail map is available at the ranger station in Atsion and the Visitor Center in Batsto.

Finding the trail: To reach Wharton State Forest, take Exit 28 on the Atlantic City Expressway and go north on US 206 to Atsion. To reach Batsto (the other end of the ride), turn right onto NJ 542 in Hammonton, about 1 mile from the Atlantic City Expressway on US 206. From the parking lot at the ranger station in Atsion, pedal past the office and turn left onto unpaved Quaker Bridge Road.

Sources of additional information:

Wharton State Forest, Atsion Office
RD 2, Route 206
Vincentown, NJ 08088
(609) 268-0444

Wharton State Forest
RD 9 Batsto
Hammonton, NJ 08037
(609) 561-0024

Notes on the trail: About 5 miles from the start, bear right at the turnaround just before the small steel bridge in Quaker Bridge; don't cross the river. For the return leg in Batsto, turn left on paved NJ 542 and go a quarter-mile. Follow the fence around Batsto Village to the trail. At Quaker Bridge, cross the steel bridge and retrace your route to Atsion. It's very easy to get lost if you venture off the roads that follow the Batsto River. You can also start the ride in Batsto and ride north to Atsion.

RIDE 79 · Lebanon State Forest

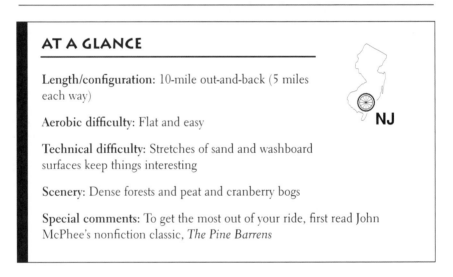

AT A GLANCE

Length/configuration: 10-mile out-and-back (5 miles each way)

Aerobic difficulty: Flat and easy

Technical difficulty: Stretches of sand and washboard surfaces keep things interesting

Scenery: Dense forests and peat and cranberry bogs

Special comments: To get the most out of your ride, first read John McPhee's nonfiction classic, *The Pine Barrens*

NJ

More than 400 miles of mostly unpaved roads crisscross 32,000-acre Lebanon State Forest in south-central New Jersey. It's the perfect place for adventurous mountain bikers to explore the Garden State's famous Pine Barrens. But be warned: There's lots to explore, and it's easy to get lost in this huge region. The mysterious Pine Barrens look much the same no matter where you are.

RIDE 79 · Lebanon State Forest

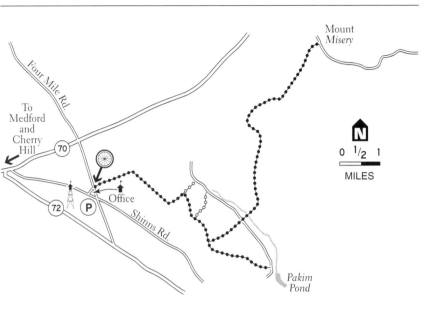

Though the barrens are flat as a pancake, don't think the riding is going to be effortless. True, you won't get blasted by any climbs, but slogging through sand and getting hammered on washboard roads can be almost as wearisome. That said, there's much to commend. First, get a copy of John McPhee's *The Pine Barrens*. McPhee, a staff writer for *The New Yorker*, captures the essence of—and the frustrations of understanding—this amorphous area of deep, slow-moving streams, swamps, pitch pine forests, deserted villages, abandoned company towns, cranberry bogs, blueberry stands, and, as the book makes clear, some very strange people. The nonfiction classic will fire you up for your visit.

Next, drive to the ranger office at Lebanon State Forest, park your car, and start riding Cranberry Trail, an easy, five-mile, one-way trek that leads to Pakim Pond, a recreation area with swimming and picnicking options. You can extend the ride by taking White Trail for a five-and-a-half-mile (one-way) out-and-back to Mount Misery. Or, if you've got a map, you'll be able to find some of the other roads that honeycomb the forest and make a loop ride out of it. Along the sandy trails you'll see huge peat bogs (they look eerie), an abandoned glass factory, and active cranberry bogs (big business in the Pine Barrens). You'll also pass through Cedar Swamp Natural Area, which is crowded with dense stands of Atlantic white cedar (up to 4,000 trees per acre), one of the characteristic trees of the barrens. Its light, soft, durable wood is used in boat building and the production of shingles, fence posts, stakes, and rustic furniture. Other plants include rare orchids, sundews, pitcher plants, and curley grass fern. The swamp is also home to many amphibians, birds, and mammals.

General location: The Pine Barrens, about 30 miles east of Philadelphia.

Elevation change: None.

Season: The best days for riding the Pine Barrens are the occasional warm days in January and February. Bugs are bad from April through October; bring plenty of insect repellent and wear long sleeves, even if it's hot.

Services: Camping is available in the state forest. Groceries are available in Browns Mills. All other services are available in Mount Holly.

Hazards: Hunting is allowed in the forest. In the fall, wear orange or ride on Sundays, when hunting isn't permitted.

Rescue index: Good; lightly trafficked paved/unpaved roads traverse the forest.

Land status: State forest.

Maps: A trail map is available at the ranger station on NJ 72, near the fire tower.

Finding the trail: Take NJ 70 east from Cherry Hill for about 25 miles. The forest is located where NJ 70 meets NJ 72, about 8 miles east of Red Lion and the intersection with US 206. Cranberry Trail starts behind the ranger station and heads to Pakim Pond. After about 2.2 miles, it connects with White Trail to Mount Misery.

Source of additional information:

Lebanon State Forest
P.O. Box 215
New Lisbon, NJ 08064
(609) 726-1191

Notes on the trail: You can ride for hours without coming across another person; give yourself plenty of time so you're not racing a setting sun at the end of the day. And bring plenty of food and water.

RIDE 80 · Delaware and Raritan Canal State Park

AT A GLANCE

Length/configuration: 128-mile out-and-back (64 miles each way); most folks do out-and-backs of varying lengths

NJ

Aerobic difficulty: Easy

Technical difficulty: Easy

Scenery: Woods and river

Special comments: Frenchtown, Lambertville, and Washington Crossing State Park are popular destinations

For nearly a century, the Delaware and Raritan Canal (D&R) was one of America's busiest navigation canals. Dug mostly by hand between 1830 and 1834 by immigrant Irish laborers, the main canal was 44 miles long, 75 feet wide, and 7 feet deep. The feeder canal along the Delaware River, originally designed to supply water to the main canal, was 22 miles long, 50 feet wide, and 6 feet deep. In the canal's peak years, during the 1860s and 1870s, 80% of the cargo was Pennsylvania coal used to fire New York City's industrial boom. Toward the end of the nineteenth century, coal use declined; the canal's last profitable year was 1892, but it continued to operate until 1932, when New Jersey rehabilitated it as a water supply system. In 1974 more than 60 miles of the canal and a small strip of land on both sides were established as a state park. Today, the D&R is one of central New Jersey's most popular recreation areas.

The towpath along the 34-mile main canal (between Trenton and New Brunswick) has either a natural or crushed-stone surface, both of which are fine for fat-tired bikes. Along the 30-mile feeder canal that parallels the Delaware River, the surface of the former railroad right-of-way is finely textured crushed stone. Both paths (which total 64 miles one-way) are flat and easy to pedal. Most folks configure out-and-backs, starting upstream so that the return leg is slightly downhill.

The park serves as an important recreational corridor rich in cultural and historic significance. General George Washington's Continental Army crossed the Delaware a few miles north of Trenton; today cyclists can stop at Washington Crossing State Park Visitor Center, which interprets the "Ten Critical Days" when the fledgling republic scored its first major victories against British forces. Nineteenth-century bridges and locktender houses, cobblestone spillways, and hand-built stone-arch culverts are reminders of the region's industrial beginnings.

RIDE 80 · Delaware and Raritan Canal State Park

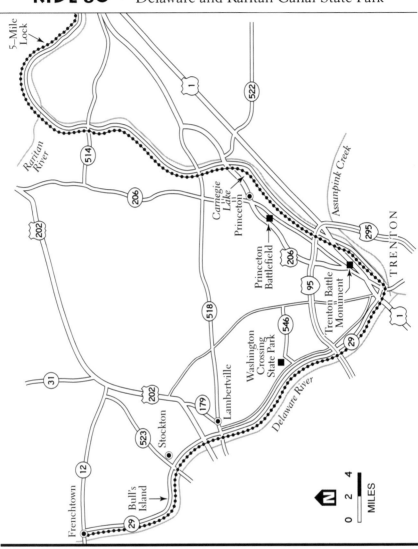

Bulls Island, a 24-acre natural area with a floodplain forest and a mixed oak and hardwood forest, is home to rare species of birds such as northern parula warbler, cerulean warbler, yellow-throated warbler, and Acadian flycatcher. You'll enjoy great views of the canal and the broad Delaware River. Frenchtown, Lambertville, and other quaint villages provide cyclists with restaurants and shops where they can get off their bikes—and spend money.

General location: Trenton.

Historic buildings add to the ambience at Washington Crossing State Park.

Elevation change: Negligible.

Season: Year-round.

Services: All services are available in Trenton and Philadelphia.

Hazards: None.

Rescue index: Excellent; the trail is extremely popular; it follows and is intersected by many roads and highways.

Land status: State park.

Maps: Maps are available by mail from the Delaware and Raritan Canal State Park.

Finding the trail: Two of the most scenic stretches of the old railroad grade along the feeder canal are from Washington Crossing State Park to Lambertville (7 miles one-way) and from Bulls Island Natural Area to Frenchtown (8 miles one-way). To reach Washington Crossing State Park, take Interstate 95 to NJ 29 and drive north about 2 miles. Bulls Island is about another 8 miles north along NJ 29.

Source of additional information:

Delaware and Raritan Canal State Park
625 Canal Road
Somerset, NJ 08873
(908) 873-3050

Notes on the trail: Visitors can reach the canal paths from small parking areas located at nearly every road that crosses them. The historic towpath along the main canal is open from Mulberry Street, just north of Trenton, to New Brunswick. Along the feeder canal, which parallels the Delaware River, a recreational trail follows the abandoned Belvidere-Delaware Railroad right-of-way from Frenchtown south to Trenton.

RIDE 81 · Round Valley Recreation Area

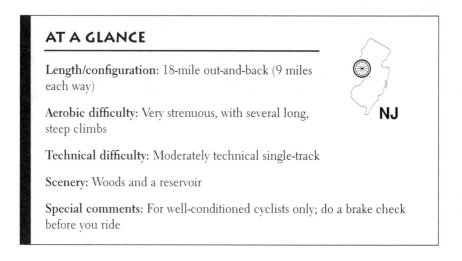

AT A GLANCE

Length/configuration: 18-mile out-and-back (9 miles each way)

Aerobic difficulty: Very strenuous, with several long, steep climbs

Technical difficulty: Moderately technical single-track

Scenery: Woods and a reservoir

Special comments: For well-conditioned cyclists only; do a brake check before you ride

NJ

It's official: You don't have to drive long distances in New Jersey to find good, hard climbing—at least, not if you're close to Round Valley. Cushetunk Trail, which wraps most of the way around a reservoir, is a nine-mile (one-way) out-and-back that will have even well-conditioned riders turning blue in the face at the tops of some of the long, steep ascents. When you're not gasping for air—and after those large dots fade from your vision—be prepared to enjoy some nice scenery. The woods in the 3,600-acre park are attractive, you get splendid views of Round Valley Reservoir, and there's an abundance of intense single-track. Technically, there's a little of everything: short stretches of rock garden; long, steep climbs; occasional deadfall to negotiate; and lots of twisting single-track. Round Valley is best suited for intermediate and advanced riders.

Navigation is a no-brainer, but because this is an out-and-back, every screaming descent becomes an eyeball-popping climb on the return. Hey, no one says you've got to go the distance. When it feels right, turn back. And don't forget to check your brakes before setting off. You'll be needing them.

General location: Lebanon.

Elevation change: Close to 1,000' one-way.

RIDE 81 · Round Valley Recreation Area

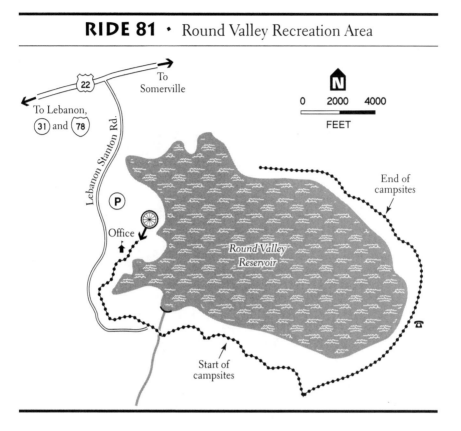

Season: Year-round.

Services: All services are available in Clinton, a few miles west on I-78. Primitive wilderness campsites, all at least a 3-mile hike from the parking area, are available at the park. Nearby Vorhees and Spruce Run State Parks offer camping with hot showers.

Hazards: Watch for horses, which are permitted along the first 6 miles of the trail. Perhaps the steepest descent occurs at the start below the earth dam.

Rescue index: Poor. The trail is fairly isolated, and after the first few miles it doesn't cross any roads. Wilderness campsites line the lakeshore for a 3-mile stretch in the middle, and a public phone is located 5 miles from the start. The Jersey Off Road Bicycle Association (JORBA) does bike patrols on some evenings and weekends. Visit their website at jorba.org.

Land status: State park.

Maps: A trail map is available at the park office.

Finding the trail: From US 22 in Lebanon, take the park access road to the parking and launch area. Cushetunk Trail—the only legal trail in the park for

The trailhead at Round
Valley looks tame,
but don't be fooled.

mountain bikes—starts at the parking lot and boat launch for wilderness
campers.

Source of additional information:

Round Valley Recreation Area
Box 45-D
Lebanon, NJ 08833
(908) 236-6355

Notes on the trail: The drop below the huge earthen dam is inelegant—it goes
120 feet straight down—what you would expect along a power-line cut rather
than in a state park. Check your brakes before taking the plunge.

Great views like this—plus challenging single-track and lung-busting climbs—await riders at Round Valley.

RIDE 82 · Allamuchy Mountain State Park

AT A GLANCE

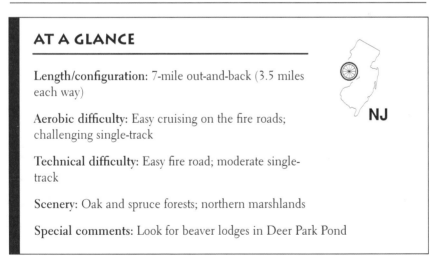

NJ

Length/configuration: 7-mile out-and-back (3.5 miles each way)

Aerobic difficulty: Easy cruising on the fire roads; challenging single-track

Technical difficulty: Easy fire road; moderate single-track

Scenery: Oak and spruce forests; northern marshlands

Special comments: Look for beaver lodges in Deer Park Pond

With its network of old farm and lumber roads, this 6,000-acre state park offers mountain bikers choices ranging from easy rambles along fire roads to challenging single-track. About 12 miles of roads and trails meander through oak and spruce forests, the northern marshlands, and Deer Park Pond.

RIDE 82 · Allamuchy Mountain State Park

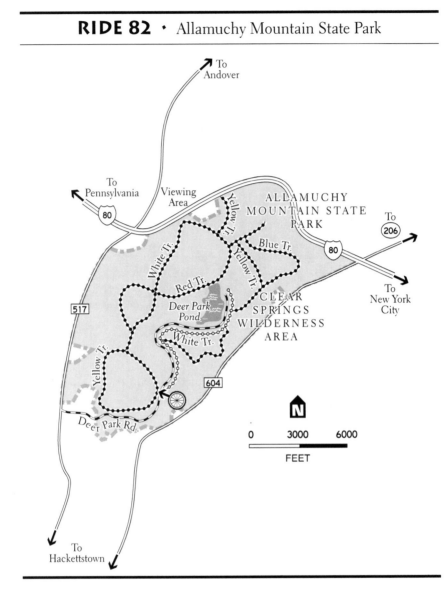

Thanks to restoration projects dating back more than 30 years, the park boasts a wide range of wildlife, including beaver, whose lodges can be seen in the pond. Ducks, osprey, and Canada geese also thrive in the small lake, and the park supports a large population of white-tailed deer. Tall stands of hemlock line the water's edge, a reminder of an era when large tracts of evergreens blanketed New Jersey.

The Delaware Indians were the area's original inhabitants, and the park's name is derived from one of their leaders' names—Chief Allamuchahokkingen, a mouthful that translates as "place within the hills." Later, after the arrival of Europeans and the customary annihilation of the natives, most of the park land became part of the Rutherford and Stuyvesant estates, descendants of Peter Stuyvesant, the last governor of New Amsterdam. Today, Allamuchy Mountain State Park is one of the most popular mountain bike destinations in this part of New Jersey.

General location: Andover.

Elevation change: About 200' total (on the dirt road to Deer Park Pond).

Season: Year-round.

Services: Andover, 10 miles north on County Road 517, has a bike shop, food, and gas. All other services are available in Hackettstown.

Hazards: Bow hunting for deer is allowed in the park; check with the park office in the fall and winter. If it's hunting season during your visit, stick to the fire roads or ride on Sundays, when hunting isn't permitted.

Rescue index: Excellent. The trails are popular, especially on weekends. They are occasionally patrolled by the Jersey Off Road Bicyclists Association (JORBA; website at jorba.org).

Land status: State park.

Maps: A trail map is available from the park office. The USGS 7.5 minute quad is Tranquility.

Finding the trail: From I-80, take Exit 19 and turn south on CR 517 toward Hackettstown. Drive 2 miles and turn left on Deer Park Road, a dirt road just past Mattars Italian restaurant. Go 0.7 mile to the park entrance, drive to the parking lot, and park your car. Pedal toward the small brown shed. The system of single-track begins with the yellow-blazed trail to the right past the trees; the wider, easier dirt road to Deer Park Pond is to the left.

Source of additional information:

Allamuchy Mountain State Park
Hackettstown, NJ 07840
(908) 852-3790

Notes on the trail: The dirt road to Deer Park Pond is 3.5 miles (one-way) and can be ridden as an out-and-back for a total of 7 miles. The single-track Yellow Trail leads to the Red, White, and Blue Trails, which can be combined and ridden in loops.

RIDE 83 · Delaware Water Gap National Recreation Area

AT A GLANCE

Length/configuration: 5-mile (one-way) out-and-back with a 5-mile loop (15 miles total)

Aerobic difficulty: Moderate, with a few easy hills

NJ

Technical difficulty: Easy paved and dirt roads

Scenery: River, farms, old stone buildings, woods, and mountains

Special comments: Peters Valley Craft Village is open daily from 10 a.m. to 5 p.m.

Located along a 40-mile stretch of the Delaware (the Eastern Seaboard's only free-flowing river), Delaware Water Gap National Recreation Area contains 70,000 acres of forest, fields, and water in New Jersey and Pennsylvania. Delaware Water Gap is a distinct, S-shaped notch more than a mile wide that the river cuts through Kittatinny Ridge. The view is spectacular. Delaware Water Gap Natural Recreation Area is popular, and more than two million people visit the park each year. Attractions include a landscape that varies from farmland and forests to rugged mountain terrain. Fast-flowing streams, waterfalls, slow-moving rivers, and still ponds tempt visitors to enjoy themselves by sightseeing, hiking, viewing wildlife, boating, fishing, hunting, picnicking, and cycling. More than 200 miles of roads wind through the park's scenic valleys, over ridges, and past historic buildings left over from when the region was a resort in the late nineteenth century. Though mountain biking isn't allowed on most trails in the park (except for Blue Mountain Lake Trail, Ride 84), off-road cyclists can enjoy scenic riding on low-traffic roads, both paved and unpaved.

This moderately hilly, 15-mile out-and-back with a loop follows the Delaware River north on the New Jersey side. You can begin your ride at the Kittatinny Point Visitor Center (the location of the Delaware Water Gap and the point where I-80 crosses the river), but if you like the feel of dirt between your knobbies, you can begin farther north at Flatbrookville on Old Mine Road. The narrow paved lane follows the river and turns to dirt in about five miles, just below the Van Campen Inn. The road is well maintained and nontechnical, passing through fields and woods and featuring plenty of river views. Keep an eye out for wildlife, like the flock of wild turkeys I surprised (and that surprised me) as I pedaled along the quiet road. You'll pass a few residences and abandoned stone buildings. The Van Campen Inn, a two-story stone house built around 1746, was restored by the National Park Service.

RIDE 83 · Delaware Water Gap National Recreation Area

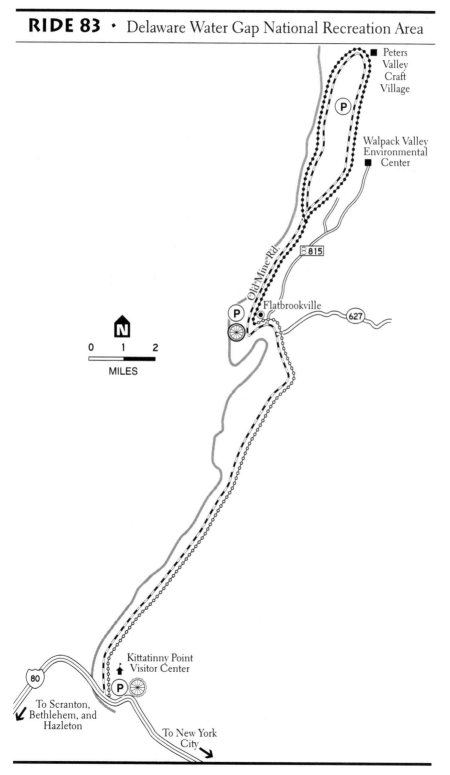

Wide, unpaved fire roads lead to breathtaking scenery at Delaware Water Gap National Recreation Area.

At Peters Valley Craft Village, open daily from 10 a.m. to 5 p.m., you can see craftspeople working in both traditional and contemporary handcrafts. Then turn back on NJ 615 south, a narrow, low-traffic paved road leading to the Walpack Valley Environmental Center. About a mile past the center, the road rejoins Old Mine Road, where you retrace your route for about five miles to your car.

General location: Delaware Water Gap National Recreation Area.

Elevation change: About 600'.

Season: Year-round. The rhododendrons bloom around July 1. The park is one of the best places to see bald eagles, which winter here; midmorning and late afternoon in January and February are the best times to spot them.

Services: Camping is available in the park at Dingmans Campground. All other services can be found in the small towns that surround the park.

Hazards: Hunting is allowed in the park, so wear orange during the fall or ride on Sundays, when hunting isn't permitted. Watch for traffic on the roads.

Rescue index: Excellent.

Land status: National recreation area.

Maps: A map is available at Kittatinny Point Visitor Center (open year-round) and park information centers throughout the park (open seasonally).

The Delaware Water Gap carves a distinct S-shaped notch more than a mile wide as the river cuts through Kittatinny Ridge.

Finding the trail: Delaware Water Gap is easily accessible from both New York and Philadelphia metro areas. From Kittatinny Point Visitor Center and I-80, drive north for 15 miles on Old Mine Road to Flatbrookville and park. Continue north along Old Mine Road on your bike.

Source of additional information:

Delaware Water Gap National Recreation Area
Bushkill, PA 18324
(717) 588-2451

Notes on the trail: You can also ride this as an out-and-back on Old Mine Road.

RIDE 84 · Blue Mountain Lake Trail

AT A GLANCE

Length/configuration: 2 double-track loops totaling about 10 miles

Aerobic difficulty: Easy to moderate

Technical difficulty: Easy to moderate

Scenery: Hardwood and spruce forest and views of 2 ponds

Special comments: Park your bike and hike to Indian Rock for a nice valley view

NJ

This system of relatively easy and scenic loops leads riders to two scenic ponds, Blue Mountain Lake and Hemlock Pond. Opened in 1998, the ten-mile trail system has a surface of pulverized stone that follows old woods roads. The easy trails, suitable for family outings, are well signed with trail markers and maps at key intersections. More experienced cyclists may want to lengthen the ride by exploring the loop trail leading to Hemlock Pond. Most of the trails pass through hardwood forest with some spruce stands to vary the mix. For a good view of the surrounding area, stash your bike and take a short hike to Indian Rocks (about a quarter-mile; no bikes allowed).

This new trail system, which is receiving a lot of use by mountain bikers, was undertaken in a collaborative effort between park managers and the Kittatinny Mountain Biking Association (KIMBA), a group of local off-road riders who helped develop and maintain the trails. A suggestion: If you ride at Blue Mountain Lake regularly, join KIMBA and volunteer for the group's trail maintenance efforts.

General location: Delaware Water Gap National Recreation Area.

Elevation change: Less than 500'.

Season: Year-round.

Services: Camping is available in the park at Dingmans Campground. All other services can be found in the small towns that surround the park.

Hazards: Hunting is allowed in the park, so wear orange during the fall or ride on Sundays, when hunting isn't permitted. Watch for other users when you're on the trail.

Rescue index: Good. A pay phone is located at Millbrook Village, 2.5 miles south of Blue Mountain Lake on Old Mine Road.

Land status: National recreation area.

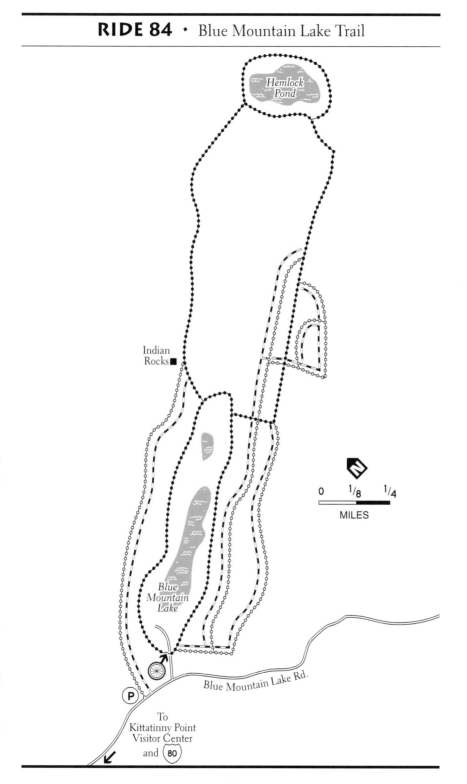

Hemlock
Pond

Indian
Rocks■

N

0   1/8   1/4
MILES

Blue
Mountain
Lake

Blue Mountain Lake Rd.

P

To
Kittatinny Point
Visitor Center
and 80

Maps: A trail map and detailed topographic maps are available at the Kittatinny Point Visitor Center (open year-round) and park information centers throughout the park (open seasonally).

Finding the trail: Delaware Water Gap is easily accessible from both New York and Philadelphia metro areas. From Kittatinny Point Visitor Center and I-80, drive north for about 14 miles on Old Mine Road to Blue Mountain Lake Road and turn right. Go about 1.5 miles to the parking lot on the left and park. The signed trailhead is at the parking lot.

Sources of additional information:

>   Delaware Water Gap National Recreation Area
>   Bushkill, PA 18324
>   (717) 588-2451
>   For information on the trail, call the New Jersey district office at (973) 948-7761.
>
>   Kittatinny Mountain Bike Association (KIMBA)
>   Beth McGatha, President
>   Oakwood Village, Building 82, Apt. 5
>   Flanders, NJ 07836
>   (973) 584-2210
>
>   Mountain Sports
>   1802 Highway 31, Suite 2
>   Clinton, NJ 08809
>   (908) 735-6244

Notes on the trail: The trail system is well signed; just be sure to stay on sections that are specifically marked for cycling. The loop around Blue Mountain Lake is relatively easy, and the 5-mile loop to Hemlock Pond is a bit more difficult and varied.

RIDE 85 · Kittatinny Valley State Park

AT A GLANCE

Length/configuration: About 10 miles of interconnected loops

Aerobic difficulty: Easy to moderate

Technical difficulty: Easy on the dirt roads and moderately difficult on the single-track

Scenery: Mostly woods with hemlock forests, old farm fields, rolling hills and ridges, and lakes

Special comments: A great destination for families on the woods roads, and for hammerheads on the single-track. Plus, not many state parks have airports

NJ

Kittatinny Valley State Park, with about 1,600 acres, is located in Andover Township in Sussex County. The park's glacially formed valleys and limestone ridges are covered with oak, sugar maple, tulip polar, and hemlock forests. Extensive wetlands provide a diversity of plant and animal life, including white-tailed deer, wild turkeys, gray and red squirrels, and chipmunks. The southern end of the park covers the Germany Flats Aquifer, an important source of groundwater.

The small park offers mountain bikers easy riding on woods roads and more challenging single-track on its ten-mile system of dirt roads, rail-trails, and old logging trails (maintained by the Iron Pony Mountain Bike Club). And scenery? Rolling hills and ridges, lots of woods, old farm fields, and several lakes. For something different in a mountain bike venue, the park is also home to Aeroflex-Andover Airport, operated by the New Jersey Forest Fire Service. Just be sure to stay off the runway, which is a restricted area.

In addition, Sussex Branch Trail (Ride 86), a 21-mile recreational mecca that offers more flat, easy, scenic riding, passes through the park. This rails-to-trails conversion was once the right-of-way of the Sussex Branch Line of the Erie-Lackawanna Railroad.

General location: Newton.

Elevation change: Less than 500'.

Season: Year-round.

Services: Most services are available on NJ 206 near the park. All other services are available in Newton.

RIDE 85 · Kittatinny Valley State Park

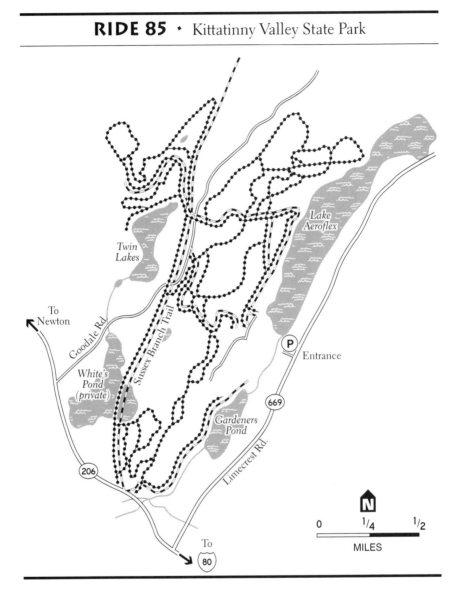

Hazards: Stay off the airport runway, which is a restricted area, and keep an eye out for planes. Watch for bears (in New Jersey!). Hunting is allowed in the park from fall through spring, so wear a Kevlar T-shirt or ride on Sundays when hunting isn't permitted.

Rescue index: Good; the park is small and surrounded by roads.

Land status: State park.

Maps: A trail map is available at the park office. The USGS 7.5 minute quads are Newton West and Newton East.

Finding the trail: From I-80, take NJ 206 north 7 miles and turn right onto Limecrest Road (look for a small sign for the park before the intersection and an Exxon station at the turn). Drive about 1 mile to the park entrance on the left. Park in the first lot just inside the entrance. The trail system starts behind the park office, between the lake and the north end of the airport.

Sources of additional information:

Kittatinny Valley State Park
P.O. Box 621
Andover, NJ 07821
(973) 786-6445

Iron Pony Mountain Bike Club
P.O. Box E
Kenvil, NJ 07847

Notes on the trail: None of the trails are marked, but getting lost shouldn't be a problem because you can't go too far without reaching a road. Another hint: the valley ridges run north to south, so keep an eye on the hills to stay oriented.

RIDE 86 · Sussex Branch Trail

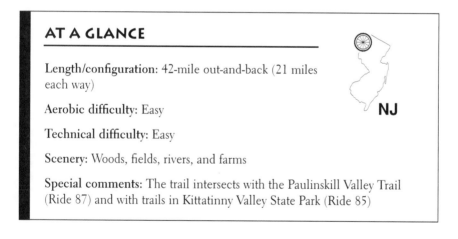

AT A GLANCE

Length/configuration: 42-mile out-and-back (21 miles each way)

Aerobic difficulty: Easy

Technical difficulty: Easy

Scenery: Woods, fields, rivers, and farms

Special comments: The trail intersects with the Paulinskill Valley Trail (Ride 87) and with trails in Kittatinny Valley State Park (Ride 85)

NJ

The 21 miles of Sussex Branch Trail lie in both the highlands and in the ridge and valley provinces in Sussex and Morris Counties. Recreational users—which include mountain bikers, joggers, hikers, runners, bird-watchers, and others—can enjoy the scenic countryside and vistas of farms, fields, and woods. As you ride the trail, keep an eye peeled for white-tailed deer, wild turkey, red and gray squirrels, and chipmunks. Oak, sugar maple, tulip poplar, and hemlock forests cover the glacially formed valley and surrounding limestone ridges.

RIDE 86 • Sussex Branch Trail
RIDE 87 • Paulinskill Valley Trail

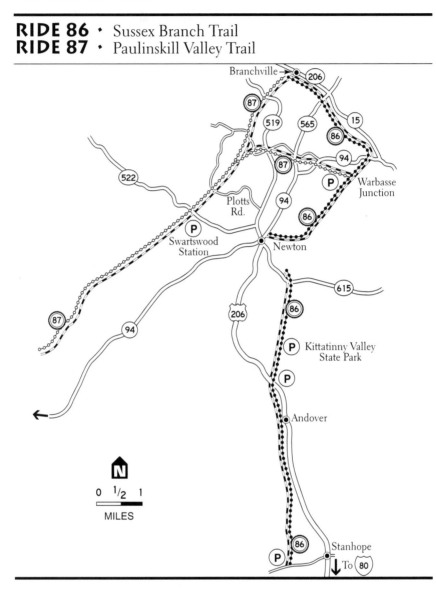

The trail was once the right-of-way of the Erie-Lackawanna Railroad, which transported iron ore, agricultural products, freight, and passengers from the mid-1800s to the mid-1900s. Until recently, Sussex Branch Trail was a series of short out-and-backs because all of the railroad bridges had been removed. No more. New bridges are in place, and cyclists and other users can enjoy the entire length of the cinder-based trail.

An added bonus: The trail intersects Paulinskill Valley Trail (Ride 87) in Warbasse Junction, adding many more miles of scenic, easy biking. In addition, the trail passes through Kittatinny Valley State Park (Ride 85) and connects with its ten-mile system of off-road, mostly single-track trails.

General location: Sussex and Morris Counties.

Elevation change: Nominal.

Season: Year-round.

Services: All services are available at towns along the trail.

Hazards: Watch for traffic at road crossings.

Rescue index: Excellent.

Land status: State park.

Maps: A map is available by mail from Kittatinny Valley State Park.

Finding the trail: From I-80, take NJ 206 north to the second traffic light, turn left, and drive 1.75 miles. Park in the lot on the right (opposite Continental Drive). Another option is to start the ride in Warbasse Junction where the trail intersects Paulinskill Valley Trail. To reach Warbasse Junction from I-80, take the NJ 206 exit, go north for 7.5 miles to NJ 94 (north of Newton), and turn right. Next, turn right onto CR 663, continue for 0.75 mile to the parking lot on the right (look for a port-a-john), and park.

Source of additional information:

Kittatinny Valley State Park
P.O. Box 621
Andover, NJ 07821
(973) 786-6874

Notes on the trail: There's a 1.5-mile interruption of the trail at Newton. If you're riding north, turn right on Hicks Avenue, which becomes CR 663. Go 1 mile to the gate on the left; the trail continues north just beyond it. If you're riding south, exit the trail at the gate, get on CR 663, and continue south. Return to the trail at Hicks Avenue.

RIDE 87 · Paulinskill Valley Trail

AT A GLANCE

Length/configuration: 54-mile out-and-back (27 miles each way)

Aerobic difficulty: Easy

NJ

Technical difficulty: Easy, with some sharp drop-offs at road crossings that can be walked

Scenery: Woods, farms, rivers, and fields

Special comments: This rails-to-trails conversion was once the right-of-way of the New York, Susquehanna, and Western Railroad

This scenic out-and-back traverses 27 miles of the Kittatinny Valley and offers fine views of farms, fields, rivers, and forest. The trail was once part of the right-of-way of the New York, Susquehanna, and Western Railroad, which was originally used to transport agricultural products and Pennsylvania coal to cities in eastern New Jersey and New York City. Today, the trail is a valuable recreational resource popular with mountain bikers, hikers, runners, bird-watchers, equestrians, and folks walking their dogs on the smooth cinder surface. Keep an eye peeled for white-tailed deer, wild turkey, red and gray squirrels, and chipmunks. Oak, sugar maple, tulip poplar, and hemlock forests cover the glacially formed valley and surrounding limestone ridges.

An added bonus: The trail intersects Sussex Branch Trail (Ride 86) in Warbasse Junction, adding many more miles of scenic, easy biking.

General location: Warren and Sussex Counties.

Elevation change: Nominal.

Season: Year-round.

Services: All services are available at towns along the trail.

Hazards: Watch for traffic at crossroads. It's also a good idea to get off your bike at road crossings with steep drop-offs.

Rescue index: Excellent.

Land status: State park.

Maps: A map is available by mail from Kittatinny Valley State Park.

Finding the trail: From I-80, take NJ 206 north to NJ 94 (north of Newton) and turn right. At CR 663, turn right and drive about 0.75 mile to the parking lot on the right (look for the port-a-john). This is also the junction with Sussex Branch Trail (Ride 86), which gives you more riding possibilities.

Source of additional information:

Kittatinny Valley State Park
P.O. Box 621
Andover, NJ 07821
(973) 786-6874

RIDE 88 · Stokes State Forest

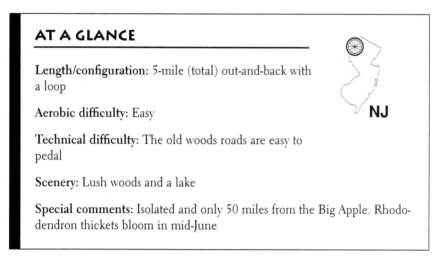

AT A GLANCE

Length/configuration: 5-mile (total) out-and-back with a loop

Aerobic difficulty: Easy

Technical difficulty: The old woods roads are easy to pedal

Scenery: Lush woods and a lake

Special comments: Isolated and only 50 miles from the Big Apple. Rhododendron thickets bloom in mid-June

NJ

Tucked away in a remote corner where New Jersey meets Pennsylvania and New York, Stokes State Forest is a 15,000-acre preserve with an Adirondack ambience. Maybe it's the lush understory of pines in the oak, birch, and maple forest or the mountain lakes lined with vacation homes. Whatever the reason, Stokes offers mountain bikers a sense of wilderness isolation that's remarkable considering it's only 50 miles or so from the Big Apple.

A system of mostly easy woods roads emanating from a lake is the basis of this easy, five-mile ramble through the western half of the state forest. The narrow, traffic-free double-track connects with a few paved roads. But traffic is usually light, and the roads serve as a link between the gated fire roads that entice fat-tired cyclists to explore them. Woods Road, which starts at the western end of Kittatinny Lake (across US 206 from the park office), is three and a half miles long and serves as the ride's start and end. It begins behind the gate with a sign that reads, "Entrance to cross-country and snowshoeing trails." Coss Road and Shay Road connect Woods Road to Struble and Dimon Roads, making a couple

RIDE 88 · Stokes State Forest

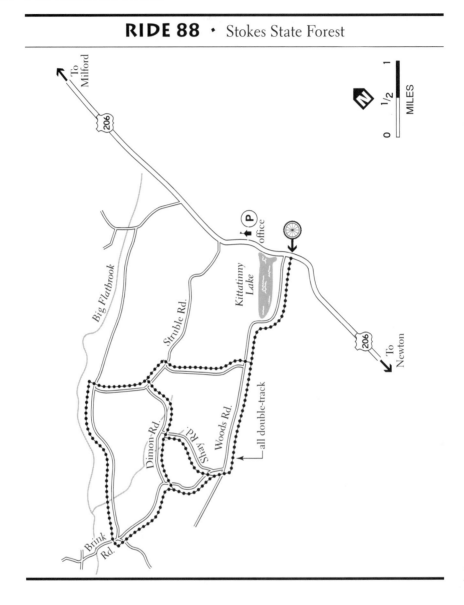

of loop combinations possible. Stoll Trail, less than a mile long and level and easy, is a pleasant single-track that runs between Coss and Dimon Roads. It's rated one of the most picturesque trails in Stokes and is lined with big specimens of beech, hemlock, white pine, and oak trees; rhododendron thickets bloom in mid-June.

Starting on Woods Road near the lake, go about a half-mile and begin making right turns on Coss Road, Stoll Trail, Dimon Road, and Brink Road, which

"Rough Road Ahead" at Stokes State Forest, but not too rough for adventurous mountain bikers.

will bring you back to Woods Road. Or lengthen the ride by taking Shay Road (which connects Brink and Dimon Roads) to Dimon Road and retracing the ride in the opposite direction along Stoll Trail and Coss Road.

General location: Newton.

Elevation change: Around 400'.

Season: Year-round.

Services: Camping is available in the forest. Groceries and motels are located along US 208, which bisects the state forest.

Hazards: Hunting is allowed in the state forest. In the fall and winter, wear orange or ride on Sundays, when hunting is not permitted.

Rescue index: Good. You're never far from paved and unpaved roads that carry traffic. Vacation houses line Kittatinny Lake.

Land status: State forest.

Maps: A trail map is available at the park office on US 206. The USGS 7.5 minute quads are Colvers Gap and Branchville.

Finding the trail: The state forest is 5 miles north of Newton on US 206; park at the park office. On your bike, cross US 206 (watch for traffic) and ride past Kittatinny Lake. Woods Road begins behind the gate.

Source of additional information:

Stokes State Forest
One Coursen Road
Branchville, NJ 07826
(973) 948-3820

Notes on the trail: An unmarked double-track off Struble Road leads to Mountain Road, an 8-mile dirt road you can ride to extend the loop. Intermediate and advanced riders will want to explore a maze of single-track trails, many of which are steep and rocky as they ascend Kittatinny Mountain Ridge to the Appalachian Trail, which begins at the Stony Lake Day Use Area; this trail system is located off Coursen Road past the park office. Mountain bikes are permitted on all trails in the state forest except for the Maine-to-Georgia Appalachian Trail, which parallels Woods Road.

RIDE 89 · High Point State Park

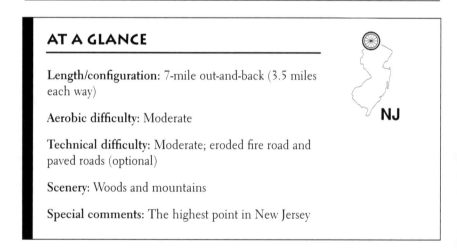

AT A GLANCE

Length/configuration: 7-mile out-and-back (3.5 miles each way)

Aerobic difficulty: Moderate

Technical difficulty: Moderate; eroded fire road and paved roads (optional)

Scenery: Woods and mountains

Special comments: The highest point in New Jersey

NJ

They don't call it High Point State Park for nothin'. The highest point in New Jersey (1,803 feet) is in High Point State Park, 14,000 acres in the Kittatinny Mountains. That's where you'll find High Point Monument, a 220-foot obelisk with a commanding view of the surrounding land, including ridges of the Pocono Mountains in Pennsylvania; Port Jervis, New York; and the Catskill Mountains. A little closer is Lake Marcia, the highest lake in New Jersey.

For mountain bikers, there's a lot more to appreciate than a pretty view from a man-made structure. Iris Trail, a three-and-a-half-mile (one-way) out-and-back, provides fat-tired cyclists with a pleasant yet mildly demanding foray along the high ridge of the Kittatinny Mountains. The trail passes through a delightful forest of oak, hickory, red maple, white ash, and young chestnut. The old forest road crosses several springs and provides views of Lake Rutherford. At the end of the ride is 20-acre Lake Marcia; in the summer you can cool off in this spring-fed lake.

General location: Sussex.

Elevation change: About 300'.

Season: Year-round. In the summer you can swim in Lake Marcia.

Services: Camping is available in the park. Lake Marcia has changing areas, showers, and a food concession. Sussex (8 miles south) has most other services.

Hazards: Plenty of rocks and tree roots make Iris Trail more technical than your typical fire road, so be careful on descents.

Rescue index: Excellent; the trails are well used, especially from spring through fall. A first-aid station is open at Lake Marcia during the summer.

Land status: State park.

Maps: A trail map is available at the park headquarters.

Finding the trail: From I-80, take NJ 23 north to the park entrance on the left. Park your car near the office on the left. On your bike, take the yellow-blazed trail at the south end of the parking lot past the small firewood shed.

Source of additional information:

High Point State Park
1480 State Route 23
Sussex, NJ 07461
(973) 875-4800

Notes on the trail: Follow the yellow-blazed trail a short distance until it merges with a white-blazed trail. After about 0.2 mile, you'll come to a three-way intersection with yellow-, red-, and white-blazed trails. Take Iris Trail, the wider, red-blazed trail, all the way to the left (look for a cement marker). From here it's a gradual, 2.5-mile descent to Deckertown Turnpike, where you can either turn around and retrace your route or make a loop on paved roads by turning right, riding 2 miles, and turning right on Sawmill Road, which takes you to NJ 23 and the park headquarters.

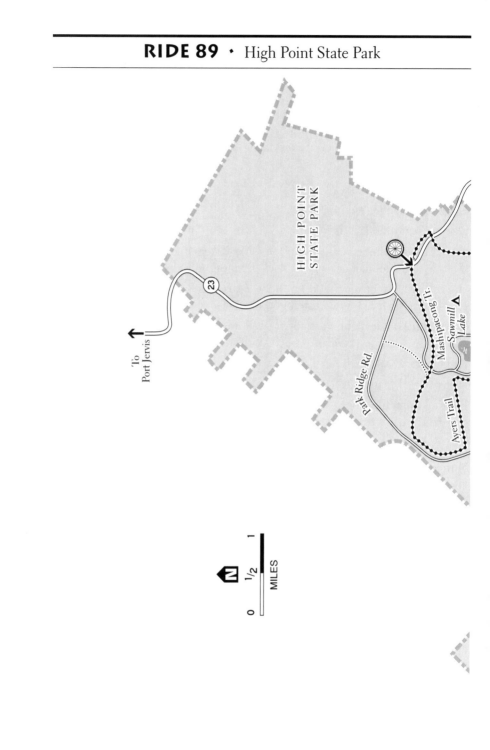

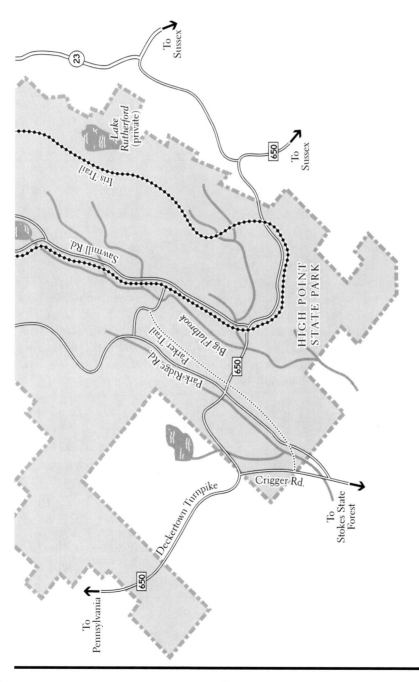

RIDE 90 · Wawayanda State Park

AT A GLANCE

NJ

Length/configuration: 8-mile loop

Aerobic difficulty: Moderate

Technical difficulty: Easy to moderate along old woods roads

Scenery: Woods, rock outcroppings, ponds, and streams

Special comments: Stay on trails open to bikes; in the summer, take a swim in the 255-acre lake

Wawayanda State Park, a beautiful 10,000-acre park in the New Jersey Highlands, is laced with old logging roads and graced with natural beauty. It's also a magnificent setting for mountain biking. This moderately challenging, eight-mile loop passes through a pristine forest of evergreens, hardwoods, and wetlands along old wooded roads. It's a New Jersey classic. Novice riders will be challenged by small hills, dips into creek valleys, and climbs up rolling ridge crests and major hilltops. Intermediate-level off-roaders will appreciate the transition zones of forest habitats and a woodscape dotted with trees, ponds, boulders, rock outcroppings, and streams. As you ride through the small river ravines, the woods alternate from the conifer-dominant wetland forest of the lower valleys to the beech, oak, and maple hardwoods sections of the higher plateau. In a word, gorgeous.

Wawayanda is nestled in the Ramapo Mountains on a level mountaintop with elevations between 1,200 and 1,300 feet. While most cyclists will find the riding challenging, most trails are fairly level. The park's maze of old logging roads left over from the heavy logging of the 1940s simply demands that you pay attention and occasionally turn on the power to make it up a climb or through a bog. And what about that name? Wawayanda, given by the Lenape Indians, means "water on the mountain"—a reference to the 255-acre lake on top of the mountain. It's a nice place to swim after a summer ride.

At the start of the ride, you pass an old charcoal furnace, all that remains of New Jersey's iron-ore industry in Wawayanda. The miles of old logging roads left behind from the bygone era give mountain bikers an opportunity to access a historic and pristine forest environment, and leave with an enchanting experience after an energetic ride through the woods.

General location: Northern New Jersey.

Elevation change: A couple of hundred feet.

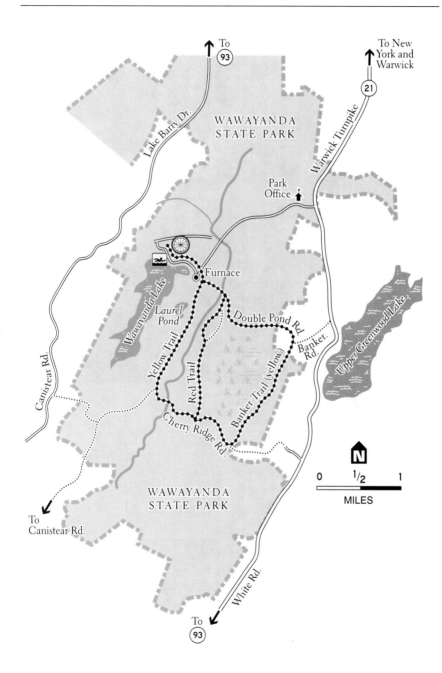

Trails on old woods roads are relatively flat at Wawayanda State Park.

Season: Year-round. During the summer, try to arrive by 9 a.m. to get a convenient parking space.

Services: Food and gas are available at Greenwood Lake.

Hazards: Watch for equestrians and hikers.

Rescue index: Good. You're never more than 3 miles from the park office.

Land status: State park.

Maps: Get a trail map at the park office. The New York–New Jersey Trail Conference's Trail Map 21, North-Jersey Trails, Western Portion, provides good detail of Wawayanda's trails; it's also waterproof and tear-proof. The map can be purchased at most outdoor outfitters in northern New Jersey. The USGS 7.5 minute quad is Wawayanda.

Finding the trail: From I-80, take Exit 53 to NJ 23 north. Go about 16 miles and turn right onto Echo Road (NJ 513). Follow NJ 513 north to its end and turn left (west) onto Macopin Road. Continue for about 4 miles and bear left at a fork onto Union Valley Road (there's a gas station on the right and a small shopping center on the left). At the next fork bear left onto White Road (there's a sign for Wawayanda State Park). This road ends at the intersection with Warwick Turnpike; turn left and continue to the Wawayanda Park entrance on the left. Go past the tollbooth and take the park road straight ahead until you see the large parking area near the beach. Turn left and park. The trail begins past the wooden barrier between the beach and the parking area.

Source of additional information:

Wawayanda State Park
P.O. Box 198
Highland Lakes, NJ 07422
(973) 853-4462

Notes on the trail: Once you're on the trail, keep hugging the lake's shoreline and continue straight—and a bit to the left—as you pass a stone dam at the end of the lake. Soon you'll come to the remnants of the old charcoal furnace at a four-way intersection. Continue across the road and keep riding; you'll be returning from the trail that leads off to the right.

RIDE 91 · Ringwood State Park

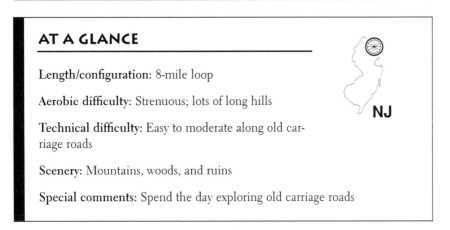

AT A GLANCE

Length/configuration: 8-mile loop

Aerobic difficulty: Strenuous; lots of long hills

Technical difficulty: Easy to moderate along old carriage roads

Scenery: Mountains, woods, and ruins

Special comments: Spend the day exploring old carriage roads

NJ

You can cruise all day on a labyrinth of old carriage roads that honeycomb Ringwood State Park, 4,300 acres in northwest New Jersey near I-87 and the New York state line. The hard-packed double-track passes through a beautiful wooded landscape that features five ponds. An eight-mile loop trail takes riders on an interesting—and, with its climbs and descents, challenging—route. The landscape is moderately hilly, but the riding is basically beginner-friendly. What once delighted turn-of-the-century (the nineteenth, that is) vacationers on horse-drawn carriages, today serves cyclists who enjoy demanding climbs, fast double-

RIDE 91 · Ringwood State Park

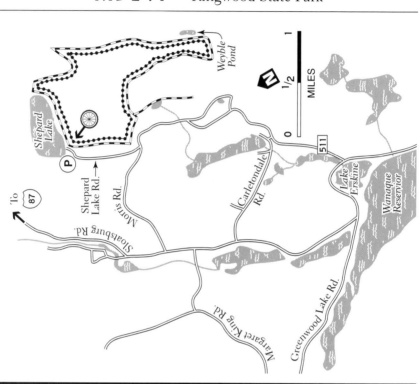

track descents, and lots of beautiful scenery. You'll see old stone ruins and walls, old stone buildings, and a stone archway that you ride through.

Ringwood Park is located in the Hudson Highlands, an ancient mountain range that rivaled the Himalayas before 500 million years of erosion reduced them to a more manageable size. Keep in mind that these are mountains; you'll encounter significant hills as you explore the maze of dirt roads. If you've got the time and energy, consider touring the historic Tudor mansions of Ringwood and Skylands after your ride. The buildings are examples of the wealth accumulated by nineteenth-century ironmasters. Mining began in the eighteenth century during the French and Indian War and continued through World War II.

General location: Ringwood.

Elevation change: Elevations range from 600' to 1,000' between valleys and ridges; most rides in the park include several climbs.

Season: Year-round. In the spring and after heavy rains, the trails get very muddy.

Services: Food is available at Ringwood Manor House from Memorial Day through Labor Day. All other services are available in Ringwood.

Hazards: Hunting in the fall and winter. Check with the park office for specific dates or ride on Sundays, when hunting isn't permitted.

Rescue index: Good. A ranger is usually available at Ringwood Manor House. The Jersey Off Road Bicycle Association (JORBA; website at jorba.org) does bike patrols on weekends.

Land status: State park.

Maps: A trail map is available at the park office. The New York–New Jersey Trail Conference's Trail Map 21, North-Jersey Trails, Western Portion, available at many outdoor outfitters, has good detail on the park trails.

Finding the trail: From I-87 in New York, take Exit 15A, which leads to NY 17. Take NY 17 north and turn left (west) onto Sloatsburg Road. Drive past Ringwood Manor, turn left on Morris Road, and go past Hewitt School and Carletondale Road. Skylands Manor House, located in the park, is 1.5 miles up Morris Road at the top of the hill. Go through the tollgate and park in area A. (If it's filled, park in area B.) Ride your bike back down the park road and past the tollgate and turn right toward Shepard Lake. Turn right at the stop sign onto a wide dirt road that passes the boat rental building and leads to a labyrinth of carriage roads and interconnecting trails.

Sources of additional information:

Ringwood State Park
RD Box 1304
Ringwood, NJ 07456
(973) 962-7031 or (973) 962-7047

Notes on the trail: Because many of the carriage roads are improperly marked or not marked at all, don't be surprised if you get lost. Luckily, it's usually not a problem, especially if you time your visit on a weekend with nice weather. That way there will be plenty of other trail users whom you can ask for directions; some may actually know where they are. The good news is that virtually all of the trails lead back to Honeysuckle Lane and the parking areas. Another key to remaining oriented is to stay on wide dirt roads and keep descending.

THE CATSKILLS AND
SHAWANGUNKS OF NEW YORK

In a two-hour drive north of the cold concrete canyons of New York City, intrepid mountain bikers are transported to the scenic Hudson Valley. Overlooking the valley to the west is Catskill Park, featuring 650,000 acres of mountains and forests and some of the best mountain biking and alpine scenery in the East. South of the park, the Shawangunk Mountains (SHOW-gums) have become a favorite destination for off-road riders.

The Hudson Valley's rich history is also a boon to mountain bikers. The region was settled in the early seventeenth century, and the many carefully carved carriage trails crisscrossing the nearby Shawangunks reflect nearly three centuries of careful use. For off-road cyclists, this translates into many miles of moderate-grade climbing through spectacular mountains. Dramatic rock outcroppings and vistas of mountain ridges and lakes mark almost every turn along many of the trails. If riding carriage trails sounds a little too tame, the Shawangunks also feature excellent single-track. For hammerheads seeking anaerobic bliss, all-day rides leading to distant peaks are easy to plan.

With New York City and populous New Jersey only a few hours away, the Shawangunks get a lot of use by hikers, and increasingly, in the last ten years or so, by mountain bikers. On a midweek morning, I found the trails in Minnewaska State Park filling up with bikers, and at least a dozen mountain bikes were being unloaded in the parking lot. The word is out: The Shawangunks are a hot destination for mountain bikers.

For scenic and easy riding, Wallkill Valley Rail Trail fills the bill. This beautiful, 12-mile hiker-biker trail passes through woods and two quaint seventeenth-century villages, skirts farms, and crosses rivers and streams. The elevated rail bed provides a view of the surrounding area, including woodland ponds, the Wallkill River, and the Shawangunk Mountains in the distance.

Hammerheads will enjoy Vernooy Kill Falls Trail, a ten-mile loop for the technically adept mountain biker. It features rough, washed-out fire roads and technical single-track. Steep climbs and long, technical descents will challenge expert riders, as will slippery wet rocks, black muck, and swamps.

RIDE 92 · Minnewaska State Park

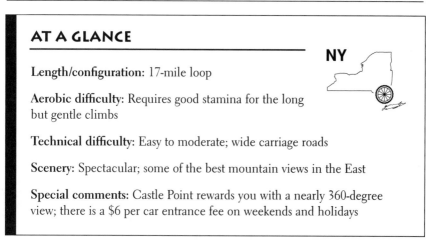

AT A GLANCE

Length/configuration: 17-mile loop

Aerobic difficulty: Requires good stamina for the long but gentle climbs

Technical difficulty: Easy to moderate; wide carriage roads

Scenery: Spectacular; some of the best mountain views in the East

Special comments: Castle Point rewards you with a nearly 360-degree view; there is a $6 per car entrance fee on weekends and holidays

For spectacular mountain scenery, this 17-mile loop may qualify as one of the best on the East Coast. The carriage roads gently switchback up the mountain face, revealing grander views of the surrounding mountains and lakes at each turn. From Castle Point, the nearly 360-degree view is breathtaking, as mountain ridges recede in the distance in all directions. The scenery never lets up.

Good news: You don't need to be super-fit to enjoy this ride. Although there are some long climbs, most of the riding is on six-foot-wide converted carriage roads with gentle grades. Bring endurance, not technical riding ability. The trails are well maintained and heavily used.

General location: Kingston.

Elevation change: 1,000'.

Season: April until the first snow in late fall, when the park closes its trails to mountain bikes.

Services: All services are available in New Paltz and Kingston.

Hazards: Watch for hikers and wheel-eating crevices on the rock formations leading to overlooks.

Rescue index: Excellent. The park is heavily used by hikers and mountain bikers, even on weekdays.

Land status: State park.

Maps: The USGS 7.5 minute quads are Gardiner and Napanoch. A trail map is available at the park entrance.

Finding the trail: From New York State Thruway (Interstate 87) Exit 18, turn left onto NY 299 west. Go through the village of New Paltz and cross the iron

RIDE 92 · Minnewaska State Park

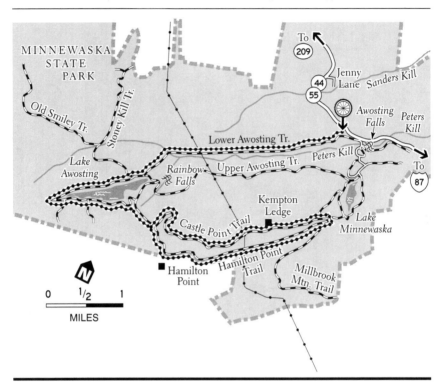

bridge. Continue on NY 299 until its end 6 miles later. Turn right on to NY 44/55. The park entrance is about 4 miles down on the left. Park in the lot and pedal out on the Lower Awosting Trail to start the loop.

Sources of additional information:

Minnewaska State Park
New Paltz, New York 12561
(914) 255-0752

The Bicycle Depot
15 Main Street
New Paltz, NY 12561
(914) 255-3859

Notes on the trail: The trails are well marked and easy to follow.

RIDE 93 · Wallkill Valley Rail Trail

AT A GLANCE

NY

Length/configuration: 24-mile out-and-back (12 miles each way)

Aerobic difficulty: Easy

Technical difficulty: Easy

Scenery: Gorgeous New York scenery at its best, with mountains in the background

Special comments: New Paltz is a charming village and a great lunch stop

This beautiful, 12-mile (one-way) hiker-biker trail passes through two quaint seventeenth-century villages, skirts farms, goes through woods, and crosses rivers and streams. The elevated rail bed provides a view of the surrounding area, including woodland ponds, the Wallkill River, and the Shawangunk Mountains in the distance. Frequently sighted wildlife include wood turtles, woodcocks, songbirds, broadwing hawks, gray horned owls, fox, white-tailed deer, and raccoons.

The well-maintained cinder trail is essentially flat and can be ridden as an out-and-back, or as a loop by returning to the start on one of 21 paved roads that cross the trail. The trail passes through the New Paltz Historical District, which features seventeenth-century stone houses and the old railroad station that served the trains on this former Conrail route. A Mexican restaurant, a bistro, a bakery, and several pizza parlors can round out a leisurely ride.

General location: New Paltz.

Elevation change: Negligible.

Season: Late spring through fall.

Services: All services are available in New Paltz. Gardiner has several bed-and-breakfasts.

Hazards: Watch for traffic at road crossings.

Rescue index: Excellent. Help can be flagged down on the paved roads that cross the trail or from nearby residences.

Land status: New Paltz and the Land Trust of Wallkill Valley.

Maps: The 7.5 minute USGS quads are Gardiner and Rosendale. Trail brochures, which include a map, are available at the town hall on North Chestnut Street in New Paltz; call (914) 255-0100.

RIDE 93 · Wallkill Valley Rail Trail

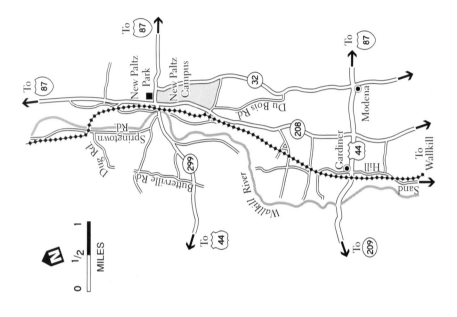

Finding the trail: From I-87, take Exit 18 (NY 299) west for 1.5 miles to New Paltz, where Wallkill Valley Rail Trail crosses the road. Park on a side street in the village or in the lot near the historic district.

Sources of additional information:

Wallkill Valley Rail Trail Association
P.O. Box 1048
New Paltz, New York 12561

New Paltz Chamber of Commerce
259 Main Street
New Paltz, New York 12561
(914) 255-0243

RIDE 94 · Vernooy Kill Falls Trail

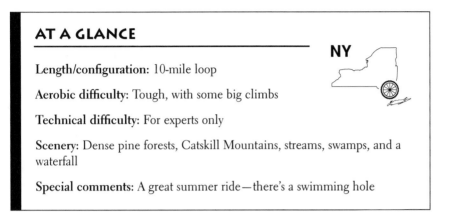

AT A GLANCE

NY

Length/configuration: 10-mile loop

Aerobic difficulty: Tough, with some big climbs

Technical difficulty: For experts only

Scenery: Dense pine forests, Catskill Mountains, streams, swamps, and a waterfall

Special comments: A great summer ride—there's a swimming hole

On this scenic ride in the mountains of Catskill Park, watch for wildlife such as bear, deer, porcupine, turkey, and birds. Other attractions include a beautiful waterfall and swimming hole surrounded by pines and shrubs about two miles into the ride. The trail passes through dense forests of pines, maples, and oaks, and by streams, waterfalls, and swamps. Don't forget to pack a fly rod; Vernooy Kill is an excellent trout stream.

This ten-mile loop is for the technically adept mountain biker. It features rough, washed-out fire roads and technical single-track. Steep climbs and long, technical descents will challenge expert riders. Additional challenges include slippery, wet rocks, black muck, and swamps. This is a ride for strong cyclists.

General location: Near Kerhonkson in the southern Catskill Mountains.

Elevation change: The total elevation gain is around 1,200'.

Season: Local riders say summer is best; it's warm enough to swim and the trails are usually dry. In the fall, the foliage is considered better than Vermont. Expect snow from November through March.

Services: All services are available in Kingston and New Paltz.

Hazards: Watch for wet, slippery rocks. On steep descents, look for other trail users.

Rescue index: Not good. The trails are all at least 5 miles from roads with residences and traffic.

Land status: State park.

Maps: The USGS 7.5 minute quads are Peekamoose Mountain, Roundout Reservoir, and Kerhonkson.

Finding the trail: Getting to the trailhead can be tough. Many road signs are obscure and handwritten, so pay close attention and be prepared to ask for directions. Take Exit 19 (Kingston) from the New York State Thruway (I-87) to

RIDE 94 · Vernooy Kill Falls Trail

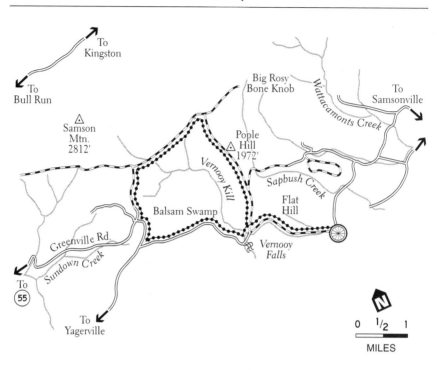

NY 209 south, toward Ellenville. Go about 16 miles through Accord; at Kerhonkson, turn right onto Pataukunk Road. At the intersection with Cherrytown Road, continue straight to Sampsonville Road. Bear left onto Lower Cherrytown Road. The name changes to Upper Cherrytown Road in Cherrytown. Continue to the parking area on the left at the state trail marker and park your car.

Source of additional information:

The Bicycle Depot
15 Main Street
New Paltz, NY 12561
(914) 255-3859

Notes on the trail: When you reach the falls at the beginning of the ride, take the trail to the right; when you return to this point on the loop, you will come from the left, crossing over a wooden hiking bridge.

POCAHONTAS COUNTY, WEST VIRGINIA

For mountain bikers who like wilderness—and lots of it—Pocahontas County is arguably the best mountain biking destination this side of the Rockies. Consider: This county in southeastern West Virginia boasts a major chunk of the 830,000-acre Monongahela National Forest, where the rugged Allegheny Mountains soar toward 5,000 feet and comprise the headwaters of eight rivers: Greenbrier, Cherry, Elk, Cheat, Gauley, Tygart Valley, Williams, and Cranberry. With 330,000 acres of state and national forests, it's not a stretch to call Pocahontas County "mountain bike heaven."

Additional high-quality wilderness attractions include Cranberry Glades Wilderness Area (closed to mountain bikes), which features 35,000 acres of bogs and forests that evoke Alaskan tundra. Underground erosion created more than 96 significant caverns in the county. The Cass Scenic Railroad, a steam locomotive–pulled train that climbs Bald Knob, the state's second-highest peak, is a spectacular trip and should not be missed. The Highland Scenic Highway extends 22 miles at altitudes of more than 4,000 feet, and its wilderness views stretch to the horizon in all directions.

So what's the mountain biking like? Scenic, varied, and virtually unlimited. While many trails are surprisingly easy (for example, Greenbrier River Trail, which is 75 miles long and virtually flat), the region is renowned for its steep and rugged trails. Be warned: Mountain biking on the foot trails in the mountains often means negotiating wet, steep, rocky, boggy, and root-tangled obstacle courses. If this isn't your idea of fun, stick to the forest service roads that lace the mountains. But if mile after mile of technical single-track turns you on, this is the place.

A word of warning to intrepid backcountry trekkers: The weather in the high mountains matches the terrain for severity and unpredictability. Mountain bikers embarking on an all-day ride should carry raingear, extra clothes, food, first-aid items, tools, a topo map, and a compass.

Mountain bike headquarters is Elk River Touring Center in Slatyfork, a small village about 20 miles north of Marlinton. Owners Gil and Mary Willis began guiding mountain bike tours in 1984 and are the resident experts in this vast area. Be sure to visit Slatyfork for the latest information on trail conditions. Also, Elk River offers lodging, an excellent restaurant, a mountain bike shop and rentals, and touring services (guided and self-guided). The Willises want to help visiting mountain bikers have a good time and spread the word about Mountain Bike Heaven. Elk River is on the Web at www.ertc.com.

Another option is Snowshoe, a huge downhill ski resort that allows mountain biking on more than 100 miles of trails in the summer and fall. In addition to two mountain bike centers, guided tours, bus service to the mountaintop, lodging, and restaurants, Snowshoe features special multiday packages to entice cyclists to visit Pocahontas County.

RIDE 95 · Greenbrier River Trail/Marlinton to Sharp's Tunnel

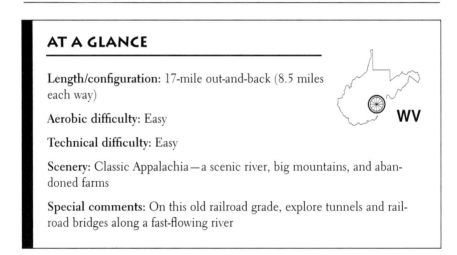

AT A GLANCE

Length/configuration: 17-mile out-and-back (8.5 miles each way)

Aerobic difficulty: Easy

Technical difficulty: Easy

Scenery: Classic Appalachia—a scenic river, big mountains, and abandoned farms

Special comments: On this old railroad grade, explore tunnels and railroad bridges along a fast-flowing river

WV

The 75-mile Greenbrier River Trail winds through a remote mountain valley along a clean, fast-flowing river that has been involved in wild and scenic river studies. Old Appalachian farms, many of them deserted and overgrown, overlook the river. On this section you can explore 511-foot Sharp's Tunnel; if the weather's warm, check out the swimming hole at the base of the trestle leading to the tunnel. The wildflower blooms in late May and early June are spectacular.

This eight-and-a-half-mile (one-way) out-and-back takes you along some of the best scenery in Pocahontas County, and, being virtually flat, it's a perfect introduction to the area. The trail, formerly a railroad right-of-way, is mostly hard-packed gravel. There are short sections of loose gravel, and washouts occasionally occur where streams and creeks empty into the river.

General location: Marlinton.

RIDE 95 • Greenbrier River Trail/Marlinton to Sharp's Tunnel

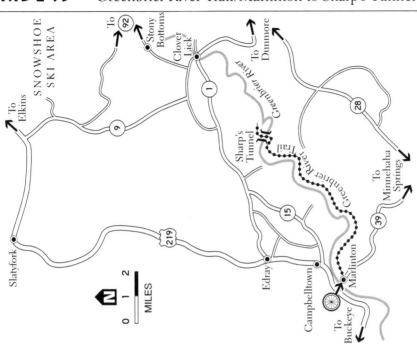

Elevation change: Nominal.

Season: The trail can be ridden from late March through late October. Spring can be muddy and cold, and expect snow from November through March. Avoid riding during deer-hunting season in late fall.

Services: Water is available at the restored railroad depot in town. Primitive camping areas ideal for cyclists are located above and below Sharp's Tunnel. Elk River Touring Center, 20 miles north of Marlinton in Slatyfork, has a mountain bike shop, lodging, food, guided tours, and shuttle service. All other services are available in Marlinton.

Hazards: Sharp's Tunnel is dark and littered with rocks; carrying a flashlight is a good idea, although not an absolute necessity (it's not very long). Watch for washouts along the trail where creeks flow into the river.

Rescue index: Fair. The trail passes through isolated country. Many of the farms in the area are remote and hard to reach.

Land status: State park.

Maps: A map of Greenbrier River Trail is available at the restored railroad depot In Marlinton. The USGS 7.5 minute quads are Marlinton and Edray.

Finding the trail: Marlinton is at the intersection of WV 39 and US 219, between Lewisburg and Elkins. Park at the Old Train Depot on Main Street (WV 39), Marlinton's Visitor Center. The trail starts behind the building.

Sources of additional information:

> Superintendent, Greenbrier River Trail
> Star Route, Box 125
> Caldwell, WV 24925
> (304) 536-1944
>
> Pocahontas County Tourism Commission
> P.O. Box 275
> Marlinton, WV 24954
> (800) 336-7009
>
> Elk River Touring Center
> HC 69, Box 7
> Slatyfork, WV 26291
> (304) 572-3771
> Email: ertc@ertc.com

Notes on the trail: From the Old Train Depot, pedal out Fourth Avenue for a half-mile to the sign for the trail on the left. This stretch of Greenbrier River Trail north of Marlinton is probably the trail's most scenic and remote. As it winds its way through the river valley, the trail passes through many villages and traverses 35 bridges and 2 tunnels.

RIDE 96 · Red Run

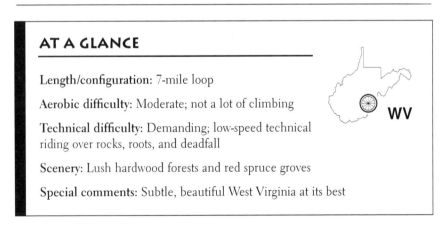

AT A GLANCE

Length/configuration: 7-mile loop

Aerobic difficulty: Moderate; not a lot of climbing

Technical difficulty: Demanding; low-speed technical riding over rocks, roots, and deadfall

Scenery: Lush hardwood forests and red spruce groves

Special comments: Subtle, beautiful West Virginia at its best

WV

While only a seven-mile loop, this stretch of fairly level single-track is demanding. The technical requirements make up for the lack of climbing. Most of the trail's surface is spongy, mossy, and wet. Rocks, wet roots, bogs,

RIDE 96 · Red Run

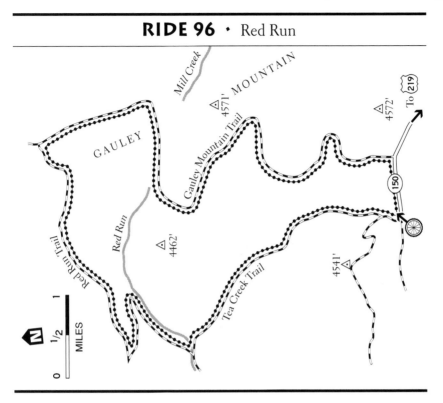

deep mud, and stream crossings make for low-speed technical riding. The trails are frequently littered with deadfall. Yet intermediate and advanced riders will be delighted by the challenges and the area's natural beauty.

The ride starts in lush hardwood forests, progresses through red spruce groves, and ends in a mixed hardwood and spruce forest. The view from the overlook at the start is of cranberry bogs and the headwaters of the Williams River. Hawks soar at eye level. This is subtle, beautiful, rugged West Virginia at its best.

General location: Marlinton.

Elevation change: The ride starts at 4,200' and varies only a few hundred feet or so.

Season: The trail is usually rideable from mid-May through early October. Avoid riding during deer-hunting season in the late fall. Expect snow from late October through March.

Services: Most services are available in Marlinton, about 10 miles from the intersection of US 219 and the scenic highway. Bike supplies, repairs, a restaurant, and lodging are available at Elk River Touring Center in Slatyfork, about 9 miles north on US 219.

Hazards: The single-track is technical with lots of slick rocks and tree roots. The weather at this altitude changes fast, so carry raingear, extra clothes, food, first-aid items, and tools.

Rescue index: Poor. This ride goes deep into the national forest; there are no farms or residences on the loop. Cars can be flagged down on the scenic highway where the ride starts.

Land status: National forest.

Maps: The USGS 7.5 minute quad is Woodrow.

Finding the trail: From Marlinton, drive north on US 219 to the intersection with WV 150, the Highland Scenic Highway. Drive 4 miles to the second overlook (Little Laurel overlook) and park. The trailhead is across the road and through the large field.

Sources of additional information:

District Ranger, Monongahela National Forest
Cemetery Road
Marlinton, WV 24954
(304) 799-4334

Elk River Touring Center
HC 69, Box 7
Slatyfork, WV 26291
(304) 572-3771
Email: ertc@ertc.com

Notes on the trail: On your bike, turn right out of the overlook parking lot and ride down the scenic highway a short distance to Gauley Mountain Trail on the left. Red Run Trail is significantly more difficult than Gauley Mountain Trail; if it gets too intense, turn back and continue on Gauley Mountain Trail to do an easier out-and-back. All of the trails in are signed and blazed, so it's an easy area to explore.

RIDE 97 · Prop's Run

AT A GLANCE

Length/configuration: 16-mile loop

Aerobic difficulty: Extreme

Technical difficulty: For experts only

Scenery: Forest and grand views of huge mountains

Special comments: Among the hard core, this is one of the best-known trails in the United States

WV

This ride shows the serious off-road enthusiast what West Virginia mountain biking is all about. Strictly for experienced, well-conditioned cyclists, Prop's Run is a 16-mile loop that climbs for 2,000 feet on a well-maintained forest service road, followed by six miles of steep, wet, and rocky downhill single-track that only expert riders will clean.

From the lookout tower on Sharp Knob, spectacular wilderness views in all directions reward the long climb. But for the truly hard core, it's the six intense miles of downhill single-track that make this ride memorable. After the hammering descent, the final spin along Elk River is quiet and peaceful, and it's a nice place to wash off your bike. It'll need it.

General location: Slatyfork.

Elevation change: Around 2,000'.

Season: Mid-May through early October. Spring is wet and usually cold. Expect snow from late October through April. Avoid riding during deer-hunting season in the late fall.

Services: Water, bicycle equipment and repairs, a restaurant, and lodging are available at Elk River Touring Center. All other services are available in Marlinton to the south or Linwood to the north. Camping is available at Tea Creek Campground and Handley Public Hunting and Fishing Area.

Hazards: You can get seriously lost in this wilderness, so be sure to carry a topo map and a compass. The weather in these mountains can change dramatically; carry raingear, extra clothing, food, water, first-aid items, and tools. The single-track is intense; don't exceed your abilities.

Rescue index: Poor. Mountain bikers aren't likely to see a soul on this ride. There are no residences, very little traffic on the forest service road, no farms, no nothing.

Land status: National forest.

RIDE 97 · Prop's Run

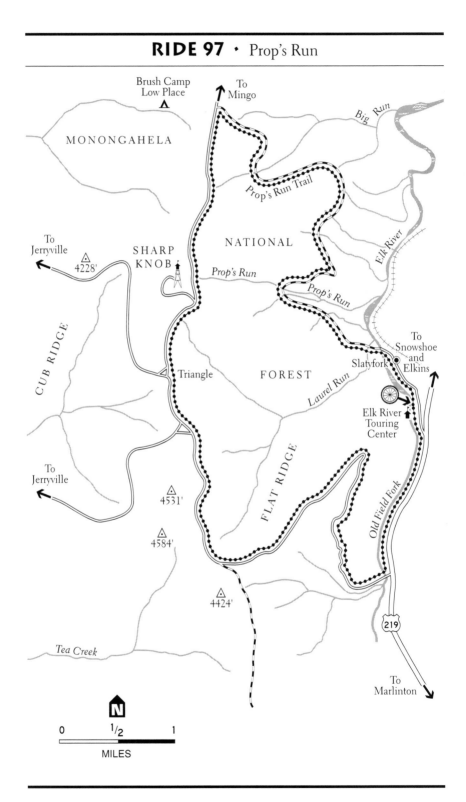

Brush Camp
Low Place

To
Mingo

Big Run

MONONGAHELA

Prop's Run Trail

To
Jerryville

SHARP
KNOB

NATIONAL

4228'

Prop's Run

Elk River

Prop's Run

CUB RIDGE

Triangle

FOREST

To
Snowshoe
and
Elkins

Slatyfork

Laurel Run

Elk River
Touring
Center

To
Jerryville

4531'

FLAT RIDGE

Old Field Fork

4584'

4424'

219

Tea Creek

To
Marlinton

N

0   1/2   1

MILES

Steep, rocky, boggy, and littered with deadfall, Prop's Run is one of the most intensely technical trails in West Virginia. It's also ruggedly beautiful.

Maps: The USGS 7.5 minute quad is Sharp Knob.

Finding the trail: The ride starts at Elk River Touring Center on US 219 in Slatyfork, about 20 miles north of Marlinton. Park in the lot past the wooden bridge. Ride from the touring center, turn right on US 219, and go 1.5 miles to Forest Service Road 24; turn right.

Sources of additional information:

District Ranger, Monongahela National Forest
Cemetery Road
Marlinton, WV 24954
(304) 799-4334

Elk River Touring Center
HC 69, Box 7
Slatyfork, WV 26291
(304) 572-3771
Email: ertc@ertc.com

Notes on the trail: Stay on FS 24; climb past several trailheads and roads on the left to the big intersection with the triangle in the middle of the road (look for pine trees growing inside the triangle) and bear right. After the lookout tower on Sharp Knob, pass through a gate and look for the Prop's Run Trail sign on the right. Then fasten your seatbelt.

At the end of the trail, cross Laurel Run, a small stream. Ride 50 yards to a T intersection and turn left to reach Elk River. Wade through the river; the old

Racing at Prop's Run: For most competitors who venture into this remote corner of West Virginia, the goal is simply to finish, not win.

ford turns into double-track. Follow it across the railroad traces, bear right, and pedal about 0.2 mile to US 219, which is paved. Turn right for the short return spin to Elk River Touring Center.

RIDE 98 · Snowshoe

AT A GLANCE

Length/configuration: More than 100 miles of trails, mostly loops

Aerobic difficulty: Easy to extreme

Technical difficulty: Easy to extreme; cyclists with good bike handling skills will get the most bang for their buck on Gauntlet and Nosedive Trails

Scenery: Beyond category; these are West Virginia mountains at their best

Special comments: You gotta pay to play ($8 a day); lodging is available on site; Snowshoe offers special mountain bike clinics throughout the season

WV

RIDE 98 · Snowshoe

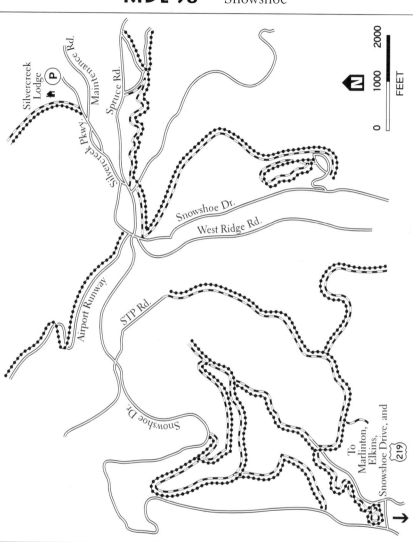

L ocated in the huge, nearly 5,000-feet-high mountains of southeastern West
Virginia, Snowshoe Mountain Resort embraces mountain biking big time
when the slopes are green. This downhill ski resort has two mountain bike centers and bike shops, lodging, restaurants, bike rentals, tours—everything a beginner, intermediate, or advanced mountain biker could want for a jaunt in some
of the most beautiful mountains in the East. Snowshoe boasts more than 100
miles of trails, all color-coded for different ability levels. Expect to find rugged
conditions on the mostly single-track trails; the plentiful rocks, bogs, stream

crossings, and other technical goodies that delight experienced off-roaders can frustrate riders a bit lower on the learning curve.

This is not your typical mountain bike destination. Because the resort is self-contained, Snowshoe offers special, multiday package deals that include breakfast and dinner, a trail pass and map, lodging, bike rentals, a helmet, and a souvenir water bottle. Snowshoe offers enough trails to exhaust even the strongest riders, but reserve time and energy to explore some of the other features of this remote corner. Pocahontas County is home to 830,000-acre Monongahela National Forest, state parks, streams stocked with native trout, wildlife galore, historical landmarks, a radio astronomy facility, virtually unlimited hiking and backpacking, spelunking, climbing, horseback riding, hundreds of miles of road cycling, restaurants and pubs, historical towns, and friendly people.

Last but not least, the Cass Scenic Railroad has a 100-year-old Shay steam locomotive still in operation, giving tours daily (in the summer and on special fall foliage weekends) up Bald Knob, the second-highest mountain in West Virginia.

General location: Between Elkins and Marlinton.

Elevation change: Up to 1,000'.

Season: Summer through fall.

Services: All services are available at Snowshoe.

Hazards: Steep descents on some trails; the weather is also a hazard. Conditions in these rugged mountains can change rapidly, so be prepared.

Rescue index: Excellent.

Land status: Private property.

Maps: A detailed trail map showing elevation gains is available at the mountain bike centers on site.

Finding the trail: From Washington, D.C., take Interstate 66 west. Then take I-81 south to Bridgewater, Virginia. From I-81 take VA 42 south to Goshen. Then head west on WV 39 to Marlinton and go north 26 miles to Snowshoe (it's well marked). You must purchase a trail pass to ride. Check with staff at the mountain bike centers for trail conditions and recommended routes that match your ability and fitness level.

Source of additional information:

Snowshoe Mountain Resort
Snowshoe Drive, P.O. Box 10
Snowshoe, WV 26209
(304) 572-5252
Website: www.snowshoemtn.com

Notes on the trail: Does the thought of grinding up 1,000 feet to a mountaintop get you down? Relax. Snowshoe provides a shuttle bus that takes riders to the mountaintop ($5 for one trip, $20 all day) and offers guided tours at 10 a.m. on weekends ($25 per person, 3 hours). Bike rentals start at $38 a day. Call the resort or check their website for schedules and current prices.

SPRUCE KNOB, WEST VIRGINIA

God knows it's a long drive from more populated areas. This mountain bike destination is about six hours from Washington, and the last 12-mile segment, which I usually drive at two in the morning, snakes up a mountain on a narrow dirt road. But it seems only natural that some of the best mountain biking in West Virginia be in the middle of nowhere. Nowhere, in this case, happens to be Spruce Knob, the highest point in West Virginia (4,861 feet), and the mountains surrounding it. Located near the center of Monongahela National Forest, the area has a well-earned reputation for ruggedness. Much of the singletrack is incredibly technical, with long obstacle courses full of rocks, roots, mud, and flowing water. Don't be put off, however, if you're not a strong rider. The terrain around Spruce Knob features meadows, open woods uncluttered by underbrush, and easy-to-follow streams and ridges. Though this is still West Virginia, the area contains enough forest service roads, off-road-vehicle trails, and well-graded hiking paths to make it attractive to all mountain bikers, regardless of their skill level.

Spruce Knob rates four stars in backcountry ambience. The area's remoteness, high altitude, and mature forests create a pristine wilderness setting. Its mountains contain the headwaters of three major river systems—the Cheat, Potomac, and Greenbrier Rivers. Wildlife ranges from the shy black bear to the wild turkey. Mosses and ferns grow in great variety on the forest floor. Rhododendron and mountain laurel add their waxy green beauty to the forest scene. Because of a variety of trees, the fall foliage is particularly riotous in these mountains.

The mountain biking possibilities around Spruce Knob are nearly endless. The Seneca Creek Trail System, just north of Spruce Knob, contains more than 60 miles of hiking trails. Using Spruce Knob Lake Campground as a base, you would need weeks to explore all the trails and forest service roads in the area. For multiday treks, ride west to Middle Mountain, west of Spruce Knob, to link up with Canaan Valley and Dolly Sods to the north and Shavers Fork and the Williams River region to the south. It's no exaggeration to say that Monongahela National Forest represents a lifetime of mountain biking opportunities.

If you can't spend a few weeks exploring this fascinating area, at least plan a long weekend (which is why people like me arrive at 2 a.m.). The three rides that follow are an excellent introduction to the mountain biking around Spruce Knob. Set up a base camp at Spruce Knob Campground and get ready for one of the best mountain biking experiences this side of Colorado.

RIDE 99 · Grants Branch to Gandy Creek Loop

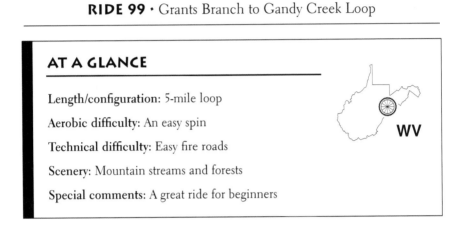

AT A GLANCE

Length/configuration: 5-mile loop

Aerobic difficulty: An easy spin

Technical difficulty: Easy fire roads

Scenery: Mountain streams and forests

Special comments: A great ride for beginners

WV

Mountain biking doesn't get easier than this fun ride in the mountains around Spruce Knob. The five-mile loop starts with a gentle descent on an abandoned railroad grade that's been converted to a wide, grassy off-road-vehicle trail. The return follows a well-maintained dirt forest service road with a gentle uphill grade.

This loop has a little of everything. The descent on Grants Branch Trail is through a mature hardwood forest. At WV 29, the ride follows Gandy Branch, a fast-moving mountain stream. On Forest Service Road 1 the trail leaves the stream and begins a gentle ascent. And on the climb, the views of the mountains get better and better.

General location: Spruce Knob.

Elevation change: The total elevation gain is around 400'.

Season: Midsummer through fall are the best seasons to ride in Spruce Knob. Spring and early summer can be cold and wet. Expect snow from November through March. Avoid riding during deer-hunting season in the late fall.

Services: Limited services—motels, small grocery stores, and gas—are available in Seneca Rocks and Riverton. The nearest bike shop is Blackwater Bikes in Davis. Camping is available at Spruce Knob Campground. All other services are available in Petersburg.

Hazards: The weather can change rapidly; carry raingear and extra clothes.

Rescue index: Fair. This is an isolated area, so the closest help is at Spruce Knob Lake Campground. Cars can be flagged down on lightly trafficked WV 29.

RIDE 99 · Grants Branch to Gandy Creek Loop

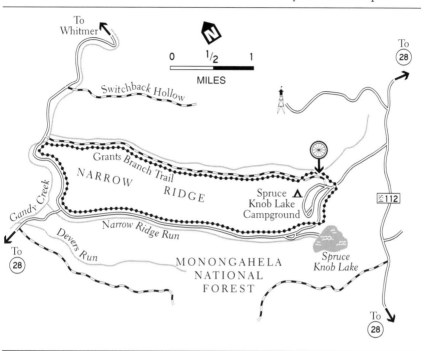

Land status: National forest.

Maps: The USGS 7.5 minute quad is Spruce Knob. The Seneca Creek Trail System, Spruce Knob Unit map complements the topo by showing more trail details.

Finding the trail: From WV 28, turn on to FS 112, 3 miles south of Riverton (there is a sign for Spruce Knob). Follow the road about 13 miles to the campground, or to Spruce Knob Lake, and park. The Grants Branch trailhead is at the campground entrance.

Sources of additional information:

U.S. Forest Service, Monongahela National Forest
Route 3, Box 240
Petersburg, WV 26847
(304) 257-4488

Blackwater Bikes
WV 32
Davis, WV 26260
(304) 259-5286 or (800) 737-1935

RIDE 100 · Big Run Loop

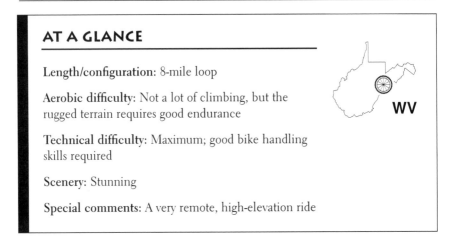

AT A GLANCE

Length/configuration: 8-mile loop

Aerobic difficulty: Not a lot of climbing, but the rugged terrain requires good endurance

Technical difficulty: Maximum; good bike handling skills required

Scenery: Stunning

Special comments: A very remote, high-elevation ride

WV

This ride is for dedicated hammerheads. While most of the riding is on forest service roads, the route's technical single-track (featuring rocks, wet roots, bogs, mud, and streams) requires good bike handling skills and endurance. Still, without a lot of steep climbing to wear you down, this ride is moderate by rugged West Virginia standards. The high elevation, remoteness, and varied terrain make Big Run Loop challenging and beautiful.

The eight-mile loop features excellent views of Spruce Knob (at 4,861 feet, it's the highest point in West Virginia) to the east and Big Run Valley. Much of the trail passes through huge, grassy meadows on the ridges. Big Run is an excellent trout stream lined with beaver ponds. The single-track near the ride's beginning is intense, with an amazing tangle of tree roots along a line of spruce trees that will challenge expert riders. More railroad grade follows, leading you through open meadows and over a couple of high fences. The last half of the ride follows a dirt forest service road.

General location: Spruce Knob.

Elevation change: About 300', but don't be deceived; this is rugged country.

Season: The best riding is from midsummer through fall. Spring and early summer tend to be wet and cool. Expect snow from November through March. Avoid riding during deer-hunting season in the late fall.

Services: Limited services—motels, small grocery stores, and gas—are available in Seneca Rocks and Riverton. The nearest bike shop is Blackwater Bikes in Davis. Camping is available at Spruce Knob Campground. All other services are available in Petersburg.

Hazards: The weather and the area's remoteness. Carry a topo map and a compass. Be prepared for severe weather and bring extra food, water, and bike tools.

RIDE 100 · Big Run Loop

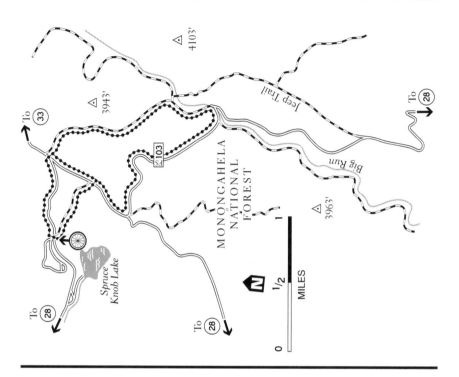

Rescue index: Poor. Mountain bikers venturing into this wilderness rarely meet other people. A vehicle could be flagged down on lightly traveled FS 103.

Land status: National forest.

Maps: The USGS 7.5 minute quad is Spruce Knob. The Seneca Creek Trail System, Spruce Knob Unit map complements the topo by showing more trail details.

Finding the trail: From WV 28, turn onto FS 112, 3 miles south of Riverton (there is a sign for Spruce Knob). Follow the road about 13 miles to the campground, or to Spruce Knob Lake, and park. The ride starts on Short Trail near the campground entrance.

Sources of additional information:

U.S. Forest Service, Monongahela National Forest
Route 3, Box 240
Petersburg, WV 26847
(304) 257-4488

Blackwater Bikes
WV 32
Davis, WV 26260
(304) 259-5286 or (800) 737-1935

Notes on the trail: After you start the ride on Short Trail (a narrow, technical single-track), turn left at FS 103 and ride a short distance to the hiking trail on the right at the intersection with FS 1.

This loop can be tricky to follow. Good map and compass skills are a must. The trail is often obscured, especially when it crosses fields and meadows. Check your map and compass regularly.

RIDE 101 · Allegheny Mountain/Seneca Creek Loop

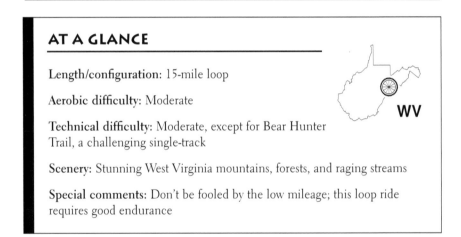

AT A GLANCE

Length/configuration: 15-mile loop

Aerobic difficulty: Moderate

Technical difficulty: Moderate, except for Bear Hunter Trail, a challenging single-track

Scenery: Stunning West Virginia mountains, forests, and raging streams

Special comments: Don't be fooled by the low mileage; this loop ride requires good endurance

WV

For a variety of terrain and views, this 15-mile loop can't be beat. It starts with the Allegheny Trail, a wide, grassy double-track that's an easy ramble along a forested mountain ridge. Bear Hunter Trail, a challenging single-track, drops through a mature forest along a small stream; next, the loop follows Seneca Creek on a gentle path through a forest that is rapidly returning to wilderness after being logged at the turn of the century. The ride ends on well-maintained, dirt forest service roads.

The single-track on Bear Hunter Trail is white-knuckle all the way, so good bike handling skills are a must. Also, this is a long ride requiring good endurance. Most of the trails are well-maintained, wide and smooth, and a joy to ride.

General location: Spruce Knob.

Elevation change: About 500'.

RIDE 101 · Allegheny Mountain/Seneca Creek Loop

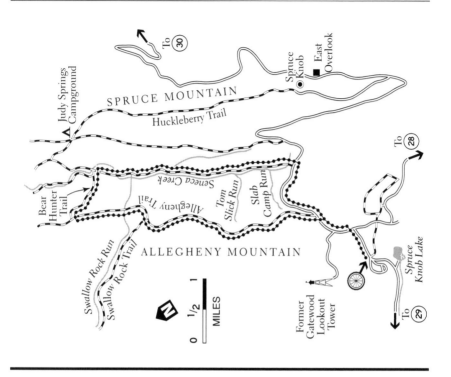

Season: Midsummer through fall. Spring and early summer tend to be wet and cool. Expect snow from November through March. Avoid riding during deer-hunting season in the late fall.

Services: Limited services—motels, small grocery stores, and gas—are available in Seneca Rocks and Riverton. The nearest bike shop is Blackwater Bikes in Davis. You can camp at Spruce Knob Campground. All other services are available in Petersburg.

Hazards: Bear Hunter Trail, with its steep and rocky descent, offers a high potential for "unscheduled dismounts" (crashes). Be prepared for rapid changes in the weather; bring extra food, water, and bike tools.

Rescue index: Poor; this is a remote area. Judy Springs Campground, on Seneca Creek Trail, is a walk-in camping area that's popular in the summer. There is light traffic on FS 112.

Land status: National forest.

Maps: The USGS 7.5 minute quads are Spruce Knob and Whitmer. In addition, the Seneca Creek Trail System, Spruce Knob Unit map complements the topo maps by showing more trail details.

Finding the trail: From WV 28, turn onto FS 112, 3 miles south of Riverton (there is a sign for Spruce Knob). Follow the road about 13 miles to the campground, or to Spruce Knob Lake, and park. The entrance to Allegheny Trail is on the left side of FS 112, past the entrance to the Gatewood lookout tower.

Sources of additional information:

U.S. Forest Service, Monongahela National Forest
Route 3, Box 240
Petersburg, WV 26847
(304) 257-4488

Blackwater Bikes
WV 32
Davis, WV 26260
(304) 259-5286 or (800) 737-1935

CANAAN VALLEY, WEST VIRGINIA

Most of West Virginia was settled by pioneers in the late eighteenth and early nineteenth centuries, but the region around the Allegheny Front—a huge geologic fault that runs north and south through Pennsylvania, Maryland, and West Virginia—wasn't settled until the 1840s and later. Pioneers avoided this region of rugged mountains, dense forests, and severe weather as they surged west into Ohio, Indiana, Illinois, and beyond. The early explorers saw the neighborhood as dark and foreboding, and they named the upper plateaus along the Allegheny Front "Canada."

Two unique geological features in this part of northeastern West Virginia are Dolly Sods and Canaan (say k'NANE) Valley. Wedged between the Allegheny Front to the east and Canaan Valley to the west, Dolly Sods is a high plateau of spruce and hemlock stands, sphagnum moss bogs, and beaver ponds. Renowned for its harsh weather—it has snowed in July, and the lowest recorded winter temperature is minus 48—the region is the unique result of heavy deforestation in the late nineteenth and early twentieth centuries, followed by fires that burned away the topsoil. What remains is a unique blend of second-growth forests, open spaces dominated by bogs and beaver ponds, and gently rolling ridges.

Canaan Valley is now a mixture of small farms, second-growth forests, and vacation homes. At 3,200 feet, this is the highest alpine valley of its size east of the Mississippi River. Surrounded by 4,300-foot ridges, the valley is considered a bit of Canada gone astray. The climate and boreal plant life are more common to northern regions than to the southern Appalachians. The northern end of Canaan Valley is 6,000 acres of wetlands and abundant wildlife such as white-tailed deer, black bear, bobcat, fisher, fox, mink, beaver, and cottontail rabbit. More than 160 species of birds and waterfowl have been identified, including great blue heron, Canada goose, black duck, woodcock, turkey, and grouse. The goshawk and common snipe have their southernmost nesting sites in the valley. In 1994, the U.S. Fish and Wildlife Service purchased land establishing Canaan Valley National Wildlife Refuge as the 500th refuge in the National Wildlife Refuge System.

With their unique features and rugged beauty, Dolly Sods and Canaan Valley are popular destinations for hikers, backpackers, birders, downhill and cross-country skiers, and, increasingly, mountain bikers. Davis, an old logging town over the mountain from Canaan Valley, is well situated for mountain biking. Off-road cyclists can ride in virtually any direction from town to the best biking in the state: flat or mountainous, single-track or forest service road, old strip mines or bogs, and, for the energetic, all of the above. Not surprisingly, Davis is one of the most popular mountain biking destinations in the East. The ramshackle old town even boasts its own mountain bike shop, Blackwater Bikes. When visiting Davis, stop in for the latest trail information. The shop also sells maps and the latest bike components, offers expert repairs, and sells and rents mountain bikes.

The trail descriptions that follow, some written with the help of former Blackwater Bikes employee Mary Morningstar, are the most popular rides around Canaan Valley. Yet they represent only a fraction of the riding in this large and fascinating section of West Virginia. Let the experts at Blackwater Bikes point you toward other great rides in this beautiful and rugged part of the Mountain State.

RIDE 102 · Plantation Trail

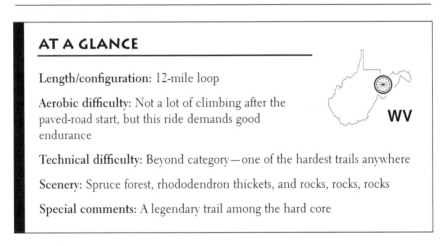

AT A GLANCE

Length/configuration: 12-mile loop

Aerobic difficulty: Not a lot of climbing after the paved-road start, but this ride demands good endurance

Technical difficulty: Beyond category—one of the hardest trails anywhere

Scenery: Spruce forest, rhododendron thickets, and rocks, rocks, rocks

Special comments: A legendary trail among the hard core

WV

Plantation Trail got its name in the 1930s when clear-cut Canaan Mountain was replanted with spruce trees. Rhododendron thickets grow rampant throughout the area, creating a glorious sight on a spring day when the bushes are in bloom and dripping with moisture from a rain shower. That's one reason this 12-mile loop, which has a shorter 9-mile option, is legendary among knowledgeable East Coast mountain bikers. The trail winds through the forests, and then the trees suddenly drop away and the trail crosses the peat bogs Canaan is so famous for. Just as quickly, the trail dives back into the thick underbrush and wooded canopy of the spruce forest. Coming around corners, keep a sharp lookout for the mother bear and cubs seen so often in these parts.

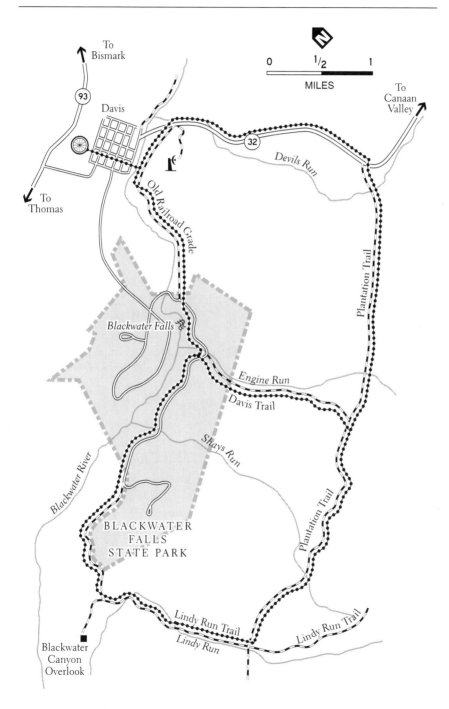

To Bismark

⑨③

Davis

To Thomas

To Canaan Valley

0   1/2   1

MILES

N

③②

Devils Run

Old Railroad Grade

Plantation Trail

Blackwater Falls

Engine Run

Davis Trail

Shays Run

Blackwater River

BLACKWATER FALLS STATE PARK

Plantation Trail

Blackwater Canyon Overlook

Lindy Run Trail

Lindy Run

Lindy Run Trail

Most of this ride is on rugged hiking trails, and good technical riding skill is required. Expect to encounter wet roots, windfall, mountain streams, short steep hills, and peat bogs. Canaan Loop Road is a graded forest service road of hard-packed rock and gravel. Warning: Don't be deceived by the low mileages. Only highly skilled mountain bikers will be able to ride all of the single-track without dismounting. This is a low-speed, highly technical ride.

General location: Davis.

Elevation change: About 520' on the paved road to Plantation Trail, which rolls along the ridge of Canaan Mountain through creeks and ravines, creating short, steep climbs and descents but losing only 300' in elevation over 5 miles.

Season: The best riding conditions are midsummer through fall. Fall has the best surface conditions and inspiring foliage. Late May through early June, although wet and often cool, offers huge thickets of rhododendron in bloom.

Services: Lodging and restaurants are available over the mountain in Canaan Valley. You can camp at Blackwater Falls State Park from spring through fall and at Canaan Valley State Park year-round. All other services are available in Davis.

Hazards: This is rugged terrain over rocks, roots, and bogs. There are steep and unexpected drop-offs and descents. Water crossings can be waist-deep when high, and the water is always cold. The weather is always unpredictable, so be prepared for the worst.

Rescue index: Not good. Blackwater Falls State Park is staffed and has phones. It is unusual to encounter anyone on the trails; occasionally four-wheel-drive vehicles can be spotted on Canaan Loop Road.

Land status: National forest and state park.

Maps: The USGS 7.5 minute quads are Mozark Mountain and Blackwater Falls. A detailed mileage guide and maps are available at Blackwater Bikes in Davis. A small map of the hiking trails is available at Blackwater Falls State Park.

Finding the trail: The ride starts in Davis (about 3.5 hours from Washington and Pittsburg and 4 hours from Baltimore). Blackwater Bikes on WV 32 is a good starting point, or park anywhere in town. Ride south on WV 32 and cross the Blue Bridge; continue riding the shoulder up Canaan Mountain to the Plantation Trail trailhead on the right.

Sources of additional information:

U.S. Forest Service
Cheat Ranger District, Nursery Bottom
Parsons, WV 26287
(304) 478-3183

Blackwater Bikes
WV 32
Davis, WV 26260
(304) 259-5286 or (800) 737-1935

Blackwater Falls State Park
Davis, WV 26260
(304) 259-5216 or (800) CALL WVA

Notes on the trail: The trailhead for Plantation Trail on WV 32 is on the right and is well signed. After turning onto the trail, you've got 2 options. The 9-mile ride turns right onto Davis Trail (2.5 miles from the start of Plantation Trail), a fairly technical trail that descends 1.5 miles into Blackwater Falls State Park. The other option (12 miles) is to continue another 2.5 miles to the intersection with Lindy Run Trail and turn right. This is a tricky, technical trail with a steep, treacherous hill.

Both trails end at Canaan Loop Road. Turn right and follow the dirt road into Blackwater Falls State Park. Turn left onto the paved road and ride about 2 miles to Falls View Gentle Trail (on the left). Turn right onto a maintenance road and then immediately left onto an old railroad grade. This leads to a settling pond on the left. Skirt the edge of the pond and follow the railroad grade back to the Blue Bridge; turn left and cross the bridge, and you're back in Davis.

RIDE 103 · Canaan Loop Road (Forest Service Road 13)

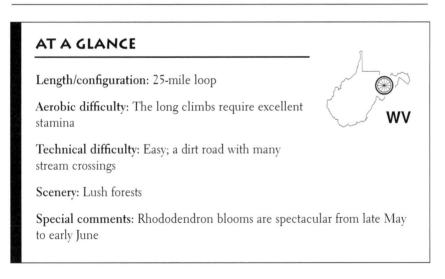

AT A GLANCE

Length/configuration: 25-mile loop

Aerobic difficulty: The long climbs require excellent stamina

Technical difficulty: Easy; a dirt road with many stream crossings

Scenery: Lush forests

Special comments: Rhododendron blooms are spectacular from late May to early June

WV

Though it's definitely not a technical ride—virtually the entire 25-mile loop follows a well-maintained forest service road and paved roads—Canaan Loop Road requires stamina. Most of the route is along rolling hills, and the last seven miles are uphill. The rewards are worth the effort. The road passes through magnificent spruce and hardwood forests and accesses trails leading to breathtaking overlooks.

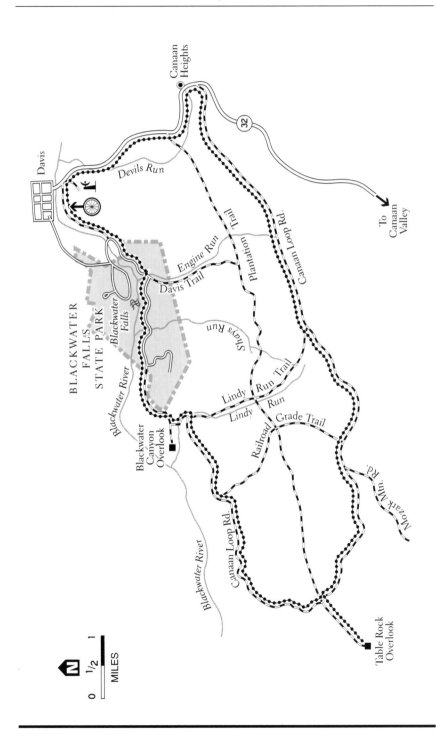

Canaan Heights

32

Davis

Devils Run

To Canaan Valley

Plantation Trail

Canaan Loop Rd.

Engine Run

Davis Trail

BLACKWATER FALLS STATE PARK

Blackwater Falls

Shays Run

Blackwater River

Lindy Run Trail

Lindy Run

Railroad Grade Trail

Blackwater Canyon Overlook

Canaan Loop Rd.

Mozark Mtn. Rd.

Blackwater River

Table Rock Overlook

N

0 1/2 1

MILES

Canaan Valley has a national reputation among mountain bike racers (and non-racers) for its rugged and beautiful terrain.

Look for spectacular rhododendron blooms in late May or early June. For a view of Blackwater Canyon, take a short spur trail at about the five-and-a-half-mile mark. (Look for a small wooden post, no sign.) Although technical, the trail is only a half-mile long and leads to a limestone outcropping overlooking the Blackwater River 860 feet below. A tougher option, but worth the effort, is the spur leading to Table Rock Overlook. Look for a sign at about the 10.5-mile mark. Stash your bike in the trees and hike the one-and-a-half-mile trail leading to an overlook of the Dry Fork River 1,635 feet below.

General location: Davis.

Elevation change: Around 1,100'.

Season: The best time to ride is midsummer through fall. The water crossings can be high in spring and winter. In all seasons, be prepared with raingear and warm clothes. The summer climate is typified by Canadian-like weather and cool temperatures.

Services: All services are available in Davis. Additional motels, restaurants, and camping are in nearby Canaan Valley.

Hazards: Changes in the weather can be sudden and brutal. Watch for traffic on the roads, especially WV 32.

Rescue index: Fair. Canaan Loop Road is accessible to two-wheel-drive, high-clearance vehicles and is a popular camping spot, so traffic can be flagged down. Blackwater Falls State Park is fully staffed.

Some areas near the mountain-biking Mecca of Davis have an unearthly look.

Land status: National forest and state park.

Maps: The USGS 7.5 minute quads are Mozark Mountain and Blackwater Falls. A detailed mileage guide and maps are available at Blackwater Bikes in Davis. A small map of Canaan Loop Road and interconnecting trails is available at Blackwater Falls State Park.

Finding the trail: The ride begins in Davis (about 3.5 hours from Washington and Pittsburg and 4 hours from Baltimore). Park near Blackwater Bikes on WV 32 or anywhere else in town. Ride south on WV 32, cross the Blue Bridge, and immediately turn right onto an old dirt road to begin the loop.

Sources of additional information:

U.S. Forest Service
Cheat Ranger District, Nursery Bottom
Parsons, WV 26287
(304) 478-3183

Blackwater Bikes
WV 32
Davis, WV 26260
(304) 259-5286 or (800) 737-1935

Blackwater Falls State Park
Davis, WV 26260
(304) 259-5216 or (800) CALL WVA

Notes on the trail: After the right onto a dirt road (an old railroad grade), follow the river and bear left; look for a settling pond on the right. Follow the railroad grade to the far end of the pond where the road forks. Turn right onto a rocky double-track that follows the fence line of the pond. The railroad grade will continue through a stream crossing and end at the intersection of a maintenance road and a paved road.

Turn left onto the paved road and continue about 2.5 miles. When the road bears left, turn right onto the dirt road marked with a wooden sign for Sled Run. This is the beginning of Canaan Loop Road, which ends at WV 32, a paved road with heavy traffic. Turn left and descend into Davis.

RIDE 104 · Camp 70 Road

AT A GLANCE

Length/configuration: 8-mile out-and-back (4 miles each way)

Aerobic difficulty: Easy; flat

Technical difficulty: Easy; dirt road

Scenery: Blackwater River, forest, and beaver ponds

Special comments: Leads out to northern Canaan Valley and our nation's 500th national wildlife refuge

WV

Camp 70 Road is a virtually flat dirt road that starts in Davis, follows the Blackwater River, and heads into the northern end of Canaan Valley. At the start of this very easy eight-mile (total) out-and-back, northern hardwoods line the road. Expect to see cherry, beech, birch, and sugar maple, all of which make this an especially enjoyable ride in the fall. Interspersed with the hardwoods are aspen groves, hemlock, spruce, and balsam fir stands. Look for blueberries, blackberries, and the unusual and delicious service (sarvis) tree berries that ripen in the summer sun.

The valley harbors a unique boreal ecosystem—a collection of plants and animals usually found much farther north. The high diversity of species and communities is the result of wet soils, high altitude, and cool climate. You could say Canaan Valley is a virtual living museum of the Ice Age in West Virginia.

General location: Davis.

Elevation change: Nominal.

RIDE 104 · Camp 70 Road

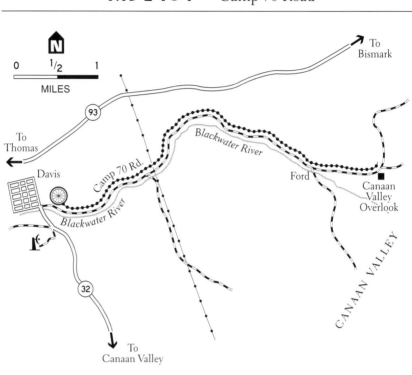

Season: The road can be ridden year-round. Midsummer is best for berry picking. In winter and early spring, the road can get very muddy.

Services: All services are available in Davis. Additional motels and restaurants are in nearby Canaan Valley.

Hazards: Watch for motorized vehicles on the road.

Rescue index: Excellent.

Land status: Private. Owned by Allegheny Power Company and open for recreational use.

Maps: The USGS 7.5 minute quad is Davis.

Finding the trail: The ride starts in Davis (about 3.5 hours from Washington and Pittsburg and 4 hours from Baltimore). Blackwater Bikes on WV 32 is a convenient place to start. Park near the shop or anywhere else in town. With a high-clearance, two-wheel-drive vehicle or a four-wheel-drive vehicle, you can drive directly onto Camp 70 Road and park anywhere. Ride south on WV 32 (Williams Avenue, the main street in Davis). When the road bears right at the convenience store/motel, continue straight onto a rough paved road that quickly

The face of veteran pro racer Roger Bird says it all about the competitive sport of mountain bike racing.

turns to dirt. Cross the bridge over Beaver Creek. This is the beginning of Camp 70 Road, which follows the Blackwater River (on the right) upstream.

Sources of additional information:

Tucker County Chamber of Commerce
Visitor Center
WV 32
Davis, WV 26260
(304) 259-5315

Blackwater Bikes
WV 32
Davis, WV 26260
(304) 259-5286 or (800) 737-1935

Notes on the trail: About 0.75 mile from Davis on the right are the remains of an old dam, a great place to swim and sun. At the 3.5-mile mark, look for a spring on the left side of the road surrounded by blueberries. At the 4-mile mark, bear left at a fork in the road and ride on to Canaan Valley. The road will begin to deteriorate and become rocky and increasingly narrow, but still easy to ride.

To reach a swinging bridge over the Blackwater River that leads to a beautiful section of Canaan Valley, look for all-terrain vehicle tracks going to the right from a point less than a quarter-mile past the fork. Follow these tracks down a gully (toward the river), bear right through a hemlock grove, and follow the

Sometimes it's faster to get off and push when racing at Canaan.

river about 150 yards to the bridge. Cross the bridge, turn left, and follow an old railroad grade that leads out across the valley floor. On all sides look for peat bogs, shrub swamps, and beaver ponds. The railroad grade may be muddy, and there are always puddles. In a couple of spots, the beaver dams have flooded the trail. But it's one of the most beautiful spots in West Virginia.

RIDE 105 · Olson Fire Tower

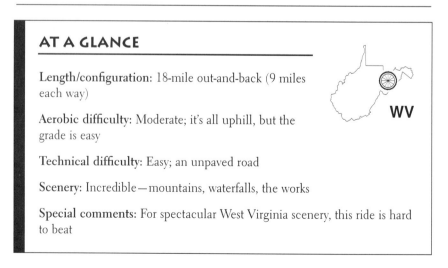

AT A GLANCE

Length/configuration: 18-mile out-and-back (9 miles each way)

Aerobic difficulty: Moderate; it's all uphill, but the grade is easy

Technical difficulty: Easy; an unpaved road

Scenery: Incredible—mountains, waterfalls, the works

Special comments: For spectacular West Virginia scenery, this ride is hard to beat

WV

RIDE 105 · Olson Fire Tower

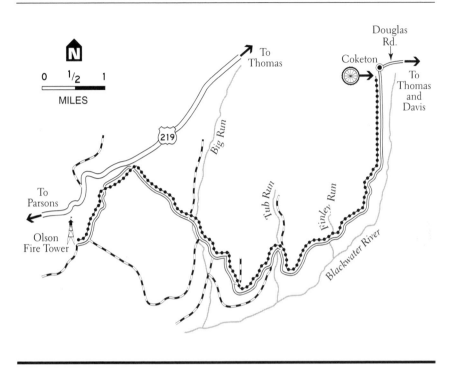

This is a great introductory ride for first-time visitors. Simply pedal on a well-maintained fire road to the top of a mountain and you're rewarded a 360-degree view of all the mountains surrounding Canaan Valley, the highest alpine valley in the East. On a clear day, you can see as far as Spruce Knob, the highest point in West Virginia. This 18-mile (total) out-and-back doesn't require any technical riding skills—just the endurance to pedal nine miles to the top. The reward, of course, is that it's all downhill on the return.

Be sure to make some stops on the ascent. About five miles up the road, look for an overlook blazed with a yellow dot on a boulder on the left. From this point, you can see Blackwater Canyon to the left and Big Run heading down to the river on your right. The entire mountainside is covered with rhododendron, an amazing sight when it's in bloom. At the 6.5-mile mark, look carefully for a trail to the left that leads to a high-elevation marshlands and bird sanctuary. An elevated boardwalk leads to the middle of the wetlands with a beaver pond and several bird houses, an unusual spot at this elevation.

General location: Thomas.

Elevation change: 920'.

Season: This ride is excellent all year. Each season has its special attractions. In the winter, when the leaves are down, there are dramatic views of the canyon. In the spring, the road isn't as muddy as other areas and the rhododendron is blooming. In the summer, the majority of the ride is in the shade; pockets of hemlock groves and cold mountain streams cool you off. In the fall, the colors are the best in Canaan.

Services: All services are available in Davis. There is a water pump near the fire tower.

Hazards: Avoid excessive speed on the return trip. Watch for blind corners; the roads are open to traffic.

Rescue index: Good. Canyon Rim Road is accessible to two-wheel-drive vehicles and is a popular spot in the summer months. But, as is the case with most of Canaan Valley, this is still remote territory.

Land status: National forest.

Maps: The USGS 7.5 minute quads are Lead Mine and Mozark Mountain. A detailed mileage log and trail guide are available at Blackwater Bikes in Davis.

Finding the trail: The ride starts at Canyon Rim Road (FS 18). From Davis (about 3.5 hours from Washington and Pittsburg and 4 hours from Baltimore), drive north on WV 32 toward Thomas. A quarter-mile past Mountain Top Market on the left, turn left onto Douglas Road. Drive 2.5 miles, crossing over 2 bridges. Park on the right immediately after the second bridge. At this point, Douglas Road turns to dirt and becomes Canyon Rim Road. Ride your bike up the dirt road.

Sources of additional information:

U.S. Forest Service
Cheat Ranger District, Nursery Bottom
Parsons, WV 26287
(304) 478-3183

Blackwater Bikes
WV 32
Davis, WV 26260
(304) 259-5286 or (800) 737-1935

Notes on the trail: The scenery on this ride is spectacular and shouldn't be missed. The view from Olson fire tower includes the entire western rim of Dolly Sods and its northern drainage. The ride can be lengthened to 28.5 miles by riding from Davis. Check with Blackwater Bikes about the route that parallels WV 32 through the woods (and away from traffic).

RIDE 106 · Canaan Valley State Park

AT A GLANCE

Length/configuration: A 10-mile system of mostly double-track loops

Aerobic difficulty: Moderate to difficult

Technical difficulty: Moderate to difficult

Scenery: Subtle; forests and northern bog and heath barren plant communities make the terrain unique

Special comments: Mountain bike rentals are available at the nature center. A bike shop at the park is planned

WV

Located on the northern edge of Monongahela National Forest, Canaan Valley State Park is a wilderness jewel with more than 6,000 acres of woodlands, meadows, hills, and streams. At 3,200 feet, Canaan Valley is the highest alpine valley of its size east of the Mississippi River, and the valley floor is approximately 12 miles long and over 2 miles wide for almost the entire length. Canaan Valley offers incredible beauty, many glimpses of wildlife (especially white-tailed deer), and solitude.

While best known to outdoor enthusiasts for its winter cross-country and alpine skiing, this park has recently started a mountain bike program in the summer months. About ten miles of trails are open to mountain bikes, and another four or five miles should be added soon. For riders who like their riding technical, Allegheny Trail is the park's top attraction. This difficult single-track connects Canaan Valley State Park to trails in and around Canaan Mountain and its Plantation Trail system (Ride 102) and serves as a link to Blackwater Falls State Park outside of Davis.

General location: Canaan Valley.

Elevation change: A few hundred feet inside the park. Allegheny Trail to Blackwater Falls State Park climbs about 400' to the top of Canaan Mountain.

Season: Summer and fall are best. In the spring and after prolonged rain, Canaan Valley is usually incredibly wet.

Services: Camping, lodging, cabins, and a restaurant are located in the park. All other services are available in Canaan Valley and in Davis (10 miles).

Hazards: Rugged trails and big mud holes. If you take Allegheny Trail to Blackwater Falls State Park, watch for rattlesnakes on Canaan Mountain. Canaan

RIDE 106 · Canaan Valley State Park

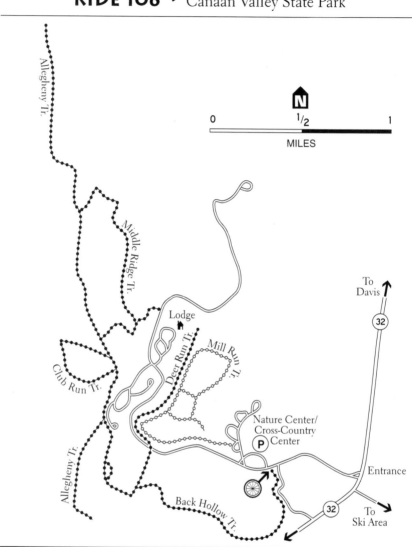

Valley State Park is the safest place to ride during the gun-hunting deer season (Thanksgiving week through mid-December), except on Sundays, when it's okay to ride in nearby Monongahela National Forest.

Rescue index: Excellent.

Land status: State park.

Maps: A trail map is available at the nature center.

Finding the trail: The park entrance is on WV 32 in Canaan Valley. Park at the Nature Center/Cross-Country Center (the first right). Back Hollow Trail starts across the main park road and connects to other park trails open to bikes. The 8-mile (one-way) Allegheny Trail is highly technical single-track that goes to Blackwater Falls State Park.

Sources of additional information:

Canaan Valley Resort and Conference Center
HC70, Box 330
Davis, WV 26260
(304) 866-4121 or (800) 225-5982 (room reservations)

Blackwater Bikes
WV 32
Davis, WV 26260
(304) 259-5286 or (800) 737-1935

Notes on the trail: Back Hollow Trail is a good warm-up and has scenic, open vistas. You can ride it as a loop by returning on the main park road or ride it as an out-and-back. It also leads to Club Run and Middle Ridge Trails. For more riding, climb up to the Plantation Trail system (Ride 102) on Allegheny Trail.

Back Hollow Trail is in open, grassy meadow and is probably as close to a beginner trail as you'll find in Canaan. Club Run and Middle Ridge are intermediate; the upper section of Middle Ridge offers the only true single-track: fast and fun going down (clockwise) and a real challenge to ride up (counterclockwise). Club Run can be ridden in either direction, but going clockwise lets you enjoy some real screamer descents.

RIDE 107 · Timberline

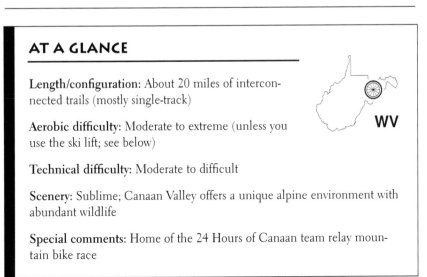

AT A GLANCE

Length/configuration: About 20 miles of interconnected trails (mostly single-track)

Aerobic difficulty: Moderate to extreme (unless you use the ski lift; see below)

Technical difficulty: Moderate to difficult

Scenery: Sublime; Canaan Valley offers a unique alpine environment with abundant wildlife

Special comments: Home of the 24 Hours of Canaan team relay mountain bike race

WV

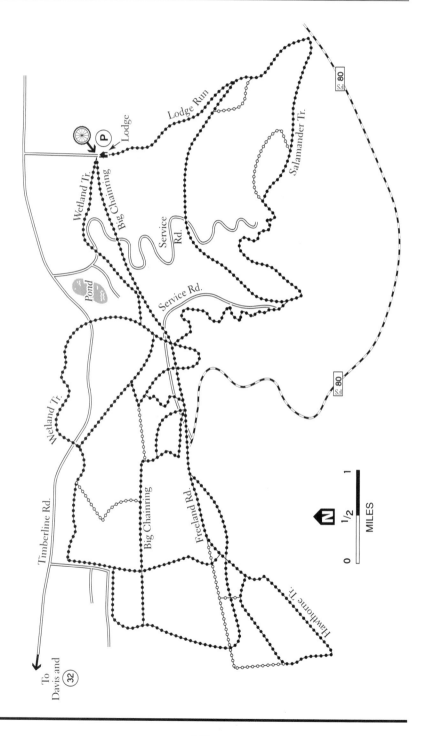

Timberline Resort hosts the "24 Hours of Canaan" team relay race each June.

Like many downhill ski resorts, Timberline Four Seasons Resort has jumped on the mountain biking bandwagon to keep visitors coming during the summer and fall months. But this resort offers something different: the unique terrain and climate of Canaan Valley, the highest alpine valley east of the Mississippi River. Located on the slopes of Cabin Mountain, Timberline offers relatively easy riding on the lower elevations and expert-level trails at higher elevations (about 20 miles total). The combination of scenic beauty, great trails, and rugged topography is also the reason Timberline has hosted the renowned 24 Hours of Canaan team relay mountain bike race. Some call it Woodstock on Wheels, as thousands of off-road fanatics converge on the resort on the first weekend in June. It's the biggest mountain bike event in the East.

General location: Canaan Valley.

Elevation change: 1,000' (unless you ride the ski lift—then it's all downhill).

Season: Memorial Day through mid-fall.

Services: Bike rentals are available at Timberline. Camping is available at Canaan Valley State Park. All other services are available in Canaan Valley and in Davis (10 miles). Lift service is available summer through fall on weekends and holidays; be sure to call first, though, if lift service is essential; sometimes the equipment is down for service.

Hazards: Incredibly rocky trails on the mountain.

Rescue index: Excellent.

Land status: Private.

Pro racer Gunnar Shogren, who holds the course record at the "24 Hours of Canaan," is fast both on and off the bike.

Maps: A trail map is available at Timberline.

Finding the trail: Timberline is located off WV 32 in Canaan Valley. Follow signs to the ski lodge and park in the lot. All trails start behind the lodge.

Source of additional information:

> Timberline Four Seasons Resort
> Route 32
> Canaan Valley, WV 26260
> (304) 866-4312 or (800) 766-9464

Notes on the trail: After parking behind the lodge, follow the signs to the bike shop, sign in, and pick up a pass to ride (free as we go to press, but don't expect that to last forever), a map, and information. As is typical with most ski resorts that offer mountain biking in the summer, the easier trails go through valley fields and woods below the mountain, and more rugged trails go straight up the ski slopes (and then wind in and out of the woods). Timberline offers lift service on weekends and holidays from 9 a.m. to 5 p.m. An all-day lift pass is $20 ($15 with a bike rental) and $5 for one ride (children ages 6 to 12 pay $3). Warning to beginners: Taking the lift to the top of the mountain doesn't mean the descent will be easy. The upper trails are extremely technical, especially if they're wet. Bike rentals start around $30 a day, including helmets (required).

GLOSSARY

This short list of terms does not contain all the words used by mountain bike enthusiasts when discussing their sport. But it should serve as an introduction to the lingo you'll hear on the trails.

ATB   all-terrain bike; this, like "fat-tire bike," is another name for a mountain bike

ATV   all-terrain vehicle; this usually refers to the loud, fume-spewing three- or four-wheeled motorized vehicles you will not enjoy meeting on the trail—except, of course, if you crash and have to hitch a ride out on one

bladed   refers to a dirt road that has been smoothed out by the use of a wide blade on earth-moving equipment; "blading" gets rid of the teeth-chattering, much-cursed washboards found on so many dirt roads after heavy vehicle use

blaze   a mark on a tree made by chipping away a piece of the bark, usually done to designate a trail; such trails are sometimes described as "blazed"

blind corner   a curve in the road or trail that conceals bikers, hikers, equestrians, and other traffic

BLM   Bureau of Land Management, an agency of the federal government

buffed   used to describe a very smooth trail

catching air   taking a jump in such a way that both wheels of the bike are off the ground at the same time

clean   while this may describe what you and your bike won't be after following many trails, the term is most often used as a verb to denote the action of pedaling a tough section of trail successfully

combination	this type of route may combine two or more configurations; for example, a point-to-point route may integrate a scenic loop or an out-and-back spur midway through the ride; likewise, an out-and-back may have a loop at its farthest point (this configuration looks like a cherry with a stem attached; the stem is the out-and back, the fruit is the terminus loop); or a loop route may have multiple out-and-back spurs and/or loops to the side; mileage for a combination route is for the total distance to complete the ride
dab	touching the ground with a foot or hand
deadfall	a tangled mass of fallen trees or branches
diversion ditch	a usually narrow, shallow ditch dug across or around a trail; funneling the water in this manner keeps it from destroying the trail
double-track	the dual tracks made by a jeep or other vehicle, with grass or weeds or rocks between; mountain bikers can ride in either of the tracks, but you will of course find that whichever one you choose, and no matter how many times you change back and forth, the other track will appear to offer smoother travel
dugway	a steep, unpaved, switchbacked descent
endo	flipping end over end
feathering	using a light touch on the brake lever, hitting it lightly many times rather than very hard or locking the brake
four-wheel-drive	this refers to any vehicle with drive-wheel capability on all four wheels (a jeep, for instance, has four-wheel drive as compared with a two-wheel-drive passenger car), or to a rough road or trail that requires four-wheel-drive capability (or a one-wheel-drive mountain bike!) to negotiate it
game trail	the usually narrow trail made by deer, elk, or other game
gated	everyone knows what a gate is, and how many variations exist on this theme; well, if a trail is described as "gated" it simply has a gate across it; don't forget that the rule is if you find a gate closed, close it behind you; if you find one open, leave it that way
Giardia	shorthand for *Giardia lamblia*, and known as the "backpacker's bane" until we mountain bikers expropriated it; this is a waterborne parasite that begins its life cycle when swallowed, and one to four weeks later has its host

(you) bloated, vomiting, shivering with chills, and living in the bathroom; the disease can be avoided by "treating" (purifying) the water you acquire along the trail (see Hitting the Trail in the Introduction)

gnarly	a term thankfully used less and less these days, it refers to tough trails
hammer	to ride very hard
hardpack	a trail in which the dirt surface is packed down hard; such trails make for good and fast riding, and very painful landings; bikers most often use "hardpack" as both a noun and adjective, and "hard-packed" as an adjective only (the grammar lesson will help you when you're diagramming sentences in camp)
hike-a-bike	what you do when the road or trail becomes too steep or rough to remain in the saddle
jeep road, jeep trail	a rough road or trail passable only with four-wheel-drive capability (or a horse or mountain bike)
kamikaze	while this once referred primarily to those Japanese fliers who quaffed a glass of sake, then flew off as human bombs in suicide missions against U.S. naval vessels, it has more recently been applied to the idiot mountain bikers who, far less honorably, scream down hiking trails, endangering the physical and mental safety of the walking, biking, and equestrian traffic they meet; deck guns were necessary to stop the Japanese kamikaze pilots, but a bike pump or walking staff in the spokes is sufficient for the current kamikazes who threaten to get us all kicked off the trails
loop	this route configuration is characterized by riding from the designated trailhead to a distant point, then returning to the trailhead via a different route (or simply continuing on the same one in a circle route) without doubling back; you always move forward across new terrain but return to the starting point when finished; mileage is for the entire loop from the trailhead back to trailhead
multipurpose	a BLM designation of land which is open to many uses; mountain biking is allowed
ORV	a motorized off-road vehicle
out-and-back	a ride where you will return on the same trail you pedaled out; while this might sound far more boring than a

out-and-back (continued)	loop route, many trails look very different when pedaled in the opposite direction
pack stock	horses, mules, llamas, et cetera, carrying provisions along the trails . . . and unfortunately leaving a trail of their own behind
point-to-point	a vehicle shuttle (or similar assistance) is required for this type of route, which is ridden from the designated trailhead to a distant location, or endpoint, where the route ends; total mileage is for the one-way trip from the trailhead to endpoint
portage	to carry your bike on your person
pummy	volcanic activity in the Pacific Northwest and elsewhere produces soil with a high content of pumice; trails through such soil often become thick with dust, but this is light in consistency and can usually be pedaled; remember, however, to pedal carefully, for this dust obscures whatever might lurk below
quads	bikers use this term to refer both to the extensor muscle in the front of the thigh (which is separated into four parts) and to USGS maps; the expression "Nice quads!" refers always to the former, however, except in those instances when the speaker is an engineer
runoff	rainwater or snowmelt
scree	an accumulation of loose stones or rocky debris lying on a slope or at the base of a hill or cliff
signed	a signed trail has signs in place of blazes
single-track	a single, narrow path through grass or brush or over rocky terrain, often created by deer, elk, or backpackers; single-track riding is some of the best fun around
slickrock	the rock-hard, compacted sandstone that is great to ride and even prettier to look at; you'll appreciate it even more if you think of it as a petrified sand dune or seabed (which it is), and if the rider before you hasn't left tire marks (from unnecessary skidding) or granola bar wrappers behind
snowmelt	runoff produced by the melting of snow
snowpack	unmelted snow accumulated over weeks or months of winter—or over years in high-mountain terrain
spur	a road or trail that intersects the main trail you're following

switchback	a zigzagging road or trail designed to assist in traversing steep terrain; mountain bikers should not skid through switchbacks
technical	terrain that is difficult to ride due not to its grade (steepness) but to its obstacles—rocks, roots, logs, ledges, loose soil . . .
topo	short for topographical map, the kind that shows both linear distance and elevation gain and loss; "topo" is pronounced with both vowels long
trashed	a trail that has been destroyed (same term used no matter what has destroyed it . . . cattle, horses, or even mountain bikers riding when the ground was too wet)
two-wheel-drive	this refers to any vehicle with drive-wheel capability on only two wheels (a passenger car, for instance, has two-wheel-drive); a two-wheel-drive road is a road or trail easily traveled by an ordinary car
waterbar	An earth, rock, or wooden structure that funnels water off trails to reduce erosion
washboarded	a road that is surfaced with many ridges spaced closely together, like the ripples on a washboard; these make for very rough riding, and even worse driving in a car or jeep
whoop-de-doo	closely spaced dips or undulations in a trail; these are often encountered in areas traveled heavily by ORVs
wilderness area	land that is officially set aside by the federal government to remain natural—pure, pristine, and untrammeled by any vehicle, including mountain bikes; though mountain bikes had not been born in 1964 (when the United States Congress passed the Wilderness Act, establishing the National Wilderness Preservation system), they are considered a "form of mechanical transport" and are thereby excluded; in short, stay out
wind chill	a reference to the wind's cooling effect on exposed flesh; for example, if the temperature is 10 degrees Fahrenheit and the wind is blowing at 20 miles an hour, the wind chill (that is, the actual temperature to which your skin reacts) is minus 32 degrees; if you are riding in wet conditions things are even worse, for the wind chill would then be minus 74 degrees!
windfall	anything (trees, limbs, brush, fellow bikers . . .) blown down by the wind

INDEX

Abbreviations
  postal service state codes, list of, 3–4
  road designation, list of, 3
Advanced rides
  long, xxiv
  short, xxiii–xxiv
Aeroflex-Andover Airport, Kittatinny Valley
  State Park, NJ, 277
Alan Seeger Natural Area, PA, 164–70,
  176–79
Allamuchy Mountain State Park, NJ,
  267–69
Allegany Mountains, Green Ridge State
  Forest, MD, 111–23
Allegheny Mountain, WV, 303, 320–22
Allegheny Trail, Canaan Valley State Park,
  WV, 337, 339
Allegheny Trail, Seneca Creek Loop, WV,
  320, 322
Andover, NJ, Allamuchy Mountain State
  Park, 267–69
Annapolis, MD, Baltimore & Annapolis
  Trail Park, 77–79
Antietam National Battlefield, MD, 55
Appalachian Excursions, Michaux State
  Forest, PA, 144–60
Appalachian Mountains
  Savage River State Forest, MD, 124–33
  Tussey Mountain to Whipple Dam, PA,
  162–64
Appalachian Trail, Michaux State Forest,
  PA, 144–60
Archer Mansion, Susquehanna State Park,
  MD, 102
Assateague Island, MD, 27–30
Atsion, NJ, Wharton State Forest, 255–58
ATV Trail, Michaux State Forest, PA,
  147–49

Back Hollow Trail, Canaan Valley State
  Park, WV, 338–339

Back Track, Switchback Trail, PA, 215–17
Bake Over Trail, Bear Gap Trail, PA, 185
Bald Eagle State Forest, PA, 180–85
Bald Knob, WV, 303, 314
Baltimore & Annapolis Trail Park, MD,
  77–79
Banner's Overlook, Stafford–East Valley
  Roads Loop, MD, 115, 116
Batsto, NJ, Wharton State Forest, 255–58
Beaches, Assateague Island, MD, 27–30
Bear Branch Nature Center, Hashawha
  Environmental Appreciation Center,
  MD, 108–10
Bear Gap Trail, Bald Eagle State Forest,
  PA, 183–85
Bear Hunter Trail, Seneca Creek Loop,
  WV, 320, 321
Bear Meadows Natural Area, PA, 167–72,
  175–79
Beginner rides, xxiii
Benson Trail, State College Epic Ride, PA,
  177, 179
Bethesda, MD, Capital Crescent Trail,
  62–65
Big Elk Creek, Fair Hill Natural Resources
  Management Area, MD, 104–7
Big Pine Flat, Long Pine Reservoir Loop,
  PA, 151
Big Run Loop, WV, 318–20
Big Run State Park, Savage River State For-
  est, MD, 131–33
Big Savage Mountain, MD, 124–33
Black Hill Regional Park, MD, 51–54
Black Locust Trail, Gambrill State Park,
  MD, 72
Blackwater Falls State Park, WV
  Canaan Loop Road, 327–31
  Plantation Trail, 324–27
Blackwater National Wildlife Refuge, MD,
  30–34
Bloede's Dam, MD, 85

Blue Marsh Lake, PA, 247–49
Blue Mountain Lake Trail, Delaware
    Water Gap National Recreation Area,
    NJ, 274–76
Blue Trail, Cedarville State Forest, MD,
    36–37
Blue Trail, Patuxent Research Refuge
    North Tract, MD, 81
B & O Railroad, 55
Broad Mountain, Weekend Warrior, PA,
    220–22
Browns Mills, NJ, Lebanon State Forest,
    258–60
Brown Trail, Cedarville State Forest, MD,
    37
Bulls Island Natural Area, Delaware and
    Raritan Canal State Park, NJ, 262, 263
BWI Trail, MD, 77, 79

Cabin Branch Trail, Black Hill Regional
    Park, MD, 54
Cabin John Trail, MD, 59–62
Cabin Mountain, Timberline, WV, 341
Caledonia State Park, PA
    Caledonia Loop, 152–54
    Mont Alto State Park Loop, 154–57
Cambridge, MD, Blackwater National
    Wildlife Refuge, 30–34
Camp Penn, PA, 158
Camp 70 Road, WV, 331–34
Canaan Loop Road, WV, 327–31
Canaan Valley, WV, 323–42
Canaan Valley State Park, WV, 326,
    337–39
Capital Crescent Trail, MD, 62–65
Carlisle, PA
    ATV Trail, 147–49
    Log Sled Trail, 147–49
Cass Scenic Railroad, WV, 303, 314
Castle Point, Minnewaska State Park, NY,
    297
Catoctin Blue Trail, Gambrill State Park,
    MD, 72
Catskill Mountains, NY, 296–302
Cattail Pond, White Clay Creek State Park,
    DE, 20
Cedar Hollow Trail, Hibernia County Park,
    PA, 244
Cedar Swamp Natural Area, Lebanon
    State Forest, NJ, 259–60
Cedarville State Forest, MD, 34–37

Chambersburg, PA, Michaux State Forest,
    144–60
Cherry Trail, Race Loop, PA, 137
Chesapeake and Delaware Canal, Lums
    Pond State Park, 15–17
Chesapeake and Ohio Canal, C & O
    Canal National Historical Park, 54
Chesapeake Bay, 26
    Blackwater National Wildlife Refuge,
    MD, 30–34
Chincoteague National Wildlife Refuge,
    VA, 27
Christmansville, PA, Summer's Loop,
    223–25
Civil War sites, Gettysburg National Mili-
    tary Park, PA, 190–92
Clearwater Trail, Cosca Regional Park,
    MD, 68
Clinton, MD, Cosca Regional Park, 66–68
Clinton, NJ, Round Valley Recreation
    Area, 264–67
Clopper Lake, MD, 48–51
Club Run Trail, Canaan Valley State Park,
    WV, 339
Coalition for the Capital Cresent Trail, 65
C & O Canal National Historical Park,
    MD, 54–59
C & O Canal Towpath, C & O Canal
    National Historical Park, MD, 54–59
Cockeysville, MD, Northern Central Rail-
    road Trail, 94–97
Codorus Creek, PA
    Spring Valley County Park, 196–98
    York County Heritage Rail Trail, 202–205
Colonial Pennsylvania Plantation, Ridley
    Creek State Park, PA, 236
Columbia, MD, Patapsco Valley State
    Park, McKeldin Area, 82–84
Combination rides, 4
Conewago Recreational Trail, PA, 208–10
Cornwall & Lebanon Railroad, Conewago
    Recreational Trail, PA, 208–10
Cosca Regional Park, MD, 66–68
Cowbell Hollow Trail, Bald Eagle State
    Forest, PA, 180–82
Cracker Bridge Trail, Bear Gap Trail, PA,
    185
Cranberry Glades Wilderness Area, NY,
    303
Cranberry Trail, Lebanon State Forest, NJ,
    259, 260

Cross Country Trail, Fair Hill Natural Resources Management Area, MD, 104–7
Cryptosporidiosis prevention, 7–8
Cunningham Falls State Park, MD, 72
Cushetunk Trail, Round Valley Recreation Area, NJ, 264, 265–66

Daniel Boone Homestead, PA, 245
Dauphin, PA, Stony Creek Wilderness Railroad Bed Trail, 205–7
Davis, WV, Canaan Valley, WV, 323–42
Davis Trail, Plantation Trail, WV, 327
Deep Creek Lake, Savage River State Forest, MD, 124
Deer Creek Trail, Susquehanna State Park, MD, 101
Deer Park Pond, Allamuchy Mountain State Park, NJ, 267–69
Delaware and Raritan Canal State Park, NJ, 261–64
Delaware River, NJ
  Delaware and Raritan Canal State Park, 261–64
  Delaware Water Gap National Recreation Area, 270–76
  Delaware Water Gap National Recreation Area, NJ, 270–73
Difficult rides, xxvi
Dolly Sods, WV, 323, 336
Dowling Farm Loop, PA, 189
Downington, PA, Hibernia County Park, 241–44
Down Track, Switchback Trail, PA, 215–17
Drinking water, 7–8
Dry Brooks Day Use Area, Blue Marsh Lake, PA, 247, 248, 249

Eastern Shore of Maryland, 26–43
Eldersburg, MD, Liberty Watershed, 97–100
Elizabethtown, PA, Conewago Recreational Trail, 208–10
Elkins, WV, Snowshoe, 312–14
Elk Lick Trail, Savage River State Forest, MD, 128–31
Elk River Touring Center, Slatyfork, WV, 303–4
Elkton, MD, Fair Hill Natural Resources Management Area, MD, 104–7
Ellicott City, MD, Patapsco Valley State Park, McKeldin Area, 82–84

Epic Ride, State College, PA, 176–79
Etiquette, trail, 6–7

Fair Hill Natural Resources Management Area, MD, 104–7
Fairmount Park—Kelly and West River Drives, PA, 227–30
Falls View Gentle Trail, Plantation Trail, WV, 327
Family rides, xxiii
Farm Road Trail, Susquehanna State Park, MD, 101
First-aid kit, 9
Flagstaff Park, Mauch Chunk Ridge, PA, 217–20
Flatbrookville, NJ, Delaware Water Gap National Recreation Area, 270–73
Flintstone, MD, Green Ridge State Forest, 111–23
Forbes State Forest, Laurel Higlands, PA, 135–43
Forest Hill Trail, Hibernia County Park, PA, 243, 244
Fort Frederick State Park, MD, 55
Frederick, MD
  Gambrill State Park, 69–72
  Greenbrier State Park, 72–75
French Creek State Park, PA, 244–46
Frenchtown, NJ, Delaware and Raritan Canal State Park, 261–64
Frostburg, MD, Savage River State Forest, MD, 124–33

Gaithersburg, MD
  Black Hill Regional Park, 51–54
  Schaeffer Farm Trail, 45–48
  Seneca Creek State Park, 48–51
Gambrill State Park, MD, 69–72
Gandy Creek, WV, 316–17
Gardiner, NY, Wallkill Valley Rail Trail, 299–300
Gauley Mountain Trail, WV, 308
Gauntlet Trail, Snowshoe, WV, 312
Georgetown Branch Trail, Capital Crescent Trail, MD, 64
Germantown, MD, Black Hill Regional Park, 51–54
Germany Flats Aquifer, Kittatinny Valley State Park, NJ, 277
Gettysburg, PA
  Gettysburg National Military Park, 190–92

Gettysburg, PA *(continued)*
  Michaux State Forest, 144–60
Gettysburg National Military Park, PA,
  190–92
Giardiasis prevention, 7–8
Glen Burnie, MD, Baltimore & Annapolis
  Trail Park, 77–79
Glen Ellen Trail. *See* Seminary Trail, MD
Glen Rock, PA, York County Heritage Rail
  Trail, 202–5
Grants Branch Trail, WV, 316–17
Grantsville, MD, Savage River State Forest,
  124–33
Grass Mountain, Penn Roosevelt State For-
  est, PA, 165
Graybark Trail, Cosca Regional Park, MD,
  68
Gray's Cotton Mill, MD, 85
Great Falls Park, VA, 55, 57
Greenbrier River Trail, WV, 304–6
Greenbrier State Park, MD, 72–75
Green Ridge MTB Trail, Green Ridge
  State Forest, MD, 112–15
Green Ridge State Forest, MD, 111–12
Green Trail, Cedarville State Forest, MD,
  37
Green Trail, Patuxent Research Refuge
  North Tract, MD, 80
Greenwood Lake, NJ, Wawayanda State
  Park, 290–93
Gunpowder Falls State Park, MD, 94–97

Hackettstown, NJ, Allamuchy Mountain
  State Park, 267–69
Hagerstown, MD, Greenbrier State Park,
  72–75
Hancock, MD, Green Ridge State Forest,
  111–23
Hanover Junction, York County Heritage
  Rail Trail, PA, 202–5
Hard Rock Trail, Black Hill Regional Park,
  MD, 54
Harpers Ferry National Historical Park,
  MD, 55
Hashawha Environmental Appreciation
  Center, MD, 108–10
Havre de Grace, MD, Susquehanna State
  Park, 101–3
Hemlock Pond, Blue Mountain Lake Trail,
  NJ, 274–76
Hibernia County Park, PA, 241–44

Hidden Valley, Laurel Highlands, PA,
  134–43
High Point State Park, NJ, 286–89
High-speed cruising rides, xxv
Historical rides, xxvi
Hopewell Furnace National Historic Park,
  PA, 245
Hudson Highlands, NJ, Ringwood State
  Forest, 293–95
Hunting Hill, Ridley Creek State Park, PA,
  236, 238

IMBA Epics, 176–79
Indian Rock, Blue Mountain Lake Trail,
  NJ, 274
Intermediate rides
  long, xxiv
  short, xxiii–xxiv
International Mountain Bicycling Associa-
  tion (IMBA), 176–79
  Rules of the Trail, 6–7
Iris Trail, High Point State Park, NJ, 287
Iron Hill County Park, DE, 12–14

Jersey Toll House, Susquehanna State Park,
  MD, 102
Jim Thorpe, PA, 211–25
John Wert Path, PA, 175–79
Jug Bay Natural Area, Patuxent River Park,
  MD, 37–40

Kain Park, PA, 198–201
Kerhonskon, NY, Vernooy Kill Falls Trail,
  301–2
Kingfisher Overlook, Seneca Creek State
  Park, MD, 50, 51
Kingston, NY
  Minnewaska State Park, 297–298
  Vernooy Kill Falls Trail, 301–2
Kittatinny Valley State Park, NJ, 277–79
Kooser State Park, Laurel Highlands, PA,
  137, 139, 141
Kuhntown Loop, Laurel Highlands, PA,
  141–43

Lake Marcia, High Point State Park, NJ,
  286–89
Lake Redman, Kain Park, PA, 198–201
Lake Shore Trail, Seneca Creek State Park,
  MD, 49, 50, 51
Lake Trail, Cosca Regional Trail, MD, 68

Lake Williams, Kain Park, PA, 198–201
Lambertville, NJ, Delaware and Raritan Canal State Park, 261–64
Laurel, MD, Patuxent Research Refuge North Tract, 79–81
Laurel Highlands, PA, 134–43
Lebanon, NJ, Round Valley Recreation Area, 264–67
Lebanon State Forest, NJ, 258–60
Lehigh Gorge State Park, PA, 212–14
Lenape Trail, French Creek State Park, PA, 244, 246
Lenape Trail, Middle Run Valley Natural Area, DE, 20
Leonardtown, MD, St. Mary's State Park, 41–43
Lewisburg, PA, Bald Eagle State Forest, 180–85
Liberty Dam, Patapsco Valley State Park, MD, 82
Liberty Watershed, MD, 97–100
Lindy Run Trail, Plantation Trail, WV, 327
Linwood, WV, Prop's Run, 309–12
Little Bennett Regional Park, MD, 53
Little Round Top, Gettysburg National Military Park, VA, 192
Little Seneca Creek, Schaeffer Farm Trail, MD, 45–48
Little Seneca Lake, MD, 52
Loch Raven Reservoir, MD
  Overshot Run Trail, 91–93
  Seminary Trail, 88–91
Log Sled Trail, Michaux State Forest, PA, 147–49
Lonberger Trail, State College Epic Ride, PA, 177, 179
Long Draught Trail, Seneca Creek State Park, MD, 49, 51
Long Mountain Trail, Penn Roosevelt State Forest, PA, 165, 177, 179
Long Pine Reservoir Loop, Michaux State Forest, PA, 149–51
Lookout Trail, Race Loop, PA, 137, 138
Loop rides, xxiv, 4
Lower Awosting Trail, Minnewaska State Park, NJ, 298
Lower Susquehanna Heritage Greenway Trail, Susquehanna State Park, MD, 101, 103
Lums Pond State Park, DE, 15–17

MAMBO. See Maryland Association of Mountain Bike Operators
Maps. See also specific trails
  list of, xi–xiii
  topographic, 3, 5–6
Maryland Association of Mountain Bike Operators (MAMBO), 76, 89, 91, 92, 99
Mather Gorge, VA, 55
Mattaponi Creek, MD, 40
Mauch Chunk Ridge, Mauch Chunk Lake Park, PA, 217–20
Meadow Mountain O.R.V. Trail, Savage River State Forest, MD, 125–27
Meeting of the Pines Natural Area, Mont Alto State Park Loop, PA, 155, 157
Mega-Dip, Iron Hill County Park, DE, 12, 13
Mercersburg, PA, Whitetail Mountain, 187–90
Merkle Wildlife Sanctuary, MD, 40
Mertens Avenue Area, Green Ridge State Forest, MD, 118–21
Michaux State Forest, PA, 144–60
Mid-Atlantic Off Road Enthusiasts (MORE), 74
Middle Ridge Trail, Canaan Valley State Park, WV, 339
Middle Run Valley Natural Area, DE, 18–20
Mid-State Trail, PA, 172
Millbrook Village, NJ, Blue Mountain Lake Trail, 274–76
Mill Dairy Trail, Tyler State Park, PA, 251
Millers Point, French Creek State Park, PA, 244, 246
Millstone Pond, White Clay Creek State Park, DE, 20
Mink Hollow Trail, Seneca Creek State Park, MD, 51
Minnewaska State Park, NY, 297–298
Monkton, MD, Northern Central Railroad Trail, 94–97
Monongahela National Forest, WV, 314
Monroe Run Loop, Savage River State Forest, MD, 131–33
Mont Alto State Park Loop, Michaux State Forest, PA, 154–57
MORE. See Mid-Alantic Off Road Enthusiasts

Mountain Bike Weekend, Jim Thorpe, PA, 212

Mount Holly, NJ, Lebanon State Forest, 258–60

Mount Misery, Lebanon State Forest, NJ, 259, 260

Mount Vernon Trail, VA, 65

Neshaminy Creek, Tyler State Park, PA, 250–252

New Freedom, PA, York County Heritage Rail Trail, 202–5

New Germany State Park, Savage River State Forest, MD, 124–33

Nolands Ferry, MD, 58

No Name Overlook, Stafford–East Valley Roads Loop, MD, 115

Northern Central Railroad Trail, MD, 94–97

North of Interstate 68, Green Ridge State Forest, MD, 121–23

North Woods Ramble, Laurel Highlands, PA, 139–41

Nosedive Trail, Snowshoe, WV, 312

Nottingham County Park, PA, 239–41

Novice rides, xxiii

Ocean City, MD, Assateague Island, 27–30

Ocean views, Assateague Island, 27–30

Old Forge State Park, Michaux State Forest, PA, 158–60

Old Tram Trail, Bear Gap Trail, PA, 183, 185

Olson Fire Tower, WV, 334–36

Orange Trail, Cedarville State Forest, MD, 37

Orienteering Trail, Greenbrier State Park, MD, 75

Out-and-back rides, xxiv, 4

Overshot Run Trail, MD, 91–93

Oxford, PA, Nottingham County Park, 239–41

Packing necessities, 7–9

Pakim Pond, Lebanon State Forest, NJ, 259, 260

Parks and History Association, 58

Patapsco Valley State Park, MD
Avalon Area, 85–88
McKeldin Area, 82–84

Patterson Viaduct, MD, 85

Patuxent Research Refuge North Tract, MD, 79–81

Patuxent River Park, Jug Bay Natural Area, MD, 37–40

Paulinskill Valley Trail, Kittatinny Valley State Park, NJ, 282–83

Paw Paw Tunnel, MD, 55, 58

Penn Roosevelt State Forest, PA, 164–66

Pennsylvania State University, PA, 161

Perimeter Trail, Cosca Regional Park, MD, 66, 68

Peters Valley Craft Village, Delaware Water Gap National Recreation Area, NJ, 270, 272

Philadelphia, PA, 226

Philadelphia Museum of Art, PA, 226, 227–30

Pine Barrens, NJ
Lebanon State Forest, 258–60
Wharton State Forest, 255–58

Pine Grove Furnace State Park, Michaux State Forest, PA, 145–47, 148–49

Plantation Trail, WV, 324–27

Pocahontas County, WV, 303–14

Pocono Mountains, Jim Thorpe, PA, 211–25

Point Lookout State Park, MD, 43

Point-to-point rides, 5

Pole Steeple Loop, Michaux State Forest, PA, 145–47

Poplar Lick O.R.V. Trail, Savage River State Forest, MD, 128–31

Postal service state codes, 3–4

Potomac River
Capital Crescent Trail, 62–65
C & O Canal National Historical Park, 54–59
Stafford–East Valley Roads Loop, 115–18

Prop's Run, WV, 309–12

R. B. Winter State Park, Bald Eagle State Forest, PA, 180–85

Raccoon Trail, French Creek State Park, PA, 244

Race Loop, Laurel Highlands, PA, 135–38

Races, relay mountain bike, 24 Hours of Canaan, 339, 341

Ramapo Mountains, Wawayanda State Park, NJ, 290–93

Reading, PA
  Blue Marsh Lake, 247–49
  French Creek State Park, 244–46
Red Run, WV, 306–8
Revolutionary War sites, Valley Forge
    National Historical Park, 233–36
Ridley Creek State Park, PA, 236–38
Rim Trial Loop, Hibernia County Park,
    PA, 244
Ringwood State Park, NJ, 293–95
Road designation abbreviations, 3
Rock Creek Park, C & O Canal National
    Historical Park, MD, 54–59
Rockport, PA, Lehigh Gorge State Park,
    212–14
Rockport Tunnel, Summer's Loop, PA, 223
Rock Run Grist Mill, Susquehanna State
    Park, MD, 101
Rock Run Y Trail, Susquehanna State
    Park, MD, 101
Rockville, MD, Cabin John Trail, 59–62
Rocky Ridge County Park, PA, 193–95
Ross Trail, Alan Seeger Natural Area, PA,
    167–70
Round Valley Recreation Area, NJ, 264–67
Round Valley Reservoir, NJ, 264–67

Sand Mountain Tower, Bear Gap Trail,
    PA, 183
Sand Spring Trail, State College Epic
    Ride, PA, 177, 179
Savage River State Forest, MD, 124–33
Scenic rides, xxv
Schaeffer Farm Trail, MD, 45–48
Schaffer Trail, Kuhntown Loop, PA, 141,
    143
Schuylkill River
  Fairmount Park—Kelly and West River
    Drives, 227–30
  Schuylkill Trail, 230–33
  Valley Forge National Historical Park,
    233–36
Schuylkill Trail, PA, 230–33
Seminary Trail, MD, 88–91
Seneca Creek, 57
  Schaeffer Farm Trail, MD, 45–48
Seneca Creek State Park, 48–51
Seneca Creek Trail, WV, 320–22
Seneca Greenway Trail, MD, 51
Sharp Knob, Prop's Run, WV, 309, 311
Sharp's Tunnel, WV, 304–6

Shawangunk Mountains, NY, 296–302
Shoreline Trail, Mauch Chunk Ridge, PA,
    218, 220
Short Trail, Big Run Loop, WV, 319, 320
Shuttle rides, xxiv
Silver Spring, MD, Capital Crescent Trail,
    62–65
Slatyfork, WV
  Elk River Touring Center, 303–4, 305,
    307, 311, 312
  Prop's Run, 309–12
Snowshoe, WV, 312–14
Somerset, PA, Laurel Highlands, 134–43
Southern Maryland, 26–43
South Mountain, Michaux State Forest,
    PA, 144–60
Spring Mountain Trail, Bear Gap Trail,
    PA, 183
Spring Valley County Park, PA, 196–98
Spruce Knob, WV, 315–22
Spur rides, 5
St. Mary's River State Park, MD, 41–43
Stafford–East Valley Roads Loop, Green
    Ridge State Forest, MD, 115–18
State College, PA, 161–79
Stepping Stone Museum, Susquehanna
    State Park, MD, 102
Stilling Basin, Blue Marsh Lake, PA, 247,
    248, 249
Stokes State Forest, NJ, 283–86
Stoll Trail, Stokes State Forest, NJ, 284, 285
Stony Creek Wilderness Railroad Bed
    Trail, PA, 205–7
Summer's Loop, PA, 223–25
Susquehanna Ridge Trail, Susquehanna
    State Park, MD, 101
Susquehanna River
  Rocky Ridge County Park, 193–95
  Susquehanna State Park, 101–3
Susquehanna State Park, MD, 101–3
Sussex, NJ
  High Point State Park, 286–89
Sussex Branch Trail, Kittatinny Valley State
    Park, NJ, 279–81
Swainn's Lock, MD, 57
Switchback Trail, Mauch Chunk Lake
    Park, PA, 215–17, 218, 219
Switchback Trail, Patapsco Valley State
    Park, MD, 82, 83, 84
Sycamore Hill, Ridley Creek State Park,
    PA, 236

Sykesville, MD, Patapsco Valley State Park, McKeldin Area, 82–84

Table Rock Overlook, Canaan Loop Road, WV, 329
Technical rides, xxiv–xxv
Thomas, WV, Olson Fire Tower, 334–36
Thomas Viaduct, MD, 85
Three Bridges Trail, Savage River State Forest, MD, 128–31, 133
Three Mile Island, PA, 193, 195
Timberline, WV, 339–42
Tools for bike maintenance and repair, 8–9
Top Mountain Trail, Bald Eagle State Forest, PA, 180–82
Topographic maps, 3, 5–6
Town Hill Mountain, Stafford–East Valley Roads Loop, MD, 115–18
Trail etiquette, 6–7
Trenton, NJ, Delaware and Raritan Canal State Park, 261–64
Tussey Mountain, PA, 162–64, 167–70
Two Top Mountain, PA, 187–90
Tyler State Park, PA, 250–52

United States Forest Service, 1, 6
United States Geological Survey (USGS), 1
topographic maps, 3, 5–6
Upper Marlboro, MD, Jug Bay Natural Area, 37–40

Valley Forge National Historical Park, PA, 233–36
Valley View Trail, Race Loop, PA, 138
Van Campen Inn, Delaware Water Gap National Recreation Area, NJ, 270
Vernooy Kill Falls Trail, NY, 301–2
Vineland, NJ, Wharton State Forest, 255–58
Virginia Memorial, Gettysburg National Military Park, PA, 191

Waldorf, MD, Cedarville State Forest, 34–37
Wallkill Valley Rail Trail, NY, 299–300
Walpack Valley Environmental Center, Delaware Water Gap National Recreation Area, NJ, 272
Walter S. Carpenter Jr. State Park. See White Clay Creek State Park, DE

Warbasse Junction, NJ
Paulinskill Valley Trail, 282–83
Sussex Branch Trail, 279–81
Washington Crossing State Park, NJ, 261, 263
Water supplies, 7–8. See also specific rides
Wawayanda State Park, NJ, 290–93
Waynesboro, PA
Mont Alto State Park Loop, 154–57
Old Forge Loop, 158–60
Weekend Warrior, Broad Mountain, PA, 220–22
Westminster, MD, Hashawha Environmental Apprecation Center, 108–10
Wharton State Forest, NJ, 255–58
Whipple Dam State Park, PA, 162–64, 170–72
White Clay Creek State Park, DE, 20–22
White Clay Creek Trail, White Clay Creek Preserve, DE, 22–25
White Deer Creek, Cowbell Hollow Trail, PA, 181, 182
White Haven, PA, Lehigh Gorge State Park, 212–14
White Oak Trail, Gambrill State Park, MD, 72
Whites Ferry, MD, 55
Whitetail Mountain, PA, 187–90
White Trail, Cedarville State Forest, MD, 37
White Trail, Lebanon State Forest, NJ, 259, 260
Wildlife Drive, Blackwater National Wildlife Refuge, MD, 32, 33
Wildlife Loop, Patuxent Research Refuge North Tract, MD, 80
Wildlife viewing rides, xxv
Williamsport, MD, C & O Canal National Historical Park, 57
Wisconsin Avenue Tunnel, D.C., 62

Yellow Poplar Trail, Gambrill State Park, MD, 72
Yellow Trail, Patuxent Research Refuge North Tract, MD, 81
York County Heritage Rail Trail, PA, 202–5
Youghiogheny River, Laurel Highlands, 134

ABOUT THE AUTHOR

Photo by Dennis Coello

JOE SURKIEWICZ, when he's not hard at work on his next mountain bike trail guide or writing yet another *Unofficial Guide* to one of America's great cities, revels in careening down twisting single-track trails, riding his road bike, and savoring the films of Carole Lombard (non-colorized). He lives in Baltimore, Maryland, with ace attorney Ann Lembo and their feline companion, Wally, The World's Smartest Cat.